# mediated moms

This book is part of the Peter Lang Media and Communication list.
Every volume is peer reviewed and meets
the highest quality standards for content and production.

PETER LANG
New York • Bern • Frankfurt • Berlin
Brussels • Vienna • Oxford • Warsaw

# mediated moms

## *contemporary challenges to the motherhood myth*

Edited by Heather L. Hundley & Sara E. Hayden

PETER LANG
New York • Bern • Frankfurt • Berlin
Brussels • Vienna • Oxford • Warsaw

**Library of Congress Cataloging-in-Publication Data**

Mediated moms: contemporary challenges to the motherhood myth /
edited by Heather L. Hundley, Sara E. Hayden.
pages cm
Includes bibliographical references and index.
1. Motherhood. 2. Social media. 3. Communication.
4. Feminism—History—21st century. I. Hundley, Heather L., editor.
II. Hayden, Sara E., editor.
HQ759.M435 306.874'3—dc23 2015029942
ISBN 978-1-4331-3167-7 (hardcover)
ISBN 978-1-4331-3166-0 (paperback)
ISBN 978-1-4539-1698-8 (e-book)

Bibliographic information published by **Die Deutsche Nationalbibliothek**.
**Die Deutsche Nationalbibliothek** lists this publication in the "Deutsche
Nationalbibliografie"; detailed bibliographic data are available
on the Internet at http://dnb.d-nb.de/.

Cover image: ©iStock.com/HultonArchive


29 Broadway, 18th floor, New York, NY 10006
www.peterlang.com

# *Table of Contents*

# *Acknowledgments*

This book was conceived in honor, admiration, and respect for all the "mothers" in our lives. We see many of our friends, family, and colleagues rejoice and struggle with the daily machinations of parenting, generally, but mothering, more specifically. At a time when women have more reproductive choices, we have also witnessed women grapple with their decisions to remain childless and to mother in nontraditional ways. In a culture where approximately 75% of the parenting and household duties remain the woman's responsibilities (regardless of whether she has a career outside of the home), we hope this anthology engages readers to question such naturalized assumptions.

Heather would like to thank her mother, Sharon Hart, for her love, care, and encouragement throughout her life. Her guidance has always been appreciated; her strength admired; and her devotion to her children venerated. Heather also expresses appreciation to others who may not be biological mothers, or are not *her* mother, but mother nonetheless. They include her "academic mothers" Leah Vande Berg, A. Susan Owen, and Jan Andersen; and her "family mothers" grandmother Bessie Hundley, stepmother Yvonne Hundley, and mother-in-law Luann Abbott; and sisters-in-law Lisa Hundley, Amy Smith, Hayley Taylor, and Anne Cordaro.

This is Sara's second edited anthology on issues related to motherhood; as before, she thanks her parents and siblings for their presence in her life. She also acknowledges the support and friendship of D. Lynn O'Brien Hallstein, whose scholarship on motherhood inspires her own. Sara thanks her partner, Scott Manning, for his constant love and support.

We extend our appreciation to the contributing authors: Beth L. Boser, Carolyn Bronstein, Patrice M. Buzzanell, Rachel D. Davidson, Suzy D'Enbeau, Tasha N. Dubriwny, Lisa A. Flores, Stephanie Gomez, Elizabeth Fish Hatfield, Natasha R. Howard, Katherine J. Lehman, Susana Martínez

Guillem, Sharon R. Mazzarella, Valerie Palmer-Mehta, Sherianne Shuler, Lara C. Stache, and Linda Steiner. Their enthusiasm, hard work, and intelligence have led to what we believe is a truly excellent collection; we hope our readers agree. We also express our appreciation to the people at Peter Lang who helped usher this project forward including Senior Acquisitions Editor Mary Savigar and Design & Production Supervisor Sophie Appel. We thank "Thea Santimo" for permitting us to use images from the Sanctimommy Facebook page. Publication of this book was supported in part by a grant from the Baldridge Book Subvention Fund in the College of Humanities and Sciences at the University of Montana and funding from Dr. Terry Ballman, Dean of the College of Arts and Letters at California State University, San Bernardino. We thank both institutions for their support.

# 1. *Introduction: Challenging the Motherhood Myth*

By Sara E. Hayden & Heather L. Hundley

You'll see them every May. Whether you're surfing the net, reading your local newspaper, or flipping through a magazine, as Mother's Day approaches you'll find this year's lists of the best and worst moms in the media. Yearly updates aside, the characteristics pundits laud or lament are remarkably consistent, and so too are some of the characters who are celebrated or deplored. "Best" mediated moms are fun (Lucy Ricardo, *I Love Lucy*, 1951–1960), cheerful (Carol Brady, *The Brady Bunch*, 1969–1974; June Cleaver, *Leave it to Beaver*, 1957–1963), and protective (Sarah Conner, the *Terminator* franchise, 1984, 1991, 2003, 2009, 2015; Ellen Ripley, *Aliens*, 1986). They are selfless and loving (M'Lynn Eatonton, *Steel Magnolias*, 1989; Clair Huxtable, *The Cosby Show*, 1984–1992). They remain upbeat and supportive in the face of moody teenagers and grumpy or bumbling spouses (Jean Weir, *Freaks and Geeks*, 1999–2000; Kitty Foreman, *That 70's Show*, 1998–2006; Jill Taylor, *Home Improvement*, 1991–1999). They offer their maternal insights and love to children who are not their own (Tami Taylor, *Friday Night Lights*, 2006–2011; Leigh Anne Tuohy, *The Blind Side*, 2009), and some are even cool enough to be their kids' best friends (Lorelai Gilmore, *The Gilmore Girls*, 2000–2007).

Worst moms, in contrast, are described as cold, cruel, and controlling (Beth Jarrett, *Ordinary People*, 1980; Margaret White, *Carrie*, 1976). They are self-serving and sexual (Peg Bundy, *Married with Children*, 1987–1997; Stifler's Mom, *American Pie*, 1999). They may engage in both physical and/or emotional abuse toward their children and/or spouses (Joan Crawford, *Mommy Dearest*, 1981; Livia Soprano, *The Sopranos*, 1999–2007; Mary Jones, *Precious*, 2009), and their actions, some of which are unlawful, may put their children in harm's way (Irina Derevko, *Alias*, 2001–2006; Gemma Teller Morrow, *Sons of Anarchy*, 2008–2014).[1]

These Mother's Day stories suggest that in the contemporary United States, we share a definitive understanding of what it means to be a good or bad mom. And indeed, the maternal characteristics described through the "best" lists and accompanying articles echo scholarly discussions of the ideology of "good" motherhood, variously termed "intensive mothering" (Hays, 1996), "patriarchal mothering" (O'Reilly, 2006), or the "new momism" (Douglas & Michaels, 2004). Andrea O'Reilly identifies six tenets that underlie this ideology:

> 1) children can only be properly cared for by the biological mother; 2) this mothering must be provided 24/7; 3) the mother must always put children's needs before her own; 4) mothers must turn to the experts for instruction; 5) the mother is fully satisfied, fulfilled, completed, and composed in motherhood; and finally, 6) mothers must lavish excessive amounts of time, energy, and money in the rearing of their children. (p. 43)

Bad mothers, of course, are defined dialectically; they are a counterpoint to intensive mothering that serves to buttress the "good mother" myth (Addison, Goodwin-Kelly, & Roth, 2009; Douglas & Michaels, 2004; Goc, 2007; Ladd-Taylor & Umansky, 1998). Moreover, as Heather Addison, Mary Kate Goodwin-Kelly, and Elaine Roth remind us, assumptions about good and bad mothering are "the yardstick by which women are judged" (p. 6); to deviate from the norms of intensive mothering "is justification for disparagement—or at least suspicion" (p. 6). Thus scholars and pundits seem to agree: In the contemporary United States, we assess maternal practices as starkly good or bad and the "best" and "worst" lists offer lessons for real-life moms about how they are expected to behave.

In spite of the clarity with which judgments of best and worst are pronounced, the contributors to this edited collection suggest that something new is taking place on the contemporary media landscape. That is, on television, movie screens, and the Internet, maternal images are deviating from the good/bad binary, providing more nuanced portraits of mothers and mothering. This suggestion is supported by Suzanna Danuta Walters and Laura Harrison (2014), who argue that "in the last few years a type of mother has emerged that seems strikingly innovative. … Neither monster nor angel, this aberrant mom is not quite a twenty-first century feminist heroine but she does upend more traditional depictions of maternal identity" (p. 40). Focusing specifically on maternal images that populate premium cable, the authors describe mothers who are "unabashedly sexual, idiosyncratic to a fault, and seriously deleterious in [their] caretaking skills" (p. 40) all the while retaining their charm and remaining basically unpunished.

Walters and Harrison's focus on cable television echoes Brett Martin's (2013) attention to the antiheroes who are central to programs such as HBO's *The Sopranos* and *The Wire*, Showtime's *Dexter*, and AMC's *Breaking Bad* and *Mad Men*. Indeed, Martin argues that *The Sopranos* marks the beginning of the Third Golden Age of Television, an era in which "difficult men" are presented as protagonists, providing viewers with the uneasy opportunity to like and root for men whose actions are often morally corrupt, criminal, and even murderous. Martin argues that the very best programs to emerge during the Third Golden Age have been "largely about manhood—in particular the contours of male power and the infinite varieties of male combat" (p. 13). The authors who contribute to *Mediated Moms* suggest that alongside the emergence of the new, more complicated set of male characters of television's Third Golden Age is a similarly nuanced and conflicted group of women, many of whom are mothers. Additionally, their work illustrates that more complicated images of mothers extend beyond high-end fictional television to basic cable, movies, reality TV, news reporting, and the Internet. The twelve chapters that follow explore these varied representations, expanding our understanding of the ever-evolving institution of motherhood that all mothers must navigate.

## *Scholarly Precursors*

By unpacking the complicated and nuanced images of mothers in the current media milieu, the contributors to this volume participate in ongoing scholarly conversations exploring mediated representations of women generally and mothers specifically. Not surprisingly, scholarly assessments of the functions of these depictions diverge. Some authors focus on the ways mediated representations reinforce oppressive norms. The essays in Addison, Goodwin-Kelly, and Roth's (2009) *Motherhood Misconceived: Representing the Maternal in U.S. Films*, for example, highlight the many ways mothers are "repeatedly demonized or deified," (p. 4) thus reinforcing the misogynistic assumptions that underlie intensive mothering. Susan J. Douglas and Meredith W. Michael's (2004) *The Mommy Myth: The Idealization of Motherhood and How It Has Undermined Women* similarly explores how various forms of media, including celebrity journalism, network newscasts, daytime television, and evening situation comedies and dramas, promote and extend the "new momism." In *Bad Girls: Cultural Politics and Media Representations of Transgressive Women*, A. Susan Owen, Sarah R. Stein, and Leah R. Vande Berg (2007) argue that although contemporary images of women in film, television, and journalism often *seem* empowering and innovative, in fact, they frequently reinforce old, oppressive norms.

Other scholars, however, find an emancipatory potential in mediated representations of women. In *Prime Time Feminism: Television, Media Culture, and the Women's Movement since 1970*, Bonnie J. Dow (1996) investigates the ways second wave feminism was incorporated into the television series *The Mary Tyler Moore Show*, *One Day at a Time*, *Designing Women*, *Murphy* Brown, and *Dr. Quinn, Medicine Woman*. Dow is careful to qualify her assessment—she recognizes the limitations of pop-culture feminism, especially the tendency to substitute feminist *identity* with feminist *politics*. Nonetheless, she also maintains that in spite of such limitations, these series helped to spread feminism's reach. Whereas Dow argues that the series she examined failed to address systemic issues, in *Defining Women* Julie D'Acci (1994) sees broader possibilities in the popular drama *Cagney and Lacey*, arguing that "a mainstream, commercial, realist text that has been subjected to all the demands and distortions of prime-time American television may nonetheless be part of a feminist project and a rallying point for pleasure *and politics*" (p. 9, emphasis ours).

Kathleen Rowe (1995) is particularly optimistic about comedy as a site where representations of women can disrupt hegemonic, misogynistic norms in *The Unruly Woman: Gender and the Genres of Laughter*. "The figure of the unruly woman," she writes, "contains much potential for feminist appropriation. … The parodic excesses of the unruly woman and the comedic conventions surrounding her provide a space to 'act out' the dilemmas of femininity … to make not only 'fantastic' and 'incredible' but also laughable those tropes of femininity valorized by melodrama" (p. 11). Several years later, Rowe Karlyn (2011) offers a somewhat more sober but still optimistic assessment of media's ability to challenge oppressive norms. In *Unruly Girls, Unrepentant Mothers: Redefining Feminism on Screen* she again explores comedy's potential to promote new, emancipatory identities; however, she similarly acknowledges that the "unruly woman's power is fragile," and that in melodrama, her "outrageousness" often shifts "from comedy to pathos" (p. 12).

Perhaps, as Amanda D. Lotz (2006) suggests in *Redesigning Women: Television after the Network Era*, these varied assessments reflect the flourishing of media texts that include women as central characters. Lotz looks specifically at television, arguing that female-centered dramas began to proliferate after the 1997 success of FOX's *Ally McBeal*. She offers a number of reasons for this proliferation, including the increased economic and cultural power (some) women achieved as a result of second-wave feminism, the shift in the television industry from the network era to a multichannel environment, which in turn led to the rise of narrowcasting aimed at niche audiences, and chance. As a result, Lotz argues that

> popular and academic critics must be wary of making the same claims or holding the same expectations of every series as they did in eras in which stories about women were more narrowly circumscribed. The changed cultural, institutional, and representational context allows characterizations and discourse of individual texts to *mean differently* than if they were the only series, or one of very few, in a given period. (p. 19)

In particular, Lotz rejects the "role model" approach to criticism, arguing that each text must be understood in terms of the broader media context in which it circulates.

## *Political Economy and the Politics of Representation*

Indeed, because of advancements in technology, specifically, compression, miniaturization, and digitalization, audiences have more programming choices than ever. Moreover, this technology provides opportunities in the Internet era allowing media audiences to become media producers. As such, a myriad of television networks and countless websites and blogs have infiltrated our media environment suggesting a great potential for content variety and a cacophony of voices and images. Thus, media has the potential to embody contradictions—not to present an either/or dichotomy but a both/and perspective (also see Mellencamp, 1992). Resultantly, "media content and representation scholars no longer limit their research questions to binary oppositions of positive/negative or biased/unbiased, but rather have achieved a high level of complexity and nuance in their studies" (Mazzarella, 2013, p. 27).

We approach this book with cautionary technological optimism. That is, despite digital progress, media producers' goal is to make a profit; therefore, they create what they think will capture viewers and users to sell to advertisers. Moreover, irrespective of the potential for increased diversity in programming, the media industry has not garnered an increase in diverse staffing, particularly writers, directors, and cinematographers ("TV industry," 2010). More specifically, in 2012 women writers working in television were underrepresented by a factor of two to one (27%) compared to men, and more significantly in film (15%) by a factor of three to one (Hunt, 2014). Female writers fare much better in cable networks representing between 43% and 50% of all writers on some networks; however, of the 292 television shows examined during the 2013–2014 season, 32 (11%) did not employ women writers at all (Hunt, 2015).

Such paltry inclusion of women extends beyond media industry writers. Interviews of 179 television workers (89% of them women) revealed that not only do men get paid more in the industry, and not only is it more difficult for women to get promoted compared to men, but "it is difficult to get back into television after a career break to have children" ("TV industry," 2010, para. 2). Considering women's employment at higher decision-making levels, they only comprised 15.1% of executive producer jobs during the 2013–2014 television season (Hunt, 2015).

While television and film paints a bleak existence for women's employment, the Internet remains an optimistic space. Initially, the Internet was dominated by White male users and creators. Yet, debatably, by 2006 women and men equally participate in creating Internet content (Lenhart & Fox, 2006). While "disagreement persists over gender equity in blog tool use" (Papacharissi & Meraz, 2013, p. 376), women increasingly engage in a variety of social and political blogs for networking and empowerment.

We are not arguing that all women (who work in the media) can speak for or better represent motherhood, but, like Hunt (2014), we find that "opportunities to tell the types of stories that are more likely to resonate with increasingly diverse audiences have been far from realized" (p. 13). We focus our attention on the institution of motherhood, because like other constructions of identity, it is a social and cultural construction rather than biologically determined (Fox-Genovese, 1991; O'Reilly, 2004b). As such, it is temporal, historical, contextual, and can be revised (Mellencamp, 1992; O'Reilly, 2004b). Accordingly, it remains important to continually explore constructed representations of identity, including motherhood.

Acknowledging the cultural constructions of motherhood illuminates the false public/private dichotomy. Indeed, motherhood not only resides within the confines of the (private) home, but it is also out in the (public) streets. As evidenced earlier in the introduction and throughout this book, numerous media outlets report on, portray, validate, judge, and punish mothers in seemingly limitless ways. In 2006, for instance, news media reported Britney Spears' "bad mothering" by driving with her infant son on her lap and then three months later inappropriately fastening him in a car seat ("Britney Spears' latest," 2006). More recently, Carrie Underwood tweeted that her dogs locked themselves and her newborn child in her car ("Carrie Underwood's baby," 2015); however, as a current fan favorite Underwood was valorized for rescuing her baby.

As the public/private dichotomy of motherhood collapses with the knowledge of its cultural construction, it becomes a political topic (Bassin, Honey,

& Mahrer Kaplan, 1994; Hamamoto, 1991; Holcomb, 1998). Because of its political nature, this volume specifically contains qualitative, critical, cultural, and rhetorical examinations of the representation of mediated mothers. Understanding how contemporary motherhood is ideologically constructed provides insight into cultural power.

Historically, scholars have argued that motherhood is a patriarchal institution (O'Reilly, 2004a; 2004b), reproduces gender hierarchy, serves the interest of men, and maintains capitalism (Hays, 1996). Clearly, not only has "American culture at large ... failed working mothers" (Matchar, 2013, p. 163), it has failed all mothers. The US, for instance, is the only country in the developed world without guaranteed paid maternity leave (Matchar, 2013). Yet, with more women writing for cable television and making significant headway online, the authors contributing to this volume argue that, to some extent, mediated multidimensional mothers are emerging. Hence, in the chapters that follow, the representations of mothers are not merely endorsing the ideologies they produce, but are simultaneously revealing relations of power and cultural practices in the institutional "material structures of power they legitimate" (Giroux, 1991, p. 90).

Akin to Owen, Stein, and Vande Berg (2007), the findings in this volume can be cautiously celebrated. While the broader array of mother portrayals are a reason for optimism, we also must note what is not obvious. Nearly all media, whether it is news, film, television, documentaries, and even the Internet, create and profit off of fictional or nonfictional drama. As media consumers, we must ask: Who benefits from these representations? Are these representations reproducing or challenging power? What power structures are being legitimized?

The chapters in this edited volume reflect this broadened environment, considering representations of mothers in fictional and reality television, in movies and documentaries, in news coverage, and in blogs. Additionally, as above, the assessments of the media texts diverge, as authors celebrate the emancipatory potential of some images and lament the regressive and oppressive implications of others. Indeed, according to several authors in this volume, the texts under study are often simultaneously emancipatory and oppressive.

Lotz (2006) maintains that "rather than calling for 'positive' representations, cultural studies theorists advocate the creation of a multiplicity of images of whatever group has been stereotyped in order to make the stereotype 'uninhabitable'" (p. 12). Not all of the authors whose work is included in this volume will agree that the stereotypes of the "good" and "bad" mothers can no longer be inhabited; however, the variety of depictions of mothers described in the chapters that follow suggest that at the least, these limited and limiting subject positions are beginning to fracture, allowing for greater variety in our understanding of motherhood.

## *Overview of Chapters*

One theme addressed in all of the chapters is intensive mothering. As other scholars have done (see, e.g., Addison, Goodwin-Kelly, & Roth, 2009; Douglas & Michaels, 2004), several contributors recognize moments when mediated representations reinforce this oppressive maternal ideology. Tasha N. Dubriwny (chapter 11), for example, begins her essay with a discussion of an episode of Anderson Cooper's daytime talk show *Anderson Live* (CNN) that focused on what is, to Cooper, the "shocking" reality that some mothers drink alcohol—an activity he intimates is as problematic as shoplifting. Similarly, in their analysis of responses to Amy Chua's *Battle Hymn of the Tiger Mother* and Dara-Lynn Weiss's *The Heavy: A Mother, a Daughter, a Diet*, Linda Steiner and Carolyn Bronstein (chapter 13) argue that although readers expressed divergent ideas about what constitutes good and bad mothering, the authors of both books were harshly condemned for taking intensive mothering "too far," thus illustrating that mothers (but not fathers) continue to be subject to intensive mothering's impossible demands.

While Dubriwny and Steiner and Bronstein offer evidence of the ongoing pressure placed on mothers to perform the new momism, contributors to this volume also point to representations of mothers who defy or otherwise transcend intensive mothering's limits. Indeed, although Dubriwny begins her essay by recounting Cooper's condemnatory segment on mothers who drink, the bulk of her chapter explores mommy blogs and mommy bloggers' books that celebrate, rather than demonize, mothers' use of alcohol. Valerie Palmer-Mehta and Sherianne Shuler (chapter 12) similarly explore the Facebook page Sanctimommy. Administered by the pseudonymous Thea Sanctimo, the page includes reposts of self-righteous memes and individual statements about motherhood accompanied by witty commentary poking fun at the intensive-mothering norms the original posts uphold. Thus while intensive mothering may be alive and well, these authors illustrate that many mothers recognize and are speaking back to intensive mothering.

Other contributors draw attention to mediated representations of mothers that defy the good/bad binary. Stephanie L. Gomez (chapter 8) explores Lifetime's reality television series *Dance Moms*, arguing that the mothers and dance instructor Abby Lee Miller variously are depicted as *both* good *and* bad. Similarly, Katherine J. Lehman (chapter 4) offers a reading of the Showtime series *Weeds* and *Nurse Jackie*, contending that although the protagonists of the series are seriously flawed—*Weeds*' Nancy Botwin deals drugs, *Nurse Jackie*'s Jackie Peyton is addicted to them—they are nonetheless depicted as multifaceted characters who love their children and display behaviors that are sometimes laudatory and sometimes condemnable. In her analysis of John Caouette's documentaries *Tarnation* and *Walk Away Renee*, Beth L. Boser (chapter 9) explores how Renee Davis's mental illness precludes her from enacting intensive mothering; nonetheless, Boser maintains that the films resist binaries associated with both good and bad mothering as well as normal and abnormal mental states. These analyses, then, illuminate depictions of mothers who are complex human beings not easily reduced by dichotomous labels.

As noted above, one of the main tenets of intensive mothering is that mothers are fully satisfied, fulfilled, completed, and composed in motherhood (O'Reilly, 2006); intensive mothering suggests that a woman's life revolves around maternity. It is significant, then, that contributors to this volume explore depictions of women who are or might become mothers but whose focus and energy lie elsewhere. Suzy D'Enbeau and Patrice Buzzanell (chapter 2) explore three nonnormative depictions of motherhood on AMC's *Mad Men*: the character Helen Bishop, a divorced mother who tends to her own interests and needs by dating men and working for a political campaign; Carla, who leaves her children in order to care for the children of another woman; and Dr. Faye Miller, an unmarried professional who chooses career over marriage and family. Elizabeth Fish Hatfield (chapter 3) similarly offers an analysis of Showtime's *Homeland*. Carrie Mathieson, the protagonist of the series, is a highly skilled CIA agent who suffers from bipolar disorder. Mid-way through the third season the narrative reveals that Carrie is pregnant; however, in defiance of intensive mothering's demands, Carrie continues to prioritize her career over her impending motherhood. As the authors of these essays make clear, there are varied reasons why motherhood is not central to the women whose lives they discuss; nonetheless, their varied depictions offer representations that challenge the common conflation of woman and mother (Hayden, 2010).

Intensive mothering is not something all women can enact. Only relatively wealthy women can afford to be stay-at-home moms and provide their children with the material goods the ideology promotes. Moreover, there is a racial element to this ideology; intensive mothers are assumed to be White (Douglas & Michaels, 2004; Ladd-Taylor & Umansky, 1998). Two of the contributors to this volume explore media depictions of mothers who undermine these class- and race-based assumptions. Sharon R. Mazzarella (chapter 7) offers an analysis of TLC's *Here Comes Honey Boo Boo*'s "Mama" June Shannon.

In many ways, Shannon is the antithesis of the intensive mother. She has four daughters, each of whom has a different father; she is poor and morbidly obese; her language is often crude compared to social standards; and she lives with her boyfriend. Nonetheless, Mazzarella argues that viewers are invited to read Shannon's maternal performances as "unruly" rather than "bad."

Natasha Howard (chapter 6) investigates how African American teenage moms are depicted in five episodes of the first four seasons of MTV's *16 & Pregnant*. Although these young women do not enact intensive mothering, Howard argues that they also are not represented through common, derogatory stereotypes typically ascribed to African American mothers. Instead, they are depicted as good moms—caring, sensitive, and intelligent people who put their families first.

While the depictions of "Mama" June Shannon and the African American teenage moms on *16 and Pregnant* offer hopeful signs that we may be moving beyond the raced and classed assumptions that underlie notions of good motherhood, two other essays suggest that these assumptions have not yet disappeared. Susana Martínez Guillem and Lisa A. Flores (chapter 5) explore media depictions of three nonnormative mothers: Sarah Linden of FX's *The Killing*; Betty Draper of AMC's *Mad Men*, and news reports about Patricia Krentcil, a New Jersey woman who was arrested for child endangerment after allegedly bringing her young daughter to a tanning booth. All three mothers defy intensive mothering; however, the authors argue that it is Krentcil, whose love of tanning transgresses racial norms who is most vigorously censured for her behaviors.

Likewise, Rachel D. Davidson and Lara C. Stache (chapter 10) read the feature film *Mammoth*'s two central female characters against one another. Ellen Vidales is a wealthy White mother and physician; Gloria is a Filipina who cares for Ellen's daughter, having left her two sons in the Philippines. Whereas both women lament the fact that they do not spend more time with their own children, as Davidson and Stache point out, it is Gloria who is more seriously punished for her "transgressions." These essays thus offer a sobering note to the larger discussion, reminding us that while the media may be beginning to depict a broader set of attributes allowable for mothers, the potential to enact those behaviors often continues to be contained by race, ethnicity, and class.

When considered as a whole, the chapters of this volume are not easily summed up in a neat package. The authors' analyses suggest that mediated depictions of mothers both reinforce and challenge intensive motherhood. They illustrate that women sometimes recognize and speak back to intensive mothering's norms, at other times they are disciplined by its rigid demands. The authors illustrate that mothers can be concurrently "good" and "bad," and they suggest that the class- and race-based assumptions that underlie intensive mothering are simultaneously being upheld and undermined. Yet, again, given the current media environment, these differences are to be expected. Perhaps, as these varied, often contradictory depictions of mothers begin to crack open the good/bad mother dichotomy, the way will be paved for real-life moms to explore motherhood on their own terms.

The twelve chapters that follow are organized loosely around genre, beginning with essays that focus on fictional television, turning to reality TV, followed by documentaries and feature-length films, and ending with blogs. However, we refer to this organizational schema as "loose" both because of author choices (Martínez Guillem and Flores focus on two fictionalized television series and news reporting about one "real" woman), and because, with Rowe Karlyn (2011), we recognize that "with increasing media convergence worldwide and the new delivery systems made possible by digital technologies, the boundaries between [various media] forms continue to soften" (p. 9). Thus we invite readers to peruse the chapters in the order that interests them most. We are confident that each chapter stands alone as an important contribution to scholarly discussions regarding representations of mothers in the media, and we believe that in conversation, the essays help explain and promote a more complicated vision of maternity.

## Note

1. For example, see Allin, 2010; Hinckley, 2015; Ramisetti, 2015; Rorke, 2012; Sacks, 2015a; Sacks, 2015b.

## References


Addison, H., Goodwin-Kelly, K. G., & Roth, E. (Eds.). (2009). *Motherhood misconceived: Representing the maternal in U.S. films*. Albany, NY: State University of New York Press.

Allin, O. (2010, May 7). The 10 best TV moms. *CNN*. Retrieved from http://www.cnn.com/2010/SHOWBIZ/TV/05/07/ten.best.tv.moms/

Bassin, D., Honey, M., & Mahrer Kaplan, M. (Eds.). (1994). *Representations of motherhood*. New Haven, CT: Yale University Press.

Britney Spears' latest parenting mishap. (2006, May 17). *ABC News*. Retrieved from http://abcnews.go.com/GMA/Entertainment/story?id=1971687

Carrie Underwood's baby accidentally gets locked in car. (2015, July 13). *CBS News*. Retrieved from http://www.cbsnews.com/news/carrie-underwoods-baby-accidentally-gets-locked-in-car/

D'Acci, J. (1994). *Defining women: Television and the case of* Cagney & Lacey. Chapel Hill, NC: University of North Carolina Press.

Douglas, S., & Michaels, M. (2004). *The mommy myth: The idealization of motherhood and how it has undermined women.* New York, NY: Free Press.
Dow, B. J. (1996). *Prime-time feminism: Television, media culture, and the women's movement since 1970.* Philadelphia, PA: University of Pennsylvania Press.
Fox-Genovese, E. (1991). *Feminism without illusions: A critique of individualism.* Chapel Hill, NC: University of North Carolina Press.
Giroux, H. A. (1991). *Disturbing pleasures: Learning popular culture.* New York, NY: Routledge.
Goc, N. E. (2007). Monstrous mothers and the media. In N. Scott (Ed.) *Monsters and the monstrous: Myths and metaphors of enduring evil* (pp. 149–166). New York, NY: Rodopi.
Hamamoto, D. Y. (1991). Nervous laughter: Television situation comedy and liberal democratic ideology. New York, NY: Praeger.
Hayden, S. (2010). Lessons from *The Baby Boon*: Family-friendly policies and the ethics of justice and care. *Women's Studies in Communication, 33,* 119–137.
Hays, S. (1996). *The cultural contradictions of motherhood.* New Haven, CT: Yale University Press.
Hinckley, D. (2015, May 8). Top 10 worst TV mothers: Betty Draper, Cersei Lannister and Kris Jenner among biggest, baddest, small-screen moms. *New York Daily News.* Retrieved from http://www.nydailynews.com/entertainment/tv/top-10-worst-tv-mothers-all-time-article-1.2211271
Holcomb, B. (1998). *Not guilty: The good news about working mothers.* New York: Scribner.
Hunt, D. (2014). *Turning missed opportunities into realized one: The 2015 Hollywood writers report* (Writers Guild of America, West Report). Retrieved from Writers Guild of America, West website: http://www.wga.org/uploadedFiles/who_we_are/hwr14execsum.pdf
Hunt, D. (2015). *WGAW 2015 TV staffing brief* (Writers Guild of America, West Brief). Retrieved from Writers Guild of America, West website: http://www.wga.org/uploadedFiles/who_we_are/tvstaffingbrief2015.pdf
Ladd-Taylor, M., & Umansky, L. (Eds.). (1998). *"Bad" mothers: The politics of blame in twentieth-century America.* New York, NY: New York University Press.
Lenhart, A., & Fox, A. (2006). Bloggers: A portrait of the Internet's new storytellers. *Pew Internet & American Life Project.* Retrieved from http://www.pewinternet.org/Reports/2006/Bloggers.aspx
Lotz, A. D. (2006). *Redesigning women: Television after the network era.* Urbana, IL: University of Illinois Press.
Martin, B. (2013). *Difficult men: Behind the scenes of a creative revolution: From* The Sopranos *and* The Wire *to* Mad Men *and* Breaking Bad. New York, NY: Penguin Press.
Matchar, E. (2013). *Homeward bound: Why women are embracing the new domesticity.* New York, NY: Simon & Schuster.
Mazzarella, S. R. (2013). Technology, convergence, and power: Current trends in text-based approaches to media studies. In A. N. Valdivia & S. R. Mazzarella (Eds.), *The international encyclopedia of media studies* (pp. 13–28). Malden, MA: Blackwell.

Mellencamp, P. (1992). *High anxiety: Catastrophe, scandal, age, & comedy*. Bloomington, IN: Indiana University Press.

O'Reilly, A. (Ed.). (2004a). *From motherhood to mothering: The legacy of Adrienne Rich's* Of Women Born. Albany, NY: State University of New York Press.

O'Reilly, A. O. (2004). *Toni Morrison and motherhood: A politics of the heart*. Albany, NY: State University of New York Press.

O'Reilly, A. (2006). *Rocking the cradle: Thoughts on motherhood, feminism, and the possibility of empowered mothering*. Toronto, Canada: Demeter Press.

Owen, A. S., Stein, S., & Vande Berg, L. (2007). *Bad girls: Cultural politics and media representations of transgressive women*. New York, NY: Peter Lang.

Papacharissi, Z., & Meraz, S. (2013). Blogging culture: Content and representation in blogs. In A. N. Valdivia & S. R. Mazzarella (Eds.), *The international encyclopedia of media studies* (pp. 367–385). Malden, MA: Blackwell.

Ramisetti, K. (2015, May 8). Top 10 TV mothers: Lucy Ricardo, Carol Brady and Marge Simpson among coolest small-screen moms. *New York Daily News*. Retrieved from http://www.nydailynews.com/entertainment/tv/top-10-tv-mothers-time-article-1.2214112

Rorke, R. (2012, May 13). TV's 10 worst moms. *New York Post*. Retrieved from http://nypost.com/2012/05/13/tvs-10-worst-moms/

Rowe, K. (1995). *The unruly woman: Gender and the genres of laughter*. Austin, TX: University of Texas Press.

Rowe Karlyn, K. (2011). *Unruly girls, unrepentant mothers: Redefining feminism on screen*. Austin, TX: University of Texas Press.

Sacks, E. (2015a, May 7). Top 10 best movie moms: From *Terms of Endearment* to *The Blind Side*, flicks to honor mom on Mother's Day. *New York Daily News*. Retrieved from http://www.nydailynews.com/entertainment/movies/top-10-best-movie-moms-article-1.2211301

Sacks, E. (2015b, May 7). Top 10 worst movie moms: From *Carrie* to *Mommie Dearest*, flicks to avoid this Mother's Day. *New York Daily News*. Retrieved from http://www.nydailynews.com/entertainment/movies/mother-day-movies-avoid-10-worst-big-screen-moms-article-1.2210954

TV industry a hostile place for working mothers, survey finds. (2010, March 15). *The Guardian*. Retrieved from http://www.theguardian.com/media/2010/mar/15/tv-industry-working-mothers

Walters, S. D., & Harrison, L. (2014). Not ready to make nice: Aberrant mothers in contemporary culture. *Feminist Media Studies, 14*, 38–55.

# 2. *Counter-Intensive Mothering: Exploring Transgressive Portrayals and Transcendence on* Mad Men

By Suzy D'Enbeau & Patrice M. Buzzanell

Contemporary discourses and media representations of gender, mothering, and caregiving often are informed by assumptions of intensive mothering, depicting mothers who either do or do not conform to these ideals. Intensive-mothering discourses place high demands on maternal performances, calling upon women to emphasize caregiving responsibilities and to disregard other aspects of their lives that do not pertain to parenting (Douglas & Michaels, 2004; O'Brien Hallstein, 2010; see also Buzzanell & D'Enbeau, 2009; D'Enbeau & Buzzanell, 2010). Moreover, intensive mothering has been both celebrated and a cause for concern. For instance, much debate in the media and in everyday conversations occurred when the "Tiger Mom" phenomenon emerged in the media as a means by which mothers could help their children acquire a competitive edge through calculated development of talents, especially talents aligned directly with high-income educational pursuits, and minimization of seemingly peripheral activities and relationships (see Bronstein & Steiner, this volume; Chua, 2011; Juang, Qin, & Park, 2013; Suissa, 2013).

Because intensive mothering adheres to widespread notions that women's primary identities are aligned with and support motherhood, nonconforming women often are trivialized, stigmatized, and punished for their pursuit of and embodiment of other identities, interests, and lifestyles (e.g., motherhood penalty in employment, Abendroth, Huffman, & Treas, 2014; Walters & Harrison, 2014). However, stigma varies across time and location, with even those deeply embedded and culturally sanctioned processes, such as intensive mothering, being socially negotiated and changeable (Meisenbach, 2010; see also Goffman, 1963) and particular discursive positionings enabling women's unconventional roles (e.g., Medved, 2009).

Popular culture provides one context in which mediated representations of gender and everyday life are constructed, contested, and can be (re)negotiated (Storey, 2003). Indeed, there are mediated representations of motherhood that do not reinforce the problematic intensive-mothering dichotomy in which mothers are either "good" or "bad," and instead offer more complicated and nuanced depictions that transgress and transcend this dichotomy (Walters & Harrison, 2014). We contend that one such popular cultural text is the hit AMC television show, *Mad Men*.

May 2015 marked *Man Men*'s seventh and final season, which followed the men and women working in the Madison Avenue advertising agencies in 1960s New York. The series explores both characters' professional and nonwork identities and relationships. The main narrative centers on Don Draper, who is, at the series' opening, the most celebrated creative director in advertising. Effective in career, Don also has a seemingly enviable personal life with a beautiful wife (Betty) and children, a well-appointed home in the suburbs, and discretionary income and time. Even at the start of the *Mad Men* series, however, viewers see the tensions, contradictions, memories, and longings for particular kinds of careers and personal lives that pervade all the characters' lives. Against the backdrop of the advertising agency (SCDP, Sterling Cooper Draper Pryce, and variations on this name), the women of *Mad Men* live with and rebel against societal strictures throughout public, relational, and private realms.

For the women of *Mad Men*, motherhood is ever present in familial aspirations, everyday experiences, and/or conditions that can thwart advancement at work or new personal relationships. Because women are associated so strongly with the private realm despite their current and prior employment, *Mad Men* offers compelling examples of motherhood in the 1960s as well as transgressive mothering portrayals. First, *Mad Men* has received critical acclaim for its contemporaneous depiction of gender, relational, and professional norms, attitudes, values, and behaviors (Lotz, 2014; Rosenberg, 2011). Further, show commentary and critique indicates that *Mad Men* offers an accurate rendition of the complexities and contradictions of gendered performances at this time (Marcotte, 2013). Second, *Mad Men* offers discerning representations of how gendered and relational practices can both constrain and transform dominant norms and constructions, in effect, paving the way for alternative, transgressive portrayals of gender (Buzzanell & D'Enbeau, 2014).

Last, these gendered renditions encourage viewers' popular memory by facilitating connections between the past, present, and future and creating a popular cultural space in which viewers can reflect on how things have changed and how much remains the same (Milestone & Meyer, 2011). The women of *Mad Men* are not unlike today's mothers whose desires for personal autonomy and career bump up against societal expectations. When mothers' career and autonomy desires conflict with normative expectations, women may find themselves fashioning justifications (Buzzanell, Meisenbach, Remke, Liu, Bowers, & Conn, 2005), struggling against forces that marginalize women's bodies in the workplace (Turner & Norwood, 2013), and contending with lower pay despite possessing appropriate credentials (Evers & Sieverding, 2014). In brief, "the 'madness' that *Mad Men* depicts … is most startling when it reminds us of our shortcomings; when it reflects back to us not only our close link to that not-so-distant past, but our own twenty-first-century versions of social—and political—madness" (Marcovitch & Batty, 2012, p. x).

With these aspects in mind, our reading of transgression and motherhood in *Mad Men* illuminates how characters operate within tensions between caregiving expectations and longings for professional success, intimacy, sensuality, and personal autonomy. Specifically, we conducted a critical discourse analysis that explores how some of the women of *Mad Men* perform mothering, gender, identity, sexuality, and femininity. We present three exemplars of transgression that detail how characters embody non-gender-conforming lifestyles, advocate for others' children, and reject mothering altogether. In this chapter, we describe these motherhood portrayals, then elucidate our method, and detail our analysis. We contribute theoretically and pragmatically to feminist change of intensive mothering by capturing moments of transformative possibility in *Mad Men* for characters and audience members and by encouraging mindfulness and dialogic engagement with others to critique and re-story motherhood starting from a difference lens.

## Motherhood in Popular Culture

Mother and mothering popular cultural portrayals often reinforce problematic and limiting gender performances, depicting, for instance, mothers in terms of "archaic oppositions of sacrifice and malevolence" (Walters & Harrison, 2014, p. 39). With regard to sacrifice, in her analysis of motherhood on the hit TV series *Lost*, Freehling-Burton (2012) traces how "the characters who survive the final struggles of and battles between 'good and evil' on the island are ones who consistently or increasingly demonstrated characteristics often ascribed to mothers—seeking peaceful solutions to differences and sacrifice for others including self-sacrifice" (p. 80). In another example, Odland (2010) explains how *Ladies Home Journal* coupled mothers' domesticity and unbridled self-sacrifice with devotion to children within the confines of the home.

In contrast, other popular cultural portrayals of motherhood emphasize deviant, destructive, and downright awful mothers. For instance, Feasey (2012) explains how mothers are shown as weak, irresponsible, and delinquent socially, financially, and sexually on most television teen dramas, like *90210*, *The O.C.*, or *Glee*. In these examples, teenagers have no choice but to cultivate their own supportive community amongst peers because the maternal figures are so tortured and troubled. Moreover, when mothers are portrayed as nonnormative or deviant, viewers are encouraged to cheer on their punishment (Walters & Harrison, 2014). Taken together, these dichotomous representations of mothers as either good or bad reinforce the maternal "notion that there is one right way to solve all dilemmas, despite conflicting discourses that tell us otherwise" (Whelehan, 2012, p. 150).

But there are possibilities and opportunities to push back on these restrictive gender narratives. For instance, D'Enbeau and Buzzanell (2014) propose a reading of *Mad Men* office manager Joan Harris as an "erotic heroine" who "takes advantage of contexts in which she is embedded ... forges her own path ... and strategically pursues a life that will offer her the most transformative possibilities" (p. 13). During the seven seasons of *Mad Men*, Joan moves from desirable single office manager and mistress of a partner to divorcee of a Vietnam veteran and protective mother who uses her (bodily) assets to secure her family's financial future by carving out an agency partnership and who relies on her uneasy relationship with her mother to provide childcare while Joan goes to the office. Throughout, Joan rejects limiting gender norms and transforms patriarchal tropes of motherhood, carving a nuanced and complicated popular cultural space in which to consider gender representations.

In examples of nonconforming representations of motherhood, Walters and Harrison (2014) and Lehman (this volume) show how mothers like Mary-Louise Parker as Nancy Botwin, the suburban mom who goes into the drug-dealing business on *Weeds*, and Edie Falco as the complicated, drug-addicted mother on *Nurse Jackie*, depict the "aberrant mom" who is "not quite a twenty-first-century feminist heroine" but who "does upend more traditional depictions of maternal identity" (Walters & Harrison, 2014, p. 40). Similarly, Peggy in *Mad Men* portrays an ambitious "Horatio Alger" character rising from secretary to agency executive with a publicly (and personally) unacknowledged illegitimate child for whom care is provided by Peggy's mother and sister. Peggy constantly tries to sort out and strategize how to be successful in her career and personal lives. In these cases, viewers see the potential, opportunities, and cautions associated with alternative maternal performances and constructions.

## *Critical Discourse Analysis*

Our reading of *Mad Men* employs a critical discourse analytic approach through which we explore power relations and hegemonic processes by analyzing the scripted talk and interactions of characters as well as the macro Discourses or cultural formations underlying such talk (Alvesson & Kärreman, 2000; Chouliaraki & Fairclough, 2010; Phillips & Oswick, 2012). Our analysis has a decidedly feminist bent as we politicize motherhood and advocate for change that envisions more nuanced, challenging, and potentially more fulfilling gender roles and relations (Buzzanell, 1994; Walters & Harrison, 2014). We explore how *Mad Men* mothers resolve, resist, and/or transcend tensions surrounding motherhood, and in so doing offer moments of transgressive possibilities in very different and character-appropriate ways.

To develop our reading of mothering in *Mad Men*, each of us took extensive notes and developed individual (and then collaborative) commentary on the episodes that form Seasons 1–7, looking for critical incidents where mothering relationships were featured. We located incidents that address how characters negotiated, perceived, and developed mothering practices and strategies and explored how these relationships and incidents intersected with gender and other cultural formations. We also examined content at both the denotative and connotative levels to highlight implications for contemporary understandings of transgressive mothering (Storey, 2003). Our reading surfaced the tensions produced by transgressive moments that could usurp the stronghold of intensive motherhood.

## *Findings and Interpretation*

Our essay is based on the assumption that the production of counterpoints to intensive mothering in *Mad Men* is not a politically neutral act that was unconsciously constructed by the writers, producers, directors, and character portrayals. Rather, *Mad Men* depicts transgressive mothering practices that are embedded within authentic representations of particular socio-historical-cultural moments in time that engage viewers' "popular memory" (Spigel, 2001), and that blur borders and boundaries of fiction and nonfiction (see Buzzanell & D'Enbeau, 2014). Indeed, numerous researchers have argued that the ways in which characters are portrayed in popular media provide insights for how viewers should and could respond to dilemmas in professional work as well as in other life realms (e.g., Cheney & Ashcraft, 2007; Hassard & Holliday, 1998; Pullen & Rhodes, 2013). Unlike many instances in lived experiences, media display the ways in which things are not what they seem, offering insights into the hidden and complex ways that women enact caregiving, particularly motherhood, and other life aspects in particular moments and over the course of their lives. These fine-grained depictions provide material through which media consumers can construct new insights into limits, possibilities, and consequences afforded by choice and agency.

Towards this end, we present three exemplars of mothering in situ that expose transgressive possibilities: (a) transgressive modeling of alternative lifestyles; (b) transgressive advocacy for others' children; and (c) transgressive anti-mothering. We note that these possibilities exist not only in mediated space where characters reside but also in the lives of viewers who might also entertain such transgressions.

## *Transgressive Modeling of Alternative Lifestyles*

To begin, transgressive mothering on *Mad Men* depicts the modeling of alternative lifestyles that contradict intensive-mothering ideals and disrupt the heteronormative status quo. By alternative lifestyles, we mean portrayals of women who do not conform to the gendered norms and ideals of the time. During the first two seasons, the wives of *Mad Men* executives and their friends live in the suburbs. Betty, then the wife of Don Draper, is talking to a psychiatrist about how she met Don, misses and hates her late mother, and does not know what to do with herself from one day to the next while her husband spends nights in Manhattan and she is lonely and alone with their children in Long Island. She describes her mother's great beauty and her mother's constant advice on weight and beauty. To her psychiatrist, Betty remarks, "I miss her [mother], I understand that. It's good and bad. She wanted me to be beautiful so that I could find a man. But then what? … Just sit and smoke and let it go until you are in a box?" ("Shoot").

Echoing the sentiments exposed by Friedan's (1963) *The Feminine Mystique*, Betty's question of "but then what?" coupled with the suburban housewives' everyday pattern—visiting each other, decorating homes and hosting parties, shopping, fixing meals, doing laundry, driving children places, supervising household help (when available), and recalling a more exciting prior life (like Betty's modeling career)—breeds boredom, underutilization of talents, and fixation on retaining the only basis of power that these women have—their marriages and their childrearing. Into this heteronormative community of traditional two-parent families enters one exception. That exception is Helen Bishop. Helen is a beautiful divorcee, college graduate, and mother of Glen. Helen also works in a jewelry shop, hires babysitters to take care of her child while she engages in paid labor and goes out on dates, takes long walks for exercise, and joins reelection political campaigns as a volunteer.

That Helen is divorced casts doubts about her character and puts fear into married women's hearts. The divorce rates of U.S. couples in the 1960s ranged from the low to mid-20 percentages (U.S. Department of Health, Education, and Welfare, 1973) but rose steadily thereafter (U.S. Census Bureau, 2011). Indeed the unwelcome and seemingly irrational fear that Helen is competition for the wives' partners and, by extension, lifestyles, is an age-old drama. She is considered "very selfish" by Betty in Season 2 because she works rather than being home with her child. At the party for Betty's children, when Helen is alone with the husbands, the wives quickly enter to forestall any further interactions. Helen's transgressions are that she disrupts the heteronormative married mother mold and engages in activities that please no one but her. She seems to enjoy being out of the home and in the world of paid employment, and she presumably has an active sex life despite her divorce, as Betty discovers when she finds The Pill, a controversial oral contraceptive for women, in Helen's bathroom cabinet. In other words, Helen is a threat to the status quo and to the security—marriage and children—to which the wives cling for social status, financial support, and spatio-temporal order in their lives.

The wives' speculations on the harms that divorced mothers can bring upon their children seem to be fulfilled when Glen acts oddly. He spends a lot of time alone at home or with babysitters. He is angry with his mother because he thinks she would rather go out on dates than care for and spend time with him. He develops a fantasy that Betty might be as attracted to and interested in him as he is to her. When Helen discovers that Glen has a lock of Betty's hair and that he ran away to hide in Betty's backyard, Helen confronts Betty and argues that "we have to talk. I don't know why he was over here but it has to stop" ("Red in the Face"). Betty and Helen do talk in one of the very rare times during the series when Betty tells the truth of her life. Betty is not a particularly patient or nurturing mother even by 1960s "custodial" mothering standards (see O'Brien Hallstein, 2010, p. 122, for a description of O'Reilly's [2004] *Mother Outlaws*). Yet Helen offers transgressive possibilities by embodying a model that seems to be even less devoted to children than Betty's. Moreover, Betty and Don's marriage has run afoul, as Betty says, "Don isn't living here," to which Helen responds that she is sorry. Helen says that she thought that with Dan, her ex-husband, out of her life she would be a better mother. But she says that Glen is right. She is not a better mother. In other words, Helen's projections about the divorcee's life—that she would carve out a more fulfilling and caring life for herself and her son when freed from marital conflict and obligations—was simply a fantasy. Helen says that it has not been all that different without her ex-husband. With this confession, the divorcee and the stay-at-home mother—two seemingly different representations of motherhood—uncover a surprising glimpse of common ground as they question the dominant gendered roles they find so limiting and constraining.

Betty continues to remark that they have not told the children and, in response to Helen's query about whether the marriage is over, Betty answers that she does not know. But Betty also explains that sometimes she feels as though she would float away if Don was not there holding her down. Helen remarks that the hardest part of being divorced is knowing that she is in charge. Not finding fulfillment (being grounded) in her own personal and familial/community life (Betty), and recognizing that the life of the divorcee involves unanticipated agency-control and self-motherhood dilemmas (Helen) provide insights into the struggles that these women and other characters in *Mad Men* routinely faced but often did not acknowledge overtly.

Helen's obvious transgressions—disregard for her primary roles in society as wife and mother—are not the main issues in these scenes. It is not simply that she is disrupting the heteronormative arrangements but more so that she models an alternative lifestyle that does not situate intensive (or even custodial) mothering and marriage at the center. Instead, she pursues other activities that are met with scrutiny, derision, and curiosity. She also creates a discursive opening for an authentic exchange between Betty and herself by being divorced and not being the "perfect" wife and mother. For a moment, Betty feels safe enough in the shelter of the stigmatized Other to disclose that her world is not ideal despite her own (and Don's) efforts to perform their roles as superficially ideal to various publics. Even so, this moment is short lived. Viewers see Betty's struggles as her world is unraveling and Helen's admissions that single motherhood is not always glamorous and fulfilling.

These transgressive portrayals of mothering situated within turbulent relational dynamics and breached societal norms offer unfulfilled openings for continued confrontations around issues of and emotions involved in intense motherhood, marital relations, and women's friendships. Shortly thereafter, Betty no longer wants to confront her behaviors when pushed to do so by Helen's remarks about Betty's interactions with Glen. Betty slaps Helen across the face at the grocery store. With this slap, Betty engages in the discursive closure process of disqualification, thereby denying Helen voice, and legitimizing Betty's (superior) social role as stay-at-home mother and wife (see Deetz, 1992). The social order is restored with this slap as the married woman disgraces the divorcee whose concern for her child is only one part of her life rather than her raison d'etre.

Furthermore, Helen is stigmatized but her son, Glen, also is stigmatized by association. For the most part, Helen's life is solitary with only an occasional show of friendship from her neighbors, as situationally demanded (e.g., invitation to a child's birthday party where neighbors were invited). She embodies the maternal sexuality that has long been depicted as threatening to the mother-child relationship. Thus, Helen's transgressive modeling of an alternative lifestyle offers a potential opening for authentic expressions that could enable exploration of more fulfilling and complex personal and relational behaviors. However, our reading suggests that for this endeavor to be realized, mothers must be willing and able to transcend the false dichotomy between good and bad, married and divorced, content and suffering, and so on, to find common ground in their diverse experiences as mothers and women.

## *Transgressive Advocacy for Others' Children*

In intensive mothering, women are considered to be the natural (or instinctively knowledgeable), primary, and devoted caregivers and nurturers of their own children (see Douglas & Michaels, 2004; O'Brien Hallstein, 2010), thus breeding conditions where mothers tend not to admit when they "have no clue" about mothering and that they resent others' advice regarding their parenting activities (see Buzzanell & D'Enbeau, 2009). Even so, mothers often transgress the unspoken rule not to give other mothers advice (unless requested) and "interfere" in parenting when conditions seem to warrant such interventions. In these cases, transgressive mothering consists both of the failure of the target mother to provide adequate or good care and of the other mothers to fill in the spaces left by the target mother.

Advocacy for others' children's welfare disrupts deep-seated assumptions that mothers are primary and the best caregivers. This assumption is the basis of contemporary divorce and child custody expectations that mothers are the parents with whom children typically should reside. This assumption also is the basis for the return of children placed in foster care for their safety to their mothers (Allard, 2006; Gerstenzang, 2007). Finally, this assumption is the basis for perceived longing by adopted children to find their birth mothers (Wadia-Ells, 1995) and for longing by society for intense mothering that presumably can solve social ills and maintain middle-class status. Because of these assumptions, women who engage in intense mothering of other women's birth children even when these women have legitimate role relations, such as legal stepmother or hired caregiver, operate in spaces of transgressive mothering. Not only are their behaviors considered nonnormative, but these women are stigmatized by evil stepmother stereotypes (Ganong & Coleman, 1995) and by their lower-class standing in relation to the birth mother (Ehrenreich & Hochschild, 2002). In this way, those who engage in other-mothering are vilified for challenging the natural or birth mother's role. Despite societal mandates not to interfere with the mother-child bond or to call into question the mother's ability to provide quality nurturing and oversight, these women transgress boundaries in ways that are not welcomed by others.

For instance, Betty's housekeeper, Carla, is a Black woman with children of her own whom she is supporting by assisting Betty with cooking, cleaning, ironing, and childcare. She is doubly transgressive in her mothering. Her own children are growing up without her presence during the weekdays and sometimes on weekends when Betty is out of town. She acts as a surrogate mother caught in conflicting demands when Betty requires a particular action and Carla attempts to comply but acts, instead, in what she believes are the children's best interests.

The conflict over appropriate mothering by behavior, emotions, and person smolders over the course of several episodes when, for instance, Carla teaches Sally, Betty's daughter, how to make French toast. Then, in the Season 4 finale when Betty is remarried to Henry Francis and preparing to move her family into his house, she reasserts her agency in one final powerful move when she fires Carla on the spot for allowing Sally to say goodbye to Glen before the relocation. Carla admits that she did not see anything wrong with the two children saying goodbye. Betty becomes agitated and defensively asks Carla what makes her their mother? Carla is clearly confused by Betty's attack that to her seems unfounded. Mixed in with racial, gendered, class, and motherhood intersectionalities, Betty's need to assert her agency and control in a context where the Other seemingly cannot resist in ways to reverse or transform the act means that Betty can insure her own power and sense of stability in a world fraught with change.

Betty takes some cash out of her purse and tries to give it to Carla as she lets her know that she no longer has a job. When Carla wants to at least say goodbye to the kids, Betty refuses and Carla leaves. The intensity of this heated exchange is confounded by the fact that Betty seems to know she did something wrong but is extremely frustrated by her circumstances and by her lack of control in most aspects of her life. By firing Carla, Betty is able to reaffirm some semblance of authority in her household. Later that evening, Henry questions Betty's decision to fire Carla. Betty explains that she wants a "fresh start" to which Henry replies that "Lives carry on." Even though he disagrees with Betty's action, Henry does not traverse the boundary of the mother knowing what is best for her child and the position of mother as in charge of the private realm.

*Mad Men* motherhood and caregiving take on different forms that defy the logics of intensive mothering. Betty does not seem to want to entertain the notion that she might not know or want to do what might be best for her children. Although not their biological mother, Carla tries to act in the children's best interests just as she did for her own children by earning a wage to support them. The core dilemma of what is best for the children is trumped by intensive-mothering ideologies that unquestioningly side with biological mothers' supposed devotion to and knowledge about their children's welfare as they forgo paid labor to affirm the privileged mother-child bond. In these episodes, Carla offers a contested site to question intensive mothering, its ironic consequences, and potentially transgressive mothering possibilities. In these episodes, Carla spans "a variety of work and family roles, complicating traditional bounded notions of both workplace and family" (Townsley, 2006, p. 149), performing family across borders and space, for her birth family and Betty's family. In this White middle-class world, Carla's behavior is doubly transgressive in that she leaves her own children for paid labor, and she confronts her (White) employer about her failings to be a good mother. As a Black woman, Carla is not permitted to perform intensive mothering. Instead, her own mothering and her paid work experiences are rendered invisible by strategic discursive positionings that pit professional, white-collar, masculine work against unpaid, reproductive, feminine labor in the home (Duffy, 2007). In this context, the paid caregiving work of non-White women that arguably facilitates the image of intensive mothering is in some cases, unacknowledged and, in many cases, vilified for undermining and challenging the role of the birth mother. And yet Carla represents a transgressive portrayal of mothering by highlighting the intersections of three structures of power in the United States: "the capitalist class structure, the patriarchal sex hierarchy, and the racial division of labor" (Rollins, 1985, p. 7). In this way, *Mad Men* reveals how the middle-class image of intensive mothering is sustained by a raced, classed, and gendered system that privileges some types of work(ers) over others.

## *Transgressive Anti-Mothering*

The final way in which we consider *Mad Men* mothering transgressions is through anti-mothering representations. Transgressive anti-mothering accounts for both the strategic and constrained choices that women make with regard to maternity, care, and work. The decoupling of woman and mother from desires for meaningful relationships and intimacy also serve as transgressive acts. Indeed, transgressive anti-mothering combats discursive conflations of "woman" and "mother," defies discourses of intensive mothering, and supports the choice to be childless (see Hayden, 2010a, 2010b).

For instance, Dr. Faye Miller is an unmarried (although she wears a wedding ring), successful strategist for a consumer-research company who is contracted to work with SCDP. She is admired by the young women in the office (e.g., Peggy looks to Faye for professional and gendered mentoring; Buzzanell & D'Enbeau, 2014). Faye is also good at her professional work, drawing upon her own femininity to encourage the unmarried secretaries in a focus group to spill their beauty routine secrets about Ponds Cold Cream that ends up being about failed relationships with men. She is powerful, autonomous, strategic, and intelligent in the public sphere.

Don and Faye engage in an affair, one that must remain private while Faye is under contract with SCDP. Don confides in her about his real and assumed identities. He is relieved to share this confidence, which Faye interprets as bringing them closer. She admits that she decided not to have children, not because she does not like children but because she prioritizes her professional career. When she resigns from her job, she contacts Don in the hopes that they can make their relationship public. But Don rejects Faye in favor of his younger, seemingly more maternal, secretary, Megan. Faye does reflect on her (potential) lack of maternal instinct, worrying that she has failed with Don's kids because she does not know how to comfort his daughter Sally after she suffers a fall in the office, whereas Megan does. Faye is honest and willing to make herself vulnerable.

It is not simply that Faye transgresses societal norms but that she decouples woman and mother to focus on what she wants and where she feels comfortable. More directly, Faye rejects women's primary role as mothers, a major transgression since the family unit of the married couple with children is sacred in that it fulfills religious and societal roles for reproductive labor. The transgressive anti-mothering is not only that Faye fractures long-term (marital) relationships and motherhood, preferring the former and rejecting the latter, but that she chooses to be childless (Hayden, 2010b). Choices to be child free are still met with sympathy, disbelief, anger, and stigmatization, especially as people move through the lifespan. The only acceptable reason to be child free is for medical reasons, and even then the woman is found wanting even if the medical condition is not of her own making (Ellingson & Sotirin, 2010).

Faye also seems to believe that she can have both relationships and a career on her terms. This is transgressive anti-mothering insofar as she nurtures others' potential, as an unwitting role model for career-oriented women, but cannot fulfill her own wishes because the fulfillment requires another party. Instead,

Faye is capable of fulfilling expectations that are under her own control, such as her own work. Faye is an example of what mothers are not, rather than all that women can be. Faye's example points to the potential of transgression to offer possibilities for nontraditional roles with the caveat that transgressions might also be the starting points for isolation, a recurring (autonomy-relationship) tension in Peggy's life. In some ways, Faye represents the stigma of the career woman left with either/or possibilities but not always able to carve out what she wants in terms of relationships without embracing the whole gendered package.

## Discussion

The beauty of *Mad Men* is found in the depth and complexities of cultural representations of motherhood.[1] These episodes can be analyzed in context for relational and cultural tensions marked by continuity and change. Although this essay examined only a few of the many transgressive mothering episodes in *Mad Men*, our critical discourse analysis contributes to feminist inquiry by showing how *Mad Men*, as a popular cultural text, portrays mothering as a contested site in which women can explore how intensive-mothering processes can be both destructive and transformative, affirming and disconfirming, and self-focused and community oriented when not carried to extremes and when situated amidst other possibilities. Our critique of mothering provides possibilities for further exploration and replication by audience members.

First, our reading of *Mad Men* delineates transgressive mothering as those gendered processes that disrupt intensive-mothering "ideals" by modeling alternative lifestyles, advocating for others' children, and engaging in anti-mothering practices. We note that transgressive mothering, at times, is highly ambiguous and ambivalent as it depicts competing ends. Modeling alternative lifestyles reinserts maternal sexuality and personal fulfillment into dominant understandings of motherhood. Advocating for others' children showcases the complex web of relationships and roles that surface in examinations of who and how care is provided to children. Anti-mothering pushes back on dominant tropes of gender, woman, and mother by redefining femininity outside of women's relationships with men, children, and the family. Taken together, these portrayals offer a multiplicity of diverse motherhood performances that disrupt binary constructions of motherhood as either evil or perfect and disavow discourses of intensive mothering. What is more, just as these "discordant images are a sign of our continued cultural confusion over motherhood and family," they also indicate that motherhood "can no longer be so narrowly defined, so reined in under a singular rubric" and are, therefore a sign of progress (Walters & Harrison, 2014, p. 51).

Admittedly, the lack of intensive mothering seems to lead to disastrous results for the children (at least in the characters' lived moments), yet the failure is that others do not step forward to fill in gaps. The men can ask their secretaries to fill in, as Don does with Megan, or can hire caregivers, thus fulfilling their fatherhood role. Moreover, the culture of intensive mothering is couched in neoliberal cultural formations or Discourses of individual choice (Reich, 2014), promoting both intensive-mothering practices and the moral default to mothers as primary stakeholders in decisions regarding their children's well-being. Mothers are considered to be experts on their own children even when others, such as Don and later Henry and Megan, question the mother's (Betty's) decisions. Further, the appearance of intensive mothering seems, at times, to be more important than the realities of a caring environment. For instance, Don tells Betty that he wishes he had a mother like her even after viewers have seen her routinely neglect and dismiss her own children's emotional needs, as she herself struggles to identify her own emotional requirements. Yet, these nonconforming depictions of mothering on *Mad Men* that contradict discourses of intensive mothering should not be read as further support for "blame the mother" tropes in which challenges around intimacy and caregiving are the sole responsibility of the mother. Put simply, transgressive mothering shifts the spotlight to the women's personal desires and activities and this is not necessarily a bad thing.

Second, our reading considers the broader historical context of *Mad Men* that is dominated by significant changes in areas of consumerism, medicine, technology, and political landscapes. Specifically, *Mad Men* depicts economic and societal changes afforded by the relative prosperity of the post-WWII economy as well as disjunctures given technological changes, political and social upheaval, uncertainties of the atomic age, and public-private divisions. In particular, *Mad Men* operates at a time when questions are just beginning to emerge about the relative absence of fathers at home, the seclusion of women and mothers in the suburbs, and structural inequalities of a modern capitalistic system. In this context, transgressive mothering operates as both opportunities and threats to the status quo during the 1960s. Our reading proposes broader, all-encompassing tensions between the past and future that surface resentments and struggle but also hopefulness for change. The 1960s and its aftermath was arguably one of the most significant times in terms of changing gender roles for women in the United States, so there is understandably ambivalence, hopefulness, pessimism, and fear that surfaced and that manifested in ironic and sometimes contradictory ways, as the show documents the erosion of male dominance and shifting gender norms (see Hundley, 2013). In this way, our analysis reveals a cautionary tale about women's (and men's) vulnerabilities and opportunities as they work through characters' transgressions and likely outcomes.

In conclusion, *Mad Men* offers a space for understanding and critique of transgressive mothering by the characters and by viewers questioning their own lives. To fulfill the transformatory potential, characters and audience members would need to engage in mindfulness about their own behaviors within the very real material conditions of their lives. By tracing why and how transgressions led to particular consequences and how the *Mad Men* stories could have been rewritten while also maintaining narrative fidelity and character coherence (see Fisher, 1985), *Mad Men* provides fodder for self- and other-instruction. However, change cannot be situated solely or even primarily at the individual level. Our analysis also reveals that transgressive motherhood in popular media offers insights into the ways mothering can be transformed through attention to difference. By using our *Mad Men* exemplars as contrastive sites for explorations and Minow's (1990) assumptions about difference as a framework for advocating how the ideology of intensive motherhood can be changed, we encourage the audience of *Mad Men* to engage in the following actions to promote transformation: consciously question what is normative, who judges and what the reference points for assessment are, how such norms and evaluations perpetuate the dominant group's interests, how to optimally incorporate the perspectives of mothers and other women, and how to work toward greater understandings and convictions that the status quo is not inevitable. Finally, engaging in critique and actions resulting from a difference lens can help make visible how intensive mothers' sole focus on their own children undermines not only possibilities for their own personal fulfillment but also community well-being (see Reich, 2014).

## Note

1. For an additional discussion of motherhood representations on *Mad Men*, see Martínez Guillem and Flores, this volume.

## References

Abendroth, A. K., Huffman, M., & Treas, J. (2014). The parity penalty in life course perspective: Motherhood and occupational status in 13 European countries. *American Sociological Review*, *79*(5), 993–1014.

Allard, P. E. (2006). Research to action: Informing policy makers about the needs of mothers and children at risk of separation. *Women & Criminal Justice, 17*, 27–42.
Alvesson, M., & Kärreman, D. (2000). Varieties of discourse: On the study of organizations through discourse analysis. *Human Relations, 53*, 1125–1149.
Buzzanell, P. M. (1994). Gaining a voice: Feminist organizational communication theorizing. *Management Communication Quarterly, 7*, 339–383.
Buzzanell, P. M., & D'Enbeau, S. (2009). Stories of caregiving: Intersections of popular gender, academic research, and one woman's experiences. *Qualitative Inquiry, 15*, 1119–1224.
Buzzanell, P. M., & D'Enbeau, S. (2014). Ambivalent, political, and erotic mentoring: Popular culture and mentor-mentee relational processes in *Mad Men. Human Relations, 67*, 695–714.
Buzzanell, P. M., Meisenbach, R., Remke, R., Liu, M., Bowers, V., & Conn, C. (2005). The good *working* mother: Managerial women's sensemaking and feelings about work–family issues. *Communication Studies, 56*, 261–285.
Cheney, G., & Ashcraft, K. L. (2007). Considering "the professional" in communication studies: Implications for theory and research within and beyond the boundaries of organizational communication. *Communication Theory, 17*, 146–175.
Chouliaraki, L., & Fairclough, N. (2010). Critical discourse analysis in organization studies: Towards an integrationist methodology. *Journal of Management Studies, 47*, 1213–1218.
Chua, A. (2011) *Battle hymn of the tiger mother.* New York, NY: Penguin Books.
Deetz, S. A. (1992). *Democracy in the age of corporate colonization: Developments in communication and the politics of everyday life.* Albany, NY: SUNY Press.
D'Enbeau, S., & Buzzanell, P. M. (2014). The erotic heroine and the politics of gender at work: A feminist reading of *Mad Men's* Joan Harris. In N. Jones, M. Bajac-Carter, & B. Batchelor (Eds.), *Heroines of film and television: Portrayals in popular culture* (pp. 3–16). Lanham, MD: Rowan & Littlefield.
D'Enbeau, S., & Buzzanell, P. M. (2010). Caregiving and female embodiment: Scrutinizing (professional) female bodies in media, academe, and the neighborhood bar. *Women & Language, 33*, 29–52.
Douglas, S., & Michaels, M. (2004). *The mommy myth: The idealization of motherhood and how it has undermined all women.* New York, NY: Free Press.
Duffy, M. (2007). Doing the dirty work: Gender, race, and reproductive labor in historical perspective. *Gender & Society, 21*, 313–336.
Ehrenreich, B., & Hochschild, A. R. (Eds). (2002). *Global woman: Nannies, maids, and sex workers in the new economy.* New York, NY: Henry Holt and Company.
Ellingson, L. L., & Sotirin, P. J. (2010). *Aunting: Cultural practices that sustain family and community life.* Waco, TX: Baylor University Press.
Evers, A., & Sieverding, M. (2014). Why do highly qualified women (still) earn less? Gender differences in long-term predictors of career success. *Psychology of Women Quarterly, 38*, 93–106.

Feasey, R. (2012). Absent, ineffectual, and intoxicated mothers: Representing the maternal in teen television. *Feminist Media Studies, 12*, 155–159.

Fisher, W. (1985). The narrative paradigm: An elaboration. *Communication Monographs, 52*, 347–367.

Freehling-Burton, K. (2012). Lost mothers: The "othering" of mothers on the TV show *Lost*. *Femspec, 12*, 66–84.

Friedan, B. (1963). *The feminine mystique*. New York, NY: W. W. Norton.

Ganong, L. H., & Coleman, M. (1995). The content of mother stereotypes. *Sex Roles, 32*, 495–512.

Gerstenzang, S. (2007). *Another mother: Co-parenting with the foster care system*. Nashville, TN: Vanderbilt University Press.

Goffman, E. (1963). *Stigma: Notes on the management of spoiled identity*. New York, NY: Simon & Schuster.

Hassard, J., & Holliday, J. (Eds.). (1998). *Organization-representation: Work and organization in popular culture*. London, UK: Sage.

Hayden, S. (2010a). Lessons from *The Baby Boon*: Family-friendly policies and the ethics of justice and care. *Women's Studies in Communication, 33*, 119–137.

Hayden, S. (2010b). Purposefully childless good women. In S. Hayden & D. Lynn O'Brien Hallstein (eds.), *Contemplating maternity in an era of choice: Explorations into discourses of reproduction* (pp. 269–290). Lanham, MD: Lexington Books.

Hundley, H. (2013). Mediated portrayals of masculinities.. In A. N. Valdivia & E. Scharrer (Eds.), *The international encyclopedia of media studies: Media effects/media psychology*, (pp. 240–262). Oxford, UK: Blackwell Publishing Ltd.

Juang, L. P., Qin, D. B., & Park, I. J. K. (2013). Deconstructing the myth of the "tiger mother": An introduction to the special issue on tiger parenting, Asian-heritage families, and child/adolescent well-being. *Asian American Journal of Psychology, 4*(1), 1–6.

Lotz, A. D. (2014, April 11). Don Draper's sad manhood: What makes *Mad Men* different from *Breaking Bad, Sopranos*. *Salon*. Retrieved from http://www.salon.com/2014/04/11/don_ drapers_sad_manhood_what_makes_mad_men_different_from_breaking_bad_sopranos/

Marcotte, A. (2013, April 5). What *Mad Men* says about women. *The Guardian*. Retrieved from http://www.theguardian.com/tv-and-radio/2013/apr/05/what-mad-men-says-about-women

Marcovitch, H., & Batty, N. E. (Eds.). Mad Men, *women, and children: Essays on gender and generation*. Lanham, MD: Lexington Books.

Medved, C. E. (2009). Constructing breadwinning mother identities: Moral, personal, and political positioning. *Women's Studies Quarterly, 37*(3/4), 140–156.

Meisenbach, R. J. (2010). Stigma management communication: A theory and agenda for applied research on how individuals manage moments of stigmatized identity. *Journal of Applied Communication Research, 38*, 268–292.

Milestone, K., & Meyer, A. (2011). *Gender and popular culture*. Cambridge, UK: Polity Press.

Minow, M. (1990). *Making all the difference: Inclusion, exclusion and the American law.* Ithaca, NY: Cornell University Press.

O'Brien Hallstein, L. (2010). *White feminists and contemporary maternity: Purging matrophobia.* New York, NY: Palrave Macmillan.

Odland, S. B. (2010). Unassailable motherhood, ambivalent domesticity: The construction of maternal identity in *Ladies' Home Journal* in 1946. *Journal of Communication Inquiry, 34,* 61–84.

O'Reilly, A. (2004). *Mother outlaws: Theories and practices of empowered mothering.* Toronto, ON: Women's Press.

Phillips, N., & Oswick, C. (2012) Organizational discourse: Domains, debates, and directions. *The Academy of Management Annals, 6,* 1–47.

Pullen, A., & Rhodes, C. (2013). Parody, subversion and the politics of gender at work: The case of *Futurama*'s "Raging Bender." *Organization, 20,* 512–533.

Reich, J. A. (2014). Neoliberal mothering and vaccine refusal: Imagined gated communities and the privilege of choice. *Gender & Society, 28,* 679–704.

Rollins, J. (1985). *Between women: Domestics and their employers.* Philadelphia, PA: Temple University Press.

Rosenberg, A. (2011, Sept. 19). TV's new nostalgia for sexism. *Salon.* Retrieved from http://www.salon.com/2011/09/19/back_to_the_sixties/

Spigel L. (2001) *Welcome to the dreamhouse: Popular media and the postwar suburbs.* Durham, NC: Duke University Press.

Storey, J. (2003). *Cultural studies and the study of popular culture* (2nd ed.). Athens, GA: The University of Georgia Press.

Suissa, J. (2013). Tiger mothers and praise junkies: Children, praise and the reactive attitudes. *Journal of Philosophy of Education, 47,* 1–19.

Townsley, N. C. (2006). Love, sex, and tech in the global workplace. In B. J. Dow & J. T. Wood (Eds.), *The Sage handbook of gender and communication* (pp. 143–160). Thousand Oaks, CA: Sage.

Turner, P., & Norwood, K. (2013). Unbounded motherhood: Embodying a good working mother identity. *Management Communication Quarterly, 27,* 396–424.

U.S. Census Bureau. (2011). *Statistical abstracts of the United States: Section 2–Births, deaths, marriages, and divorces.* Washington, DC.

U.S. Department of Health, Education, and Welfare. (1973). *100 years of marriage and divorce statistics, United States 1867–1967.* National Vital Statistics Series 21, Number 24. Washington, DC.

Wadia-Ells, S. (Ed.). (1995). *The adoption reader: Birth mothers, adoptive mothers, and adopted daughters tell their stories.* Seattle, WA: Seal Press.

Walters, S. D., & Harrison, L. (2014). Not ready to make nice: Aberrant mothers in contemporary culture. *Feminist Media Studies, 14,* 38–55.

Whelehan, I. (2012). "Shit and string beans," boredom and babies: Bad mothers in popular fiction since 1968. In E. Podnieks (Ed.), *Mediating moms: Mothers in popular culture* (pp. 147–166). Montreal, QC: McGill-Queen's University Press.

# 3. *Motherhood and Mental Health: Carrie Mathison's* Homeland *Pregnancy*

By Elizabeth Fish Hatfield

The mass media's portrayal of pregnancy and parenthood often demonstrates an unrealistic view of these experiences, idealizing intensive mothering and promoting a pronatalist viewpoint. One recent depiction of pregnancy breaking the Hollywood mold is that of Carrie Mathison on Showtime's *Homeland*. The Central Intelligence Agency (CIA) officer's pregnancy became a storyline in the show's third season for many reasons—the married, terrorist father, Carrie's nontraditional career, her reaction to the pregnancy, and her ongoing struggle with mental illness. Carrie's character brings up many questions about capable parenting, inviting viewers to consider their own opinions. Research has shown the media significantly impact how people think about mental health issues, particularly audiences who do not have personal experience with the subject (Gerbner, Gross, Morgan, Signorielli, & Shanahan, 2002; Philo, Secker, Platt, Henderson, McLaughlin, & Burnside, 1994; Signorielli, 1989). Additionally, a correlation has been found between television viewing and intolerance to people with mental health issues (Granello & Pauley, 2000; Sieff, 2003). However, in creating protagonist Carrie, show writers have positioned audiences to support and empathize with her struggle—humanizing the challenges of bipolar disorder even as they simultaneously dramatize them. The show highlights Carrie's periodic struggles to manage her own care by depicting issues with medication dosages and problems with her career. However, by introducing a pregnancy into the storyline, the show asks viewers to question Carrie's ability to parent.

This chapter analyzes Carrie Mathison's pregnancy in the television show *Homeland* as an atypical pregnancy. In this study, I look at how the pregnancy becomes a narrative tool that invites audiences to consider social norms surrounding motherhood and mental health. With an idealized good mother as a pillar of our culture, Carrie's pregnancy immediately characterizes her form of motherhood as alternative. Her mental health issues and refusal to prioritize prenatal care position her as a bad mother even during pregnancy, reflecting the dichotomy that is motherhood, with two extreme choices rather than a continuum of capability. The first three complete seasons of the show were analyzed thematically to argue that Carrie's character offers a transgressive form of motherhood as she balances career, mental health issues, and a pregnancy. In their review of research examining mental health depictions in the media, Stout, Villegas, and Jennings (2004) identified gaps in the literature relating to mass media depictions of mental illness, stigma, and audience reception. They noted the field had incredible room to grow. A decade later, many scholars have answered their call, expanding the body of research on stigma, studying how exposure to mental health issues changes perceptions, and analyzing mediated representations (see Caputo & Rouner, 2011; Corrigan, Watson, Gracia, Slopen, Rasinski, & Hall, 2005; Klin & Lemish, 2008; McGinty, Webster, & Barry, 2013). This chapter contributes to that research by connecting the relationship with mental health and motherhood in fictional media. Ultimately, Carrie Mathison's *Homeland* pregnancy presents a nonnormative motherhood possibility that reinterprets the challenges of work, family, and mental health.

## *Mental Health, Motherhood, and the Media*

Over the course of three seasons, *Homeland* received mixed reviews for its depiction of mental health, and specifically, bipolar disorder. *The Guardian* called the first season "a step forward" (Whitehead, May 7, 2012, headline) and a "vast improvement on much of what's gone before" (Whitehead, May 7, 2012, para. 1). Praise for the show's depiction of mental health continued through the next two seasons, as reviewers called the show "groundbreakingly realistic" (Lacob, April 10, 2012, para. 3), "the best example we've seen to date" (Reyers, 2014, para. 1), and "not only accurate, but ... commendable" (Sifferlin, October 8, 2013, para. 2). Yet, the storyline's progression also brought criticism, as reviewers found that Carrie, played by Clare Danes, depicted a stereotypical "crazy" person that inaccurately portrays the condition (Havrilesky, March 12, 2013; Rouleau, 2014; Shoals, September 25, 2013). Consistent across these contrasting reviews was an awareness that the narrative brings mental health to mainstream media in the form of a heroic, yet flawed, main character—allowing life with a bipolar diagnosis to become part of the national conversation. Sifferlin (October 8, 2013) argues that while "entertainment value can still get in the way of a completely accurate portrayal" (para. 6), current media depictions of mental health shift "away from those showing the mentally ill to be primarily psychotic" (para. 7). Indeed, Carrie leads a successful life as *Homeland's* protagonist, often demonstrating signs of genius in her role as a CIA agent.

Fifteen years ago, research found that television characters with mental illness did not display the mental capacity of a typical person, instead being portrayed as slow, disoriented, or simple (Wilson, Nairn, Coverdale, & Panapa, 1999), but Carrie's narrative presents a new role model for viewers dealing with similar issues (Sifferlin, 2013), as well as the opportunity to change cultural perspectives surrounding mental illness (Stout, Villegas, & Jennings, 2004). Presenting a likable protagonist with a mental health diagnosis results in audience members decreasing their social distancing behaviors according to Caputo and Rouner (2011). They found stigma regarding mental health concerns was reduced for their participants because the character becomes relatable.

This concept of stigma weaves through much of the research on mental illness. Researchers consistently note the existence of both public stigma and self-stigma regarding bipolar disorder (Elgie & Morselli, 2007; Vasquez, Kapczinski, Magalhaes, Cordoba, Lopez Jaramillo, et al., 2011; Wahl, 1992), highlighting the impact stigma has on an individual's self-concept and path to success. The media offer most people's primary source of information about health issues (Edney, 2004), and especially for heavy viewers, media messages become reality (Gerbner et al., 2002). The media often present characters stereotypically, framing people with mental health conditions as unpredictable, dangerous, violent, and bizarre or abnormal (Caputo & Rouner, 2011). Early research on Carrie's *Homeland* character identified the use of the "hysterical woman" stereotype in her depiction (Rouleau, 2014), and hegemonic, normative gender role schemas as her mental illness undermines her professional success (Murray, 2014). Carrie both adheres to and contrasts existing stereotypes about bipolar disease, which may be why popular media offered such a diversity of opinions on the show's portrayal of mental health. Her intellectual capabilities contrast earlier media portrayals of someone living with a bipolar diagnosis, yet her actions reinforce stereotypes about unpredictability, irrationality, and personal capability.

The stigma experienced by people living with bipolar disorder becomes more complex and emotional upon entering parenthood (for a discussion of the challenges of motherhood combined with mental illness, see Boser, this volume). Season Three of *Homeland* reveals a complicating storyline—Carrie's unplanned pregnancy. Though the character engages in promiscuous sex, the pregnancy results from her relationship with main character Nicholas Brody. The genetic nature of bipolar disease and the heavy medications required to manage the symptoms of the disease make a pregnancy storyline inherently dramatic. For pregnant women who suffer from bipolar disorder, health risks can exist for both the mother and child whether taking medication or purposefully refraining from doing so (Gentile, 2012). Even so, most women with serious mental illnesses like bipolar disorder, do have biological children, as these risks are relatively low (Montgomery, Mossey, Bailey, & Forchuk, 2011). However the social stigma experienced by women with bipolar disorder multiplies, as women must adhere to a new set of challenges and pressures.

Douglas and Michaels (2004) analyzed the modern motherhood environment, noting that the media create an unrealistic vision of good mothering that includes success in career, hands-on parenting, and physical attractiveness. Impression management is frequently reported as a way women maintain their public persona as a "good mother" (Christopher, 2012; Collett, 2005; Douglas & Michaels, 2004; Johnson & Swanson, 2006) demonstrating the panoptic nature of parenthood (Blackford, 2004). Adherence to good mother stereotypes occurs in a variety of ways across class, race, and gender, but is notably consistent as a part of motherhood. One challenge facing today's American mother is the continued cultural perception that staying home with young children represents truly devoted motherhood (Cohn & Caumont, 2014; Garey, 1995; Gorman & Fritzsche, 2002). However, with 71% of women working outside the home, this vision of motherhood represents the smallest group in the current era (Cohn & Caumont, 2014). Instead this ideal serves as a culturally restrictive goal, unattainable by most women and yet desired by many who seek public approval as a good mother.

Along with all the perceptions and pressures faced by typical mothers about their performance, mothers with bipolar disorder report feeling a greater sense of social stigma than they usually feel as a person with mental illness alone, noting increased impression management as they attempt to adhere to "good mother" norms (Davies & Allen, 2007). The pressures of motherhood also elevate a secondary form of stigma from which women with bipolar struggle: self-stigma. This personal stigma layers self-doubt about inability onto society's existing, critical perceptions (Dolman, Jones, & Howard, 2013). One part of impression management for mothers with bipolar disorder includes a fear of asking for help—reflecting a concern that others might judge them as unsuitable caregivers (Diaz-Caneja & Johnson, 2004). In their qualitative study of mothers with BP, Diaz-Caneja and Johnson (2004) found participants' greatest fears surrounded custody and the possibility of having children taken away from them. Even as recently as the 1970s, many believed that women with severe mental health issues should not have children (David, Styron, & Davidson, 2011). Only with the introduction of medication-based treatments and social support has our culture begun to accept that women with bipolar disorder can be capable mothers (Howard & Hunt, 2008). The joys of motherhood impact women with bipolar disorder much like they do typical women: Diaz-Caneja and Johnson's (2004) participants reported feeling motherhood gave them a greater purpose, significant joy, and improved self-esteem. However, the authors discussed the challenges still facing women with severe mental health issues who become mothers:

> Contrary to hopes they may have of achieving a normal and fulfilling life and integration into the community through this role, the motherhood of mentally ill women does not appear to be highly valued in the way motherhood is in general. Rather, it seems to be viewed by the public and by professionals as inherently problematic. (p. 480)

Diaz-Caneja and Johnson's argument reflects the slow-changing perception of parenting with mental illness for much of society. In particular, they draw attention to a devalued type of motherhood that breaks cultural norms for what constitutes a good mother.

## *The* Homeland *Pregnancy*

The research on pregnancy, mental illness, and motherhood points to the challenges faced by women managing these intersecting identities and responsibilities. In *Homeland*, audiences see one example of this intersection—a mediated storyline that presents motherhood as a situation overshadowed by mental illness and career ambitions. The audience first learns about Carrie's pregnancy in the sixth episode of Season Three when the character casually opens her bathroom cabinet, gets out a pregnancy test from a large box, and takes the test. Seeing a positive result, she opens her bathroom drawer filled with dozens of used pregnancy tests, also positive, and sets it in the pile. The character looks into the mirror, then lies down in bed. No mention of the pregnancy occurs, no other characters in the series are informed, and viewers are left puzzled. Once the bathroom drawer closes, viewers receive no additional information. The large pile of pregnancy tests alerts viewers to the fact that Carrie's pregnancy is well underway, even though no other clues to this fact had been made available during the previous five episodes of Season Three. Had the episode not been aptly titled "Still Positive," viewers might wonder what they really saw. The next few episodes following Carrie's pregnancy reveal include only one scene each referencing the pregnancy, sometimes quite abstractly, such as Carrie throwing up or seeing her reflected figure. As such, Carrie's pregnancy is abnormal from its onset.

Unlike the dramatic pee-on-the-stick pregnancy scenes that make up much of popular media, Carrie's highly routinized test-taking actions indicate her mental separation and isolation. Emotionless, Carrie continues her life unchanged, avoiding the fact that she must at some point deal with this pregnancy that will not go away, no matter how many tests she takes. Only after being hospitalized from a gunshot wound to her shoulder does someone else learn Carrie's news. Carrie unwillingly shares the news of her pregnancy, just as she unwillingly shared her bipolar diagnosis, because controlling that information is critical to controlling the way others see her. Though Carrie's pregnancy does not elicit the type of conversation typical between characters of television drama, the predicament pregnancy places on Carrie's work life mirrors much of what other fictional television does: using an unwanted pregnancy for dramatic effect as a character struggles to choose between abortion, adoption, and motherhood.

Zara (2013) argues that depictions of abortion remain highly controversial in fictional television, making producers timid to introduce such storylines. Though the number of abortions performed in the United States since the 1973 *Roe v. Wade* decision has grown, media depictions of women considering, but choosing not to abort, have risen (Orr, 2014). Instead, women on television disproportionately choose to keep the baby (Orr, 2014). For Carrie, her avoidance and denial of the pregnancy and its demands on her body ultimately allow the producers to avoid discussion of abortion, by allowing the pregnancy to progress past the period when that is an option. Instead, Carrie's fictional depiction of pregnancy fosters what some label "mandatory motherhood" ("Mandatory Motherhood," n.d.; Wolf, 2011) on television. TVTropes.com ("Mandatory Motherhood," n.d.) defines this common television scenario: "We have a character who, while fertile, very much does not want children. But society, or the law, or destiny, will not let her get away with that easily" (para. 1). Instead, a transformation of women who become mothers is assumed. As women have children, their identity shifts as the mother identity becomes dominant, and previous identities such as work or marital status recede (Rogers & White, 1998).

## *Data and Method*

Data for the current study included all episodes from the first three seasons of *Homeland*, with a particular focus on Season Three. Data collection yielded 36 one-hour-long episodes, as well as transcribed scripts for every episode available publicly online. The project's emphasis on Carrie's pregnancy targets the narratives of pregnancy, mental illness, and cultural expectations of motherhood that this storyline produced: How does Carrie's pregnancy deviate from typical pregnancy narratives? How does it position her career as prioritized over her family (future baby)? From the moment Carrie's pregnancy enters the narrative, her resistance and nonconforming approach to motherhood is seen.

The literature reveals that Carrie's bipolar disorder, secrecy about the pregnancy, and desire to give the baby up make her a bad mother, even before she has the baby—circumstances that piqued my interest as a researcher. This chapter seeks to understand how Carrie's pregnancy transgresses typical pregnancy narratives in the media, the cultural assumptions about pregnancy and parenthood that emerge within this narrative, and how Carrie's bipolar diagnosis and intense career serve as counterpoints to her pregnancy. To consider these goals, thematic analysis was conducted (Braun & Clark, 2006). Rather than addressing all aspects of *Homeland*, I focused on a smaller group of themes related to a single subject within the series: Carrie's potential for motherhood. Braun and Clark (2006) identify this approach to thematic analysis as one that can:

> provide a more detailed and nuanced account of one particular theme, or group of themes, within the data. This might relate to a specific question or area of interest within the data. (p. 83)

*Homeland* offers a rich text, applicable to many disciplines and forms of study. Here, early episodes serve as a background for the character's development, particularly in light of her bipolar diagnosis. Season Three was closely analyzed for themes surrounding Carrie's representation of pregnancy and anticipated motherhood. Scenes sharing information about Carrie's family life, maternal nature, interactions and discussions of family relationships, diagnosis and health concerns, and pregnancy received the most attention. This included a close reading of the text in search of culturally normative expectations, talk, and behavior regarding pregnancy and potential motherhood. Several distinct scenes depict Carrie's ongoing pregnancy and nontraditional reactions to it. Each episode was explored to determine what messages the show produces about mental health and parenting, as well as how Carrie transgresses assumptions typically linked to pregnant women.

With Braun and Clark's (2006) approach, the researcher first must familiarize him/herself with the text in question. Next, initial codes are made while themes will be both inductive and deductive. Initial codes produce themes that should be teased out, mapped, and organized. One of the strongest elements of Braun and Clark's (2006) method is their attention to detail—noting the researcher's obligation to assess all events/scenes equally rather than allowing one dramatic scene to take over (what they call an anecdotal approach). For this project, early seasons provided a surprising amount of background information about Carrie's maternal nature and contributed to the analysis much more than initially expected.

Upon completion of analysis, organizing themes allowed the researcher to see how they fit together as a cohesive study, including the project's relationship with existing literature. Indeed, Carrie's *Homeland* pregnancy very much transgresses typical media narratives of pregnancy as the protagonist treats the pregnancy as a threat to her hard-earned career and emotional stability. These themes surrounding pregnancy, career, and mental health create a place in our media environment for understanding this minority voice that goes against a typical type of mandatory motherhood. Rather than shock, joy, or other emotions, viewers see Carrie almost completely removed from the experience of pregnancy for much of Season Three. Carrie continually struggles to understand and prove her own capability as a person diagnosed with bipolar disorder, is unwilling to make her work identity subordinate to a potential new mother identity, and refuses to allow her pregnancy to overtake her body.

## *Capability and Bipolar Disorder*

In the first episode of the series, audiences learn that Carrie manages her bipolar disorder under the close watch of her sister, who is a doctor. The diagnosis must be hidden from her job at the CIA to allow Carrie to maintain her high-level security clearance. Bridging mental illness with an intense career invites viewers to consider cultural assumptions about capabilities and mental illness. Can a bipolar person be a successful CIA agent? Unlike previous mediated versions of the mentally ill, viewers are shown a complicated, but ultimately positive, answer in Carrie Mathison. She continually disobeys orders, takes wild risks, and puts her own body in the way of potential harm. Yet her irrational decisions often lead to great progress in her career. For example, she pursues a suspect the agency dismissed. Her pursuit initiates a romantic relationship with a suspected terrorist (Brody), which allows her to gain critical intelligence on his activities even as she is falling in love with him. Carrie fits the characteristics found by other researchers of media depictions of the mentally ill—irrational, unpredictable, dangerous—but transforms these moments into her greatest work successes. Though Carrie's illness is under control, audiences are to conclude that her mental illness offers an explanation for irrational behavior rather than other personality traits (like bravery or dedication). Audiences can even overlook some of Carrie's behavior by shifting the blame to her condition, rather than Carrie herself. Actions that might have alienated viewers become reframed through the lens of mental illness, and allow Carrie to remain likeable even while she behaves in socially unacceptable ways. Her bipolar diagnosis is ultimately presented as both a weakness and a strength, acting as both a constant threat to her career and an explanation for her career success.

Carrie, for the most part, actually does a good job managing her care for the first two seasons. She regularly takes her medications as prescribed. The bipolar episode she experiences at the end of Season One occurs because she must hide her illness from her work, not because she refused to follow her sister's orders. The cause is situational rather than a result of Carrie's management of the disorder. This fact may be overlooked for casual viewers because the show purposely builds the tension of managing bipolar and life as a CIA agent. But Carrie's breakdown occurs because she was in a bomb blast that sent her to the hospital and cut off her private supply of lithium. With hospital staff unaware of her condition, she effectively went off her medications, resulting in a manic episode. Carrie does not have another unprovoked episode in the series, though viewers see her edging closer to the manic mindset periodically, allowing the threat of mental illness overtaking her to remain constant for audiences.

The great effort Carrie exerts to hide her bipolar diagnosis reflects the high priority she places on her professional career. Having bipolar disorder for Carrie goes beyond stigma to societal control. Rules governing the CIA dictate that CIA agents cannot have bipolar disorder and effectively do their jobs. Yet, Carrie is a talented, intuitive CIA agent. Knowing these workplace restrictions, Carrie continually works to balance her mental health with her mental capacity. She often refers to "missing something" when analyzing terror suspects—a reference alluding to the impact on memory and concentration that is a common side effect of bipolar treatment drug lithium (Micromedex, 2014). Her feeling that taking lithium clouds her judgment and perception becomes a stumbling block for her superseding belief in her own capability as a CIA agent. Carrie works to balance the two so that she can continue her career.

This confidence in her ability as an agent does not appear in her discussions of relationships and potential motherhood. Discussing her mental illness during Season Two, Carrie tells Brody that he should be scared of her illness, that "It's hard. It's ugly" (Season 2, Episode 12). At one point, she fears being alone forever, while later she argues with Saul, her CIA mentor and boss, about her desire to build a family. This waffling about family continues during her pregnancy, as she considers keeping the baby with Brody. Once he dies, these considerations shift to her conclusion that she cannot parent. Self-stigma and self-doubt resurface as she envisions being a single parent with bipolar disorder. She wants to have the baby adopted to continue working towards her career goals, discussing her situation with a coworker:

Carrie: It took getting this far, to the fucking endgame, to realize it's, it's impossible.

| | |
|---|---|
| Quinn: | Why? |
| Carrie: | Quinn, I can't be a mother. |
| Quinn: | Because? |
| Carrie: | Because of me. Because of my job. Because of my problems. |
| Quinn: | Everyone has problems. |
| Carrie: | I'll be a great station chief. I'll be fearless, obsessed, ruthless if I have to be—all the same reasons I can't … (Season 3, Episode 12) |

Rather than engage in dialogue of the possibility of parenting, Carrie takes control by choosing not to parent. She argues the symptoms of her disease—which audiences have come to expect—complement her work outcome, but will hinder her parenting. This self-stigma and self-doubt manifest later in her own evaluations of her competency with family members. Her "problems" undermine any feeling of capability she entertained with Brody, and instead, she uses a preference for career over family as the rationale for her choice. This nonnormative media outcome identifies Carrie as different from typical depictions of motherhood on television that encourage the transformation to the domestic, rather than the inclusion of the domestic as part of a more dynamic identity (Kornfield, 2014). In Carrie's case, she rejects the domestic identity completely.

Of her desire to give the baby up for adoption (Carrie's only choice, so late in the pregnancy), Carrie tells her father and sister: "It's sick, I know. But I can't [keep the baby]" (Season 3, Episode 12). In this comment, she refers not to her health, but to her decision to choose work over family—a telling comment highlighting her awareness of the mandatory motherhood our culture supports. Communicating the perceived unnaturalness of the decision, as pressured by social norms about motherhood, Carrie feels a constraint on her capability and a necessary choice between work and motherhood. She operates within various stigmas including those surrounding mental illness and capability, and chooses the immediate stigma of not wanting her child over the potential future stigma of bad motherhood.

### Managing the Body: Mental Illness and Pregnancy

While Carrie actively manages her bipolar diagnosis, audiences do not see the same behaviors surrounding her pregnancy. A "second 9–11" happens at the end of Season Two when a bomb destroys the CIA building, killing over 200 people. Season Three starts with Carrie blaming her failure to predict the blast on the bipolar medication. While she was conscientiously managing her disorder in the first two seasons, at the start of Season Three she stops taking it and instead begins a "holistic" program (supposedly under the care of a new doctor, but more likely at her own discretion) for managing bipolar disorder that includes plenty of sleep, running, and heavy doses of tequila. Off the medications, Carrie shows signs of another possible manic episode. However, the potential vulnerability of having others discover her bipolar condition becomes secondary to the need to succeed in her job.

Five episodes later, the audience learns not only that Carrie is pregnant, but she has been the entire season. She refuses to accept this fact, evidenced in the numerous pregnancy tests she takes potentially hoping for a negative outcome. This transforms the narrative, creating a critical lens that repositions Carrie's body as a continued site of struggle and her behavior as nonnormative. As Kornfield (2014) argues, in many ways "pregnancy essentializes women to their bodies" (p. 184) and she demonstrates that pregnancy discourse intersects with notions of difference, treating pregnant women as less capable. For Carrie, already managing the stigma of a bipolar diagnosis, the possibility of further limiting others' perceptions of her (as well as her own) may be unthinkable. While typical Hollywood movie scenes involving home pregnancy tests serve as catalysts for character interactions and discussions about the situation (Leavett, 2006), zero dialogue about the pregnancy occurs for two more hour-long episodes. The first interpersonal discussion of the pregnancy happens at the obstetrician's office, where the doctor questions Carrie's behavior.

Specifically, Carrie continues to drink, smoke, and engage in casual sex even after she knows of her pregnancy. Strict social norms govern expectations of pregnant women and their fetal care; discourses of personhood, fetal rights, and prenatal care privilege the unborn child as "precious cargo" (Lupton, 2012, p. 337). Lupton argues that women must adhere to rigid prenatal guidelines ensuring the unborn baby's health as part of a social trend emphasizing the importance of the perfect baby, noting that this occurs as the "mind should control the body" (p. 337). In other words, vigilant self-control should be used as part of an ethical obligation to the unborn child. Carrie's disregard for positive prenatal behaviors positions her motherhood as abnormal. Audiences can easily read Carrie's behavior as destructive in light of this lens, one constructed as part of good mother ideologies. Upon learning of Carrie's pregnancy, audiences may seek to reinterpret her earlier choice to stop taking lithium at the beginning of Season Three (seeing it as a prenatal care observation, rather than a work-related choice). However, Carrie's continued argument that her medication choices reflect her need to succeed at work erodes this possibility. As a result, the only typical part of Carrie's pregnancy is the drugstore standard, white pregnancy test itself.

Carrie's visit to her doctor, the only scene referencing the pregnancy in Season Three's eighth episode, focuses on the doctor's stern advice for behavior modification. When the doctor tells Carrie she needs to start taking care of herself and the baby, Carrie positions work as her primary responsibility before prenatal care:

| | |
|---|---|
| Doctor: | Are you telling me you wish to terminate? |
| Carrie: | I just want to know what the tests say. If things are okay. |
| Doctor: | Well you're iron deficient. We can fix that. But your blood pressure's very high. |
| Carrie: | I've been really stressed at work. |
| Doctor: | Well, you really should be taking it easy. |
| Carrie: | Yeah, I'll try. |
| Doctor: | Carrie, we can manage this. Keep you and the baby healthy. It's not magic, it's a process. You want to leave it to chance, that's up to you. Otherwise you need to modify your behavior. Not in a week or two, or when it's convenient. Now. |
| Carrie: | What I'm doing, it has to do with the father. I need to make some things right. It matters to a lot of people. |
| Doctor: | But this is different, Carrie. You're not on your own anymore. |
| Carrie: | Yes. (Season 3, Episode 8) |

For Carrie, work continually supersedes adapting to the pregnancy—even while simultaneously paired with questions of the baby's welfare. The doctor's position reflects normative parenting expectations—an adherence to prenatal care and trying to reduce overall stress for the baby's well-being. The concept of the greater good and belief that freedom for the pregnant body is significantly restricted by the superior need to prioritize the fetus often govern discussions of prenatal care (Lupton, 2012).

As Carrie visits the doctor, she indicates a form of prenatal care is occurring, even as she simultaneously continues to drink and smoke. These contrasting behaviors purposefully blur the character's true intentions within the storyline, maintaining the pivotal question of what will happen to the baby. What remains clear for audiences is that Carrie's pregnant behavior is atypical and socially unacceptable. Audiences learn this as various characters discover Carrie's pregnancy; each criticizes her behavior and pressures her to change her lifestyle for the good of the baby. These interactions serve to remind viewers that their own expectations fit within the cultural norm, putting the burden on Carrie for responsible prenatal decisions and presenting her as transgressive in her approach to the pregnancy. Carrie therefore becomes "other" as a mother—one who does not adhere to cultural notions of good parenting. Viewers are invited to doubt Carrie's ability to parent as participants in a pronatalist culture that emphasizes fetal health. Her unwillingness to follow the "rules" of good pregnancy behavior do not deviate from what audiences know of the character's personality, seen earlier in her workplace behavior and risk-taking acts.

## *Prioritizing Career over Family*

As briefly indicated in her discussion with her doctor, Carrie's prenatal care (or lack thereof) competes with her notions of serving a greater purpose. As Carrie refuses to submit to prenatal cultural imperatives, she instead positions her potential to protect a larger public from physical harm as critical to national security. The value of a single human life, even that of her own child, is not greater than that goal. As a result, discussions of family in the series often serve as useful tools for understanding the demanding environment of the CIA. Saul, Quinn (her coworker), David Estes (the CIA director), and Carrie all demonstrate that working at the CIA does not support having a family. In the first season, audiences learn Carrie missed her niece's birthday due to work and never spends enough time with her sister or father, who live nearby. Saul, David, and Quinn's families all broke up as a result of their dedication to work, something they each disclosed as regretting. In *Homeland*, the message is clear and consistent: working at the CIA and having a healthy family life is not feasible.

In many ways, the CIA itself becomes a substitute for family—easily seen in the father-like role Saul takes on with Carrie, coworker Quinn as a pseudo-sibling, and once Brody works there, he as her spouse. The dominance of a job requiring undercover, life-threatening work alienates those who are part of that world from their non-CIA counterparts. With much cultural discussion of work-life balance and women having it all, Carrie's narrative departs from this possibility, instead forcing on a strict choice rather than an integration of roles. Seeing many role models before her love and lose, Carrie opts out of parenting (or tries to) as a reflection that she truly cannot have it all and must, instead, make the best choice for her.

Carrie's narrative offers *Homeland's* audiences an emotional conflict—the social expectation that she should want the baby versus her work life and mental illness, which already consume much of the character's energy. Carrie demonstrates maternal instinct at times, as she secures an infant who must be left alone at a crime scene, greets her nieces who clearly adore her, and communicates her knowledge of the deep love parents have for their children. But much more for Carrie, children symbolize a weakness—an Achilles heel impacting those who love them. Her character returns again and again to this theme—the title of an episode focused on this concept in Season One. The theme repeats as Carrie targets a Saudi diplomat by threatening his favorite daughter; with Tom Walker (a Marine turned terrorist) who risks everything to call his family; as Brody puts off his terrorist acts at the behest of daughter Dana, and at the core of the narrative, for Abu Nazir, whose son Issa was killed in a drone strike, launching his terrorist mission for Brody. Carrie actively uses the threat of harm to children to break down their parents, as seen in this interrogation:

| | |
|---|---|
| Carrie: | Mr. Al Zahrani, I'd like to remind you, you love your children very much, don't you? Do you have a favorite? |
| Al Zahrani: | No, of course not. |
| Carrie: | I think Janine is your favorite. |
| Al Zahrani: | She is a very remarkable young woman, but all of my children are remarkable. |
| Carrie: | Not one of your other children is a sophomore at Yale majoring in political philosophy. Not one of your other children was a National Merit Scholar. Not one of your other children has spent two full days with you at the Phillips Gallery, happily looking at your beloved Impressionists. We would deport her. And we would make sure that she was not welcome in England, or Germany, or France, or Italy, or even all-forgiving Scandinavia. We would make sure that she had no choice but to go back to Saudi Arabia and get fat and wear a burkha for the rest of her miserable life. (Season 1, Episode 10) |

After this, Al Zahrani gives in and provides Carrie with the information she seeks. As Carrie considers having a child herself, she must also consider the vulnerability this creates for her as an agent.

Carrie entertains the possibility of keeping the baby only for a short period in Season Three, when she believes there might be a chance for her and Brody to come home together after the current mission. Instead, Brody, killed for his actions, does not come home. After that, Carrie consistently communicates her desire to take on a new, more challenging role abroad and give up the baby. While cultural assumptions position (and research supports) motherhood as women's primary and most important identity, Carrie negates this imposed necessity to choose family over work. Influenced by her diagnosis and single parenthood, Carrie chooses to pursue her career goals instead. For audiences, this decision may be less alienating due to the continued stigma surrounding motherhood and mental health; her choice may actually affirm what audiences presumed—that the mentally ill cannot mother. This false notion, and harmful stereotype, may be just what producers needed to keep their main character's decision within socially acceptable boundaries.

## Discussion

Carrie Mathison's *Homeland* pregnancy creates a space within discussions of pregnancy and parenthood for audiences to see another perspective. Carrie's Season Three narrative culminates with the impending decision facing Carrie: to keep or give up the baby. Her mental health and intense job at the CIA serve as complicating factors for keeping the baby, though keeping the baby presents the normative, socially acceptable behavior. Audiences are shown that this life choice is not simple and cannot be taken lightly. Yet Carrie's line of work and ability to take care of just herself positions her as potentially unable to parent, especially under the demands of our culture's intense notions about what constitutes a good mother.

This series brings up issues surrounding mental illness that tease out cultural assumptions about capability at work and home. The relationship between mental health and work in the series sends mixed messages, as Carrie's bipolar disorder occasionally interferes with her role as a CIA agent, yet ultimately positions her as more skilled for the job because of her self-concept. For audiences who know little about bipolar disorder, the character positively frames the ability of the mentally ill to hold challenging jobs overall. Carrie's mental illness ultimately threatens her position at the CIA, but it does not eradicate it. Instead, her success stems from her intelligence and intense emotions, which offer insight and clarity at times.

While viewers can read the character Carrie as capable at work, the interpretation of her potential motherhood may be more ambiguous. Poor prenatal care, as communicated through Carrie's emotion, drinking, and smoking, positions her as failing to meet cultural expectations that place the fetus's needs above her own. Carrie refuses to let the pregnancy control her identity or impact her work output, a series of decisions that may alienate her from viewers whose culturally developed notions of parenthood clash with Carrie's enacted version.

Carrie's pregnancy comes as a complicating factor, rather than a planned choice. The existing stigma Carrie feels as a person with bipolar disorder makes the potential vulnerability parenthood introduces seemingly impossible for her. She communicates her desire to opt out of parenting, choosing instead to continue in her career. All of this presents a narrative on motherhood in great contrast with general notions of social obligation and naturalness—quite consistently presenting Carrie as unfit or unprepared for parenthood. The nonnormative nature of Carrie's behavior highlights significant social norms for capable and good motherhood. So while Carrie's professed choice to give the baby up for adoption goes against social norms for mandatory motherhood, the choice is acceptable as understood through stereotypes about mothering with mental illness. Carrie takes control of her situation by choosing the path least complicated—at least in terms of her own obligation.

## *Concluding Thoughts*

Despite Carrie's transgressive pregnancy, she conforms to standard mediated narratives. From previews of *Homeland's* fourth season, audiences learn Carrie keeps the baby, but takes a new position in Istanbul (presumably the child is born between Season Three and Four). She leaves the child under the care of her sister and father. Mandatory motherhood triumphs and Carrie will be a mother. But this narrative seems far from over, and as previews allude, Carrie's motherhood remains a challenge for her career goals and capability. Through close reading and thematic analysis of the first three seasons of *Homeland*, this chapter identifies Carrie Mathison's pregnancy as transgressive, intersecting competing notions about motherhood and mental health. Cultural beliefs about mandatory motherhood are challenged by stereotypes and stigma surrounding mental health capability. In these competing ideologies, audiences see that our culture contradicts itself, forcing an examination of norms and preconceptions for women. Carrie represents the crossroad our culture currently faces in discussions of work-life balance, ableist discourse, and gender roles. Rather than exist in the center of competing dialogues about motherhood, work, and mental health, audiences see Carrie bypass the drama and pick two out of three. In some ways, her choice shows audiences the need to keep talented women in the workforce—because as the show's protagonist, Carrie acts as the most intuitive CIA agent in the show. As Quinn notes, "I have never seen a better intelligence officer" than Carrie (Season 2, Episode 12). Yet, her mental illness flaws her, undermining her decision as not one of choice, but of necessity. While Carrie embodies several contradictory messages, her character presents audiences with a new form of feminism and motherhood that puts personal goals before motherhood as a service to the greater good, one possibly more valued than motherhood—national safety. And that is an interesting message for all who look at how cultural norms situate those who choose alternative paths as "other"—recentering these people's choices as a more human, realistic, and valuable part of a diverse society.

## References


Blackford, H. (2004). Playground panopticism: Ring-around-the-children, a pocketful of women. *Childhood, 11*(2), 227–249.

Braun, V., & Clarke, V. (2006). Using thematic analysis in psychology. *Qualitative Research in Psychology, 3*(2), 77–101.

Caputo, N. M., & Rouner, D. (2011). Narrative processing of entertainment media and mental illness stigma. *Health Communication, 26*(7), 595–604.

Christopher, K. (2012). Extensive mothering employed mothers' constructions of the good mother. *Gender & Society, 26*(1), 73–96.

Cohn, D., & Caumont, A. (2014, April 8). 7 key findings about stay-at-home moms. Retrieved from http://www.pewresearch.org/fact-tank/2014/04/08/7-key-findings-about-stay-at-home-moms/

Collett, J. L. (2005). What kind of mother am I? Impression management and the social construction of motherhood. *Symbolic Interaction, 28*(3), 327–347.

Corrigan, P. W., Watson, A. C., Gracia, G., Slopen, N., Rasinski, K., & Hall, L. L. (2005). Newspaper stories as measures of structural stigma. *Psychiatric Services, 56*(5), 551–556.

David, D. H., Styron, T., & Davidson, L. (2011). Supported parenting to meet the needs and concerns of mothers with severe mental illness. *American Journal of Psychiatric Rehabilitation, 14*(2), 137–153.

Davies, B., & Allen, D. (2007). Integrating "mental illness" and "motherhood": The positive use of surveillance by health professionals. A qualitative study. *International Journal of Nursing Studies, 44*(3), 365–376.

Diaz-Caneja, A., & Johnson, S. (2004). The views and experiences of severely mentally ill mothers. *Social Psychiatry and Psychiatric Epidemiology, 39*(6), 472–482.

Dolman, C., Jones, I., & Howard, L. M. (2013). Pre-conception to parenting: A systematic review and meta-synthesis of the qualitative literature on motherhood for women with severe mental illness. *Archives of Women's Mental Health, 16*(3), 173–196.

Douglas, S., & Michaels, M. (2004). *The mommy myth: The idealization of motherhood and how it has undermined all women*. New York, NY: Simon and Schuster.

Edney, D. R. (2004). Mass media and mental illness: A literature review. Retrieved from http://www.ontario.cmha.ca/content/about_ mental_illness/mass_media.asp

Elgie, R., & Morselli, P. L. (2007). Social functioning in bipolar patients: The perception and perspective of patients, relatives and advocacy organizations—a review. *Bipolar Disorders, 9*(1–2), 144–157.

Garey, A. I. (1995). Constructing motherhood on the night shift: "Working mothers" as "stay-at-home moms." *Qualitative Sociology, 18*(4), 415–437.

Gentile, S. (2012). Bipolar pregnancy: To treat or not to treat? *BMJ*. doi: 10.1136/bmj.e7367

Gerbner, G., Gross, L., Morgan, M., Signorielli, N., & Shanahan, J. (2002). Growing up with television: Cultivation processes. In J. Bryant, D. Zillman, & M. B. Oliver (Eds.) *Media effects: Advances in theory and research* (pp. 43–67). Mahwah, NJ: Lawrence Erlbaum.

Gorman, K. A., & Fritzsche, B. A. (2002). The good-mother stereotype: Stay at home (or wish that you did!). *Journal of Applied Social Psychology*, *32*(10), 2190–2201.

Granello, D. H., & Pauley, P. (2000). Television viewing habits and their relationship to tolerance toward people with mental illness. *Journal of Mental Health Counseling*, *22*, 162–175.

Havrilesky, H. (2013, March 12). TV's new wave of women: Smart, strong, borderline insane. Retrieved from http://www.nytimes.com/2013/03/17/magazine/tvs-new-wave-of-women-smart-strong-borderline-insane.html?hpw&_r=1&

Howard, L. M., & Hunt, K. (2008). The needs of mothers with severe mental illness: A comparison of assessments of needs by staff and patients. *Archives of Women's Mental Health*, *11*(2), 131–136.

Johnston, D. D., & Swanson, D. H. (2006). Constructing the "good mother": The experience of mothering ideologies by work status. *Sex Roles*, *54*(7–8), 509–519.

Klin, A., & Lemish, D. (2008). Mental disorders stigma in the media: Review of studies on production, content, and influences. *Journal of Health Communication*, *13*(5), 434–449.

Kornfield, S. (2014). Pregnant discourse: "Having it all" while domestic and potentially disabled. *Women's Studies in Communication*, *37*(2), 181–201.

Lacob, J. (2012, April 10). *Homeland* and *Shameless*: Television tackles bipolar disorder with realism. Retrieved from http://www.thedailybeast.com/articles/2012/04/10/homeland-and-shameless-television-tackles-bipolar-disorder-with-realism.html

Leavitt, S. A. (2006). "A private little revolution": The home pregnancy test in American culture. *Bulletin of the History of Medicine*, *80*(2), 317–345.

Lupton, D. (2012). "Precious cargo": Fetal subjects, risk and reproductive citizenship. *Critical Public Health*, *22*(3), 329–340.

Mandatory motherhood. Retrieved from http://tvtropes.org/pmwiki/pmwiki.php/Main/MandatoryMotherhood

McGinty, E. E., Webster, D. W., & Barry, C. L. (2013). Effects of news media messages about mass shootings on attitudes toward persons with serious mental illness and public support for gun control policies. *American Journal of Psychiatry*, *170*(5), 494–501.

Micromedex. (2014). Lithium (Oral Route). Retrieved from http://www.mayoclinic.org/drugs-supplements/lithium-oral-route/side-effects/drg-20064603

Montgomery, P., Mossey, S., Bailey, P., & Forchuk, C. (2011). Mothers with serious mental illness: Their experience of "hitting bottom". *ISRN Nursing*, *2011*, 1–8.

Murray, S. C. (2014). *The deceptions of powerful female roles: A feminist critique of* Homeland (Undergraduate Thesis, California Polytechnic State University, San Luis Obispo).

Orr, R. (2014). Breaking the taboo of abortion on TV and film. Retrieved from http://www.independent.co.uk/arts-entertainment/films/features/abortion-on-screen-shes-not-having-a-baby-9647952.html

Philo, G., Secker, J., Platt, S., Henderson, L., McLaughlin, G., & Burnside, J. (1994). The impact of the mass media on public images of mental illness: Media content and audience belief. *Health Education Journal, 53*(3), 271–281.

Reyers, C. (2014). *Homeland*: An upfront look at bipolar disorder. Retrieved from http://www.nami.org/Content/NavigationMenu/Top_Story/_em_Homeland_em_An_Upfront_Look_at_Bipolar_Disorder.htm

Rouleau, J. (2014). Keep it right—*Homeland*: The female body, disability, and nation. Retrieved from http://www.rds.hawaii.edu/wp-content/uploads/2014/06/RDS-v10iss1and2.pdf#page=17

Rogers, S. J., & White, L. K. (1998). Satisfaction with parenting: The role of marital happiness, family structure, and parents' gender. *Journal of Marriage and the Family, 60*(2), 293–308.

Shoals, B. (2013, September 25). Calling out *Homeland*'s bipolar bs. Retrieved from http://www.gq.com/blogs/the-feed/2013/09/calling-out-homelands-bipolar-bs.html

Sieff, E. (2003). Media frames of mental illnesses: The potential impact of negative frames. *Journal of Mental Health, 12*(3), 259–269.

Sifferlin, A. (2013, October 8). *Homeland* and bipolar disorder: How TV characters are changing the way we view mental illness. Retrieved from http://healthland.time.com/2013/10/08/homeland-and-bipolar-disorder-how-tv-characters-are-changing-the-way-we-view-mental-illness/

Signorielli, N. (1989). The stigma of mental illness on television. *Journal of Broadcasting & Electronic Media, 33*(3), 325–331.

Stout, P., Villegas, J., & Jennings, N. (2004). Images of mental illness in the media: Identifying gaps in the research. *Schitzophrenia Bulletin, 30*(3), 543–561. Retrieved from http://schizophreniabulletin.oxfordjournals.org.ezproxy.uhd.edu/content/30/3/543

Vázquez, G. H., Kapczinski, F., Magalhaes, P. V., Córdoba, R., Lopez Jaramillo, C., Rosa, A. R., … & Tohen, M. (2011). Stigma and functioning in patients with bipolar disorder. *Journal of Affective Disorders, 130*(1), 323–327.

Wahl, O. F. (1992). Mass media images of mental illness: A review of the literature. *Journal of Community Psychology, 20*(4), 343–352.

Whitehead, R. (2012, May 7). *Homeland*'s depiction of mental illness has been a step forward for TV. Retrieved from http://www.theguardian.com/commentisfree/2012/may/07/homeland-mental-illness-bipolar-tv

Wilson, C., Nairn, R., Coverdale, J., & Panapa, A. (1999). Mental illness depictions in prime-time drama: Identifying the discursive resources. *Australian and New Zealand Journal of Psychiatry, 33*(2), 232–239. doi: 10.1046/j.1440-1614.1999.00543.x

Wolf J. B. (2011). *Is breast best? Taking on the breastfeeding experts and the new high stakes of motherhood.* New York, NY: New York University Press.

Zara, C. (2013). 40 years after *Roe v. Wade*, depictions of abortion on TV are still taboo. Retrieved from http://www.ibtimes.com/40-years-after-roe-v-wade-depictions-abortion-are-still-taboo-television-1031332

# 4. *Addicted to Danger: The Fierce, Flawed Mothers of* Nurse Jackie *and* Weeds

By Katherine J. Lehman

It's just another day in the emergency room of New York's All Saints Hospital. Wearing plain scrubs and coifed with a cropped haircut, Nurse Jackie Peyton (played by Edie Falco) approaches her job with a mixture of compassion and cynicism. She weathers the tirades of an uptight administrator, mentors a new nurse, and metes out justice to an abusive patient. She indulges in a tryst with the hospital pharmacist, who slips her pills to treat her aching back. She and a colleague talk shop in the chapel, surrounded by statues of saints. As she trudges home to Queens at twilight, Jackie muses about practical sainthood. "If I were a saint," she says in a voiceover, "I would be like Augustine. He knew there was good in him and he knew there was some not so good. And he wasn't going to give up his earthly pleasures before he was good and ready." Upon entering her home, Jackie reaches in her pocket to put on her gold wedding band, and warmly greets her daughters and husband. "Make me good, God, but not yet," she prays inwardly, as her husband embraces her and the sorrowful theme from *Valley of the Dolls* plays (Brixius, Wallem, Dunsky, & Coulter, 2009).

*Nurse Jackie*, which completed its seventh and final season in June 2015, is noteworthy in its portrayal of a working mother as equally saintly and self-indulgent. The gradual revelation of Jackie's identity in the pilot episode allows viewers to recognize her as a healthcare professional before she is understood as a mother. The episode also underscores Jackie's efforts to keep her home and work identities separate, to the point of slipping off her wedding ring at the beginning of each shift and allowing her colleagues to assume she is single. As the series progresses, Jackie struggles to maintain this division; for her, as for most working mothers, "children impinge on work place and time, and work impinges on family space and time" (Johnston & Swanson, 2006, p. 510). Jackie's reference to "earthly pleasures" could refer to her extramarital affair or her addiction to prescription painkillers—a secret she conceals from her family and closest friends.

As this volume explores, Jackie Peyton is far from the only imperfect mother on television, as she joins many female characters who challenge normative family ideals and juggle multiple identities. Her series shares much in common with its predecessor *Weeds* (Showtime, 2005–2012), which features a newly widowed mother of two who sells marijuana for a living. While both programs revolve around the sale and consumption of illicit drugs, they are equally noteworthy for their provocative portrayals of modern mothers as danger junkies. Just as Jackie is drawn to the adrenaline rush of the emergency room and the jolt of the drugs to her system, *Weeds'* protagonist Nancy Botwin (played by Mary-Louise Parker) embraces the physical and emotional pitfalls of the drug trade, as it provides escape from stifling suburbia.

Some viewers and critics have castigated these characters as "bad mothers," both for their connection to illicit drug use and their tendency to prioritize their careers above their children (Chozick, 2010; Fallon, 2010; Fernandez, 2014; Meredith, 2013). Jackie and Nancy often question their own worth as mothers, blaming themselves for their children's anxieties, addictive behaviors, and antisocial tendencies. Yet as Nancy helps her sons through personal crises or Jackie soothes a frightened child in the emergency room, they emerge as compassionate parents and their struggles to maintain family harmony and mediate conflict are both comedic and poignant. While media tend to portray mothers as either "saintly sacrificers" or "viperous spiders," *Weeds* and *Nurse Jackie* provide complicated "antiheroines" who are not so easily categorized, and who model alternatives to the traditional nuclear family (Walters & Harrison, 2014, p. 39). Viewers can turn to those characters for absolution of their own imperfect parenting and find a thrill in seeing female protagonists defy domestic expectations.

## Media and the "Intensive-Mothering" Ideal

Nancy and Jackie are subversive characters who resist dominant models of parenting. The ideology of "intensive mothering" claims a proper mother should be the central caregiver for her children, "lavishing copious amounts of time, energy, and material resources" on them and always putting their needs first (Hays, 1996, p. 8). Naturally, many women fall short of this unattainable ideal and are taught to blame themselves and harshly judge each other for their failings (Douglas & Michaels, 2004, p. 26). Scholars argue that this model of parenting has an inherent White middle-class bias, as it presumes mothers have flexible schedules and financial resources and excludes other models of parenting, such as the extended kinship networks more common in communities of color (Baker & Carson, 1999; Collins, 1994). Furthermore, those who advocate intensive mothering often assume that women have choices about how to spend their time and energy. Media coverage of the "mommy wars" and "opt-out revolution" exaggerate differences between working and stay-at-home moms, framing the decision to work as a moral one (Douglas & Michaels, 2004; Press, 2011). Of course, many mothers who work full-time are motivated by financial necessity as much as personal ambition. Those who cut back on their work hours may do so reluctantly, citing the lack of adequate childcare and support from their partners (Owen, Stein, & Vande Berg, 2007). As mothers judge themselves and others for their faults as caregivers, they neglect to challenge a social system that demands perfection from mothers yet denies them needed resources such as universal childcare or workplace flexibility (Douglas & Michaels, 2004; Warner, 2005).

Nancy and Jackie also challenge conventions of "good" parenthood through their very lifestyles. Ladd-Taylor and Umansky (1998) note that particular groups have historically been categorized as bad mothers: "those who did not live in a traditional nuclear family; those who would not or could not protect their children from harm; and those whose children went wrong" (p. 3). Nancy is widowed at the beginning of *Weeds*, and makes repeated failed attempts at remarriage. When Jackie's husband discovers her illicit behaviors in the third season of *Nurse Jackie*, the two divorce. Single mothers face greater cultural scrutiny than partnered parents: Female-headed households are thought to deprive children of male role models and predispose children to poverty and psychological troubles (McLanahan & Sandefur, 2009). At the same time, single mothers may actually feel "less accountability to the intensive mothering model" (Christopher, 2012, p. 91), as financial necessity dictates that they work, and feel less guilty than their married counterparts in articulating the need for time away from the kids.

Jackie's prescription drug use and Nancy's dangerous drug trade also mark them as unconventional television mothers. Drug addicts like Jackie easily fulfill the cultural stereotype of a "bad mother," as their behavior is thought to be selfish and harmful to children. Recovering addicts interviewed in a research study did blame themselves for "failing to fulfill their role as socially acceptable mothers when they put their children in danger, when they were unavailable for their children, and when they lacked control over them. … They accepted, at least in part, the parameters of the dominant ideology of intensive mothering" (Baker & Carson, 1999, p. 356). However, these women defined themselves as good mothers, citing their deep care and concern for their children and willingness to seek help. In a similar study, mothers in recovery questioned the common practice of removing children from homes in which drug use is present, arguing that their children were harmed greatly by this forced separation (Reed, Greaves, & Poole, 2008). Scholars urge attention to the ways in which marginalized groups articulate their identities and "create for themselves more inclusive boundaries for acceptable mothering practice" (Baker & Carson, 1999, p. 361).

As they are driven by their career ambitions, Nancy and Jackie also depart from television's tendency to minimize women's work roles. For female media protagonists, entering the public sphere itself represents a transgression against the dominant order (Owen, Stein, & Vande Berg, 2007). Women in television comedy have historically been defined by domesticity, as classic family sitcoms of the early 1960s elevated the nuclear family, delineated separate spheres for men and women, and presented nurturing and housework as effortless endeavors for the suburban housewife (Haralovich, 1989). The television industry's turn toward relevance and tentative engagements with feminism from the 1970s onward enabled depictions of single working women as well as mothers who worked outside the home. Yet even career-oriented series such as *The Mary Tyler Moore Show* placed heroines in feminized roles within workplace families (Dow, 1996). Comedies featuring working mothers such as *Roseanne* and *The Cosby Show* downplayed the conflicts most women face in balancing work and home responsibilities, both by minimizing the time characters spent in the workplace and depicting fathers as actively involved in parenting and housework. This "postfeminist" programming trend emphasizes women's choices and personal ambitions, suggesting that individuals can easily fulfill social expectations at home and at work (Press, 2011). Even today, comedies such as *Modern Family* are criticized for largely portraying single-income families with discretionary income in an age of dual-income households and economic recession (D'Addario, 2013).

Dramatic series that emerged in the 1980s and 1990s offered more complex portraits of working women's lives, often presenting heroines as "flawed yet authentic professionals struggling with family commitments and occupational demands" (Lotz, 2006, p. 3). The expansion of cable in the 1990s provided more avenues for women's stories to be told and prompted experimentation with program formats, including the emergence of hybrid comedy-dramas or "dramedies" that foregrounded women's concerns (Lotz, 2006, p. 107). Cable networks such as Showtime have the freedom to narrowcast to specific audience segments rather than appealing to viewers of diverse demographic and ideological backgrounds (Lotz, 2006). Thus, professional women who appreciate irreverence may enjoy Showtime offerings while those who prefer more conventional models turn to TLC for example. Even network television has offered complex portraits of working mothers in recent years, including the harried, dysfunctional clan on *Desperate Housewives* and the ambitious lawyer on *The Good Wife*. On both the public airwaves and premium cable, we see the rise of a new kind of female protagonist in television: an independent-minded woman who is compelling if not always likeable (Fernandez, 2014).

## *Connecting with Female Viewers*

Jackie and Nancy are part of a broader programming trend on Showtime, a premium cable network that is actively courting female viewers and creating a niche for complex portrayals of middle-aged women (Chozick, 2010). In recent years Showtime has offered series such as *The Big C* and *United States of Tara*, featuring mothers battling diagnoses of cancer and multiple personality disorder, respectively. The *Wall Street Journal* described Showtime's strategy as "attracting big-name actresses, of a certain age and experience, who are hard-pressed to find juicy, challenging, starring roles elsewhere" (Chozick, 2010, para. 3). Bradshaw (2013) suggests that "complicated" women with "female problems" (p. 167) are part of Showtime's branding strategy; in advertisements for *Weeds* and *The Big C*, characters talk to one another over a picket fence, emphasizing the disjuncture between their lives and the suburban ideal and forging comparisons between the series. Bradshaw (2013) argues such series enact a resistance to conventional family life, yet their reliance on humor and irony softens their subversive edge.

*Weeds* and *Nurse Jackie* owe their popularity not only to new programming tends but also innovative female authorship. *Weeds* was created by Jenji Kohan, who had previously written for comedian Tracey Ullman and a host of conventional sitcoms. With *Weeds*, Kohan wanted to create an outlaw who was neither heroic nor villainous ("Weeds Spreads," 2006). More recently, Kohan launched the Netflix prison comedy *Orange Is the New Black*, which expands upon *Weeds*' criminal themes while also offering thoughtful portrayals of mothers behind bars. *Nurse Jackie*'s creators were concerned not only with increasing female representation on television beyond stereotypical wives and mistresses but also bringing stories of addiction and recovery to the small screen (Carmon, 2010). Producers Liz Brixius and Linda Wallem, as well as Falco herself, have spoken openly about their own histories of alcoholism and addiction, and their experience adds empathy and realism to the series

(Bergen, 2011; Carmon, 2010). As an *Entertainment Weekly* reporter mused about Showtime's female-centric series:

> Perhaps it takes women to make comedies about mothers that are both so empathetic and so brutal. They understand that one can feel like (and be) a good or a bad mother on alternate days or in alternate minutes, that one woman's mitigating circumstance can be another's dishonest self-justification, that the question "Am I being a good mother?" is one that many women ask and re-ask with every action they take—and can never answer to their own satisfaction. (Harris, 2009, para. 3)

On some level, Nancy and Jackie are far from average. Jackie, whom producers describe as "intensely good, but intensely unsentimental" (Nayberg & Richardson, 2009) is a force for moral justice in the midst of a flawed medical system. She stands up against arrogant doctors and stingy insurance policies, ensuring that patients get the care they need, and often goes beyond duty to help people (for example, giving a young patient her personal phone number, or bringing groceries to a man undergoing chemotherapy.) As a worker, Jackie comes across as "very smart and very much in control" (Fallon, 2010, para. 7), despite her drug habit. A comprehensive study on nursing portrayals declares Jackie to be "probably the best nurse in television history, a tough clinical virtuoso who excels at physical and psychosocial care, patient advocacy, and mentoring. She regularly saves lives" (Summers & Summers, 2014, p. 67). However, researchers also appreciate that Jackie is not an "angel" whose successes stem from her innate goodness, but rather a skilled professional with a sarcastic attitude (Summers & Summers, 2014).

In *Nurse Jackie*'s initial seasons, she boasts about her ability to handle strong drugs and stay in control, much as a man might brag about holding his liquor. She casually sprinkles strong drugs as "sweetener" in her morning coffee. While addiction is often framed as a weakness, for Jackie it is one component of her unsentimental approach to work and parenting. When her daughter's friend spots her snorting the contents of a prescription pill and asks questions, Jackie covers up her drug use by telling the child it is merely "a trick that nurses use to dry up their tear ducts. We see a lot of pain and suffering during the day and the last thing we want to do is come home and cry in front of our families" (Cleveland & Taylor, 2010). She then gives the suspicious girl a hug, thwarting the judgmental line of questioning and reasserting her authority as mother (Walters & Harrison, 2014).

Nancy in *Weeds* is an entrepreneur, bringing her once-small suburban drug trade into ever larger and more dangerous territory. She is defined by her sexuality more than Jackie is, accentuating her milky skin and lanky frame with heels and miniskirts. Nancy's beauty and fashion-forward sensibilities may soften the transgression of her criminal activities and unconventional approach to parenting (Press, 2011), but it also fits with a third-wave feminist understanding of sexuality as a source of empowerment. Nancy often uses her sexuality to advance her career goals, sleeping with rival dealers and DEA agents alike. Beyond her sexual appeal, her ambition and no-nonsense approach commands respect from the men with whom she does business. Over the course of several seasons, she opens a bakery to sell pot-laced goods and develops her own proprietary marijuana blend. When business goes south due to rival dealers, she moves her family to the Mexican border to get a cut of a larger importing business. She is frequently at the mercy of gangsters but uses her charm and strategizing to emerge unscathed. When given opportunities to live a quieter, more respectable life, she rejects them. As actress Mary-Louise Parker describes Nancy's motivations: "She's one of those people who thinks, 'OK, once my situation is better, I'll do some charity work and be a better parent.' She's putting off being a good person until later" (Shaw, 2009, p. 3).

Some argue that Jackie's addiction and Nancy's profession make them implausible characters whose experiences differ greatly from the average viewer's. After all, most widows with money issues do not turn to drug dealing, and Jackie's role as a drug-abusing mother and nurse makes her a controversial character. However, popular accounts suggest that these women may not be too far outside the norm. For instance, mainstream magazines such as *Parents* (2011, November) and *Working Mother* (2010, October) have acknowledged an escalating trend of alcoholism and prescription-drug abuse among working mothers. In 2008, more than 18 million women in their late 20s and older used prescription drugs for non-prescribed purposes; the number of people seeking treatment for narcotic-painkiller addiction quadrupled between 1998 and 2008 (Barbalich, 2011). *Working Mother* reported that more than 10 percent of children in the United States live with an alcoholic parent. Experts argue that working mothers are particularly vulnerable to addiction given their schedule pressures and drive for perfection, and are more likely to hide their habits than men (DeGregory, 2010). Nor is addiction a recent trend: Valium was prescribed heavily to housewives starting in the 1960s, and was the nation's most widely prescribed drug for more than a decade (DeGregory, 2010). Acknowledging this historical context, *Nurse Jackie* alludes to *Valley of the Dolls*, a late 1960s novel and film that featured ambitious women who popped pills to cope with both sorrow and success (Susann, 1966; Weisbart & Robson, 1967).

These days, when a White suburban female drug dealer makes the news, she's invariably compared to *Weeds'* protagonist. Two recent cases ended more tragically than Nancy Botwin's, with dealers being arrested for their crimes or even murdered by rivals (Anderson & Feuer, 2013; Duell, 2011). However, a 2011 *Mother Jones* feature offered less sensational stories of suburban drug dealers, noting that the economic recession had forced many middle-class, otherwise law-abiding families to enter the trade (D'Souza, 2011). The *Washingtonian* further documented a growing marijuana trade among the upper crust of Washington, D.C., in which fashionable suburbanites sell THC-laced baked goods, much like Nancy in *Weeds*' early seasons. The article predicted the market would only increase as marijuana laws become more lenient (Robbins, 2012).

Kinnick (2009) argues that the "outlandish plots" on series such as *Weeds* obscure the real issues facing modern mothers, like "family-work-life balance, the glass ceiling, and latchkey children" (p. 4). However, *Weeds*' Nancy also holds professional roles beyond drug dealing, making her more relatable to a mass audience. As an unskilled single mother, she often bides her time in low-wage, low-status jobs such as retail clerk, secretary, and hotel maid. In one season she becomes a marketing representative for a synthetic marijuana pill, putting her talents to work in a legal realm. Thus, many viewers may relate to Nancy's struggles with the tedium and indignity of low-wage work and understand why she would rather be a lucrative outlaw than an underpaid employee. Her financial struggles may resonate with women who have experienced poverty in the wake of divorce or a spouse's death (Fallon, 2010).

## *Mediating Motherhood*

Historically, media narratives typically provide binary representation of mothers, associating good mothers with self-sacrifice and nurturance and portraying bad mothers as "self-centered, neglectful, preoccupied with career, or lacking traditional femininity" (Kinnick, 2009, p. 9). In both these series, Nancy and Jackie fulfill Ladd-Taylor and Umansky's (1998) description of "bad mom" stereotypes—they work long hours, expose themselves and their children to illegal activities, and fail to create the idealized nuclear family. Furthermore, these women defy the dictates of intensive mothering, which suggest that parenting should be their primary identity and concern (Hays, 1996). That said, their status as middle-class White women makes them more potentially sympathetic to mainstream audiences; it's hard to imagine that narratives featuring minority mothers as drug pushers or addicts would work as comedies or have the same subversive edge. *Weeds* in particular relies on racialized humor, as Nancy's criminal lifestyle represents a rebellion against the stifling conformity of her stifling White suburb. The series perpetually calls attention to Nancy's Whiteness; for example, the minority men in her drug trade call her names like "blanca" and "snowflake."

Although motherhood is only one facet of these women's identities, it is an important one. Viewers first meet Nancy at an elementary-school PTA meeting, heading up the "healthy children" initiative to ban sugared soft drinks from the school vending machines. Ironically she is later seen selling drugs to other parents at her son's soccer game: a spin on the suburban soccer mom who became visible as a voting bloc in the early 2000s. Yet rather than serving as a selfless chauffeur and cheering her children's every success on the field, she is focused on her own business ambitions. At the start of *Weeds*, Nancy is the mother of two boys, 15-year-old Silas and 10-year-old Shane, and has found herself suddenly single after her beloved husband's heart attack. (Over the course of the series she gives birth to another son, Stevie.) Her husband's brother Andy, an underemployed wisecracker, moves in to help Nancy with parenting, although at times Nancy complains he's more of a liability than a help. He cooks for the family and helps the boys with their problems, further distinguishing the family from the dominant parenting model in which *mothers* provide nurturance and moral guidance (Hays, 1996).

Pot dealing begins as a way to preserve Nancy's California suburban lifestyle, a secret she carefully guards from her sons. "I'm not a drug dealer. I'm a mother who distributes illegal products," she explains (Platt, Safchik, & Sanford, 2005). This rhetorical strategy positions Nancy as a mother making ends meet rather than a criminal mastermind, although as the series progresses it is clear she finds the dangerous drug trade alluring. Obtaining her supply forces her to travel into the ghetto, where her Whiteness is conspicuous and drive-by shootings are common. As the series develops, the risks grow with her ambitions, as later Nancy is actually driving the gangsters' car and navigating an underground passage to Mexico. Even then, motherhood remains foundational to her identity. She sells a marijuana blend named "MILF weed," which boasts her identity as a "Mother I'd Like to Fuck," and links her maternal role and sexuality to an illicit pleasure. She subsequently runs a maternity shop in a border town, the backroom of which contains a tunnel that her comrades use to traffic drugs from Mexico. Later she is saved from certain death at the hands of a Mexican drug lord, Esteban, when she produces the ultrasound photo proving she carries his son.

Nancy ultimately serves a stint in jail as a means to preserve her own life, as well as the lives of her children. As Walters and Harrison (2014) argue, this is a rare moment when Nancy's needs and those of her children intersect. Despite her claim she is a "mother lion" who will do anything to protect her offspring, she also imagines life without them. Early in the series she uses a fake ID, reveling in the opportunity to be a woman without encumbrances. She also approaches parenthood with a crass cynicism. While caring for her infant son, Stevie, she describes motherhood as a shitty endeavor: "Wiping shit. Keeping them away from shit. Minimizing the external shit." The love, she concedes, is there, "it's just buried under all the shit" (Kohan, Kelly, & Trim, 2009). In such scenes, Nancy refutes what Douglas and Michaels (2004) call the "mommy myth" that "motherhood is eternally fulfilling and rewarding … and that if you don't love each and every second of it there's something wrong with you" (pp. 3–4). Although Nancy eventually marries Stevie's father, Esteban, she hesitates to take his last name for fear that her own, independent identity will be lost. In an episode, for instance, she jokes about hyphenating her last name and laments that she will no longer be Nancy Botwin but rather "Mrs. Esteban Reyes. Mrs. Somebody … Somebody Else. Isn't that weird?" (Reisen, 2009).

Jackie is initially successful at establishing a work identity independent of motherhood, to the point of not telling most of her coworkers that she has a husband and two young daughters (the secret is exposed in Season Three when her husband shows up at the hospital). Actress Edie Falco describes Jackie as someone trapped in a maternal role, explaining: "There are women who are not meant to be mothers … they have fallen into it because it was what was expected of them, and it was easier to do that than to figure out what you'd really like to do. And by that time, you have a child and someone who depends on you for everything" (Bolonik, 2013, para. 30). Despite her ambivalence, many episodes are framed by the mornings and evenings she spends with daughters Gracie and Fiona at the beginning of the series, and her work shifts are punctuated by school meetings and phone calls to sort out family problems.

Jackie's maternal identity carries into her job, where she often compassionately intervenes on behalf of mothers and children. This aspect of the series suggests that, try as she might, she cannot shed her maternal identity at work. The presentation of Jackie as an empathetic and effective nurse reveals a depth of compassion beneath her addictive behavior and illicit sexual impulses, and perhaps makes her behavior more palatable to viewers. Even her addiction is framed in terms of motherhood: in one episode she hides a stash in her daughter's outgrown glove, cradling it as she retrieves her pills.

## *Mocking Family Ideals*

These series fault their characters for flawed parenting; for example, Jackie's husband sarcastically refers to her as "Mother of the Year" upon learning the extent of her drug habit. However, the series also emphasize the impossibility of living up to cultural ideals of motherhood and family life. As Douglas and Michaels (2004) argue, many women aspire to maternal perfection even as they recognize cultural ideals as "utterly ridiculous and oppressive" (p. 4). *Weeds*' theme song is the folk ballad "Little Boxes," which presents the suburbs as a bleak place where people work, study, and play in lockstep. Even as Nancy clearly values her comfortable life, her drug excursions offer a welcome escape from the racial homogeneity and conservatism of her neighbors. *Weeds*' second season ends with a deeply symbolic act. When a drug dealer starts a fire that sets the suburb aflame, Nancy douses her family home in gasoline to make sure it goes up in smoke. Her broad grin upon leaving the scene reveals she is relieved to release the albatross of suburban life, even as she verbally apologizes to her deceased husband for failing to live up to the ideal. By freeing herself from the suburban home, she rids herself of stifling conformity and the need to manage a traditional household—not to mention the pressure to pay her mortgage. Her family spends much of the remaining series itinerant, living in family members' homes, hotels, and even an RV.

*Weeds* also mocks family ideals in its depiction of dysfunctional family dinners. In an early episode, Nancy feels out of touch with her sons and turns to her supplier, an older African American woman named Heylia, for advice. Heylia recommends instituting a family dinner tradition, casually referencing research that links the family dinner table to better communication and less rebellion among teens (Fulkerson, Story, Mellin, Leffert, Newmark-Sztainer, & French, 2006). Nancy stops for a bucket of fried chicken on her way home. Her efforts to get her sons to sit at the table and connect through conversation are a running joke throughout the remaining series. "We're gonna be a family if I have to kill all of you!" she bellows at her rebellious brood (Kohan & Zisk, 2006). When she invites guests over, her younger son, Shane, refuses to eat a vegetarian dish, using choice swear words to describe it before leaving the table. In later seasons her family table expands to include her friends and fellow drug-runners. At the culmination of one rough day, they sit around the table with bruises and black eyes, dining in sullen silence. This scene offers an alternate model of kinship, even if it fails to resemble a Norman Rockwell painting.

At the beginning of the final season, Nancy hosts an elegant outdoor dinner at her new Connecticut estate and raises a toast to family togetherness, only to be felled by a sniper's bullet (she survives, but barely.) The ill-timed bullet emphasizes that Nancy can never truly "have it all," and may also represent narrative punishment for her earlier crimes. The sniper strike happens just as Nancy's family has achieved some degree of stability, and suggests that old patterns will follow them into their new lives. Family members struggle to solve the crime, debating which of Nancy's many enemies pulled the trigger.

Unconventional family dinners are also a given in *Nurse Jackie*. Husband Kevin owns and operates a neighborhood bar, and most evenings the daughters dine at the bar while their mother works a late shift. Jackie's anxiety is less about preparing and eating meals than creating meaningful traditions with her daughters, such as dance lessons. When she catches part of a film featuring a tap-dancing Shirley Temple, Jackie signs up for a dance class with her daughter Grace. But Grace can't keep up with the steps, and the two are soon tossed out of the class when Jackie loses her temper at another rude mother. The tap-dancing fiasco becomes symbolic for her generally askew relationship to parenting.

As the first season ends and Jackie fears her affair will soon be revealed, she descends to the hospital basement and stretches out on the cold floor. In a drug-induced fantasy, she sees herself as Florence Nightingale in a starched white uniform, gazing upon an equally antiquated image of her family in glowing suburban perfection. Grace reenacts the Shirley Temple film, happily tap dancing in a flouncy dress. For Dolan (2013), the scene reveals Jackie's ambivalence about her assigned social role: "Is Jackie afraid of being trapped in the conventionality of her domestic family life? … Is she smart enough to want to resist the banalities of middle-class, White heterosexuality, even if she's clearly, at an earlier point in her life, decided to acquiesce to it?" (p. 66). The dream ends abruptly when Jackie sees the silhouette of a rat running inside the fluorescent light above her, an ugly reminder of her less-than-glamorous reality. Jackie's hallucination reminds us that maternal perfection is out of reach for her as an addict and cheating spouse. Yet, as Dolan (2013) suggests, Jackie resists the cookie-cutter suburban life depicted in her dream.

The following season, Jackie takes a rare day off work and takes her family on an impromptu vacation. She becomes jittery when she loses the pills she is addicted to and even more anxious when the only place to stay at the seashore is a bed and breakfast with a nosy proprietor who recognizes her withdrawal symptoms. On edge and uncomfortable in the B&B, the family makes a hasty retreat for home, and the trip ends with Jackie and her husband in a terrible fight about finances. Although Jackie's misfortune is due largely to her drug use and deceptive practices, this darkly comedic episode may resonate with viewers who have ever endured a disastrous family vacation. The trip that started out as "quality time" with her family prompts the first of many fights that lead to Jackie's divorce.

## *Like Mother, Like Child*

While these series narratively acknowledge the challenges that working mothers face, they also hold mothers responsible for influencing children's behavior. Repeatedly, these series suggest that the mothers' character, poor choices, or work ambitions make their children rebellious and unhappy. These themes draw from a familiar cultural tendency to blame mothers for a host of children's maladies, conveniently discounting other social, financial, and psychological factors at work (Thurer, 1995). The series' tendency toward mother-blame is in some ways problematic, yet these series do not provide one-dimensional "bad mothers." Rather, these are portraits of women continually making amends for their mistakes and compassionately dealing with their children's long-term issues.

On *Weeds*, Nancy's son Shane grows from a sweet 10-year-old with trusting brown eyes into a hardened criminal. He is sexually precocious, losing his virginity at 13. When his mother tries to discipline him, he accuses her of being a "slap-happy drug dealer" and asks her to "stop pretending to be a mom" (Morrow & Robinson, 2008). Shane's true transformation takes place in the fifth season, when the 14-year-old spends afternoons with his Mexican stepfather's bodyguard, Ignacio. He admires Ignacio's strength but is shocked to see him violently attack a man with a golf club at the slightest provocation. At the end of Season Five, Shane overhears a conversation in which a powerful politician named Pilar threatens to kill him and his brother. Following his mentor's example, he steps out of the shadows with a croquet mallet and strikes a fatal blow to Pilar's head, smiling at her demise. Although the series provided early hints that Shane was unhinged, Nancy's absent parenting and inability to protect her son from poor role models contributes to the crime.

Nancy takes responsibility for Shane's crimes—to the point of taking blame and serving jail time for Pilar's death. She tries to remind Shane of his childhood innocence: for example, spending the day with him at a town fair riding rollercoasters. Furthermore, she reforms her ways a bit for her younger son, Stevie. When a doctor suggests that Stevie's irregular bowel movements are an indicator of stress, Nancy trades a freewheeling life on the road for a more stationary existence in Seattle. She later creates a blended household with her sister's family, providing Stevie more parental figures and support. (The fact that she and her sister dislike each other ultimately takes a backseat to Stevie's needs.)

*Nurse Jackie* is equally direct in blaming mothers for their children's afflictions. In an early episode, Jackie's family stops at a donut shop on the way to the subway station. Jackie reaches in her pocket for a tissue, accidently sprinkling the contents of a medicine capsule on daughter Fiona's donut. Horrified at the prospect of drugging her daughter, she pretends to see a bug and knocks the donut out of her hand. The slip up suggests that Jackie's drug use has the potential to directly harm her children, or at the very least, poison the time they spend together.

Fiona may be saved from her mother's missteps, but Grace is not so lucky. Early in the series, 10-year-old Gracie shows signs of a mental disorder. She watches documentaries about doomsday scenarios and washes her hands obsessively. Jackie is in denial, chalking up her daughter's behavior to preteen moodiness, but her husband and the school psychologist intervene to make her take Grace's condition seriously. In a particularly ugly fight, husband Kevin blames Jackie for making their daughter's anxiety worse by working long hours and then trying to "fix" things when she returns home (Brixius, Wallem, & Feig, 2010). Even Jackie indulges in this line of thinking, blaming her absence for Gracie's anxiety. "You're right: I'm not here. Not in the way you are," she tells her husband. "When they fall down they run to you" (Brixius, Wallem, & Feig, 2010). A *Los Angeles Times* reviewer drew the connection, writing, "I'm not saying that Jackie's life of distance and deception caused Grace to be obsessive and morbid, but it certainly could have stoked the fires already there" (Hanson, 2011, para. 2). The series takes a similar tactic, addressing OCD as a medical condition but linking Grace's behavior to her mother's actions.

Not surprisingly, Jackie is resistant to putting Grace on medication, signing her up for therapy instead. When Grace locks herself in the bathroom to hide her latest compulsion—pulling out her hair—Jackie takes her wounded daughter in her arms and hypocritically cries, "We cannot have secrets in this house" (Hurdis & Feig, 2010). Grace's condition is thus connected to Jackie's secret addiction. However, savvy viewers recognize that Jackie is a nurse struggling to come to terms with a mental illness that is not easily cured. Taking cues from an elderly patient who feeds soup to her dying husband, Jackie buys chicken soup for Grace and feeds her spoonfuls of the warm broth. The scene emphasizes that a mother's attention and nurturance can be powerful medicine—even if Jackie didn't bother to cook the soup herself.

Developments in Season Five further underscore the belief that, as *Nurse Jackie*'s producers put it, "the apple doesn't fall far from the tree" (Smith, 2014). Jackie goes through rehab and gets divorced, fighting her husband for shared custody of her daughters. Meanwhile, Grace becomes increasingly rebellious, sneaking off to spend time with an older boyfriend in Manhattan; she startles her mother with her foul mouth and charcoal-rimmed eyes. Jackie tries to control her daughter's appearance and romantic life, mostly unsuccessfully. Learning that Grace is hiding a stash of the amphetamine Adderall in her backpack spurs more radical changes. Jackie forces her daughter to spend a day with her at work, both to see the injurious effects of drug use and to better understand her mother's pressures. Grace nevertheless blames her now-sober mother for her drug use, telling her in a sharp, accusatory tone: "I took [drugs] and I still did everything I was supposed to do. You know what that's like, right?" (Flahive & Peretz, 2013). While Jackie's husband chalks up Gracie's behavior to adolescent rebellion, Jackie heeds the warning signs. She gives up her hard-won shared custody of the girls, insisting they should live full-time with their father because she is a bad influence. By the sixth season, however, Gracie has become a full-fledged addict and Fiona acts emotionally needy. The trauma of the divorce and separation from their mother seems to have worsened the problem, echoing the perception that children are harmed by forced separation from their mothers (Reed, Greaves, & Poole, 2008).

## *Mothers at Work*

Jackie's bad influence may well extend beyond her family. One blogger accused *Nurse Jackie* and similar series of fueling cultural antagonism towards working moms. "If the only working mother that the media displays is one that works until they need drugs to get them through the day ... then of course people are going to be against the idea of working moms," she argued (Meredith, 2013, para. 3). However, to some viewers Jackie and Nancy are welcomed alternatives to earlier, more respectable working mother narratives in which the "competitive go-getter" transforms effortlessly into the "selfless doormat at home" (Douglas & Michaels, 2004, p. 12).

Although both women clearly love their jobs, these series present moments in which busy work schedules interfere with healthy family life. Jackie's husband urges her to take more time off work, claiming that her physical and emotional absence from the household is harming their children. Grace even bribes her mom not to go into work, telling her she wishes the hospital would burn to the ground. Jackie's long work hours become even more consequential in divorce proceedings: Her 60-hour weeks are used as a strike against her, and she is forced to rearrange her schedule to facilitate a joint custody agreement. Yet Jackie herself points out her husband's hypocrisy in valuing her income but not her labor: "You didn't mind my long hours when they were paying for your bar," she tells him (Straw & Mitchell, 2013). She clearly recognizes the value of her work to the family and refuses to let her husband dictate her priorities. The emergency room is a realm in which she is praised for her acumen, a welcome respite from the guilt and recrimination waiting for her at home. Much like the working mothers' dilemma described by Hochschild (1997), Jackie finds her long work hours more appealing than returning home to the "second shift" of household responsibilities and the "third shift" of trying to appease her husband's and daughters' demands for more family time (p. 83).

In *Weeds*, Nancy's guilt is doubled, as her erratic, dangerous job means extended absences from her family and the ever-present threat of leaving them motherless. In one episode, she misses her son's 18th birthday celebration, instead driving to a meeting with Mexican drug dealers who have threatened to kill her. Her parting gift to her son, Silas, is a card that acknowledges her absence from his upbringing. "Congratulations on raising yourself," she writes. "You've done a great job" (Kohan & Zisk, 2008). In a later season, when she tearfully embraces her toddler son, Stevie, after a lengthy separation, she muses on how motherhood is more complex than presence or absence. "Someone accused me of only being aware of what's right in front of me," she says in a voiceover. "It isn't true. [It's] the opposite. Any moment—eating lunch, washing my hair—I'm aware of all my people, wherever they are. I carry them, you know?" (Falk & Trim, 2011). This quotation refutes the idea that a mother's presence is foundational to good parenting (Johnston & Swanson, 2006), and highlights her care and concern for her children as evidence of good-enough motherhood. The scene also suggests that Nancy never gives up her maternal identity, even as she appears to act out of sheer self-interest.

Furthermore, these series conceive of mothering as a role that expands beyond one's own family. Jackie's exceptional nursing entails not only expert medical care but also comforting and respecting children, who are often brushed off or trivialized in an ER setting. As a *Los Angeles Times* reporter noted: "Jackie is essentially mom to a hospital full of people, including the staff" (Hanson, 2011, para. 1). Nancy's line of work is hardly child friendly, but she makes crucial decisions on behalf of youth. When she learns the drug-smuggling operation that she is involved in also traffics young women across the border for sex work, Nancy begins to have blinding migraines and images of a young woman in peril. Her conscience prompts her to report the operation to U.S. authorities and have it shut down, at the expense of her own safety. She also performs charity on a small scale: When she is hospitalized in *Weeds*' last season, she distributes marijuana free of charge to patients in need of herbal pain relief. These actions make Jackie and Nancy more sympathetic as they counter the characters' self-serving behavior in other domains of life. Audiences see evidence of *Weeds*' creator Kohan's claim that Nancy operates from her own moral code rather than letting the justice system or drug cartel dictate her limits (Bolonik, 2007). As they take moral responsibility for patients, coworkers, and complete strangers, Nancy and Jackie point to a definition of mothering that extends beyond the nuclear family.

## *Judging the Other Mothers*

In the world of *Weeds* and *Nurse Jackie*, "being a parent means always being subjected to unfairly harsh judgment, not least from your kids and from yourself" (Harris, 2009, para. 2). These series acknowledge a climate of "maternal surveillance" in which all mothers continually police themselves and others for weaknesses (Podnieks, 2012, p. 14). Warner (2005) further suggests that oppressive mothering ideologies spur women to direct anger at themselves and other mothers, rather than blaming the system or reigning experts who set the standards in the first place. Thus Nancy and Jackie, themselves imperfect parents, frequently criticize the attitudes and actions of fellow mothers. Such scenes may appear to fuel the "mommy wars" (Douglas & Michaels, 2004), but they also challenge easy assumptions about what makes a good mother.

Nancy lacks a maternal role model; viewers learn that both her parents died when she was in her early twenties, and she rarely speaks of her childhood. Nevertheless, she seems educated in parenting techniques. When her son Stevie is born she tries to breastfeed exclusively, bragging that she did so with both of her older sons. (Her plans go by the wayside as formula becomes an easy substitute). When she spots another pregnant woman eating a fast-food sandwich in the obstetrician's waiting room, she lectures her about nitrates and proper prenatal nutrition. However, Nancy's harshest judgment is reserved for nosy neighbor Celia. Celia maintains a facade of control but has an unhappy marriage and an unhealthy relationship with her daughters. In the pilot episode, Celia finds out her teenage daughter is pregnant and forces her to move out; throughout the series she is cruel to her younger daughter Isabel, who is both overweight and has lesbian tendencies. Nancy's somewhat lax approach to parenting seems psychologically healthier than Celia's harsh approaches.

While White suburban Celia illustrates dysfunctional parenting, Nancy's working-class African American supplier provides a stronger model of motherhood. Heylia provides a home for her grown daughter and nephew, sharing her business with them, and is not judgmental about her daughter's unwed pregnancy. Heylia's family fits the African American kinship model Collins (1994) describes in which childcare responsibilities are shared among extended family members and family members provide reciprocal means of support. (In this case, Heylia's daughter and nephew help her run her home business). Her mutually supportive relationship with her grown children contrasts with Nancy's isolated efforts to keep her nuclear family afloat. Heylia initially runs the business out of her home, neatly merging the domestic and professional roles that Nancy endeavors to keep separate (Ganz, 2013).

However, critics struggle with whether Heylia and her family play into or refute stereotypes. Ganz (2013) sees in Heylia's appearance, accent, and sassy attitude a reflection of the historical mammy and matriarch stereotype of Black women, but also suggests an oppositional reading of her character. After all, Heylia emerges as a wiser mother than Nancy, often outsmarts her in business transactions, and offers a family stability unparalleled by Nancy's dysfunctional clan (Bolonik, 2007).

*Nurse Jackie* seems to reserve its harshest judgments for privileged mothers, particularly those whose vanity harms their children. For example, when a preteen suffers brain injury in a skateboarding accident, Jackie is initially compassionate toward the White middle-class mom and broaches the issue of wearing a helmet. The mother admits that she had asked her son to remove his helmet during a skateboarding photo shoot, to show off his long hair. Jackie is aghast: "Your job is to protect him," she seethes (Brixius, Wallem, & Zisk, 2009). In another episode, Jackie deals with a snippy Park Avenue mom who noticed her sons had head lice and strategically chose a distant ER to avoid embarrassment. "I don't even want to touch them," she scowls, looking at her louse-ridden sons. Anticipating the sons' need for continual treatment—and wanting to expose the mother's secret—Jackie phones a drug store and asks that multiple boxes of lice shampoo be delivered to the woman's swanky building (Shepherd & Feig, 2009). Jackie is decidedly more compassionate toward mothers with fewer resources, such as the Latina mother whose son is critically injured from a playground fall (Season 1, Episode 4) or the mixed-race family facing a cystic fibrosis diagnosis (Season 2, Episode 2). The series' running commentary on motherhood suggests that those with fewer privileges may be better parents and makes Jackie—who is practical, earthy, and at least tries to protect her children—appear more compassionate than the narcissistic, self-serving wealthy moms. The series decouples the association of wealth with good parenting, and warns White women against the dangers of investing too much of their identities in their children.

A memorable episode of *Nurse Jackie* features Rosie Perez as a sassy Puerto Rican woman admitted to the ER who appears to be close to giving birth (Season 4, Episode 4). Viewers soon learn she only looks pregnant because she has two deadly tumors growing inside her that she calls her "slow-growing monsters." The woman admits she gets a kick out of "riding the subway 'pregnant' with a cigarette in one hand and malt liquor in the other" (Fairey & Mann, 2012). The episode reminds audiences not to judge by appearances—and also comments on how motherhood is a public activity in which women's bodies, behaviors, and attitudes are subject to constant scrutiny. Much like the antiheroines on Showtime, Perez's character takes pleasure in defying social expectations.

## *Conclusion*

Just as these series offer complex narratives about motherhood, they decline to offer easy answers and happy endings. Jackie makes it through one year of sobriety but at the end of the fifth season swallows a single pill in a moment of weakness, reviving her addiction. In the following season, her daughter Grace becomes distant and develops a full-fledged addiction to prescription pills, and the relapsed Jackie starts to make mistakes at work. Her ex-husband notices Jackie's erratic behavior and bars her from seeing their children. In the sixth season finale, she crashes her car into an ambulance and is arrested for drug possession and driving under the influence. She nearly loses her nursing license as a result, but remains at the hospital in a probationary position.

Recovery is a key theme of *Nurse Jackie*'s final season, as she finally enters a rehab program and strives to remain sober. Her recovery is initially motivated more by her career than her family. "I can't *not* be a nurse," she declares. "I need my life back" (Phillips, Salzman, & Walsh, 2015). However, her gradual reconnection with her daughters also contributes to her changed behavior. When Jackie is offered a line of cocaine at a vulnerable moment, she resists temptation and calls to check in with daughter Grace instead. She is, quite literally, "saved by Grace," at least this once (Newman, 2015, para. 8). Ultimately, once her nursing license is reinstated, the pull of addiction becomes too strong to resist. Jackie surreptitiously pops pills and uses a patient's heroin in the series finale, collapsing in an apparent overdose. Her colleagues try to revive her. While her fate remains ambiguous, it's clear that even if Jackie survives she has lost her nursing career and the trust of family and friends who believed her to be sober.

*Weeds* ended in 2012 on an ambivalent note, imagining the Botwin family ten years in the future, when marijuana is legal nationwide. Nancy winds up a wealthy businesswoman with marijuana cafes in multiple cities. Her now far-flung family gathers at her Connecticut estate for her son's bar mitzvah. She is still a single mom to Stevie, a surly teen who has decided to go to boarding school. Her troubled son Shane is a bitter, alcoholic police officer, and her happiest son Silas prefers to keep her at a distance. She is saddened by the strained relationships, but her brother-in-law Andy urges her to embrace her new phase of life: "You're free; you did your job, now it's done. [There's] no one there to answer to ... no one to hold you back from becoming the person you always wanted to be, doing only what you want to do" (Kohan & Trim, 2012). As the series ends, Nancy sits alone on her porch as snow falls. Her children come out of the house to join her, passing a joint around, the family laughs remembering their shared misadventures. Motherhood remains a source of both sustenance and struggle, with a flawed but fascinating woman at the center.

These somber conclusions offer some evidence of redemption. Nancy has finally achieved financial success and decides to sell her business, leaving the pot trade for good. Her grown children function independently of her, and she is symbolically freed from the responsibility of parenting them. In the final season of *Nurse Jackie*, college-bound Grace attends a prospective students' weekend at UPenn, and younger Fiona rehearses her confirmation ceremony in the family's Catholic church. These events grant Jackie moments of maternal pride, and also suggest she has imparted wisdom and morality to her daughters despite her failings. In Jackie's final scene, as she lies on the cold hospital floor, her protégé, Zoey, tells her that she is "good"—acknowledging her saintly qualities. As always, *Weeds* and *Nurse Jackie* blur the boundaries between good and evil, and they allow us to understand these characters as multifaceted women, not merely mothers (Walters & Harrison, 2014). Nancy and Jackie may fall far short of the "intensive-mothering" ideal, but ultimately their moral journeys lead them to riches and redemption.

## *References*

Anderson, J., & Feuer, A. (2013, June 7). She rode horses, drove an S.U.V. and, the authorities say, farmed marijuana. *The New York Times.* Retrieved from http://www.nytimes.com/2013/06/08/nyregion/scarsdale-ny-woman-is-charged-as-marijuana-farmer.html?pagewanted=all&_r=0

Baker, P., & Carson, A. (1999). "I take care of my kids": Mothering practices of substance-abusing women. *Gender and Society, 13*(3), 347–363.

Barbalich, A. (2011, November). Moms on drugs: The prescription pill epidemic. *Parents.* Retrieved from http://www.parents.com/parenting/moms/healthy-mom/prescription-drug-addiction/?page=1

Bergen, J. (2011, February 20). *Nurse Jackie*'s Edie Falco on her new roles. *WebMD.* Retrieved from http://www.webmd.com/women/features/nurse-jackie-edie-falco-on-her-new-roles

Bolonik, K. (2013, April 14). Edie Falco: I took *The Sopranos* home with me. *Salon*. Retrieved from http://www.salon.com/2013/04/14/edie_falco_i_took_the_sopranos_home_with_me/Salon.com

Bolonik, K. (2007). *In the Weeds*. New York, NY: Simon Spotlight Entertainment.

Bradshaw, L. (2013). Showtime's "female problem": Cancer, quality, and motherhood. *Journal of Consumer Culture, 13*(2), 160–177.

Brixius, L., & Wallem, L. (Writers), & Feig, P. (Director). (2010). Years of service. [Television Series Episode]. In R. Jackson (Producer), *Nurse Jackie*. New York, NY: Showtime.

Brixius, L., & Wallem, L. (Writers), & Zisk, C. (Director). (2009). Sweet 'n all [Television Series Episode]. In R. Jackson (Producer), *Nurse Jackie*. New York, NY: Showtime.

Brixius, L., Wallem, L., & Dunsky, E. (Writers), & Coulter, A. (Director). (2009). Pilot [Television Series Episode]. In R. Jackson (Producer), *Nurse Jackie*. New York, NY: Showtime.

Carmon, E. (2010, March 19). Women aren't interesting? *Jackie* begs to differ. *Jezebel.com*. Retrieved from http://jezebel.com/5497343/women-arent-interesting-jackie-begs-to-differ

Chozick, A. (2010, March 19). Showtime's bad girls make good. *Wall Street Journal*. Retrieved from http://online.wsj.com/articles/SB10001424052748704743404575127472943944014

Cleveland, R. (Writer), & Taylor, A. (Director). (2010). Candyland [Television Series Episode]. In R. Jackson (Producer), *Nurse Jackie*. New York, NY: Showtime.

Christopher, K. (2012). Extensive mothering: Employed mothers' constructions of the good mother. *Gender and Society, 26*(1), 73–96.

Collins, P. H. (1994). Shifting the center: Race, class, and feminist theorizing about motherhood. In E. Glenn, C. Chang, & L. R. Forcey, (Eds.) *Mothering: Experience, ideology and agency* (pp. 45–66). New York, NY: Routledge.

D'Souza, T. (2011, November/December). The new dealers. *Mother Jones*. Retrieved from http://www.motherjones.com/politics/2011/12/tony-dsouza-marijuana-growers

D'Addario, D. (2013, September 24). *Modern family* is a class-blind fantasy world. *Salon*. Retrieved from http://www.salon.com/2013/09/24/modern_family_is_a_class_blind_fantasy_world/

DeGregory, L. (2010, October). Addicted moms: Everybody knows somebody. *Working Mother*. Retrieved from http://www.workingmother.com/special-reports/addicted-moms-everybody-knows-somebody

Dolan, J. (2013). *The feminist spectator in action: Feminist criticism for stage and screen*. New York, NY: Palgrave MacMillan.

Douglas, S., & Michaels, M. (2004). *The mommy myth: The idealization of motherhood and how it has undermined all women*. New York, NY: Free Press.

Dow, B. J. (1996). *Prime-time feminism: Television, media culture, and the women's movements since 1970*. Philadelphia, PA: University of Pennsylvania.

Duell, M. (2011, May 13). Tragedy of a real-life *Weeds* mom. *Daily Mail.* Retrieved from http://www.dailymail.co.uk/news/article-1386331/Real-life-Weeds-mother-Krista-Dittmeyer-brutally-murdered-drugs.html

Fairey, E. (Writer), & Mann, S. (Director). (2012). Slow growing monsters [Television Series Episode]. In R. Jackson (Producer), *Nurse Jackie.* New York, NY: Showtime.

Fallon, K. (2010, August 16). Showtime: Television for women, for everyone? *The Atlantic.* Retrieved from http://www.theatlantic.com/entertainment/archive/2010/08/showtime-television-for-women-for-everyone/61535/

Falk, S. (Writer), & Trim, M. (Director). (2011). Object impermanence. [Television Series Episode]. In J. Kohan (Producer), *Weeds.* New York, NY: Showtime.

Fernandez, M. E. (2014, July 26). TV's new leading ladies: Don't call them likeable. *NBC News.com.* Retrieved from http://www.nbcnews.com/pop-culture/tv/tvs-new-leading-ladies-dont-call-them-likable-n163101

Flahive, L. (Writer), & Peretz, J. (Director). (2013). Heart [Television Series Episode]. In R. Jackson (Producer), *Nurse Jackie.* New York, NY: Showtime.

Fulkerson, J., Story, M., Mellin, A., Leffert, N., Newmark-Sztainer, D., & French, S. (2006). Family dinner frequency and adolescent development: Relationships with developmental assets and high-risk behaviors. *Journal of Adolescent Health, 39*(3), 337–345.

Ganz, J. (2013). Mammies, maids and mothers: Representations of African-American and Latina women's reproductive labor in *Weeds.* In D. Davis-Maye, A. D. Yarber, & T. Perry (Eds.), *What the village gave me: Conceptualizations of womanhood* (pp. 19–36). Lanham, MD: University Press of America.

Hanson, A. (2011, May 9) *Nurse Jackie* recap: World's greatest mom. *Show Tracker.* Retrieved from http://latimesblogs.latimes.com/showtracker/2011/05/nurse-jackie-recap-worlds-greatest-mom.html

Haralovich, M. B. (1989) Sitcoms and suburbs: Positioning the 1950s homemaker. *Quarterly Review of Film and Video, 11*(1), 61–83.

Harris, M. (2009, August 28). TV's great bad mommies. *Entertainment Weekly.* Retrieved from http://www.ew.com/ew/article/0,,20301501,00.html

Hays, S. (1996). *The cultural contradictions of motherhood.* New Haven, CT: Yale University Press.

Hochschild, A. R. (1997). *The time bind: When work becomes home and home becomes work.* New York, NY: Metropolitan Books.

Hurdis, M. (Writer), & Feig, P. (Director). (2010). P.O. box [Television Series Episode]. In R. Jackson (Producer), *Nurse Jackie.* New York, NY: Showtime.

Johnston, D., & Swanson, D. (2006). Constructing the "good mother": The experience of mothering ideologies by work status. *Sex Roles, 54*(7–8), 509–519.

Kinnick, K. (2009). Media morality tales and the politics of motherhood. In A. Hall, & M. Bishop (Eds.), *Mommy angst: Motherhood in American popular culture* (pp. 1–28). Santa Barbara, CA: Praeger.

Kohan, J., & Kelly, B. (Writers), & Trim, M. (Director). (2009). Suck 'n' spit [Television Series Episode]. In J. Kohan (Producer), *Weeds.* New York, NY: Showtime.

Kohan, J. (Writer), & Trim, M. (Director). (2012). It's time. [Television Series Episode]. In J. Kohan (Producer), *Weeds*. New York, NY: Showtime.

Kohan, J. (Writer), & Zisk, C. (Director). (2006). Corn snake [Television Series Episode]. In J. Kohan (Producer), *Weeds*. New York, NY: Showtime.

Kohan, J. (Writer), & Zisk, C. (Director). (2008). If you work for a living, then why do you kill yourself working? [Television Series Episode]. In J. Kohan (Producer), *Weeds*. New York, NY: Showtime.

Ladd-Taylor, M., & Umanksy, L. (1998). *"Bad" mothers: The politics of blame in twentieth-century America*. New York, NY: New York University Press.

Lotz, A. (2006). *Redesigning women: Television after the network era*. Champaign, IL: University of Illinois Press.

McLanahan, S., & Sandefur, G. (2009). *Growing up with a single parent: What hurts, what helps*. Cambridge, CT: Harvard University Press.

Meredith, B. (2013, September 25). The misrepresentation of working moms on television. *My take on TV*. Retrieved from http://www.mytakeontv.com/2013/09/25/the-misrepresentation-of-working-moms-on-television/

Morrow, V. (Writer), & Robinson, J. A. (Director). (2008). Love circle overlap. [Television Series Episode]. In J. Kohan (Producer), *Weeds*. New York, NY: Showtime.

Nayberg, K., & Richardson, S. (Producers). (2009). All about Edie. On *Nurse Jackie: Season one* [DVD]. Santa Monica, CA: Lionsgate.

Newman, M. (2015, May 17). *High noon. Entertainment Weekly*. Retrieved from http://www.ew.com/recap/nurse-jackie-season-7-episode-6

Owen, A. S., Stein, S. R., & Vande Berg, L. R. (2007). *Bad girls: Cultural politics and media representations of transgressive women*. New York, NY: Peter Lang.

Phillips, C., & Saltzman, T. (Writers), & Walsh, B. (Director). (2015). Clean [Television Series Episode]. In R. Jackson (Producer), *Nurse Jackie*. New York, NY: Showtime.

Platt, M., & Safchik, B. (Writers), & Sanford, A. (Director). (2005). Dead in the nethers [Television Series Episode]. In J. Kohan (Producer), *Weeds*. New York, NY: Showtime.

Podnieks, E. (2012). *Mediating moms: Mothers in popular culture*. Montreal, QC: McGill-Queens University Press.

Press, A. (2011). Gender and family in television's golden age and beyond. *The Annals of the American Society of Political and Social Science*, *625*(1), 139–150.

Reed, C., Greaves, L., & Poole, N. (2008). Good, bad, thwarted, or addicted? Discourses of substance-abusing mothers. *Critical Social Policy*, *28*(2), 211–234.

Reisen, V. (Writer), & Trim, M. (Director). (2009). A modest proposal. [Television Series Episode]. In J. Kohan (Producer), *Weeds*. New York, NY: Showtime.

Robbins, A. (2012, 2 February.) High society: Washington's love affair with marijuana. *Washingtonian*. Retrieved from http://www.washingtonian.com/articles/people/high-society-washingtons-love-affair-with-marijuana/

Shaw, G. (2009, May 21). Mary-Louise Parker on momhood and marijuana. *WebMD*. Retrieved from http://www.webmd.com/parenting/features/mary-louise-parker-on-momhood-and-marijuana

Shepherd, J. H. (Writer), & Feig, P. (Director). (2009). Nosebleed [Television Series Episode]. In R. Jackson (Producer), *Nurse Jackie*. New York, NY: Showtime.

Smith, S. (Producer). (2014). A sober Jackie. On *Nurse Jackie: Season five* [DVD]. Santa Monica, CA: Lionsgate.

Straw, T. (Writer), & Mitchell, J C. (Director). (2013). Luck of the drawing [Television Series Episode]. In R. Jackson (Producer), *Nurse Jackie*. New York, NY: Showtime.

Summers, S., & Summers, H. J. (2014). *Saving lives: Why the media's portrayal of nursing puts us all at risk*. New York, NY: Oxford University Press.

Susann, J. (1966). *Valley of the dolls*. New York, NY: Bernard Geis Associates.

Thurer, S. (1995). *Myths of motherhood: How culture reinvents the good mother*. New York, NY: Penguin Books.

Walters, S. D., & Harrison, L. (2014). Not ready to make nice: Aberrant mothers in contemporary culture. *Feminist Media Studies, 14*(1), 38–55.

Warner, J. (2005). *Perfect madness: Motherhood in the age of anxiety*. New York, NY: Riverhead Books.

*Weeds* spreads to Pittsburgh (2006, November 21). *Pittsburgh Post-Gazette*. Retrieved from http://www.post-gazette.com/ae/tuned-in/2006/11/21/Weeds-spreads-to-Pittsburgh/stories/200611210189

Weisbart, D. (Producer), & Robson, M. (Director). (1967). *Valley of the dolls* [Motion picture]. United States: Twentieth Century Fox.

# 5. *Maternal Transgressions, Racial Regressions: How Whiteness Mediates the (Worst) White Moms*

By Susana Martínez Guillem & Lisa A. Flores

"World's Worst Mom!" "Worst Mom Ever!" These are proclamations that would seem to bring shame, defeat and condemnation and perhaps be used only in rare occasions. Yet interestingly, amidst the clamors of intensive mothering and the new momism, discourses that ask women to commit themselves to that "natural" calling—motherhood, we see as well a host of pronouncements hailing some mothers as worst ever! At times, the label is clearly an indictment, a marker of failure and transgression. Consider, for instance, the current spate of "worst mom in the world" photo essays available online, such as the one published by *IJReview*, which include photographs of women, typically with their children, in poses suggesting poor maternal judgment ("15 women compete," 2014). The label "worst mom ever" would seem to capture a transgression so great that it cannot easily be undone, such as that alleged against Jennifer Marie Vargas, who reportedly yanked her son's genitals so hard that she tore them and then attempted to glue them back together (Gray, 2013). Or the too-many instances of mothers who kill or attempt to kill their children.[1] Some of these transgressions may well qualify as "worst ever."

"Worst" would seem to be a selective category, a marker of absolute failure. But today, "worst mother ever" has become a name so common that it even produced a television series, *World's Worst Mom*, which featured parents whose main transgression was their over-protectiveness.[2] It has become, as well, a label that is self-imposed, mostly in ways that invite struggling mothers to come together in commiseration and forgiveness over our failures. Seemingly fueled by social media and technology as well as by contemporary discourses on mothering, these proclamations center that "perfect madness" that Judith Warner (2005) details in which women strive for while also resisting the consumptive demands of contemporary White mothering. Here, women such as Tammy, in her blog "World's Worst Moms: We all screw up. It's the cleanup that matters ..." explore and expose what she labels "worst mom moments." The list includes such failures as when you inappropriately snap at your child or almost accidently reveal the "truth" about Santa Claus or the Easter Bunny. It brings together the many, many other mothers, whose failings, which range from spending too much time at the office to being late to pick up their children, seem counter intuitive to a label that relies upon the superlative form of bad.

The cultural ease with which we indict women as the worst ever or the world's worst indicates that something rhetorically is at play at the intersections of mothering and success/failure. Perhaps this is not surprising given the long history of mother as a category steeped in expectations of natural and innate selflessness and the cultural constructions still present today, despite feminist attempts to trouble them, that to mother is to fulfill the highest ideals of woman. These cultural constructions have long situated mothering as both a natural instinct and a compulsory calling (Barnett, 2006; Gibson & Heyse, 2010) in ways that indicate mothers occupy a contested category. Historically, mediated representations of mothering have perpetuated narrow and even trite caricatures, with good mothering reduced to an almost-complete sacrifice of self in the presumed joy of caring for others and bad mothering equally reductively captured in selfishness and bitterness. These cultural parameters of mothering emerge and shape both news media and entertainment media, which in recent years have converged in rhetorically complex ways. Mediated ideals of mothering shift and flow, in ways that account for and often accommodate intersecting national conversations—about gender and feminism, work and labor, politics and representation.

Where second wave feminist and gender politics enabled spaces for conversations about super women, who balanced work and family, and struggling women, who divorced and learned to single parent, contemporary intersections struggle with a different set of seeming (im)possibilities. The fairly recent popular literature on the opt-out generation or the 2009 bestseller, *Bad Mother*, which claims to offer a humorous account of the competing demands for a contemporary pure mothering, exemplifies this current trend. Across these contradictory accounts what emerges is the persistent crisis of mothering, an overtly gendered crisis that is alternately laden with discourses of class, race, and labor.

In this chapter, we trace contemporary narratives of maternal transgressions in news/entertainment media. While they are often positioned differently in terms of "fictional" and "real," we treat here those two spheres as operating in an indissoluble relationship characteristic of the current postmodern sensitivity. In this sense, the boundaries between these two genres blur into the similar investment in constituting, rather than reflecting, a particular kind of reality that builds on and constitutes different cultural ideals (Baudrillard, 1983; Lang, 2008).

Within our analysis, we look to the ways that cultural narratives of race and class intersect with and inform gendered depictions of mothering. We do so around three mothers who have been named, either by themselves or by others, as the "worst mom ever" but whose transgressions seem, if not trivial, at least also not that superlative, worst. Consider, for instance, Betty Draper of *Mad Men*, who was named the "worst mother in TV history" for failings that surround her quick temper and often caustic comments (Friedman, 2010). Or Sarah Linden, of *The Killing*. Coming in as number one on Yahoo TV's annual Mother's Day list of the ten worst TV moms, Linden's failings surround her investment in her career and its impact on her son (Segal, 2012). And then there is Patricia Krentcil, commonly known as "tan mom," a deeply tanned New Jersey woman arrested for child endangerment after allegedly taking her young daughter into a tanning booth. Ranked number 7 on a list titled "Mother's Day 2012: The Ten Worst Moms in the History of Ever," Krentcil exploded into a contemporary celebrity as images of and commentary on her extensive tanning circulated widely (Sentenac, 2012).

With a host of failings that include and exceed mothering, these three mothers transgress in ways that are both markedly different and interestingly interrelated. We turn to these three mothers, two television characters and one "real" person, for the insights they offer us into the intersections of race and gender, post-feminism and post-racialism, intertextuality, caricature and complexity. These three exemplars of "worst" mother are significant, we argue, both for their marked differences in their transgressions, as well as for how their failings converge in racialized ways. What emerges from this reading is that maternal transgressions rely upon assumptions of an ideal that, in its naturalness and its perfection, is grounded in Whiteness and patriarchy in ways that link transgression to race. In addition, we suggest that as instantiations of "worst," all three mothers must necessarily be caricatured. Yet interestingly, the rather privileged characters of Draper and Linden are offered greater complexity than the more peripheral, not quite White, Krentcil. This contrast is a telling reminder of the ways in which Whiteness may act as a mediating mechanism that marks transgression while at the same time allowing for its deconstruction.

### *From Best to Worst—the Contentious Category of Mother*

From the proverbial question about whether a good mother stays at home with her children or "goes to work," motherhood as both an identity and role has a long and contested history. Scholarly accounts of mothering suggest that discourses capturing both ends of the spectrum—ideal mother versus base mother—circulate widely (Douglas & Michaels, 2004). Whether captured in iconic representations, such as the Virgin Mary and Medea, or more contemporary manifestations of these ideals, the extremes of mothering—both best and worst—are easily identified and delineated. The poles, which Fixmar-Oraiz (2014) names virtuous motherhood and pathological motherhood, signal the heaviness of the categories. That is, notions and representations of mothers and motherhood are deeply steeped in assumptions of im/morality and sacrifice/self-absorption, or what Robson (2005) identifies as the "weight of responsibility" (p. 219) for perfect mothering that by necessity produces failure. As Quiney (2007) so aptly concludes, mothers exist in an "unforgiving context" (p. 25).

Perhaps given the impossibility of maternal perfection, contemporary pop feminism seems invested in, if not obsessed by, what it means to mother today, in an era that motherhood texts emphasize as fraught with contradictions and im/possibilities. If mothering debates in the 1960s were characterized by the "feminine mystique," contemporary popular accounts of ideal mothering are best captured by what Sharon Hays (1996) has named "intensive mothering" and others reference as the new "momism" (Douglas & Michaels, 2004; O'Brien Hallstein, 2011). Hays explains that intensive mothering is a cultural approach to mothering that is "child-centered, expert-guided, emotionally absorbing, labour-intensive and financially expensive" (p. 69). Reminiscent and perhaps a contemporary manifestation of the ideals captured in the "feminine mystique" (Friedan, 1963), intensive mothering draws on postfeminist ideals of women's free choice to work outside of the home or stay at home and to share the joys of child-raising with their pro-feminist husbands (Douglas & Michaels, 2004). As Hayden (2011) explains, the rhetorical force of intensive mothering lies in part in its promise that in mothering women can escape consumerist mentalities and return to a familial space that values "unselfish, loving, and altruistic relationships" (p. 2). Douglas and Michaels (2004) argue similarly, noting that the trend inspired by the ideology likely has such wide appeal for the ways that it appears to celebrate mothers and mothering.

Despite the wide cultural appeal of the new momism, feminist and cultural critics note the ways that intensive mothering exacerbates the seemingly inescapable tensions that surround mothers and mothering (see e.g., O'Brien

Hallstein 2010). Grounded in assumptions that mothering is both natural, a divinely ordained and biological calling, *and* inherently insufficient, always in need of expert guidance, the ideology of intensive mothering perpetuates the tension between best and worst. As Andrea Press (2006) explains, "Momism is the ethic that has impossibly raised the levels of time and expertise needed to meet the rapidly rising minimum level of 'good-enough-mothering" (p. 235), even as it promises to mothers that, guided by our natural instincts and rewarded by the endless joys of self-less sacrifice, mothering is our calling and our fulfillment.

Given its framing of mothering, it is not surprising that intensive mothering centers a particular figure of ideal. In ways that are remarkably parallel to the silences and absences surrounding race, class, and privilege in Friedan's early account of the feminine mystique, the popular literature on and the mediated accounts of intensive mothering today rarely account for the deep investments in race and class privilege that surround both ideals of maternal perfection and the specific manifestations of intensive mothering and attachment parenting. Through the ideals expressed—continuous self-sacrifice, relentless *positive* attention to children and their seemingly insatiable needs and wants—the category of good mother is, as Shome (2011) so clearly argues, deeply grounded in Whiteness. Indeed, if the "best" mothers are White and privileged, popular media regularly reminds us that the "worst" mothers are not. Functioning as caricatures of selfishness and excess in ways that make them hypervisible, these (non-White) bad mothers rhetorically sustain and make necessary discourses of White maternal perfection (Carpenter, 2012; Fixmar-Oraiz, 2014).

In this chapter, we hope to contribute to this consistent critique of White mothering as ideal that simultaneously positions mothers of color as inherently deficient. Our goal is to complicate this dichotomy by carefully examining the mediation of bad White mothers, both fictional and real, and exploring what they tell us about the ever-evolving contours of mothering in the U.S., as well as how race and class combine in complex ways to both delineate and potentially expand these gendered borders. To guide us, we turn to scholarly accounts of myth.

## *Mothering, Media, and Myth*

In order to navigate the space between real and fictional maternal transgressions, as well as their broader cultural implications, we draw on Roland Barthes to conceptualize mothering as myth. Our starting theoretical point is that the signification processes that accompany discourses and practices of mothering are also, inevitably, naturalization processes. As Barthes (2012) puts it, "myth has the task of giving a historical intention a natural justification, and making contingency appear eternal" (p. 254). In this sense, myth both includes and goes beyond false belief and ideology, which, far from debilitating it, makes it all the more pervasive. Rather than lies, myths are insistently repeated distorted truths that can neither be rejected nor uncovered, and thus inherently lend themselves to appropriation in defense of particular interests.

One specific arena where these strategic appropriations take place is popular culture. As Paulson (2005) explains, "Whether film, television, or print [and social] media, popular culture does not serve the function of representing the real world so much as it reveals, reinforces, and shapes the cultural beliefs, values and myths held about the 'real world'" (p. 135). Following this assumption, our critique in this chapter builds on Barthes to foreground the narrative, multifaceted components of mothering as a concept that takes many different forms as it "transforms history into nature" (Barthes, 2012, p. 240).

The myth of mothering is well documented in feminist media studies literature as a mechanism that helps sustain current unequal social arrangements. Some of its manifestations include idealizing stay-at-home mothers (Hall, 1998); demonizing childless women (Paulson, 2005); representing non-White mothers as deviant (Carpenter, 2012; Young, 2010); or coupling (Western) Whiteness with ideal motherhood (Lang, 2008; Shome, 2011). As Simon (2014) puts it: "good mothers are almost always rich, white women" (p. 51). Similarly, in the case of "bad" mothers, the mothering myth works to deprive this concept of its history, thus ignoring the broader culture that has given rise to, for example, mothers' sense of overwhelm, mental instability, or even harmful conduct toward their own children (Barnett, 2006; Naylor, 2001). Ultimately, the figure of the bad mom regulates the behavior of mothers through the "individualization of responsibility" as it also relies upon and reifies ideal (White) femininity as the site of mothering (Robson, 2005, pp. 217–218).

In contrast with these more essentialist portrayals of ideal vs. deficient, good vs. bad moms, there have also been, in the last decades, alternative representations of women who would seem to be distanced from the ideal of mothering, or from mothering altogether, but at the same time not suffering extreme social punishment, thus disrupting binary thinking about women. These would be the heroines of TV shows such as *Sex in the City*, *Desperate Housewives*, or *Girls*, and movies like *Bridget Jones' Diary*, or *The Devil Wears Prada*. Across these varied texts, women are figured as active consumers and sexual subjects who prioritize their personal needs and wants, who can be feminine *and* feminist, or have a choice to distance themselves from the rigid standards of feminism altogether, thus embracing the contradictions of their times. Many critics, however, see this as part of a backlash against feminism (Akass, 2013), or of a more subtle "postfeminist" sensitivity that tries to go beyond "old-fashioned" feminism by both embracing and mocking it—a move that ultimately diminishes its emancipatory potential (Owen, Stein, & Vande Berg, 2007; Thornham, 2007).

A slightly different media figure enabled by the current "post" sensibility is that of the women who do have children but explicitly resist the cultural expectations associated with mothering. The discourse enabled by these mothers usually comes in the form of what Quiney (2007) labels "maternal confessional writing" (p. 21). This "confessional" genre is characterized by self-reflection and awareness of the extreme demands associated with mothering that push the women who embrace them towards inescapable failure. As Quiney puts it, "Maternal confessional writers confess their own vulnerability to a powerful and paradoxical ideological synthesis that fuses the mythography of the selfless Good Mother with the clashing capitalist discourses of individual achievement and productivity" (p. 33).

Importantly, the "post" ideological landscape that enables both fictional and real versions of these transgressive women does not only have to do with gender, but also with race. Thus, even if we acknowledge the subversive potential of some of these narratives, we still need to ask: what is allowing for these kinds of "rebellious mothering"? (Holland, 2009). A quick look at the examples above suggests that race—and more specifically, Whiteness—as well as class and sexual orientation, emerge as relevant factors. As Thornham (2007) succinctly summarizes: "women of color [...] do not feature so readily as postfeminist heroines" (p. 17). Conversely, critiques of White middle-class motherhood emerge mostly from White middle-class, heterosexual circles. It seems, therefore, that only certain transgressions are available to certain women. In the next section we address some of these dynamics as we explore different representations of bad White moms.

## *(Un)Fictional Femininity: White Moms Break Bad*

Representations of mothers—named good and bad—abound in public and popular media. Indeed representations of, and commentary about, mothers and mothering are as compulsory as motherhood itself. Here, we turn our attention to three publicly mediated mothers—Betty Draper, Sarah Linden, and Patricia Krentcil—whose public presence as mothers seems mired in critique and censure and whose transgressions, while seemingly dramatically different, are bound together within racialized norms and ideals. We argue that these three cases figure transgression in similar kinds of ways as they also invite quite different public responses. More specifically, we suggest that *Mad Men* and *The Killing* constitute two interesting examples of how the figure of the transgressive, "bad" White mom has recently gained relevance on television as a potentially rich source of complexity that may allow writers and audiences to explore new territories with regards to female character representation in general, and mothering in particular. In contrast, "bad" White mom, Patricia Krentcil, is discursively secured within a reductive narrative that protects the Whiteness of ideal mothering through the caricature of Krentcil as irrevocably "bad". Here, we introduce these mothers and their failings.

## Mad Men, *Mad Moms?*

*Mad Men* is a television drama focusing on the New York City advertising world of the late 1950s and early 60s. The series premiered on AMC in 2007 and aired its seventh season and final episode May 2015. The show's main character is Don Draper, a self-made ad man who has been described as representing a "meditation on what it means to be a White middle-class man in a period of rapid social change" (Étienne, n.d.), and even a "representation [...] of American society" (Rosin, 2014, para. 27). During its seven years of existence, *Mad Men* has been repeatedly acclaimed for its careful, high-quality production and efforts to accurately represent a convulsed era in the U.S.

In spite of its title and central focus on Don Draper, we argue that *Mad Men* is at least as much about women as it is about men. And among all the different femininities represented in the show, Don Draper's wife—and later ex-wife—Betty (Draper) Francis stands out as particularly relevant and controversial, both within and outside of the show (for further discussion of transgressive mothering on *Mad Men*, see D'Enbeau & Buzzanell, this volume). In a 2014 interview with Matthew Weiner, creator of *Mad Men*, the writer expressed his puzzlement at predominant audience reactions to the character of Betty (Draper) Francis in the series. To the question "who do people hate the most on the show?" Weiner answered: "People are very, very hard on Betty. I think it's because she behaves that way [not properly], and she's beautiful. There are lots of factors. Don cheated on her for years, and people hated her. I never understood that" (Rosin, 2014, para. 44).

Regardless of Weiner's perplexity and attempts to distance his own understanding of Draper from that of the audience, we argue that there are plenty of textual features within *Mad Men* that encourage viewers' dislike for her. Most notably, Draper's characterization as a bad mom relies on the myth of mothering to act as a metonymic mechanism by which a particular role—and her inadequacy at performing that role—comes to define her as a person. Thus, since being a bad mother is equated to being a bad person, predominant audience hostility is guaranteed.

When viewers first encounter Betty Draper (Season 1, Episode 1), she embodies a textbook case of what Betty Friedan (1963) famously described as "the problem that has no name." A White, middle-class housewife with a comfortable life, including a nice house in the suburbs of New York and (from her perspective) a loving, professionally successful husband who provides for her and their two small children, Draper would seem to have it all. And yet, throughout the first episodes of Season 1, viewers start getting indicators that this socially rewarded domesticity is not fully satisfying for Draper, but also, and importantly, that her own personal flaws are a main cause of this dissatisfaction.

In the second episode of Season 1 viewers learn that Draper suffers from episodes of incontrollable hand shaking and numbness ("Ladies Room"). Her husband Don encourages her to see a psychiatrist, thus pointing at a possible physical manifestation of a psychological condition. The psychiatrist's diagnosis (unprofessionally) shared with Don, deserves to be quoted fully: "She seems consumed by petty jealousies and overwhelmed with everyday activities. We're basically dealing with the emotions of a child here." In short, he dismisses her illness as "childishness" ("Red in the Face"). This is not the only instance in which characters in the show position Draper as a child, either by the way they talk to her (especially her husband, Don Draper), or by directly pointing out how she is consistently excluded from adult conversations and activities. For example, when Don is doing business with Bobbie Barrett (and also having an affair with her), Bobbie's husband breaks this news to Draper with a laconic "look at us, over here at the kids' table" ("The Gold Violin").

One could argue, as many commentators have, that the main purposes of particular characters and lines such as the ones quoted above is to accurately capture, as well as to denounce, the rampant sexism of the times. However, we suggest that it is not only through the lens of her psychiatrist, her husband, and other men in the show that Betty's childishness is constructed. Rather, this depiction is consistent—and even worsens—throughout the show's seven seasons, since most of Draper's own actions and words, far from challenging it, reinforce the assumption that she is immature and dependent. As Ono (2013) argues with reference to racial representations in *Mad Men*, this kind of strategy by which the show's narrative and structure reproduce the biases of its characters serves the double purpose of producing "a historically realist representation" while at the same time "unnecessarily and objectionably" producing particular subjects—such as a childish Draper—"for television viewers now" (p. 306).

The "child" frame through which viewers are encouraged (not) to relate to Draper is intrinsically related to another salient trait of hers: bad mothering. Thus, even though both her social status and physical appearance would make it possible for Betty (Draper) Francis to occupy the space of the ideal mother, her words and actions consistently deviate from cultural expectations of motherhood, both past and present. Draper's child-like, immature personality, which includes frequent episodes of jealousy, cruelty, selfishness, emotional instability, or lack of empathy, thus shapes her strained relationship with her children. At the same time, she consistently exercises her power over them with direct commands, threats, or psychological and physical violence. This display of authority is especially acute whenever her daughter Sally intentionally or unintentionally violates gender expectations. This makes it difficult for Draper to be perceived solely as a victim, since she is also an active participant in the perpetuation of the gendered dynamics that produced her.

## *Good Cop, Bad Mother*

*The Killing* is a crime drama series set in contemporary Seattle that first aired on AMC in 2011. The show is an adaptation from the successful Danish production *Forbrydelsen*, and during its first two seasons it narrated the unsolved murder of Rosie Larsen, mostly from the perspective of Seattle police officer Sarah Linden, who plays the lead role on the show. *The Killing* then deviated from its original plot to offer two more seasons investigating different murder cases, as well as with detective Linden's struggle managing her professional and personal life.

Agent Linden embodies a present-day and less traditional kind of femininity compared to *Mad Men*'s Betty (Draper) Francis. Whereas Draper is described in the show as "looking like a princess," and has been compared by commentators to former actress and real-life princess Grace Kelly, Sarah Linden lacks most conventional features of femininity: she wears no make-up, rarely changes her turtleneck sweater and jeans, does not style her hair beyond a clumsy ponytail, and constantly chews gum. In many ways, this character is a prototype of the professionally accomplished "new capitalist" mother (Quiney, 2007, p. 31) who has to deal with the tensions arising from the fact that she cannot enjoy a fulfilling job, a good relationship with her thirteen-year-old son, and a stable partner/family all at the same time.

For *The Killing*'s writer, Veena Sud ("*The Killing's*," 2011), Sarah Linden is "a very complex, dark, really interesting female lead of the kind we haven't seen in a long time," a portrayal that Sud finds "refreshing" (para. 2). In this same interview, Sud recognizes the difficulties of developing a police drama with a female as main character—an obstacle that, according to her, is overcome by the capacity of female leads to be "real." As she explains: "The female leads are very human and very real and very flawed, yet are good cops" (para. 6).

An important part of this being "very real and very flawed," for Sarah Linden, emanates from her deficiencies as a mother. As with *Mad Men*'s Draper, the signs of "bad mothering" are quite clear for this female lead: When audiences encounter her in the first season, she is on her way to quit her job in Seattle and move to Sonoma with her fiancée, far from the stress and long hours of homicide cases, and towards a quiet life of "writ[ing] speeding tickets." Viewers also learn that she is a single mother of a teenage son, who, in Sarah's words, is "bitching about changing schools," although, according to her, "he'll live" (Pilot).

However, her gradual obsession with the Rosie Larsen case leads detective Linden to break off her engagement and stay in Seattle, where her constant neglect of her son in favor of her own needs not only damages her relationship with him, but eventually puts him in danger when, unsupervised, he starts to consistently skip school and is even reported missing for a whole day ("Missing"). Eventually, and with Child Protective Services threatening to take her son away, Linden ends up accepting his request to move to Chicago and live with his biological father.

In the case of detective Linden, being a bad mother is part of a more general (and widely documented) way of representing women who step into "male" narrative roles and the broader public sphere of masculinity through genres such as the thriller, the police series, or the legal and political dramas. As Kaplan (1983) points out, the price females pay for being cast in these roles is to lose any "traditional" feminine characteristics, such as kindness, humanness, and especially motherliness. In most cases, the development of the plot and the usually negative consequences for these female characters act as a second form of punishment. Thus, "[f]or a female character to become the hero of such series she must appropriate agency, action, command, the occupation of public sphere, discursive authority and the control of the investigative face. All of these, of course, run counter to the norms of femininity" (Thornham, 2007, p. 69).

## *Not Natural, Not Mom*

If Draper is chided for her childishness and Linden for manliness, what do we make of a mother whose primary failing is her love of tanning, or what commentators dubbed her tanorexia? Such is the accusation that surrounds Patricia Krentcil, notoriously dubbed the "tan mom." Admittedly, Krentcil exploded onto the media scene in May of 2012 not because of her tanorexia but because tanorexia compromised her parenting. She was arrested on child endangerment charges after allegedly taking her then 5-year-old daughter into a tanning bed. In the initial days following her arrest, media quickly and immediately denounced and ridiculed Krentcil, accusing her of child abuse and mocking her ruthlessly for her appearance. By the time charges were dismissed, Krentcil was firmly established as a caricatured character and most references to her children had disappeared from the public commentary.

Almost instantly from the time of her arrest, Krentcil became something of a contemporary media celebrity. News of her arrest and her appearance became fodder for public discussion, and not only in news media. Her arrest prompted jokes by Jimmy Kimmel, Jimmy Fallon, Anderson Cooper, Jay Leno, and Kelly Ripa. *Saturday Night Live* spoofed her, and Hero Builders, a company that designs and sells dolls, even created a tanorexic action figure, inspired by Krentcil, that they intentionally designed as "hideous" (Araiza, 2013). The frenzy that continues to surround Krentcil seems deliberately fostered by her. She has a Twitter feed, @RealTanMom, a Facebook page, which shows that she joined Facebook on May 4, 2012, just days after her arrest, and a long list of ventures that include a part in a gay porn film, both a book and a film about her life, a self-tanning lotion, and two music videos. Across these many manifestations of the spectacle that surrounds Krentcil is the persistent reduction of her identity to "tan mom." Yet while she is consistently named "mom," the commentary that surrounds her is only minimally explicitly about her mothering. Instead, what most likely prompted and now sustains her bizarre celebrity status is her appearance: "she's achieved a color that's simply not found in nature" (Dorfman, 2012, para. 12).

In the initial media attention to Krentcil, the two transgressions—alleged child endangerment and what would come to be called tanorexia—collapsed in accounts of and responses to Krentcil. Consider this collapse: "I DON'T know what I found more shocking: the grotesque pictures of 'tanorexic' Patricia Krentcil's mahogany skin, or the allegations that she allowed her five-year-old daughter to suffer burns by taking her into the tanning booth" (Nanjiani, 2012, para. 1). For some, it is her questionable love of tanning that signals her inability to mother appropriately. Here, Young Turk Cenk Uygur's response to the arrest in which he names Krentcil guilty because of her appearance is revealing: "I have a decision: guilty. Look at her. I mean what kind of freak is that?" (qtd. on "Sterilize," 2012). What becomes quite clear, particularly in the months that follow, is that for much of the public, Krentcil is a bad mom because she tans herself in ways that violate social assumptions. Her freakish tan becomes a means through which the excesses of transgression frame public understanding of her character, and by extension of her mothering. The guilt through appearance turn is so pointed that reporters comment on it. As one reporter concludes, "The question isn't: Did she or didn't she [take her daughter into a tanning bed]? The question is: Could this woman be a tanorexic?" (Lynch, 2012, para. 1). Another account frames it this way: "Her unnatural tan shocked the world *as much* as the allegations that she took her five-year-old daughter into a sunbed booth" (Reilly, 2012, para. 1, emphasis added).

As noted above, these frighteningly pervasive accounts of Krentcil's appearance either become the evidence of her bad mothering or are the only focus of the narrative. She names herself a wonderful mom, detailing the care she provides for her children and her husband (e.g., Martinez, 2012; Putney, 2012; Stableford, 2012). Both her husband and her attorney are also widely cited with proclamations of her good mothering (e.g., Eugenios, 2012; "Nutley mom," 2012). But otherwise, while Krentcil is regularly dubbed a bad mom, audiences learn more about Krentcil's tanning habits than about her mothering. For instance, media accounts regularly commented on the amount of time Krentcil spent tanning, noting again and again the reports that she tanned 20 times a month, likely visited multiple tanning salons, or was banned from several salons. They never linked mothering and tanning, never asked about whether she tanned while her children were in school or if she hired sitters so that she could tan (e.g., Friedman, 2012; Martinez, 2012). Reports also returned repeatedly to the initial arrest but mostly as a way to remind readers of how Krentcil emerged in the spotlight. Early reports include testimony from neighbors that Krentcil continued to tan while pregnant (see, e.g., Cunningham, Twelves, & McShane, 2012). Beyond that one comment, readers learn almost nothing about Krentcil as a mother aside from the initial arrest in May 2012 and the February 2013 decision by the New Jersey grand jury *not* to indict. Instead, what occupies almost all the mediated attention is Krentcil's tanning.

Across the mediated accounts of Krentcil, perhaps what most frames the narratives and becomes the defining transgression is excess. Not surprisingly, it is the excessive darkness of her skin that prompts the most intense media scrutiny and ridicule. That is, media accounts offer vivid commentary on Krentcil's look, regularly identifying her as, in the words of one account, "disturbingly dark" (Cunningham, 2012, para. 6). Elsewhere touted as "scarily dark," Krentcil "epitomizes the word ugly" (McShane, 2012, para. 2; "Melanie Harvey," 2012, para. 7). The focus on excess emerges across the narrative as Krentcil becomes not just ugly or a freak but an addict. The most overt framing of the addiction conversation centers on the notion of tanorexia, the relatively recent term used to describe (and mock) people who appear overly and unnaturally tan. Such references are pervasive in the discussion of Krentcil. For instance, clinical dermatologist Dr. Richard Glogau concludes: "She's overdone it ... She's drained the bank" (qtd. in Lynch, 2012, para. 9), while dermatologist Dr. Joshua Zeichner proclaims, "I have never encountered anything like this" (Zeichner, 2012, p. 1). Elsewhere, coverage reminds us that tanorexia is akin to addiction, explicitly noting that it is much like addiction to alcohol (Ridley, 2012), and accounts widely credit the Krentcil case with the passage of a New Jersey law restricting teen access to tanning salons and with greater media attention to the dangers of both tanning beds and spray tans (Hayes, 2013). Interestingly Krentcil is not just named a tanorexic, but is compared to celebrity tanorexics in ways that signal that she is more excessive and more ridiculous than the other excessive tanners (Cunningham, Twelves, & McShane, 2012; Mitchell, 2012).

Excess broadly and tanorexia more specifically function rhetorically to both separate and collapse Krentcil the person with/from Krentcil's mothering. That is, we are invited to view her excessive tanning as representative of her character and thus of her mothering. In short, as a person, Krentcil becomes equated with her excessive tanning. This collapse occurs both through the ease with which her tanning makes for easy ridicule and the continuous emphasis on her seemingly endless list of transgressions. For instance, along with reporting her excesses in tanning, accounts regularly narrate a long history of transgressions which include prior arrests for theft and forgery as well as of multiple judgments or liens against her (e.g., Cunningham, 2012; "Probation dropped," 2012). Moreover, Krentcil is regularly reduced to a rude, if not out of control, drunk. Reports chronicle her public drunkenness and her stay at a drug and alcohol rehabilitation facility (Eby, 2013; Giambusso, 2013). She was described and quoted as yelling, screaming, ranting, howling, and raving at those around her, particularly in the days following her arrest (e.g., Cunningham, 2012; McShane, 2012). Reports generally cover her alcohol abuse, identifying those instances in which she was allegedly staggering and slurring while in public (e.g., Ashenmacher, 2013; Garvey, Niemietz, & Cartwright, 2013; Rosario, Fenton, & Oliveira, 2012; "'Tanning Mom': I was set up," 2012).

Too childish, too manly, too dark. While certainly the attention to bad mothering for Draper, Linden, and Krentcil exceeds these three failings, in many ways audiences are invited to hate these women for their particular excesses that are also articulated as at odds with good mothering. Importantly, in all three cases, these women's deficiencies as mothers are not depicted as isolated negative traits but are treated as determinant factors in a generalized lack of fulfillment in their lives that also affects their relationships with their partners, coworkers, family, or friends. When placed in the general context of the public commentary, the potentially transgressive deviations from the "natural mother" and "intensive-mothering" expectations that these women embody is shuttered by the coupling of these transgressions with undesirable attributes like the incapacity to develop healthy relationships, generalized psychological instability, addiction, and, for both Linden and Krentcil, even criminal activity. In other words, these women's "rebellious mothering" (Holland, 2009) is resolutely disciplined within the narratives of *Mad Man* and *The Killing*, as well as the public frenzy surrounding Krentcil. This kind of disciplining, as Thornham (2007) claims, acts as public sanctioning of the fantasies that could "subvert conventional gender positionings" (p. 56), thus working to contain the "unruly excess" of desire.

## *Reading Patriarchy, Consuming Whiteness*

Based on the discussion above, it would seem like narrating bad mothers constitutes a rather straightforward way in which contemporary popular culture texts contribute to the broader cultural construction of Good Mothers (Simon, 2014), and the mothering myth as a whole. Certainly, we contend that this is in part what these representations are doing. However, and importantly, figures such as Betty (Draper) Francis, Sarah Linden, and Patricia Krentcil are also creating space for interesting public discussions about feminism and patriarchy—or, to use Barthes's terminology, for "myth reading." We thus end our discussion by sketching some important aspects of these broader debates, as well as reflecting on the contemporary conditions that (do not) enable them.

Public commentary on Betty (Draper) Francis, Sarah Linden, and Patricia Krentcil has systematically critiqued their mothering abilities. Accompanied by statements such as the hyperbolic and already discussed "worst [TV] mom," or its ironic versions such as "mother of the year" (O'Brien, 2010; Ryan, 2013), these women consistently feature in the top 10 of most "worst moms on TV" rankings offered by different television-oriented blogs and online newspaper columns. In the case of Betty (Draper) Francis, the theme of childishness identified above is often brought up by (re)viewers as the main reason why she is a deficient mother. Thus, commentators use words like "self-centered," "a spoiled brat," or "cruel," together with "a terrible mother," "TV's iciest matriarch" or "a hideous person" to refer to Draper (Agirre, 2014; Miller, 2010; Ryan, 2013). A similar process of regulation of desire through coherence can be observed with regards to critiques of Sarah Linden. Thus, commentaries do not only condemn her "absentee parenting," or see her as "wrapped up in her career;" they also repeatedly associate these unmotherly characteristics to other faults, thus referring to her as a "bad cop" and "bad girlfriend" and discussing "her failings as a friend and a human being" (Delahaye, 2011; Paskin, 2012; Ryan, 2013). With Krentcil, the collapse occurs through a broader discussion of bad—and selfish—choices. It is her bad taste, bad dress, and bad music videos that sustain her fame as a bad person thus a bad mother. In some ways, Krentcil is deemed guilty by association.

However, in the case of Draper and Linden, these are not the only ways viewers and critics have engaged with the characters. In fact, the pervasive, direct, and strong negative reactions quoted above have been consistently critiqued in various outlets as manifestations of a broader misogynist, antifeminist, or sexist cultural climate. As a whole, these commentators push back against the dominant readings of the bad mom/bad person figure, thus marking "how the socially constructed mother can be used against women by demanding not only that they embody the ideal maternal figure, but also that to fail to do so is to undermine one's very identity as a woman" (Ruthven & Mádlo, 2010, p. ix).

Even though they are anchored in a rather straightforward rejection of conventional gender roles—past and present—a careful look at these critiques suggests that something other than a defense of transgressive ways to mother is at play here. Rather, the presence or naming of patriarchy in these commentaries is made possible through a significant absence: race—and more specifically, Whiteness. This fostering of Whiteness's invisibility as a way to advance feminist claims permeates these discourses and, we argue, constitutes an important discursive location to explore the dialectical relationship between reproduction and transformation, transgression and regression.

One way in which the myth of Whiteness is consumed in these critiques is through the discussion of the characters as unproblematically representing all women and their experiences, either in the 1960s or nowadays. For example, sympathetic readings of Draper point to her pedagogic function as a reminder to viewers of the overt sexism of the times and its pervasive consequences, without acknowledging that this is a particular kind of sexism that may not have been experienced by every woman, and that will elicit different responses depending on viewers' locations.

In an article titled "Why *Mad Men* Is TV's Most Feminist Show," the show is described as "one of the most sympathetic to women," and its author justifies the "rampant chauvinism of virtually all its male characters (and some of its female ones)," or Draper's "attempts to appear the perfect wife [that] render her incapable of fully knowing her children" as a "much needed lesson" for viewers, and a laudable effort of historical accuracy in portraying the sexism of that era. And she concludes: "*Mad Men*'s writers aren't sexist. The time period was" (Coontz, 2010, para. 5).

Similarly, in a piece titled "In Defense of Betty," Harris (2013) claims to be "troubled" by the "pervasive hostility towards Betty," arguing that, even though she is "unlikeable," "emotionally distant [...] from her own children," "often peevish and self-centered," she should be seen as a "victim of her time and circumstances" (para. 9). According to Harris: "that's how it works, and that's how you make a show about sexism: You show the deformities. Because otherwise, you're selling it short; you're not acknowledging the worst consequences of that era's brand of sexism" (para. 9). The text concludes with a critique of the audiences' inability to engage in this self-reflexive reading, which the author sees as a reflection of the sexist values that permeate society even today. As she puts it: "The fact that we all seem stuck blaming, even hating, the victim makes me wonder just how far we've come" (para. 9).

The most striking feature of these commentaries is the persistent unmarkedness of terms like "women", "victim", or "sexism", as well as the assumption of an equally unmarked gaze from the audience's perspective. In these readings, a White woman like Draper can stand for women and sexism as a whole; she is assumed to embody a generalized victim position, and an equally uniform viewer is expected to both recognize and identify with what she symbolizes. In both cases, the fierce critique of patriarchy rests on the invisibility of Whiteness.

Similar strategies can be observed in feminist readings of Sarah Linden, who is presented as a symbol of the ways capitalist mothers are doomed to failure, both in fiction and in real life, without considering how Whiteness may be an important factor shaping these (im)possibilities. In an article tellingly titled "*The Killing* and the Misogyny of Hating Bad Mothers" (Kolb, 2013), the author describes "vilifying mothers" as a "national pastime" and critiques the double standard that makes audiences relate to "complex, fallible male characters," while at the same time criticizing or blaming "women with the same depth of characterization—especially mothers" (para. 11)—a move that she considers "blatantly obvious" when it comes to Sarah Linden" (para. 11).

Linden's character is then described as a realistic, "accomplished single mom striving to keep her son out of trouble all while maintaining her demanding career," and according to the author, the predominantly negative reactions to her are a painful reminder of how, "when audiences see female characters, they think primarily in critical terms, especially about their roles as mothers and wives" (Kolb, 2013, para. 26). Once again, Linden's experience is generalized as a way to critique society's treatment of women and mothers as a whole, without considering how roles and expectations associated with femaleness *and* Whiteness give shape to both Linden's character and the persistent hostility towards her. In her powerful marking of the predominantly male world of television antiheroes, and society's incapacity to accept similar faults in women, this critique fails to acknowledge that it is not only masculinity, but also Whiteness that inevitably shapes the experiences of these bad moms.

The particular, rather privileged locations of the women in *Mad Men* and *The Killing* enable a kind of critique that could not be possible otherwise—and in fact is not present in Patricia Krentcil's case. Krentcil's love of (addiction to?) tanning produces a condemnation of her mothering that serves as a guise for its condemnation of her racial transgression. She becomes, both in mediated accounts of her and her own performances, a caricature. Flattened by and reduced to excess, Krentcil comes to represent the horrors of otherness, or in the words of one account, "unnatural" (Reilly, 2012). As we detail above, both journalists and public commentaries almost obsessively conclude that Krentcil is too dark. This fixation on her "disturbingly dark" skin intersects with similarly obsessive attention to her crassness in ways that come to define her entirety: "she epitomizes the word ugly for me. Not just the way she looks, but the manner she has" ("Melanie Harvey," 2012, para. 7).

This attention to the "manner she has" signals her choice, her agency. Krentcil is guilty because she repeatedly and knowingly makes bad choices. That Krentcil is depicted as and presents herself as choosing to be "tan mom" protects the sacred character of ideal mother. It is not the category that doesn't work, it is this particular misguided woman, made "real" in ways that Betty (Draper) Francis and Sarah Linden, always situated as fictional characters, are not. It is this "realness" that requires the caricature in Krentcil. She must be reduced to absolute ridicule as a means of containing the threat she poses. Yet, she must also serve as a regulatory figure, bringing us back into line. Here, the emphasis on her tanning addiction and the alleged spread of tanorexia as a social problem, which includes both repeated references to how often she tans and to the seeming explosion of tanning abuses everywhere, serves as a reminder to White readers who might also be guilty of excess that they must regulate their dark desires. Combined with the excessive attention to her excessive body—a body that exudes crassness and rudeness, Krentcil's too-dark skin and thus Krentcil herself function as the rhetorical reminder that darkness pollutes and threatens. If left unchecked that darkness will reproduce.

## *Conclusions*

The myth of mothering, like the myth of Whiteness, relies on its naturalness and its superiority, and thus on its natural superiority. Iconic in its force and function, the ideal mother figure stands for both beauty and self-sacrifice. Yet like all mythical constructions, that ideal perfection, Barthes tells us, must be relentlessly produced, and produced as natural. A distorted truth, if repeated over and over again through a variety of channels, will eventually deprive its signs of memory, and become "frozen purified, eternalized, made absent" (Barthes, 2012, p. 234). Through these modes of writing and representations, a myth accomplishes a "double function: it points out and notifies, it makes us understand something, and it imposes it on us" (Barthes, 2012, p. 226). The complex phenomena that accompany practices such as mothering are reduced in this process to a few traits that are taken as definitive. In other words: they constitute themselves as common sense.

But of course, like all ideals, the ideal of the perfect joyful mother is neither attainable nor sustainable. And lest we, as women, forget that despite our individual failings, we must continue to strive for that teleological perfection, media relentlessly remind us of the penalties of transgressions and failures. Will we, like Betty (Draper) Francis, in a recent season, ask, "Am I a good mother?" "Why don't they love me?" Will our children, like Sarah Linden's son, ask to go live with their fathers? When we fail, as of course we will, will we be subject to ridicule and scorn, reduced to our all-too-visible ugliness? In many ways, these varied and disparate representations of women's vulnerabilities and failings function both to sustain the perfection of the ideal and to cultivate our compliance with it. They do so with the reminders of the costs of failings and the perception of a possibility to be better that enables the public's judgment.

As Barthes (2012) explains: "one never tries anybody but analogues *who have gone astray*" (p. 266). And as one commentator on *Mad Men* puts it, "the tragedy of Betty Draper is that she has the potential to be happy" (Wright, 2013, para. 1). However, the capability to be read as an "analogue," as well as the so-called "potential to be happy" are not equally accessible to all mothers. Rather, as our discussion has shown, they seem to be more accessible to those mothers who are closer to the ideological center of Whiteness. As the characters of *Mad Men* and *The Killing* demonstrate, the expectation of their possible perfection, as well as the deconstruction of the myth it relies on, are made greater through their location *within* Whiteness. Unlike women in more peripheral positions, like Patricia Krentcil, who can never fully occupy the site of the ideal mother, these women could.

In an early interview, Krentcil is asked to comment on a claim attributed to "Octo-mom" that Krentcil needs parenting help. She responds by proclaiming, "In the name of God, I am the best mother in the whole entire world" (Krentcil, qtd. in "Patricia Krentcil, 'Tanning Mom,'" 2012). The circulation of that quote stands against the greater reflexivity and awareness attributed to Draper and Linden, who are at least occasionally depicted as sensing their own failings. Herein perhaps we begin to see the entailments of Whiteness with class and patriarchy. These characters make some space for conversations about representation and misogyny. From their privileged positions, they invite White women to think about their choices, particularly the obvious ones, like work versus family, and to do so in ways that gently remind women of the alleged ugliness of selfishness. That gentleness, however, requires viewers to see past (or through) the Whiteness that sustains the misogyny. In contrast, Krentcil's identity as disturbingly dark forces attention to her racialized actions, choices, and behaviors. The public is asked to laugh at, to mock, to ridicule, and thus we are allowed to distance ourselves from Krentcil in ways that are akin to the reductionist racialized caricatures of bad non-White mothers. Indeed, if these comparisons of maternal transgressions tell us anything, it is that security lies in Whiteness while danger comes in darkness.

## *Notes*

1. Barnett (2006) estimates that in the U.S. a parent kills a child at the rate of "nearly one child per day" (p. 411).
2. The short-lived series was produced by Cineflix and aired for one season.

## *References*


Agirre, K. (2014). "Am I supposed to say how shocked I was?" Audience responses to *Mad Men*. *European Journal of Cultural Studies, 17*, 631–646.

Akass, K. (2013). Motherhood and the media under the microscope: The backlash against feminism and the mommy wars. *Imaginations, 4*, 47–69.

Araiza, K. (2013, July 1). NJ tanning mom inspires tanorexic doll. Retrieved from www.nbcphiladelphia.com/news/local/Tanning-Mom-Inspires-Tanning-Doll-150597995.html

Ashenmacher, W. (2013, June 14). "Tan mom" in detox after Minneapolis airport incident. *Saint Paul Pioneer Press*. Retrieved from proquest.com.libraries

Baudrillard, J. (1983). *Simulations*. New York, NY: Semiotext(e).

Barnett, B. (2006). *Medea* in the media: Narrative and the myth of newspaper coverage of women who kill their children. *Journalism, 7*, 411–432.

Barthes, R. (2012). *Mythologies. The complete edition, in a new translation*. New York, NY: Hill and Wang/Farrar, Straus and Giroux.

Carpenter, T. R. (2012). Construction of the crack mother icon. *The Western Journal of Black Studies, 36*, 264–275.

Coontz, S. (2010, October 10). Why *Mad Men* is TV's most feminist show. *The Washington Post.* Retrieved from www.washingtonpost.com/wp-dyn/content/article/2010/10/08/AR2010100802662.html

Cunningham, J. H. (2012, May 4). Patricia Krentcil, tanorexic New Jersey woman, cites dark forces behind her arrest. *New York Daily News.* Retrieved from www.nydailynews.com/news/national/patricia-krentcil-tanorexic-new-jersey-woman-cites-dark-forces-behind-arrest-article-1.1072017

Cunningham, J. H., Twelves, M., & McShane, L. (2012, May 03). Ma's toast! Hey, N. J. lady, when Snooki calls you "crazy," maybe it's time to quit. *New York Daily News* Retrieved from http://0-search.proquest.com.libraries.colorado.edu/docview/1010783298?accountid=14503

Delahaye, G. (2011, May 23). Detective Sarah Linden: The worst police officer on earth? *Videogum.* Retrieved from www.videogum.com/308221/is-detective-sarah-linden-the-worst-police-officer-on-earth/top-stories/

Dorfman, S. (2012, May 5). "Tanning mom" sends salons, "tanorexia" into the limelight. *Palm Beach Post.* Retrieved from proquest.com.libraries

Douglas, S., & Michaels, M. (2004). *The mommy myth: The idealization of motherhood and how it has undermined all women.* New York: Free Press.

Eby, M. (2013, July 6). "Tan mom" Patricia Krentcil hospitalized for seizure inside rehab facility. *Daily News.* Retrieved from http://www.nydailynews.com/entertainment/gossip/tan-mom-patricia-krentcil-hospitalized-seizure-article-1.1391789

Étienne, M. (n.d.). Why everyone wants to be Don Draper … Except Don Draper. Retrieved from www.askmen.com/entertainment/austin_300/345_why-everyone-wants-to-be-don-draper-except-don-draper.html

Eugenios, J. (2012, May 21). New Jersey "tan mom": Leave my family alone. *Today News.* Retrieved from www.todaycom/id/47502597/ns/today-today_news/t/new-jersey-tan-mom-leave-my-family-alone/#.VMrKYMIQig

15 women compete for title of "Worst Mom in the World" by taking disturbing selfies with their kids. (2014). *IJ Review.* Retrieved from http://www.ijreview.com/2014/05/138217-worst-moms-world-pose-kids-disturbing-inappropriate-selfies/

Fixmar-Oraiz, N. (2014). (In)conceivable: Risky reproduction and the rhetorical labors of "Octomom." *Communication and Critical/Cultural Studies, 11*, 231–249.

Friedan, B. (1963). *The feminine mystique.* New York, NY: Norton.

Friedman, A. (2012, May 6). N.J. tanning mom: "I love to tan," but didn't burn my daughter in a salon bed. *Star-Ledger.* Retrieved from http://www.nj.com/news/index.ssf/2012/05/nj_tanning_mom_i_love_to_tan_b.html

Friedman, R. (2010, August 22). *Mad Men*: Betty Draper now officially worst mom in TV history. *Showbiz 411.* Retrieved from http://www.showbiz411.com/2010/08/22/mad-men-betty-draper-now-officially-worst-mom-in-tv-history

Garvey, M., Niemietz, B., & Cartwright, L. (2013, June 2). Diary of a mad "housewife." *New York Daily News.* Retrieved from proquest.com.libraries.

Giambusso, D. (2013, June 15). N.J. tanning mom sent to detox facilty after being found allegedly drunk in airport. *nj.com*. Retrieved from http://www.nj.com/news/index.ssf/2013/06/nj_tanning_mom_sent_to_detox_facility_after_being_found_allegedly_drunk_in_airport.html

Gibson, K. L., & Heyse, A. L. (2010). "The difference between a hockey mom and a pit bull": Sarah Palin's faux maternal persona and performance of hegemonic masculinity at the 2008 Republican National Convention. *Communication Quarterly, 58*, 235–256.

Gray, M. (2013, October 24). "Worst mother ever allegedly tears kid's genitals then tries to superglue them back together." *Time*. Retrieved from newsfeed.time.com

Hayden, S. (2011). Constituting savvy aunties: From childless women to child-focused consumers. *Women's Studies in Communication, 34*, 1–19.

Hayes, A. (2013, April 2). "N.J. bans minors from tanning beds." *CNN Health*. Retrieved from www.cnn.com/2013/04/02/health/new-jersey-tanning-minors/

Hays, S. (1996). *The cultural contradictions of motherhood*. New Haven, CT: Yale University Press.

Hall, P. C. (1998). Mothering mythology in the late twentieth century. Science, gender lore, and celebratory narrative. *Canadian Woman Studies, 18*, 59–63.

Harris, P. (2013. May 5). In defense of Betty. *Speakeasy*. Retrieved from http://blogs.wsj.com/speakeasy/2013/05/05/in-defense-of-betty/

Holland, M. (2009). Morality in a (TV) box, or, "I'm Not Your F[]cking Mommy!": Lessons on media and mothering from *The Ring* and *The Ring Two*. *Journal of Popular Culture, 42*, 680–698.

Kaplan, E. A. (1983). *Women and film: Both sides of the camera*. New York, NY: Methuen.

Kolb, L. (2013, July 10). *The Killing* and the misogyny of hating bad mothers. *Bitch Flicks*. Retrieved from www.btchflcks.com/2013/07/the-killing-and-the-misogyny-of-hating-bad-mothers.html#.VGgW5odHo-l

Lang, L. (2008). Big brother meets the "Alpha Mom": Tensions in the media standardization of motherhood. *Lore*, N. Retrieved from www.lorejournal.org

Lynch, R. (2012, May 3). "N.J. tanning bed mom: Tanorexic? Or victim of a witch hunt?" *Los Angeles Times*. Retrieved from articles/latimes.com/2012/may/03/nation/la-na-nn-nj-tanning-bed-mom-is-she-tanorexic-20120503

Martinez, E. (2012, May 10). "Tanning mom" Patricia Krentcil banned from over 60 tanning salons, report says. *CBS News*. Retrieved from http://www.cbsnews.com/news/tanning-mom-patricia-krentcil-banned-from-over-60-tanning-salons-report-says/

McShane, L. (2012, May 9). "Tanorexic" mom, Patricia Krentcil, banned from New Jersey salons. *New York Daily News*. Retrieved from www.nydailynews.com/news/national/tanorexic-mom-patricia-krentcil-banned-new-jersey-salons-article-1.1074929

Melanie Harvey … the last word. (2012, May 7). *Daily Record*. Retrieved from http://0-search.proquest.com.libraries.colorado.edu.docview/1011134317?accountid=14503

Miller, J. (2010, July 23). *Mad Men*: No sympathy for Betty Draper. *The Atlantic*. Retrieved from www.theatlantic.com/entertainment/archive/2010/07/mad-men-no-sympathy-for-betty-draper/60287

Mitchell, J. (2012, May 21). Pauly D loves gtl, but "tan mom" goes too far. *MTV News.* Retrieved from mtvnews.com/news/1685527/pauly-d-tan-mom

Nanjiani, S. (2012, May 7). Give sunbeds the ex-factor. *The Sun.* Retrieved from http://0-search.proquest.com.libraries.colorado.edu/docview/1011300188?accountid=14503

Naylor, B. (2001). The "bad mother" in media and legal texts. *Social Semiotics, 11*, 155–176.

Nutley mom accused of putting 6-year-old daughter in tanning bed pleads not guilty. (2012). *CBS New York.* Retrieved from http://newyork.cbslocal.com/2012/05/02/nutley-mom-in-court-on-charges-she-put-6-year-old-daughter-in-tanning-bed/

O'Brien Hallstein, D. L. (2010). Public choices, private control: How mediated mom labels work rhetorically to dismantle the politics of choice and white second wave feminist successes. In S. Hayden & D. L. O'Brien Hallstein (Eds.), *Contemplating maternity in an era of choice: Explorations into discourses of reproduction* (pp. 5–26). Lanham, MD: Lexington Books.

O'Brien Hallstein, D. L. (2011). She gives birth, she's wearing a bikini: Mobilizing the postpregnant celebrity mom body to manage the post-second wave crisis in femininity. *Women's Studies in Communication, 34*, 111–138.

O'Brien, M. (2010, July 26). Betty Draper, Mother of the Year. *Picket Fence Post.* Retrieved from http://picketfencepost.blogspot.com/2010/07/betty-draper-mother-of-year.html

Ono, K. A. (2013). *Mad Men*'s postracial figuration of a racial past. In L. M. E. Goodlad, L. Kaganovsky, & R. A. Rushing (Eds.), *Madmen, madworld: Sex, politics, style and the 1960s* (pp. 300–319). Durham, NC: Duke University Press.

Owen, A. S., Stein. S. R., & Vande Berg, L. R. (2007). *Bad girls: Cultural politics and media representations of transgressive women.* New York, NY: Peter Lang.

Paskin, W. (2012, March 28). Hating *The Killing*. Retrieved from www.salon.com/2012/03/28/hating_"the-killing"/

Patricia Krentcil, "tanning mom," poses braless for paparazzi. (2012, May 17). *Huffington Post.* Retrieved from www.huffingtonpost.com

Paulson, L. E. (2005). Mama bears, bitches and monsters: Motherhood and violence in popular film. In E. Cole, & J. Henderson Daniel (Eds.), *Featuring females. Feminist analyses of media* (pp. 131–141). Washington, DC: American Psychological Association.

Press, A. L. (2006). The mommy myth: The idealization of motherhood and how it has undermined women. *NWSA Journal, 18*, 235–236.

Probation dropped against tanned N.J. mom. (2012, May 04). *Bennington Banner.* Retrieved from http://0-search.proquest.com.libraries.colorado.edu/docview/1011012727?accountid=14503

Putney, L. (2012, May 2). She says she's a good mom. Retrieved from http://newyork.cbslocal.com/2012/05/02/nutley-mom-in-court-on-charges-she-put-6-year-old-daughter-in-tanning-bed/

Quiney, R. (2007). Confessions of the new capitalist mother: Twenty-first-century writing on motherhood as trauma. *Women: A Cultural Review, 18*, 19–40.

Reilly, J. (2012, June 5). Fresh-faced and natural: Glamour shots reveal what "tanning mom" looked like two decades before she hit the sunbeds. *Mail Online*. Retrieved from www.dailymail.co.uk/news/article-2154770/Fresh-faced-natural-Glamour-shots-reveal-tanning-mom-looked-like-decades-hit-sunbeds.html

Ridley, J. (2012, June 28). "I banned my tan." *New York Post*, Retrieved from nypost.com/2012/06/28/i-banned-my-tan/

Robson, K. (2005). "Canada's most notorious bad mother": The newspaper coverage of the Jordan Heikamp inquest. *Canadian Review of Sociology & Anthropology, 42*, 217–232.

Rosario, F., Fenton, R., & Oliveira, P., Jr. (2012, May 4). Tan-trum ma red in the face rips "ugly" and "jealous" haters. *New York Post*. Retrieved from http://0-search.proquest.com.libraries.colorado.edu/docview/1010980099?accountid=14503

Rosin, H. (2014, March 19). *Mad Men*'s creator: Don Draper represents American society. *The Atlantic*. Retrieved from www.theatlantic.com/entertainment/archive/2014/03/-em-mad-men-em-s-creator-don-draper-represents-american-society/284529/

Ruthven, A., & Mádlo, G. (Eds.). (2010). *Illuminating the dark side: Evil, women & the feminine*. Oxford, UK: Inter-Disciplinary Press.

Ryan, A. (2013). The 7 worst moms in TV history. *The Globe and Mail*. Retrieved from www.theglobeandmail.com/life/parenting/mothers-day/the-7-worst-moms-in-tv-history/article11637384/

Segal, C. (2012, May 11). The 10 worst moms on TV. *Yahoo TV*. Retrieved from https://tv.yahoo.com/photos/mothers-day-the-10-worst-moms-on-tv-this-season-slideshow/sarah-linden-mireille-enos--photo-1336762710.html

Sentenac, H. (2012, May 11). Mother's Day 2012: The ten worst moms in the history of ever. *Miami New Times*. Retrieved from http://blogs.miaminewtimes.com/cultist/2012/05/final_the_top_ten_worst_moms_o.php?page=4

Shome, R. (2011). "Global motherhood": The transnational intimacies of white femininity. *Critical Studies in Media Communication, 2*, 388–406.

Simon, J. M. (2014). Disciplining drunken mothers: Media representations of women's use of alcohol. *The Communication Review, 17*, 45–64.

Stableford, D. (2012, May 21). Tanning mom: "I'm sorry, I'm tan. I like to be tan. It just feels good." *Yahoo! News*. Retrieved from http://news.yahoo.com/blogs/sideshow/tanning-mom-m-sorry-m-tan-tan-just-141447643.html

Sterilize Patricia Krentcil the "tanning mom." [Video file]. (2012, May 3). *The Young Turks*. Retrieved from https://www.youtube.com/watch?v=awZwgC4PwlU

Tanning mom: "I was set up in this whole mess-it's not true" Patricia Krentcil denies taking her six-year-old daughter tanning and says she hasn't sunned herself in six months. (2012, September). *mail online*. Retrieved from www.dailymail.co.uk/femail/article-2201615/Tanning-Mom-I-set-mess---true-Patricia-Krentcill-denies-taking-year-old-daughter-tanning-says-sunned-months.html

*The Killing's* Veena Sud. (2011, June 19). Retrieved from deadline.com/2011/06/emmys-the-killings-veena-sud-141342/

Thornham, S. (2007). *Women, feminism, and media.* Edinburgh, UK: Edinburgh University Press.

Warner, J. (2005). *Perfect madness: Motherhood in the age of anxiety.* New York, NY: Riverhead Books.

Wright, J. (2013, April 8). Is Betty Draper doomed? *Jezebel.* Retrieved from http://jezebel.com/is-betty-draper-doomed-471172318

Young, C. C. (2010). Monstrous mothering from *Boys' N' the Hood* to *Precious*: Damaged mothers on screen. In A. Ruthven, & G. Mádlo (Eds.), *Illuminating the dark side: Evil, women and the feminine* (pp. 33–38). Oxford, UK: Inter-Disciplinary Press.

Zeichner, J. (2012, May 2). Dermatologist says Patricia Krentcil's "tanorexic" condition is "craziest thing I've ever seen." *New York Daily News.* Retrieved from www.nydailynews.com/life-style/health/dermatologist-patricia-krentcil-tanorexic-condition-craziest-article.1.1071641

# 6. 16 and Pregnant *and Black: Challenging and Debunking Stereotypes*

By Natasha Howard

In 2011 an infamous picture featuring two young African American girls posing in the bathroom showing off their pregnant stomachs, with a caption that revealed them as being 14 and 15 years old, circulated through social media outlets such as Facebook and Tumblr (Atlien, 2011). That same year news stories circulated about a Memphis high school where 90 students were either pregnant or had given birth all within the same year (Eng, 2011). A few years prior to that, in June 2008, another major news story regarding teen pregnancy came to national attention when *Time Magazine* published a story about a group of 17 teenage girls in Gloucester, Maine, who made a pact to get pregnant (Kingsbury, 2008). In the article, Kingsbury (2008) described that upon getting the news of their pregnancies the girls would often give each other high-fives and cheers. While teenage pregnancy is not a new social issue, altogether the girls' actions in these stories suggest a growing acceptance of and, in some cases, a desire to be a young parent or create a family at a young age in today's society.

Undoubtedly, teen pregnancy and single motherhood are realities in the United States today. The March of Dimes (2009) reports that an average of "3 out of 10 teenage girls become pregnant at least once before age 20" (p. 1). Additionally, approximately 1 in 4 teenage mothers are likely to become pregnant again within 2 years of the birth of their first child (March of Dimes, 2009). The realities of this issue are far reaching in terms of society and future generations. Statistics reflect that many young mothers do not go onto college and therefore do not have the educational background to pursue and attain high-paying careers (Centers for Disease Control, 2011).

In fact, only 40 percent of teenagers who become parents before they are 18 years old graduate from high school compared to 75 percent of teenagers the same age from the same socioeconomic background (March of Dimes, 2009). Often, as a result of having their education cut short, the teen parents are not able to find high paying jobs, which can lead to financial dependence on the family or the government. In fact, "teen mothers are more likely to live in poverty than women who delay childbearing, and more than 75 percent of all unmarried teen mothers go on welfare within 5 years of the birth of their first child" (March of Dimes, 2009, p. 2). Additionally, the results of teen pregnancy potentially have lasting effects on children of teen mothers who are more likely to become teen parents themselves, drop out of high school, exhibit behavior problems, have lower cognitive abilities, and go to jail as juveniles (Centers for Disease Control, 2011).

While the mothers' socioeconomic background or pre-existing financial difficulties prior to the pregnancy can influence the extremity of teen mothers' financial hardships, there are some additional difficulties that many teenage mothers, regardless of race, often have in common. Aside from health issues (as many teen mothers give birth prematurely and their children, as a result, may have low birth weights or face other health complications), teen mothers often have to sacrifice their educational or career goals and sometimes face alienation or isolation from their peers (March of Dimes, 2009). Further, the responsibilities and decisions that accompany being a teenage parent often result in teenage mothers feeling isolated because they spend so much time taking care of their child and are alienated from their peers who are not parents (Donnelly & Voydanoff, 1996).

Images of teenage pregnancy are increasingly portrayed in television programming. In 2015, MTV alone aired several unscripted reality television shows, *16 and Pregnant* and its spinoffs *Teen Mom*, *Teen Mom 2*, and most recently *Teen Mom 3*, which feature the day-to-day lives of pregnant teenagers and teenage mothers. Created in 2009 by Lauren Dolgen, Executive Vice-President of Series Development for MTV, the premise of *16 & Pregnant* and its spin-offs is to "serve as a cautionary tale about the consequences of unprotected sex, and the reality of becoming a parent too early" (Dolgen, 2011, para. 12). Prior to the *16 and Pregnant* and *Teen Mom* franchises, images of teenage pregnancy and motherhood were not often portrayed on television. Therefore MTV proposed, with the creation of *16 & Pregnant*, that the show would go against this trend by actually featuring pregnant teenagers both before and after they gave birth:

> MTV's *16 and Pregnant* is an hour-long documentary series focusing on the controversial subject of teen pregnancy. Each episode follows a 5–7 month period in

> the life of a teenager as she navigates the bumpy terrain of adolescence, growing pains, rebellion, and coming of age, all while dealing with being pregnant. Each story offers a unique look into the wide variety of challenges pregnant teens face: marriage, adoption, religion, gossip, finances, rumors among the community, graduating high school, getting (or losing) a job. Faced with incredibly adult decisions, these girls are forced to sacrifice their teenage years and their high school experiences. (MTV's *16 & Pregnant*, 2009, para. 1)

However, there are critics who disagree with the assertion that these shows have been helpful in serving as a warning to teenagers about teen pregnancy and parenthood (Dockterman, 2014; Majeski, 2013). One of the biggest criticisms of *16 & Pregnant* is that it glamorizes teenage pregnancy as opposed to showcasing the consequences and hardships teen parents face (Dinh, 2010). Due to the fact that the mothers receive a paycheck and fame, Dolgen (2011) notes that some people have accused the show of inspiring copycat behavior, leading to an increase in the teenage pregnancy rate.

Yet on the other hand, there are those such as Bill Albert, a spokesperson with the National Campaign to Prevent Teen and Unplanned Pregnancy, who assert that the show "helps broaden insight into teen pregnancy" (Dinh, 2010, para. 3). Additionally, studies report that the rate of teenage pregnancies in the U.S. decreased to an all-time low in 2009, with some linking this statistic to the premiere of *16 & Pregnant* in the same year (Centers for Disease Control, 2011; Dinh, 2010; Guttmacher Institute, 2010; National Bureau of Economic Research, 2014). Despite the fact that teen pregnancy rates are declining, the Centers for Disease Control and Prevention (2011) reveals that the teen pregnancy rate for Black and Latina teenagers is still more than twice that of other racial groups. Moreover, often when images and news stories of young African American mothers have been in the media they have been negative portrayals of "bad mothers," and modern-day reflections of the stereotypical welfare queens (Douglas & Michaels, 2004). To date there have not been many reality television shows featuring African American teen mothers. However, in an effort to reflect real-life common consequences of teenage mothers, *16 & Pregnant* has included Black and Latina teenage mothers, although they represent a small number in comparison to the total number of White mothers featured on the show.

In general, while the media cannot entirely be blamed for the phenomenon of Black teenage pregnancy, the messages in the media about teenage pregnancy, motherhood, and Black women bear closer examination. As a show that has been known to draw over 31 million viewers, many of whom are girls and women between the ages of 12 and 34 (Seidman, 2009), the potential impact that *16 & Pregnant* can have on its audiences, in regard to how it portrays the realities of teen pregnancy, renders it one that should be analyzed. It is especially important to consider the role that race plays in these depictions, as Black teen moms have stereotypically been considered the face of teen pregnancy. However, to my knowledge there have not been any studies examining how Black teen mothers are portrayed in reality television.

Although studies have explored the effects of watching television, including music videos specifically, with regard to attitudes and behaviors regarding sex and relationships in adolescents (see, e.g., Brown, 2002; Brown & Keller, 2000; Eyal & Kunkel, 2008; Gruber & Thau, 2003), few studies have investigated media representations of teenage pregnancy. As the media, including television, are sources of information for many teenagers, and teen pregnancy rates among Black and Hispanic teenagers persist (Centers for Disease Control, 2011), analyzing how Black teen mothers are depicted is important. Thus, I critically examined five episodes of *16 & Pregnant* that feature pregnant Black teenaged girls to expose the consequential themes. Then I compared the consequences of their pregnancies to the aforementioned consequences noted in various reports and studies. In the results I explore what challenges these mothers face and whether the show glamorizes and encourages, or perhaps denigrates and discourages teen pregnancy. Furthermore by examining Black teen mothers, I argue they are not stereotypically portrayed as bad mothers but rather are depicted as caring, sensitive, and intelligent people who put their family first. As such, *16 & Pregnant* thwarts long-established stereotypes and begins to offer a new version of Black mothers.

## *Television's Effect on Teenagers*

Much has been written about the effects the media can have on their audiences, both young and old (see Brown, 2002; Brown & Keller, 2000; Eyal & Kunkel, 2008; Gruber & Thau, 2003). Out of all the demographics, teenagers and young adults consume and utilize the media and all its corresponding technology, particularly television, the most (Vahlberg, 2010). As a result of this television consumption, scholars have identified correlations between ideas, values, and behaviors that teenagers have with themes in the programming they consume (Besley, 2008; Emmers-Sommer, Pauley, Hanzal, & Triplett, 2006). For example, Emmers-Sommer et al. (2006) found that when viewing media with sexually violent images, teenage girls were likely to believe and abide by traditional ideas and roles of women in relationships suggested by these same media. Additionally, Besley's (2008) research on media use and human values evidenced a positive correlation between consumption of entertainment television and reinforcement of traditional roles and customs—a finding he refers to as conservation values. Altogether, past research implies that the images in television can influence the ideas teenage girls and young adults have in terms of what is acceptable and encouraged, regardless of whether the message is positive or not.

## *Sexual Images in the Media and the Effects on Teenage Audiences*

Sex in the media is not a new phenomenon. In fact, studies have revealed that in television shows, the chance that characters will converse about or mention sex is higher than 50 percent (Kunkel, Cope, & Biely, 1999). In particular, American television content is considered "highly sexual" with many images reflecting casual sex or sex occurring outside of a committed relationship (Gruber & Thau, 2003). In light of the fact that adolescents make up a large part of television viewing audiences, analyzing whether these images depict some of the consequences that can arise from unprotected sex is possible (Vahlberg, 2010). As adolescence is a time when people begin to develop an understanding of society, sex, and a myriad of other topics, the influence of television shows such as *16 & Pregnant*, that propose to demonstrate the reality of teenage pregnancy and parenthood, is particularly important. The premise of this idea has been embraced by health advocates who seek to work with the media in terms of creating "entertainment education" and shows with "embedded messages" to promote healthier sexual behavior (Keller & Brown, 2002, pp. 66–69).

Despite the fact that only one-fourth of adults in the U.S. have stated that they receive information regarding sex from the media, there are many opportunities for the media to be utilized for this purpose (Keller & Brown, 2002). Under the assertions of Gerbner's Cultivation Theory, television as a medium reinforces the values and norms of real life (Gerbner & Gross, 1976; Pietila, 2005). As such, audiences can come to believe that the images portrayed in the media are a reflection of reality. Essentially, as Gross and Morgan (1985) found, "the more time one spends living in the world of television, the more likely one is to report conceptions of social reality that can be traced to television portrayals" (p. 226). In terms of teenage pregnancy and parenthood, by simply showing teen pregnancy, the media have the opportunity to cultivate a better understanding of the consequences and issues associated with teenage pregnancy and parenthood. Additionally, because teen mothers and, more specifically, Black mothers have often been portrayed negatively in the good-versus-bad mother spectrum (Douglas & Michaels, 2004), analyzing the depictions of how these Black teen mothers' lives are affected by pregnancy and motherhood can add to the conversation. Considering the effect that television can have on their young audiences, images that reflect the reality of sexual interactions for teenagers of different ethnicities from across the country are salient as the possibility of a cultivating effect is probable.

## *Perceptions of Black Teen Mothers*

Historically, Black women have been categorized and represented by a number of different archetypes in popular culture and the media at large. Three particular archetypes include the Mammy, the Sapphire, and the Jezebel (hooks, 1981). The Mammy archetype was used to characterize some Black women as naturally maternal and loyal to the White families they worked for and served (Parks, 2010). The Sapphire, on the other hand, was known as "harsh, loud, and uncouth" and was representative of "the myth that Black women are invulnerable and indefatigable" (Jones & Shorter-Gooden, 2003, p. 3). Both the Mammy and the Sapphire archetypes were characterized as being asexual and not particularly attractive. The Jezebel character, however, was the one known to represent the "oversexed, carefree, and immoral" attributes prescribed to Black women in popular culture (Jones & Shorter-Gooden, 2003, p. 30). The Jezebel archetype has often been used to describe Black teen mothers, as their status as young, unmarried mothers served as evidence of the "hypersexual" nature of Black women.

Adding to these archetypes have been the media's depictions of Black mothers. As Douglas and Michaels (2004) point out, in the media's representation of motherhood, the examples of bad mothers were nearly all "African American and were disproportionately featured as failed mothers in news stories about 'crack babies,' single teen mothers, and welfare mothers" (p. 40). As a result, the media created a dichotomy between what they seemed to consider "good" and "bad" mothers, including "welfare mothers, working-class mothers, and teenage mothers" that were often divided on the basis of race (Douglas & Michaels, 2004, p. 41).

In addition, stereotypes about young mothers, particularly those of color, suggest they are a burden to society and are unreliable. For example, Kennelly (1999) examined how White employers view Black women and relays that a majority of them automatically equate Black women as single mothers and consider the possible issues related to childcare as a hindrance to Black women being good employees. Unfortunately, stereotypical images of Black women can serve to reinforce and influence audiences' perceptions of them (Ford, 1997).

## *Intensive Mothering*

Representations of motherhood in the media span a spectrum from good to bad; in contemporary society, the "best" mother is the one who exhibits characteristics of "intensive mothering" (Hays, 1996). The concept of intensive mothering, which Hays (1996) notes has evolved over centuries, essentially supports the idea that a good mother is "hands-on" and focuses all of her care, attention, time, and money on her child. As Douglas and Michaels (2004) further explain, according to ideals held up by the media about motherhood "to be a 'remotely decent mother' a woman has to devote her entire physical, psychological, emotional and intellectual being 24/7 to her children" (p. 15).

Inherent in this idea is that a good mother has the resources that allow her to provide these necessities for her children, whether she is a working mother or not. As a result, many teenage mothers in general fall outside of this category due to their lack of education and financial stability. The stereotype of Black women as bad mothers would seemingly place them outside of the intensive-mothering category as well. Therefore, if the qualities of intensive mothering seem to be the opposite of the stereotype of Black teenage mothers, examining how these young women handle the challenges of motherhood will add to the dialogue about whether their depictions add to pre-existing stereotypes or contradict them. In order to address this, I posed the following research question:

> RQ1: How does the television show *16 & Pregnant* portray the consequences of teenage pregnancy and motherhood for Black girls?

## *The Text:* 16 & Pregnant

The TV show *16 & Pregnant* began airing on the MTV network in June 2009. With just 6 episodes in the first season, the show aired a total of 61 episodes by the end of the 5th season in July 2014. Additionally, each season ended with a reunion show, and some of the mothers have even gone on to be featured in the spinoff series *Teen Mom* (recently renamed *Teen Mom OG*), *Teen Mom2*, and *Teen Mom3*.

Each episode of this hour-long documentary style series follows a different teen during a five-to-seven-month period of her life both before and after she gives birth. The setup of each show begins with the pregnant girl narrating and describing where she was from, the day-to-day habits and activities she enjoyed doing, and then saying that her life was about to change because she was pregnant. The rest of the episode switches back and forth between her narration and scenes of her in different situations such as at school, at work, with her child's father, with her parents, or just at home taking care of her child. In the last scene of each episode the teen talks directly to the camera reflecting on how her life had changed since she became pregnant and later a mother, her feelings about becoming pregnant at a young age, choosing motherhood, and her thoughts about what the future would bring.

## *Method*

The five episodes featuring Black teenage mothers that aired during the first four seasons of *16 & Pregnant* were studied to address my research question. To do this, the images and dialogue were carefully examined in each episode, focusing specifically on how they portrayed and reflected the consequential concerns of teenage pregnancy and motherhood. For the purposes of this study, the description "Black" was applied to any teen mother who identified herself or one of her parents as Black or of African descent through conversation in the course of the episode. As a result of this definition a total of five mothers, two of whom were biracial, were included in this study. These five mothers included: Ebony Jackson, age 17 (Season 2, Episode 4); Markai Durham, age 16 (Season 2, Episode 14); Cleondra Carter, age 17 (Season 3, Episode 5); Kianna Randall, age 17 (Season 3, Episode 8); and Jordan Howard, age 17 (Season 4, Episode 6). While two additional girls from the show appeared to be biracial, they did not discuss or allude to their ethnicity or that of their parents on the episode or disclose their ethnicity in their cast biography; therefore, they were not included in this study. Additionally, in order to be examined, each episode needed to feature a teenager who not only decided to give birth, but also who decided to keep her child.

Within each episode, I analyzed the images and dialogue of the featured teenage mothers interacting with their families, friends, and babies. In the first round of examination, I took notes regarding the various details of the lives and relationships of the different teenage mothers. In particular, I noted and analyzed images and dialogue that revealed the concerns and problems each teenage mother faced in terms of their pregnancies and motherhood. I then coded and categorized the images and dialogue and compared them with the existing research on the consequences of teenage parenthood.

In the second round of coding, I examined examples of how each of these themes was presented. Primarily these themes were either mentioned during the mother's narration, portrayed as the topic in a conversation the mother was seen having with a friend or family member, or shown depicting the mother in a situation exhibiting this consequence. During this portion of coding and analysis, I took copious notes of the depictions. Finally, I examined the question of whether the mother expressed regret with her pregnancy and her decision regarding motherhood.

## *Results*

After viewing the selected episodes, four major themes emerged related to the consequences the mothers faced: sacrifice of career/educational goals, social isolation/alienation, financial hardship, and changes in relationships. These teen mothers were portrayed as struggling to deal with the changes in their lives that motherhood brought, and having to adjust to how their realities sometimes differed from what they expected. Yet regardless of the issues they faced, each teenage girl was portrayed as a mother who was determined to do what was necessary to overcome obstacles she faced in order to be a good mother. Thus I argue that *16 and Pregnant* neither encourages nor discourages teenage motherhood. Instead, the show thoughtfully illustrates real issues that mothers (regardless of age or race) endure such as self-sacrifice, isolation, financial stress, and evolving relationships.

## *Sacrifice of Career/Educational Goals*

The first major theme that each of the teenage mothers faced was the realization that they would either have to adjust or completely sacrifice the plans they had to continue their education and pursue the careers they desired. The first example of this was Ebony Jackson, who was depicted as having to come to terms with having to sacrifice her post–high school career plans (Episode 4, Season 2).

Of primary importance to Ebony, who like her fiancé Josh came from a military family, were her goals to finish high school and join the Air Force. The majority of the first half of the episode involved her talking about what she envisioned would happen after she had her baby. One example of this was her narration about her plans for the future, which was followed by a scene of her talking to her guidance counselor about what she would need to do to graduate on time. The pivotal scene, however, was when she and her fiancé met with the Air Force recruiter who informed them that because they were having a child and were a couple, one of them would be disqualified from enlisting because there was a child involved. At that moment Ebony realized that her career goal would have to be forfeited in order for her boyfriend to enlist so he could support her and the baby.

Further examples of this sacrifice of educational and career goals for Ebony were in her discussions with her fiancé after the baby was born. By that time in the episode she had decided to enroll in night school and relied on him to take care of the baby when he got out of school so she could get to class on time. One scene depicted her telling him that she needed him to get home on time so that she could get to class and ultimately graduate on time. Her goal of trying to finish her education was also reflected in scenes with her reading homework while in the waiting room for a doctor's appointment and also trying to read at home while holding the baby.

Markai Durham also dealt with her pregnancy and motherhood interfering with her career plans (Season 2, Episode 14). Markai, who was a 16-year-old senior in high school during the November 16, 2010 episode, had aspirations of becoming a veterinarian. Prior to her pregnancy, she was part of a program at her high school that was designed for students interested in that field. Because she was pregnant, however, she shared via her narration that her doctor said that she could not continue to work with animals because the pregnancy made her more susceptible to viruses from the animals.

In addition to not being able to participate in the program to the extent that she did before, basic logistics of her pregnancy required Markai to take time off from school. In the scene early in the episode before she gave birth, she was shown talking to her caseworker about how she planned to have a friend bring her the work she missed from school while she was out of school on pregnancy leave. Later, after she has had the baby, however, she narrated that in the time that she had been out of school she ended up falling far behind with her class work. Her strained finances also led her to realize that she would have to put her career goals on hold, which she reflected on when she shared that she would have to end up being a cashier a little longer than she originally intended.

Seventeen-year-old Cleondra Carter also had to deal with sacrificing her career and educational goals (Season 3, Episode 5). The high school senior, whose episode originally aired on May 17, 2011, had been considered the "smart" and "responsible" daughter in her family. Prior to giving birth to her child, Cleondra helped her mother take care of her two-year-old niece due to her sister's absence, so she had ample experience taking care of children; however, the toll of having to be responsible for her own child weighed on her. As an honor-roll student, Cleondra was determined not to let pregnancy and motherhood prevent her from her goal of graduating from high school, which she promised her mother she would do. She stated in the beginning of the show that her career goal was to become a physical therapist. She discussed with her friends her plan to only take two weeks off from school after she gave birth due to the fact that she would be out of school for Christmas break when her daughter was scheduled to be born. Despite talking about how difficult it was to keep up with school work because her daughter was taking up all her time, Cleondra was still consistently depicted doing homework, often getting assistance from her family. In one scene she was able to have her older sister watch the baby while she went to take a midterm. Through narration and scenes depicting her taking the baby to different relatives, Cleondra disclosed that her family and the family of the child's father, Mario, were able to keep the baby while she attended school. While Cleondra did not indicate having to change her career plans, she did disclose that upon learning she was pregnant, Mario canceled his career plans to join the Army and, instead, took a full-time job at a local tire shop so he could be present and bring in money for his new family.

Upon finding out that she was pregnant, the main concern for Kianna Randall, a 17-year-old high school senior, was her future (Season 3, Episode 8). Through her narration, Kianna described how she was deliberating between giving her child up for adoption or keeping the child and raising it herself. The first half of the episode depicted her having conversations with her friends and her child's father about not being sure what to do. Her concerns regarding sacrificing her goals for the future and balancing school and her future goals came to fruition as she found herself trying to manage motherhood duties with her school obligations after her child was born. In an effort not to fall behind with her goal of graduating from high school, Kianna revealed in the beginning of the episode that she had switched to a new high school for her senior year. This particular school offered free daycare for students who were parents and helped students graduate early. Shortly before Kianna gave birth she was confined to bed rest due to her health, and that, combined with the time off she took after her baby was born, led her to fall behind with her school work. Later, after the baby was born she was shown trying to work on her computer while the baby was beside her. She was also seen getting up early, dressing her son, and dropping him off at the school daycare. Speaking to the camera, she informed viewers that it was hard trying to balance school with taking care of a newborn and expressed doubts about whether she would be able to reach her goal of getting a veterinarian degree.

The primary conflicts that 17-year-old Jordan Howard faced were mostly about the individual issues her mother had with her child's father, Tyler (Season Four, Episode 6). However, she also dealt with the common consequence of possibly sacrificing her career/educational goals. Aside from the interpersonal issues between Tyler and her mother, Jordan's fear regarding having to sacrifice her future goals was also a key theme within the episode. She revealed during her narration at the beginning of the show that she hoped to attend a trade school and become a dental hygienist. The reality of balancing childcare with attending school, nonetheless, became an issue. Jordan was talking to her friends in one scene about how childcare would be necessary in order for her to attend school or work. She vocalized her need for her mother's assistance with taking care of her child. Tyler's absence and lack of assistance was frustrating to Jordan because he left her to struggle with the balance of taking care of her child and doing coursework. She stated in her narrative that it would take her some time to learn to balance and get used to motherhood. At the end of the episode, when talking to some friends about her plans the following year, she revealed that she would be dropping out of school.

While each of these teen mothers had plans for their future, each faced the reality of how motherhood changed their lives. Discussions and images revealed each of them trying to adjust to these changes; clearly these teen mothers struggled with re-imagining their goals and navigating how to achieve those goals. They additionally portrayed how hard teenage mothers had to work to balance school work with the responsibilities of motherhood. Despite voicing and displaying frustration at how their lives had changed, each teen mother resigned herself to working towards a better future for her and her child, regardless of the setbacks that arose.

### *Social Isolation/Alienation*

In addition to mothers having to sacrifice their career and educational goals, social alienation was another theme identified throughout several of the episodes examined in this study. However the extent of the social isolation/alienation and the circumstances regarding the relationships in the mothers' lives all varied. For example, Ebony disclosed that some classmates at school were understanding of her situation while others were not (Episode 4, Season 2). This preceded a scene in which she was handing out invitations to the baby shower and then later was in the midst of a classroom discussion on teen pregnancy. This particular classroom scene featured two classmates who vocalized strong views regarding teen pregnancy. One boy shared how his sister became a teen parent and it ruined her life. Another said that "girls should keep their legs closed" in response to the phenomenon of teen pregnancy. In a different scene, the alienation Ebony faced is shown when she was not allowed to participate in the school drill team, which she had joined in the beginning of the year. In one scene where they were practicing, she sat in the bleachers watching them. In the end when the captain asked the team to applaud her for still coming out in support regardless of not being able to participate, the students were shown clapping. Yet despite sitting on the bleachers with them, she was off to the side separated from them. The episode ended with her narrating how much she had to sacrifice to have her child, including not being able to walk at graduation, not being able to join the Air Force, and not being able to be a teenager.

Cleondra also was depicted as coping with social isolation and alienation (Season 3, Episode 5). Aside from having to adjust to the day-to-day responsibilities of having her own child, Cleondra also expressed feeling left out of activities that she participated in before she got pregnant. During part of her narration she shared how she loves to dance and would have to give up being on the school dance team after having only been on the team for a year. In scenes with her friends and her siblings and mother's boyfriend, respectively, she was also seen discussing the fact that she would have to give up activities. She revealed that these sacrifices were amplified by the fact that in addition to no longer being able to do what she enjoyed, she also would not be able to be with her peers and have fun. Essentially, she disclosed, she would not be able to be a part of everything she was a part of before her pregnancy. An additional aspect to this alienation was the disbelief and shock that her friends expressed in one scene where they discussed how they found out about her pregnancy. The sentiment conveyed was that they did not expect that of her because she was always looked at as "responsible." As a result they looked at her differently because of this new role she held.

The alienation and isolation that these mothers faced reflected the reality of what can happen when teenagers have the life-altering experience of motherhood. The conversations and situations that these teen mothers were depicted in where their peers reacted to their pregnancies and motherhood showed how family and friends of teen mothers can sometimes view teen mothers. While teen pregnancy is not a new phenomenon, when it does occur it can elicit different reactions from friends, families, and peers of the teen mothers. These reactions can often make the teen mothers feel alienated because of how this experience has made them be perceived, and sometimes treated, differently. Although all of the teen mothers in this analysis were not depicted as facing this, the ones that did reflected one of the consequences that many mothers face.

## *Financial Hardship*

The third major theme found in this analysis of Black teenage mothers was that of financial hardship. While the concern over money was consistently expressed throughout each of the episodes, for some of the mothers this concern was especially pronounced. For example, Markai consistently discussed her desire to be able to find a place for her, her boyfriend James, and their child to live as a family together (Season 2, Episode 14). The consistent issue of money, however, existed because her boyfriend did not have a job and seemingly appeared to not have a place to live. While Markai had a part-time job working at a grocery store, she had to take a leave of absence right before her due date and for a time period afterward, which made her completely dependent on her mother, with whom she lived. In addition to this, her car broke down during the episode while she was driving her boyfriend around to apply to jobs, which became an additional expense.

Markai frequently disclosed to her friends her frustration over James's unemployment. Markai drove James to businesses such as Dairy Queen and Burlington Coat Factory so he could inquire if they were hiring or follow up on job applications. Additionally, one scene depicted her talking to the school-appointed case worker questioning whether she could help her find a place for James to live. Later she called her father, who is described as having been primarily absent throughout her life, asking for his help to find James a place to live. Following this, Markai's mother, who had been against the idea of James living with them, agreed to allow James to stay in the house and help with the baby. This conversation as well as the fact that James's family and home were not alluded to, suggest that James was homeless.

Kianna also struggled with the concern about her pregnancy causing a financial hardship (Season 3, Episode 8). In the beginning of the episode Kianna disclosed, via her narration, that she considered abortion and adoption because she doubted whether she could count on her child's father, Zack, to help take care of their child and assist with their financial needs. Part of this was because Zack was 15-years-old and lived with his family in a different town that was 30 minutes away from her. Early in the episode Kianna shared with him her misgivings about how they could afford to keep their child and Zack assured her that everything would work out and he would help her. However, after the baby was born and Kianna questioned Zack about money, Zack told Kianna that it was not easy to get a job at his age. In other scenes when Kianna tried to voice her concerns regarding how they would ever be able to get enough money to be together as a family she appeared frustrated with him for not listening to her but rather playing with the baby when she tried to voice her concern.

Kianna's interactions with her mother also reflected the difficulties that her pregnancy and motherhood brought into her life. For example in one scene after Kianna had returned from a doctor's visit, her mother told her how the doctor's visit caused her to go in debt and that Kianna needed to think about how she could get a job because she did not intend on having the full burden of Kianna's financial responsibilities falling on her. Later after the baby was born her mother is seen in the kitchen talking to her about the cost of the bottles and formula that she bought for the baby. She then asked Kianna how much Kianna now owed her, indicating that she expected Kianna to pay her back. In a separate scene where Kianna was talking to one of her friends she disclosed how even though she and her mother do not have much money, her mother still helped out a lot, which is needed because neither she nor Zack had jobs.

The conversations and scenes where the teen mothers were shown dealing with financial concerns reflected the reality of how becoming a parent also means incurring more financial obligations. These teen mothers, however, were portrayed as taking on that responsibility directly as they deliberated about how to find a more permanent way to achieve financial stability. Whether they received help from their families, their child's father, or focused on jobs for themselves, each teen mother stepped up to the challenge. The concern each displayed over future career goals revolved around their focus on being financially stable. The struggle to do this, however, ended up being one of the biggest trials teenage parents faced, and its pervasiveness as a topic amongst loved ones affected their relationships.

## *Relational Changes*

A common issue that each of the Black teen mothers faced was the change in their interpersonal relationships. Primarily these changes were with their boyfriends. For example, the issues Jordan and her boyfriend Tyler had regarding her mother's misgivings about Tyler took a toll on their relationship after the baby was born and Jordan decided to live with her mother. For Jordan, the change in her boyfriend Tyler came as a complete shock to her, particularly since she was living with his family before she gave birth. He stated that his doubts regarding her mother's authenticity about allowing him over made him not come and visit. In one scene when he did come over to see the baby he and Jordan ended up arguing and Tyler left cursing in reference to her entire family, which led her brothers to chase him out of the house. The episode ended with them essentially estranged.

Cleondra's relationship with her boyfriend Mario also was affected negatively by her pregnancy in that after giving birth Cleondra felt that Mario did not want to help her because she would not agree to stay with him. Because Cleondra lived with her mother, her mother's boyfriend, her older sister and brother, and her niece, Mario believed that she had "too much going on" in her house. In separate scenes he was seen discussing with his father and mother respectively how he did not like the idea of Cleondra's older sister and brother being around their child. He further stated that he did not foresee his relationship with Cleondra working out if she did not move in with him. The tension between the two continued as Cleondra confided in her mother that she felt as though he did not care about her anymore. In the end of the episode, however, she narrated that he had started helping more and the two planned to eventually live together and get married.

Kianna and Markai also experienced changes in the relationships that they had with their mothers as a result of their pregnancies. Both girls had mothers who were also young mothers. Both of their mothers indicated their disappointment in their daughters following in their footsteps. Markai's mother's disappointment was so deeply felt by Markai that she talked about how her pregnancy had impaired her relationship with her mother. In the narration Markai shared that her mother used to be like her best friend, but after her pregnancy she felt alienated from her and did not talk to her the way that she once did. For Kianna, this change was felt in the sense that by the end of the episode she began to wonder how much longer she would be able to rely on her mother. This marked a change from earlier in the episode when she told a friend that despite how little they had, she knew that she could depend on her mother.

## *Discussion and Conclusion*

The purpose of this study was to analyze the portrayal of the consequences of Black teenage pregnancy and motherhood on the television show *16 & Pregnant*. Historically negative stereotypes permeate society regarding teenage mothers overall and Black mothers specifically. Analyzing the depictions of these mothers and the consequences of teen pregnancy provided an opportunity to ascertain if newer images of this demographic were present. Positive images of Black teenage mothers in the media that go against the stereotype of them as irresponsible "welfare queens" who are bad mothers are needed because of the potential impact that such images have on how audiences may view Black teenage mothers.

Overall, as evidenced in the episodes under scrutiny in *16 & Pregnant*, the show represented an accurate portrayal of the consequences some Black teenage mothers faced compared to information provided in March of Dimes (2009) and Centers for Disease Control and Prevention (2011) literature. The depiction of them struggling with sacrificing their career and educational goals, facing isolation and alienation from their peers, as well as dealing with financial hardships correlate with findings from these sources regarding teenage mothers (Centers for Disease Control, 2011; March of Dimes, 2009). Additionally, the direct involvement, care, and sacrifice presented in *16 & Pregnant* revealed a contrast to the historically negative media portrayals of teenage mothers, especially Black teenage mothers. Each mother under investigation was not only shown as being the primary caregiver of the child, but was often depicted as trying to balance childcare with household duties. Contrary to the myth of the "welfare queen," these mothers, while concerned about money, were shown working or looking for employment and studying and trying to find work and school options that would allow them to work towards a better future for themselves and their children. The concept, then, of the "bad mother," which teenage mothers and Black mothers have been historically portrayed as in the media, was not evident with these Black teenage mothers.

While they were not "bad mothers," the girls in this series were not necessarily portrayed as "good intensive mothers" either (Hays, 1996). Even though the show is about mothering and these girls were featured enacting motherhood, they did not focus all their time, care, attention and money on their children. Instead they depicted a more balanced persona engaging in relationships with their parents, friends, and boyfriends. Their devotion to their children was evident as was their devotion to themselves and their extended relationships. Moreover these young mothers were also seen investing in themselves either by completing high school or seeking employment to begin their careers. This suggests that being a "good" mother, as defined by Hays (1996) and later, Douglas and Michaels (2004) is not ideal since it is far from healthy or possible to devote your "entire physical, psychological, emotional and intellectual being 24/7 to children" (p. 15). Indeed, not only did the young Black mothers on *16 and Pregnant* upend media stereotypes, but they also dismissed the illustrations of "good" and "bad" moms, offering up a more realistic portrayal of motherhood.

Rhetorically, this television show presented a glimpse into the realities of teenage pregnancy and motherhood. Each episode portrayed the mothers both visually and verbally engaging in hardships and changes they faced as a result of their pregnancies and decisions to become teenage mothers. Additionally, the final scene in each episode featured each mother summing up her feelings about becoming pregnant as a teenager, the changes in her life, and her thoughts about the future and the decisions she made. Out of the five teenage mothers examined, none expressed regret regarding her decision to have her child and become a mother. Instead each teen mother reflected on her self-described careless behavior in terms of what led her to get pregnant and how becoming a mother forced her to grow up and mature. Rather than expressing sadness or happiness with their choices, the young mothers acknowledged the reality of the sacrifices they made and the changes in their lives that resulted.

Overall, the episodes of *16 & Pregnant* examined in this study succeeded in refuting their critics' claims and debunking Black teen mom stereotypes.

The issues these teenagers faced were not glamorized, but were instead portrayed as real obstacles that had to be faced and worked to overcome. The episodes did not provide happy endings or show the moms' problems resolving. Instead, much as in real life, the challenges and situations the teenage parents faced were left open-ended as they struggled to make adjustments and figure out how to deal with their challenges. This honest depiction of teenage parenthood provided by *16 & Pregnant*, therefore allows this show to be a useful media tool with the potential of having a positive cultivating effect.

Despite the fact that the stereotype is of Black teens being the face of teenage pregnancy, a majority of the girls featured on *16 & Pregnant* are Caucasian. Regardless, as the synopsis of the show suggests, each of the girls featured on the show struggled with adjusting to motherhood and the changes to their lives that resulted (MTV's *16 & Pregnant*, 2009). The episodes featuring the Black teen mothers' circumstances depicted the common issues that teen mothers as a whole reflect (Centers for Disease Control, 2011; March of Dimes, 2009). Additionally, each of these mothers defied the stereotype of being irresponsible and lazy in that each of these girls was shown actively taking care of her child and seeking ways to balance motherhood, financial responsibilities, and education.

## References

Atlien. (2011, October 7). Facebook fail … are these your daughters? (For discussion) [Blog post]. Retrieved from http://straightfromthea.com/2011/10/07/facebook-fail-are-these-your-kids-for-discussion/

Besley, J. (2008). Media use and human values. *Journalism and Mass Communication Quarterly*, *85*(2), 311–330.

Brown, J. D. (2002). Mass media influence on sexuality. *The Journal of Sex Research*, *39*(1), 42–45. Retrieved from http://www.jstor.org/stable/3813422

Brown, J. D., & Keller, S. (2000). Can the mass media be healthy sex educators? *Family Planning Perspectives*, *32*(5), 255–256. Retrieved from http://www.jstor.org/stable/2648180

Centers for Disease Control and Prevention. (2011). Teen birth rates declined again in 2009. Retrieved from http://www.cdc.gov/Features/dsTeenPregnancy/

Dinh, J. (2010, December 22). MTV's *16 and Pregnant* credited for decline in teen pregnancy rates. Retrieved from http://www.mtv.com/news/articles/1654818/mtvs-16-pregnant-credited-decline-teen-pregnancy-rates.jhtml

Dockterman, E. (2014, January 13). Does *16 and Pregnant* prevent or promote teen pregnancy? Retrieved from http://time.com/825/does-16-and-pregnant-prevent-or-promote-teen-pregnancy/

Dolgen, L. (2011, May 4). Why I created MTV's *16 and Pregnant*. Retrieved from http://articles.cnn.com/2011-05-04/entertainment/teen.mom.dolgen_1_teen-pregnancy-teen-mom-teen-mothers/2?_s=PM:SHOWBIZ

Donnelly, B. W., & Voydanoff, P. (1996). Parenting versus placing for adoption: Consequences for adolescent mothers. *Family Relations*, *45*(4), 427–434. Retrieved from http://www.jstor.org/stable/585172

Douglas, S. J., & Michaels, M. (2004). *The mommy myth: The idealization of motherhood and how it has undermined women*. New York, NY: Free Press.

Emmers-Sommer, T. M., Pauley, P., Hanzal, A., & Triplett, L. (2006). Love, suspense, sex, and violence: Men's and women's film predilections, exposure to sexually violent media, and their relationship to rape myth acceptance. *Sex Roles*, *55*, 311–320. doi: 10.1007/s11199-006-9085-0

Eng, J. (2011). 90 Pregnancies at one high school. Retrieved from http://usnews.msnbc.msn.com/_news/2011/01/14/5841767-90-pregnancies-at-one-high-school

Eyal, K., & Kunkel, D. (2008). The effects of sex in television drama shows on emerging adults' sexual attitudes and moral judgements. *Journal of Broadcasting & Electronic Media*, *52*(2), 161–181. doi: 10.1080/08838150801991757

Ford, T. E. (1997). Effects of stereotypical television portrayals of African-Americans on person perception. *Social Psychology Quarterly*, *60*(3), 266–278.

Gerbner, G., & Gross, L. (1976). Living with television: The violence profile. *Journal of Communication*, *26*(2), 173–199.

Gross, L., & Morgan, M. (1985). Television and enculturation. In J. R. Dominick & J. E. Fletcher (Eds.), *Broadcasting research methods* (pp. 221–234). Boston, MA: Allyn & Bacon.

Gruber, E., & Thau, H. (2003). Sexually related content on television and adolescents of color: Media theory, physiological development, and psychological impact. *Journal of Negro Education*, *72*(4), 438–456. Retrieved from http://www.jstor.org/stable/3211195

Guttmacher Institute. (2010, January 26). Following decade-long decline, U.S. teen pregnancy rate increases as both births and abortions rise. Retrieved from http://www.guttmacher.org/media/nr/2010/01/26/index.html

Hays, S. (1996). *The cultural contradictions of motherhood*. New Haven, CT: Yale University Press.

hooks, b. (1981). *Ain't I a woman: Black women and feminism*. Boston, MA: South End Press.

Jones, C., & Shorter-Gooden, K. (2003). *Shifting: The double lives of Black women in America*. New York, NY: Harper Collins.

Keller, S., & Brown, J. (2002). Media interventions to promote responsible sexual behavior. *The Journal of Sex Research*, *39*(1), 67–72. Retrieved from http://www.jstor.org/stable/3813427

Kennelly, I. (1999). That single-mother element: How White employers typify Black women. *Gender & Society*, *13*(2), 168–192.

Kingsbury, K. (2008, June 18). Pregnancy boom at Gloucester High. *Time Magazine.* Retrieved from http://www.time.com

Kunkel, D., Cope, K., & Biely, E. (1999). Sexual messages on television: Comparing findings from three studies. *The Journal of Sex Research, 36*(3), 230–236. Retrieved from http://www.jstor.org/stable/3813434

Majeski, A. (2013, March 14). Has *Teen Mom* lost its original message? Retrieved from http://www.today.com/popculture/has-teen-mom-lost-its-original-message-1C8866403

March of Dimes. (2009). Professionals & researchers, quick reference: Fact sheets. Retrieved from http://www.marchofdimes.org/materials/teenage-pregnancy.pdf

MTV's *16 and Pregnant.* (2009). Full summary and description of series. Retrieved from http://www.mtv.com/shows/16_and_pregnant/season_1/series.jhtml

National Bureau of Economic Research. (2014 January). *Media influences on social outcomes: The impact of* MTV's 16 and Pregnant *on teen childbearing.* Retrieved from: www.nber.org/papers/w19795

Parks, S. (2010). *Fierce angels: The strong Black woman in American life and culture.* New York, NY: Ballantine.

Pietila, V. (2005). *On the highway of mass communication studies.* Cresskill, NJ: Hampton Press.

Seidman, R. (2009, June 30). MTV greenlights season two of hit series *16 & Pregnant.* Retrieved from http://tvbythenumbers.zap2it.com/2009/06/30/mtv-greenlights-season-two-of-hit-series-16-pregnant/21672/

Vahlberg, V. (2010). Fitting into their lives: A survey of three studies about youth media usage. *Newspaper Association of America Foundation.* Retrieved from https://www.americanpressinstitute.org/wp-content/uploads/2013/09/NIE_Fitting_into_their_lives.pdf

# 7. *"It Is What It Is"*: Here Comes Honey Boo Boo's *"Mama" June Shannon as Unruly Mother*

By Sharon R. Mazzarella

> Cross-cut by race, class, and sexuality (and, importantly, marital status), interwoven with changing psychological and biological theories and fantasies, tied up with nation-building and citizenship claims, images of motherhood remain both template and signpost upon which we project our desires for kinship and care and our most vexed understandings of womanhood and femininity.
>
> —Walters and Harrison (2014, p. 38)

In their recent analysis of cultural representations of what they term "aberrant mothers," Walters and Harrison (2014) remind us that the hegemonic, binary construction of mothers as either "sacrificial saints [or] demonic destroyers of hearth and home" (p. 51) has long permeated the cultural landscape. In opposition to these motherhood "myths" and binaries, Walters and Harrison (2014) argue that "novel counter-images have surfaced, especially in television" (p. 40). "Aberrant mothers," as they term the phenomenon, "upend more traditional depictions of maternal identity" (p. 40). While the authors identify Nancy Botwin in Showtime's *Weeds*, Betty Draper of HBO's *Mad Men*, as well as other fictional mothers in "high end … cultural venues much beloved by critics and advertisers looking for viewers with sophistication and disposable income" (p. 40), I argue producers also present audiences with such aberrant, transgressive, and/or complex maternal representations in the more low-brow reality television genre. Specifically, in this chapter, I focus on "Mama" June Shannon, the mother on TLC's hit reality program *Here Comes Honey Boo Boo* (*HCHBB*), which premiered to great controversy in August 2012.

## *Background*

Described initially by TLC as "'unapologetically outrageous'" (Cox, 2012), the program is a spinoff of the network's hugely popular reality television program *Toddlers & Tiaras* (*T&T*). *HCHBB* was originally intended to focus on 6-year-old[1] child beauty pageant contestant Alana (aka "Honey Boo Boo") Thompson, but it wasn't long before Mama June[2] became the "star" of the program as the focus shifted away from pageants and toward family dynamics including Mama June's unconventional relationship with her four daughters and live-in boyfriend, Mike ("Sugar Bear") Thompson.[3] Mama June's four daughters, ranging in age during Season 1 from 6 to 17 all have different fathers,[4] and at the start of that season, it was revealed that 17-year-old Anna ("Chickadee") Shannon was pregnant, unwed, and living at home. By the end of the first season Anna had made the 32-year-old Mama June a grandmother, and the baby's father was not in the picture. The other daughters, 12-year-old Lauren ("Pumpkin") Shannon and 15-year-old Jessica ("Chubbs") Shannon, like their mother and younger sister, were noticeably overweight (and even heavier by the second season), representing a dramatic contrast to the typical anorexic-looking adolescent girls who populate contemporary U.S. television programs. The program is filmed in the family's modest home in rural McIntyre, GA, where a freight train frequently runs through the backyard and the family proudly proclaim themselves to be "rednecks." Taken together, these programmatic elements had the blogosphere abuzz with negative reaction that began even before the program premiered when, during an episode of *T&T*, Mama June was seen giving Alana "Go Go Juice" (a homemade concoction of Mountain Dew and Red Bull) to rev the child up for pageant performances. From that point on, Mama June was branded a "bad mother," and the press had a field day.

The premier episode drew 2.25 million U.S. viewers (Bibel, 2012), while the highest-rated first season episode drew nearly 3 million (Kondolojy, 2012). Viewership dropped overall during the second season, however, the highest-rated episode of all four seasons was the final episode of Season 2, Mama June and Sugar Bear's commitment ceremony (3.21 million viewers) (Kondolojy, 2013). By the third season, viewership was averaging under 2 million with a range of 1.44 to 2.39 million viewers per episode ("Here Comes," n.d.).

The program was cancelled in October 2014 after four seasons when reports surfaced that Shannon was dating Mark Anthony McDaniel, a registered sex offender, recently released after serving 10 years in prison for aggravated child molestation (Hare, 2014). According to Shannon's oldest daughter, McDaniel molested her when she was eight-years-old (France, 2014). Shannon denied the accusations she was dating McDaniel (Hare, 2014). While the "real-life" issues being raised in the press are serious, the purpose of this chapter is to focus solely on the persona ("character") of "Mama June" as constructed in the episodes of the program. It does not address June Shannon's mothering in real life.

## ***Literature Review***

### *Reality Television*

Critical academic scholarship of reality television has exploded over the past decade, paralleling the proliferation of such programs. Much of the recent scholarship on reality television has addressed how such programs work to construct a particular group or place—for example, working class men (Fleras & Dixon, 2011; Mazzarella, 2008), wealthy, White women (Lee & Moscowitz, 2013); "Gypsies" (Tremlett, 2013); Women with a physical disability (Carlson, 2013); "Africa" (Steeves, 2008), and so on (also see Gomez this volume). That critical scholars would turn their attention to the politics of representation in this genre is not surprising since, as Winslow (2010) asserts, "more so than fictional television dramas, situational comedies, daytime talk shows, or news magazines, RTV programs are politically loaded because they occupy a more privileged position in relation to the representation of the real than overtly fictional forms" (p. 268).

While Walters and Harrison (2014) note that reality television "has the potential to create space for new and progressive representations of real mothers," for example, they argue "it instead routinely presents a stage for the public flogging of 'bad' moms" (p. 44). Similarly, in his analysis of reality television programs *Wife Swap* and *Trading Spouses*, Brancato (2007) asserts:

> these shows reveal social anxieties over caring relationships, and turn those anxieties into spectacle for mass consumption and, one can speculate, mass catharsis or perhaps identification, since the shows' mode of address obviously encourages viewers to measure themselves against the standards of the participants as well as idealized social norms. (p. 51)

I argue that in the "character" of Mama June, *HCHBB* offers a multidimensional representation of mother that transcends the binaries. Instead, Mama June functions as a transgressive mother, demonstrating a deep, abiding love for her children, yet simultaneously "mothering" them in a way that some would define as "bad"—feeding them primarily junk food, encouraging farting/burping and other indecorous behavior, allowing herself to be the butt of her children's jokes and playful banter, becoming a grandmother at such a young age, having four children out of wedlock herself, living with the baby daddy of her youngest child while refusing to marry him, not encouraging her children's school work, and a host of other behaviors that the culture at large would look down upon.

## *Mediated Constructions of Social Class*

One cannot analyze this program or the people who populate it without putting it into the broader context of a long, problematic history of mediated representations of the working class. Butsch (2010, 2005), for example, documents both the underrepresentation of working-class characters on U.S. television, as well as the tendency to portray them as loud, overweight, slovenly, lazy, and unintelligent. Similarly, in her book on *Framing Class*, Kendall (2011) asserts "Although the middle and upper classes may be caricatured in some media representations, people in the working class are particularly vulnerable to media framing that overemphasizes or misrepresents their appearance or behavior to produce an exaggerated or comic effect and turn them into objects of ridicule" (p. 142). Nowhere is this more evident than in the plethora of "trash" talk shows that populated daytime television during the 1990s—talk shows that typically featured women, people of color, and working-class guests being put into situations where they were shown reacting in a loud, physically confrontational manner as they were framed as unable to control their emotions (notably anger) and desires (Grindstaff, 2002). As Grindstaff (2002) explains, "Class, especially in the context of television, is also a performance, a social script involving, among other things, language use, mannerisms, and dress" (p. 31).

The intersections of class and gender have been addressed in recent critical scholarship examining mediated representations of working-class women. According to Ringrose and Walkerdine (2008), for example, working-class women are often the subject of television makeovers because they fail to meet standards necessary to be a "subject/object of desire and consumption" (p. 228) as defined by cultural dictates. One way in which the mediated figure of the working-class woman has been examined has been through the critical lens of the unruly woman (Rowe, 1997), the key theoretical concept guiding the analysis in this chapter.

## *Unruly and Transgressive Women*

Drawing from the psychoanalytic theories of Freud and Cixous, mythology, and Bakhtin's theorizing of spectacle and the grotesque, Kathleen Rowe

(1997) defines the "unruly woman" as "a topos (a 'place' or stock rhetorical theme) of female outrageousness and transgression which often evokes such ambivalence—on the one hand, delight; on the other, unease, derision, or fear" (p. 30). Applying the characteristics of the unruly woman to analyze the persona of TV comedienne Roseanne Arnold,[5] Rowe (1997) documents how "the topos of the unruly woman ... reverberates whenever women disrupt the norms of femininity" (p. 30). Inspired by the work of historian Natalie Davis, Rowe identifies "an inventory of [8] qualities associated with female unruliness" (pp. 30–31), including "dominating or trying to dominate men"; manifesting an excessively fat body; demonstrating "quantity, content, and tone" excess in speech; joking and laughing at herself; and association with dirt, liminality and taboo (p. 31). In this analysis, I focus primarily, but not exclusively, on the body signifiers, since, as Rowe (1997) observes: "the transgressive, round female body is also the maternal body" (p. 63). It's not surprising then that June Shannon is more often than not referred to both in the show and in the popular press as "Mama June."

Somewhat related to Rowe's concept of the unruly woman are the mediated "bad girls" and "transgressive women" deconstructed by Owen, Stein, and Vande Berg (2007). Owen, et al. (2007) are self-admittedly conflicted about the female characters they analyze, asserting that seemingly transgressive representations of female television and movie characters such as Ripley in the *Alien* film series and Ally McBeal in the television program of the same name can actually function to perpetuate *post*feminist messages that in reality work against women's progress. Like Rowe (1997), however, I argue portrayals of unruly women function in the opposite way—seemingly regressive on the surface, but actually progressive in the way such women lay claim to their own agency and subjectivity. I draw more from Gronbeck's foreword to Owen et al. in which he asserts such women "transgress social and institutional norms of thought and behavior" such that their representation has the potential to be "transformative" (Gronbeck, 2007, p. xvi).

## *Mama June Wars*

The Mommy Wars (see, e.g., Douglas & Michaels, 2000) are alive and well in the press coverage and broader public dialogue about Mama June's transgressive and unruly mothering style. Many have taken to the Internet and popular press to defend Mama June from others who have, in those same venues, criticized her mothering. For example Shana Aborn's (2012) article on the Walt Disney-sponsored website *Babble* offers ten reasons why Mama June is a good mother including that she "adores her children," "teaches self-acceptance," "teaches her children compassion," "doesn't judge her kids," and "believes in family togetherness" (para. 6–7, 9–11).

While the framing of articles/posts in the popular press is typically grounded in the hegemonically constructed good mother/bad mother binary, this chapter goes beyond the knee jerk "Is she or isn't she?" question. Grounded primarily in Rowe's (1997) theorizing of working class "unruly women" and informed by Walters and Harrison's (2014) deconstruction of "aberrant mothers," this chapter is a theoretically grounded textual analysis of the figure of Mama June Shannon in Seasons 1 and 3 of *HCHBB*.[6] By drawing from the theoretical concept of the "unruly woman," this chapter complicates the analysis of the construction of motherhood by adding the element of social class. Specifically, I argue that it is her construction as an agentive unruly woman that enables her character to transgress cultural good mother/bad mother binaries and function as an unruly *mother*.

## "As a Mom I Try to Teach My Girls Good Habits"

From the first episode of Season 1, the complex and contradictory construction of Mama June as mother becomes apparent. In that episode, Mama June asserts to the off-camera interviewer, "As a mom I try to teach my girls good habits,"[7] a scene that is immediately juxtaposed with images of her daughters eating cheeseballs for breakfast (what audiences hear Mama June jokingly refer to as the "breakfast of champions"). In this instance, TLC is engaging in what Lee and Moskowitz (2013) refer to as "the wink"—juxtaposing an on-camera quote from a reality television "character" with a clip of that same person engaging in contradictory behavior. This strategy, according to Bravo executive Andy Cohen, is employed in the various programs of the *Real Housewives* franchise to let "'the audience in on the fun'" (as quoted in Lee & Moskowitz, 2013). Lee and Moskowitz (2013) argue such tactics are gendered in that "they are designed to expose and reduce female characters and engage the viewing audience in the process" (p. 68). So whether it is the upper-class "housewives" of Bravo or the working-class "redneck" females of *HCHBB*, the use of the wink serves to "create the irony of hypocrisy" (p. 73). In fact, Lee and Moskowitz (2013) argue this is a particularly pervasive tactic when dealing with reality TV representations of mothers, with the result that such programs "construct these real mothers as ineffective, neglectful, selfish, superficial, and juvenile" (p. 75).

Scenes related to the family's diet, eating, and playing with food are main focal points of many episodes. For example, the producers include Mama June's cooking as a topic of several episodes, notably the infamous "Time for Sketti" episode (Season 1, Episode 7). Sketti, viewers are told, is "an old family recipe"—a concoction of spaghetti, ketchup and butter—which is the family's "favorite meal" (Season 1, Episode 7). As Mama June reports "I try to like cook like at least every day of the week." Moreover, the extreme couponer Mama June says, "I feed them on about $8 a week. And that's just buying cheaply" (Season 1, Episode 7). Almost as if she knows the audience is going to reprimand her for her family's eating habits, Mama June tells the off-camera interviewer: "They don't look like they're going hungry. They look pretty healthy. They enjoy what I cook" (Season 1, Episode 7).

If the viewer focused solely on the family's eating habits as shown in the program—a penchant for road kill, eating candy for breakfast, a pantry full of junk food, a stated disdain for vegetables other than corn and potatoes, huge restaurant meals, Mama's famous multi-meals (hand-mixed one-pot meals consisting of meat, sides, and sauce), the fact that they are shown eating their meals in the living room or standing up in the kitchen, where, as Mama June herself acknowledges she doesn't "enforce table manners" (Season 1, Episode 7)—the viewer could easily fall into the trap of labeling Mama June as a "bad" mother. Yet, despite TLC's attempt to construct Mama June as a controversial even hypocritical figure, there is an underlying consistency to her words and actions as she frequently reminds audiences, "We are who we are" (Season 1, Episode 3).

## *"Their Personalities Are Very Big"*

The assertion stated in the subheading also serves as a recurring counterpoint to TLC's attempts to construct the family through the gaze of outside observers. In her analysis of the British reality television program *My Big Fat Gypsy Wedding*, Tremlett (2013) focuses on the roles of the program's narrator and dressmaker, each of whom serve to comment on and construct for the audience an "authentic" and one-dimensional gypsy identity. While *HCHBB* has no actual narrator, the producers often feature aside commentary from various others who have encountered the family including the horrified etiquette instructor Mama hires to teach Alana and Pumpkin etiquette (Season 1, Episode 2); the overwhelmed spa aesthetician who pampers the family during a spa day (Season 1, Episode 3); the bemused proprietor at a wig shop (Season 1, Episode 6); the tickled clerks at the neighborhood convenience store (Season 1, Episode 7); the shocked former Miss Georgia who has lunch with Alana and Mama June (Season 1, Episode 8); the baffled candy store clerks they encounter while on vacation (Season 3, Episode 3); and the beleaguered realtor showing them houses (Season 3, Episode 6) among others. The comments these family outsiders make serve as an attempt to construct the family, and Mama's oversight of them, as outside of the norm, outrageous, and shocking. For example:

| | |
|---|---|
| AESTHETICIAN: | Their "personalities are very big. Very big" ... "It was an experience. I think I'm gonna go home now" (presumably because the experience of working with them has been just too overwhelming for her.) |
| WIG STORE PROPRIETOR: | "This particular family is kind of outside the box." She laughs and asserts their visit has been "more on the interesting side" than the regular wig fittings. "It was different, but it was fun." |
| STORE CLERK #1: | Proclaims the convenience store would go out of business if not for this family. |
| STORE CLERK#2: | "The family ads a lot of flavor to the city of McIntyre." |
| MISS GEORGIA: | Tells the camera that Alana's manners need work; that she never thought she herself would say the word "fart" on camera, and that Alana "has a lot of refining to do." |

To such reactions, Mama June is prone to respond, "I raised my kids to be who they are. Like us or love us. I don't really care" (Season 1, Episode 10). Indeed, this indifference to social norms, cultural dictates, and the judgment of others is a hallmark of the unruly woman. Unlike Cixous's concept of the "'well-adjusted woman" (as cited in Rowe, 1997, p. 31), the unruly woman is not invisible. "Through her body, her speech, and her laughter, especially in the public sphere, she creates a disruptive spectacle of herself. ... Ultimately, the unruly woman can be seen as prototype of woman as subject—transgressive above all when she lays claim to her own desire" (Rowe, 1997, p. 30). By asserting that she doesn't "really care" what people think about her, her family or the public spectacle they create, Mama June is laying claim to her agency and to her right to raise her daughters how she sees fit, whether or not that violates social conventions for appropriate female behavior and, as shown in the next section, appearance. Moreover, Mama June is refusing to allow herself and her family to be held hostage by the ridicule that often characterizes mediated representations of the working class in general (Kendall, 2011) and working class females in particular (Ringrose & Walkerdine, 2008).

## *"Mama Says Pretty Comes in All Different Sizes"*

When Alana quotes her mother in the third episode of Season 1 that "pretty comes in all different sizes," she sets the stage for the program's recurring messages about size acceptance. On one level, statements like this juxtaposed with images of less-than-ideal female bodies could seem to be mocking. On the other, they are said/reinforced with such genuineness that it's difficult to believe otherwise. For example, in the first episode of Season 1, Mama June (weighing 309 pounds at the time) acknowledges she may not be "the most beautimous" woman in the world, but she confidently claims she cleans up well.

> JUNE: You know, I just put, like, a little bit of paint on the barn. And dressed up a little bit for family photos. It is what it is. [She smooches the camera.] ... Beauty comes within. I mean, if you got a great personality and everything, I mean, it shines through on the outside. It doesn't matter. Big, small, little. It's the eye, the ... beauty is the eye, eye of the beholder. I mean, you know, skinny, fat, it doesn't matter." (Season 1, Episode 10)

In her analysis of Roseanne Arnold as an unruly woman, Rowe (1997) refers to the large-sized Arnold's "supreme ease with her body" (p. 64), "an ease which triggers much of the unease surrounding her because it diminishes the power of others to control her" (p. 64). Mama June displays this same ease with her own body when Pumpkin wants her mother to go on a diet with her. Mama June replies "I'm pretty happy with myself, but for support for you, I'll do it" (Season 1, Episode 1). In this one statement, Mama June sends her daughter two important messages, one of size/self-acceptance and one of motherly support. Interestingly, two seasons later, Pumpkin, who has noticeably gained a great deal of weight, looks at herself in the mirror and declares, "I don't really even need makeup. I'm so pretty" (Season 3, Episode 9).

Mama June, who refers to herself as voluptuous (Season 1, Episode 6), often makes comments about her own weight, but they are not derogatory or self-effacing. Rather they just "are" such as the multiple times over the series when she asserts in the heat of the Georgia summer, "heat and fat don't mix." Rowe (1997) continues, "Ease with one's body is the prerogative of the upper classes. For the working classes, the body is more likely to be a source of embarrassment, timidity, and alienation" (p. 64). Like Arnold, Mama June "rejects what that coding signifies" (Rowe, 1997, p. 64). Not only is Mama June comfortable in her own body, but so are her daughters. No matter what can be said about the health ramifications of being obese, the fact of the matter is that the program sends a very powerful message about size acceptance and transgresses cultural dictates for ideal female body size and for social class. Unlike the typical reality television fare featuring working-class women who undergo makeovers to fit the cultural standards of objects of desire (Ringrose

& Walkerdine, 2008), Mama June and her daughters exhibit no discomfort in or dissatisfaction with the size of their bodies.

While Mama is at ease with her own size, she does maintain standards of decorum for what is/isn't appropriate attire for large-sized women. When the family attends the Redneck Games during Season 1, Mama complains about the "voluptuous" women there with their "vajiggle jaggle" hanging out, and asserts they should put on some clothes. Similarly, while accepting her physical size, Mama June is quite conscious of and embarrassed by her "forklift foot," which is first referenced in Season 1, Episode 3 when she and the girls go to a spa. As she tells it, a forklift ran over her foot at work years earlier. As a result, she has a deformed toe that she always keeps covered in socks. In fact, she even has the pedicurist paint nail polish on her socks covering her toes. Two episodes later when Mama June takes the girls to a water park, she has her socks on, but after teasing and nagging by the girls, she takes off her sock and the audience sees the shocked/revolted looks on the girls' faces before the camera cuts to a shot of Mama June's deformed toe with gnats buzzing around it. Alana screams "That's disgusting," while Pumpkin declares that if she had a toe like that she'd "chop it off." While such verbalizations might seem an inappropriate way for daughters to talk to their mother, they are in keeping with the way the family banters with, teases, and jokes with each other, so there are no visible repercussions from these outbursts.

Despite being self-conscious about her own deformed toe, Mama shows no such concern when daughter Anna gives birth to granddaughter Kaitlyn who has two thumbs on one of her hands. Mama June tells the off-camera interviewer that the family has embraced it. "And she's more special to me. It is what it is" (Season 1, Episode 10). Again, the message of acceptance is reinforced.

As in the case of Kaitlyn, this message of accepting people for who they are transcends just self-acceptance. One of the more interesting examples of this occurs in Episode 10 of Season 1 when viewers first meet "Uncle Poodle"—Sugar Bear's younger brother, Lee. Lee is gay, and Alana calls all gay people "poodles," hence his affectionate nickname.[8] Alana and the family, including Mama June, are excited when they learn Lee is coming for a visit, and he eventually becomes a much more regular "character" by the third season when he accompanies the family on most of their outings, vacations, and excursions. As Alana proclaims to the off-camera interviewer when Lee visits "Ain't nothing wrong with bein' a little gay. Everybody's a little gay." This remark and the program's "portrayal" of family acceptance of Lee garnered a nomination for a GLAAD Award after its first season. Indeed, one hallmark of the unruly woman is the ways in which she "draws attention to the construction of gender"

(Rowe, 1997, p. 31). While typically accomplished through the unruly woman's often androgynous appearance, Mama June's unconditional acceptance of Lee works toward a progressive construction of gender, a construction that is furthered in the way she discusses various bodily topics with her daughters as shown in the next section.

## *"Ta-tas, Biscuits, Fruit Loop, Vajiggle Jaggle"*

It's not surprising that in a house of three teenage girls and one emerging tween opportunities will arise to have assorted sex talks. While on the one hand June and the girls (including Alana) use euphemisms such as "biscuit"[9] and "vajiggle jaggle" to refer to female body parts, June makes a sincere effort to educate her girls, especially once the two older girls, Anna and Jessica, both have boyfriends. In Episode 2 of Season 3, June tells the off-camera interviewer she is worried about one of her girls coming home pregnant. She admits "I don't really talk to the girls about sex," but she knows it's time, and begins with her version of the birds and the bees. As she tells the girls, girl and boy meet and fall in love. "They love each other for two days. And the boy tries to get the girl's fruit loop." Jessica asks why it's always about food with Mama, and June explains to the off-camera interviewer, "A fruit loop is your biscuit, your vaginal area, vagenital area." She continues explaining to the girls: "Let me tell you, boys, they try to park their motor boat into your fruit loop." June then goes through all the female body parts for the off-camera interviewer: "Ta-tas, biscuits [Jessica in the background ads gluteus maximus], fruit loop, vajiggle jaggle, tingalings, weed whacker, tic tacks, bungalow which is butthole" (Season 3, Episode 2). "See," she adds "we have different names for different parts" (Season 3, Episode 2). By the end of what is an awkward and uncomfortable conversation, June and her daughters are all snuggling, gabbing, and bonding in bed together. Indeed, scenes of Mama June and her girls hugging, snuggling, and cozying up together punctuate many important moments in the series, demonstrating that while her mothering style may transgress cultural norms, she has crafted what appears to be a close and loving relationship with her daughters.

Later in Season 3, after she catches Alana playing with maxi pads, she decides it is time to educate Alana about menstruation, and promptly begins to use a piñata as a metaphorical example. June tells Alana that a period is like a piñata so full of candy that every month it needs to spill some of the candy (aka blood). She then pours water into a maxi pad to demonstrate for Alana how it works. Alana exclaims for the off-camera interviewer: "All I know is a period belongs at the end of a sentence. I know English." The scene returns to the living room:

| | |
|---|---|
| JUNE: | And sometimes it stinks. So it's like smelly, sour candy. |
| ALANA: | [Points to her belly] "So you have smelly, sour candy right here?" |
| JUNE: | [Laughs] Kinda. I'll teach you more whenever it happens. [As Alana leaves the room.] (Season 3, Episode 12) |

In general, *HCHBB* is rife with references to body parts, bodily functions, bodily fluids, and other "taboo" subjects. Mama and the girls discuss these topics often and, as seen above, the language used to do so is often crude, humorous, and stereotypically masculine. As Rowe (1997) notes, one characteristic of the unruly woman is that her "speech is excessive, in quantity, content, or tone" (p. 31). This is one more way in which the unruly woman upsets the dictates of propriety for females, enabling her to claim agency. In the case of Mama June and her daughters, it's more than just talking about such taboo subjects. The program often shows them belching, farting, vomiting, sneezing visible snot, smelling armpits, and more. According to Rowe (1997):

> Farting, belching, and nose-picking convey a similar failure—or refusal—to restrain the body. While boys and men can make controlled use of such "uncontrollable" bodily functions to rebel against authority, such an avenue of revolt is generally not available to women. But, as Henley suggests, "if it should ever come into women's repertoire, it will carry great power, since it directly undermines the sacredness of women's bodies." (p. 64)

Clearly, Mama June and her girls are able to "make controlled use" of stereotypically masculine language and bodily functions, and therefore lay claim to the power of their own bodies. They physically take up space with their bodily size and draw attention to themselves through their language and behaviors.

## *"Guess Whose Breath"*

Toward the end of the final episode of Season 1, with the family surrounding her, Mama June proclaims, "As long as we are havin' fun, makin' memories, and together as a family, that's all that really matters." The girls all agree and pile on to hug June. In a follow-up with the off-camera interview, she continues: "We have fun together. We don't take things too seriously. Whatever the future holds is whatever's out there is possible. You ride with the flow. And when it's over you get off and start your next adventure. Peace. It is what it is."

The central theme of family togetherness and fun is demonstrated right from the first episode when Mama June informs viewers that Sugar Bear works seven days a week, so it's usually just she and the girls hanging out together. Over the course of the two seasons studied, the family, sometimes with/without Sugar Bear, goes to the "Redneck Games," (Season 1, Episode 7), four-wheelin' with friend "Crazy Tony" (Season 1, Episode 4), a water park (Season 1, Episode 5), "the local department store" (aka town dump) (Season 1, Episode 6), Bingo ("Mama's sport"), (Season 1, Episode 8), a blueberry festival (Season 3, Episode 6), camping (Season 3, Episode 9), and an amusement park (Season 3, Episode 12) where Pumpkin throws up on a ride prompting Mama June to utter: "You're not gonna have fun at the amusement park until somebody throws up."

Family togetherness is shown often in Season 3 starting with the third episode titled "Familymoon." Season 3 picks up after Sugar Bear and Mama June's Season 2 commitment ceremony, and instead of the couple going off on a honeymoon, they take the kids and Uncle Poodle on a "familymoon" in a rented RV. Throughout the episode, everyone reiterates that the best part is being all together. The trip is expensive for the family, but Mama asserts "My kids may not be perfect, but it's pretty good to spoil 'em every once in a while. That's what this trip is all about, makin' memories as a family" (Season 3, Episode 3).

Staying consistent to her "we are who we are" and "it is what it is" mantras, Mama June lets the girls be who they are and have fun doing things many parents would not allow. For example, she constructs for them a "redneck slip-n-slide" (trash bags, oil, water hose) in the backyard (Season 1, Episode 3) while exclaiming, "If you're not having fun and makin' memories it's not worth the experience." And to those who would look down on a redneck slip-n-slide in the backyard, she repeats, "We are who we are." In another episode, while she's initially upset that the girls have TP'd the house while she was out, she eventually laughs, and it is revealed that her displeasure is not over the mess, but rather over the waste of her iconic stash of free toilet paper. Similarly when the girls build a mud hole in the front yard as a way to have fun and cool off (Season 3, Episode 5), Mama isn't outraged or even upset, although she does suggest they get summer jobs to earn money to buy a real pool. This isn't the only episode when the girls play in mud. It's highlighted in multiple episodes including the mud belly flop at the Redneck Games (Season 1, Episode 1; Season 3, Episode 1) as well as four-wheeling through mud (Season 1, Episode 4), and Mama has no problems with dirt. Rowe (1997) argues that the unruly woman "is associated with dirt, liminality (thresholds, borders, or margins), and taboo" (p. 31). While Mama June herself, isn't typically shown playing in mud or getting dirty, she is supportive and encouraging of her daughters' behavior in this regard. Similarly, as discussed earlier, her use of language to talk about body parts and sex, especially in front of her daughters, breaks taboos for the way parents and children talk to each other.

In the same way Mama is not put off by dirt, behaviors that others would label as gross are also acceptable to her. For example, in Season 1, Episode 7, the family plays "Guess Whose Breath"—a made-up game where they each (including Mama and Sugar Bear), take turns being blindfolded while the other family members breathe heavily directly into the face of the blindfolded person. The goal is to guess whose breath it is. In this lengthy segment, they act grossed out and horrified by the various breaths, but they all, adults included, have a blast.

Overall, in all of these various family bonding activities, the family doesn't hold back with the yelling and hollering at each other, but they also laugh at and with each other, with Mama June laughing the heartiest, and evidencing the self-deprecating joking and humor that often characterizes the unruly woman (Rowe, 1997).

## *"I Wear the Stretch Pants in the Relationship"*

When narrating introductions of each of the family members in the first episode of Season 1, Alana announces "the boss of the family is Mama." Such a declaration, coming in the first episode of the series, sets the tone for how Mama June's character will be constructed, in particular as it concerns her relationship with partner Sugar Bear. Moreover, it is directly relevant to the trope of the unruly woman, who, according to Rowe (1997), "creates disorder by dominating, or trying to dominate, men" (p. 31). The unruly woman, according to Rowe (1997) "is unable or unwilling to confine herself to her proper place" (p. 31).

Physically, Mama is a more imposing figure than Sugar Bear, standing 6–7 inches taller (Season 1, Episode 4) and clearly outweighing him. At one point in the third season, she informs the audience that she "wears the stretch pants in the relationship" (Season 3, Episode 1). In fact, her daughters inform viewers that "Mama doesn't appreciate the things that Sugar Bear does for her" (Season 1, Episode 3).

While June acquiesces somewhat and agrees to the commitment ceremony that concludes Season 2, the lack of a physically intimate relationship between her and Sugar Bear is a recurring topic for the whole family across the two seasons analyzed. Unlike the quintessential unruly woman (as defined by Davis as cited in Rowe, 1997), and despite having four children, June shows no interest in sex. There are less than a handful of times in the seasons viewed when physical intimacy between Mama June and Sugar Bear is implied. For example, in Episode 4 of Season 3, the two spend the night alone at a honeymoon hotel during the familymoon trip. Narrating that experience, June tells the off-camera interviewer: "You know I don't give it up too often, but because I do it so well so I don't have to do it a lot. It keeps him going for the next six months."

Later in that season, Sugar Bear announces he wants him and Mama June to have another baby. She exclaims "No, my biscuit is closed for business" (Season 3, Episode 7). In that same episode Sugar Bear says he has "to figure out how to get more spice back in our lives." He goes on to assert, "I never know how June's gonna react to my swoo with her. She's an unpredictable woman, but that's the reason I love her ... I just swoo how I think she wants me to swoo, but hey, every single time I do it, something goes wrong" (Season 3, Episode 7). At that point, June comes into the bedroom and tells him it smells "like crap" (the candles), and she needs to use the bathroom. Eventually, they go to couples counseling, and the episode ends with them kissing on the bed. While there are more scenes of Mama June and Sugar Bear engaged in physically intimate behavior during this season than in others, their rarity across the series is notable, and June's comments about sex evidence that withholding sex is one way in which she wields power over Sugar Bear and maintains a dominant place in their relationship. Again, such dominance is a key characteristic of the unruly woman (Rowe, 1997).

I argue, however, that there is more going on here than simply sex as a power ploy. The fact that the producers focus so much attention on Mama June's lack of interest in sex serves to further construct her as an (unruly) *mother* rather than just an (unruly) *woman*. Drawing from Weaver's concepts of god and devil terms, Lindal Buchanan (2013) asserts that "Mother" functions as a god term, "an ultimate expression to which all others are subordinate" (p. 8) and which "diminish" the force of other terms" (p. 8). Devil terms, according to Weaver (as cited in Buchanan, 2013) provide contrast to god terms by inviting reproach and repulsion. "Woman," Buchanan (2013) asserts, is such a term. She argues that "Mother," as a god term, is associated with children, home, love, nourishment, strength, and the reproductive body among other related rhetorics. In contrast, "Woman" is associated with childlessness, work, self-centeredness, sex, and the sensual body, among other related concepts. So, for example, when asked by her daughters why she's "scared" to marry Sugar Bear, Mama June replies "Relationships come and go, but my kids will always be forever" (Season 1, Episode 7). In doing so, she frames herself as a mother, not a wife/partner/lover. Moreover, there is one key attribute of Rowe's (1997) unruly woman inventory from which Mama June deviates, and that is the trait of an excessive, overindulgent, even loose sexuality. Deviating from this one characteristic enables Mama June to be constructed as an unruly mother rather than an unruly woman.[10]

## *Conclusion: Mama June as Unruly Mother*

Overall, throughout the seasons studied, Mama June emerges as a complex and multidimensional figure who transcends good/bad mother binaries through her construction as what I have argued is an unruly mother—manifesting many of the characteristics of Rowe's (1997) unruly woman, but going further by modeling those traits for her four daughters. First, by manifesting an excessively obese body, Mama June refuses to remain invisible and demonstrates an ease with her body that, according to Rowe (1997) is usually more the "prerogative of the upper classes" (p. 64). As a mother, her actions and words in this regard send a powerful message to her daughters who are shown exhibiting the same ease with their own bodies. Similarly, by displaying what can be described as "excess" in "quantity, content and tone" of speech/language (Rowe, 1997, p. 64), Mama June demands to be heard, as do her daughters, who themselves talk loudly, argumentatively, and often. Related to the concept of excess speech is her association with dirt, liminality, and taboo, both in terms of behavior and language. Her use of slang, often "masculine" language to talk about body parts and sex, especially in front of her daughters (who themselves use the same language), breaks taboos both for the way women in general talk and the way mothers and children talk to each other. Moreover, through her relationship with Sugar Bear, Mama June upends the traditional gender dynamics in female-male heterosexual relationships. Like the unruly women studied by Rowe (1997), Mama June asserts and exhibits her dominance over Sugar Bear, further demonstrating for her daughters the importance of claiming agency. On the other hand, her lack of interest in sex enables her to be positioned more as Mother than Woman.

Walters and Harrison (2014) conclude their analysis of television's aberrant moms on a "strangely hopeful" note, taking "issue with critics who see only the overweening force of the market and renewed anti-feminism in contemporary images" (p. 51). While they see the diversity in mediated portrayals of mothers as "progress," they also worry these portrayals of aberrant mothering "can be easily morphed into a new version of that tired classic 'blame the mother'" (p. 51). Certainly, that was the initial reaction by many in the popular press to Mama June. On the other hand, Walters and Harrison (2014) assert "we are in dire need of some tough, messy, non-normative renegades to blast a few more holes in the maternal shrouds we've been wearing for far too long" (p. 51). In this chapter, I have argued that, through her construction as an unruly mother, Mama June is just such a "tough, messy, non-normative" mother figure.

## Notes

1. Ages listed are from Season 1.
2. Following Rowe (1997), I use "Mama" or "Mama June" to refer to the "character" constructed in episodes of *HCHBB*. I use "Shannon" to refer to June Shannon, the public personality constructed in news reports.
3. Shannon and Johnson split in September 2014 after nearly a decade together (Hare, 2014).
4. While popular press articles originally published this information originating from Shannon, stories published during the fall of 2014 (e.g., France, 2014) alleged that the father of two of the girls was the same man, convicted sex offender Michael Anthony Ford.
5. At the time of Rowe's analysis, the comedienne was married to Tom Arnold and had changed her last name from Barr to Arnold. While she no longer goes by Arnold, this chapter refers to her by that name to be consistent with Rowe (1997).
6. I selected these seasons to include both the first and most recent season aired at the time of this writing. While Season 3 was the most recent season at the time of my analysis, a fourth season has since aired.
7. Because the producers use subtitles to "translate" most of the family's conversations/interview comments, the majority of quotes in this chapter are typed verbatim from the content of those subtitles.
8. In an article published in the *Huffington Post* (Sieczkowski, 2012), Lee explains the origins of why he's "Uncle Poodle." While talking about some gay friends, Alana's pageant coach reportedly said "I love all my poodles." Alana thought the coach was talking about real dogs until Lee explained that she was talking about gay people. From then on, he has been "Uncle Poodle."
9. In Season 1, Episode 2, June explains why they call the vaginal area a "biscuit"—"because it looks like a biscuit." Later that season (Season 1, Episode 10) when Anna goes into labor, she exclaims that unborn baby Kaitlyn is "hurting my biscuit."
10. While I have focused in this chapter solely on how the program itself works to construct Mama June (the character), it is impossible at this point not to speculate that one reason why the program was canceled after allegations surfaced that June Shannon (the news persona) was dating a convicted sex offender is that June Shannon had crossed the line between unruly mother and unruly woman—a taint that couldn't help but spread to the Mama June character. As Buchanan (2013) asserts "Positioning a woman toward the Mother end of the continuum typically elevates her ethical standing; situating a mother toward the Woman end of the continuum usually erodes it" (p. 121).

## References

Aborn, S. (2012, September 19). 10 reasons *Honey Boo Boo*'s Mama June is (yes!) a good mom. *Babble*. Retrieved from http://www.babble.com/celebrity/10-reasons-honey-boo-boos-mama-june-is-yes-a-good-mom-photos/

Bibel, S. (2012, August 9). Wednesday cable ratings: *Dallas* wins night, *Here Comes Honey Boo Boo*, *Restaurant Impossible*, *Daily Show*, *Melissa & Joey*, *Futurama*, *The Exes* & more. Retrieved from http://tvbythenumbers.zap2it.com/2012/08/09/wednesday-cable-ratings-dallas-wins-night-here-comes-honey-boo-boo-restaurant-impossible-daily-show-melissa-joey-futurama-the-exes-more/144373/

Brancato, J. (2007). Domesticating politics: The representation of wives and mothers in American reality television. *Film & History, 37*(2), 49–56.

Buchanan, L. (2013). *Rhetorics of motherhood.* Carbondale IL: Southern Illinois Press.

Butsch, R. (2010). Ralph, Fred, Archie, and the King of Queens: Why television keeps recreating the male working-class buffoon. In. G. Dines & J. M. Humez (Eds.), *Gender, race and class in media: A critical reader* (3rd ed.) (pp. 101–109). Los Angeles, CA: Sage.

Butsch, R. (2005). Five decades and three hundred sitcoms about class and gender. In G. Edgerton & B. Rose (Eds.), *Thinking outside the box: A contemporary genre television reader* (pp. 111–135). Lexington, KY: University Press of Kentucky.

Carlson, L. (2013). Wired for interdependency: *Push Girls* and cyborg sexuality. *Feminist Media Studies, 13*(4), 754–759. doi: 10.1080/14680777.2013.805591.

Cox, K. L. (2012, July 23). *Here Comes Honey Boo Boo*: There goes TLC. Retrieved from http://southinpopculture.com/2012/07/23/here-comes-honey-boo-boo-and-there-goes-tlc/

Douglas, S. J., & Michaels, M. (2000, Feb./Mar.). The mommy wars: How the media turned motherhood into a catfight. *Ms. Magazine.* Retrieved from http://www.ms-magazine.com/feb00/mommywars1.asp

France, L. R. (2014, November 13). *Honey Boo Boo*'s Mama June admits relationship with another sex offender. Retrieved from http://www.cnn.com/2014/11/13/show-biz/celebrity-news-gossip/mama-june-sex-offender-honey-boo-boo/?cid=ob_articlesidebarall&iref=obnetwork

Fleras, A., & Dixon, S. M. (2011). Cutting, driving, digging, and harvesting: Re-masculinizing the working-class heroic. *Canadian Journal of Communication, 36*(4), 579–597.

Grindstaff, L. (2002). *The money shot: Trash, class, and the making of TV talk shows.* Chicago, IL: University of Chicago Press.

Gronbeck, B. E. (2010). Foreword: The politics of representation. In A. S. Owen, S. R. Stein, & L. R. Vande Berg Eds., *Bad girls: Cultural politics and media representations of transgressive women* (pp. xiii–xix). New York, NY: Peter Lang.

Hare, B. (2014, October 14). TLC ends production on *Honey Boo Boo.* Retrieved from http://www.cnn.com/2014/10/24/showbiz/tv/honey-boo-boo-tlc/

*Here Comes Honey Boo Boo.* (n.d.). Wikipedia. Retrieved from http://en.wikipedia.org/wiki/Here_Comes_Honey_Boo_Boo

Kendall, D. (2011). *Framing class: Media representations of wealth and poverty in America.* Lanham, MD: Rowman & Littlefield.

Kondolojy, A. (2012, August 30). Wednesday cable ratings: *Here Comes Honey Boo Boo* wins night, + FOX RNC coverage, *Storage Wars Texas*, *Royal Pains*, *American Hoggers*, *Daily Show* & more. Retrieved from http://tvbythenumbers.zap2it.com/2012/08/30/wednesday-cable-ratings-here-comes-honey-boo-boo-wins-night-fox-rnc-coverage-storage-wars-texas-royal-pains-american-hoggers-daily-show-more/146753/

Kondolojy, A. (2013, September 12). Wednesday cable ratings: *Duck Dynasty* Wins Night + *Modern Dads*, *Here Comes Honey Boo Boo*, *Royal Pains*, *The Challenge: Rivals* II & more. Retrieved from http://tvbythenumbers.zap2it.com/2013/09/12/wednesday-cable-ratings-duck-dynasty-wins-night-modern-dads-here-comes-honey-boo-boo-royal-pains-the-challenge-rivals-ii-more/202249/

Lee, M. J., & Moscowitz, L. (2013). The "rich bitch." *Feminist Media Studies*, *13*(1), 64–82. doi: 10.1080/14680777.2011.647971.

Mazzarella, S. R. (2008). Men, media, and machines: Fabricating masculinities in *American Chopper*. *Popular Communication: International Journal of Media and Culture*, *6*(2), 68–84. doi: 10.1080/15405700801977434.

Owen, A. S., Stein, S. R., & Vande Berg, L. R. (2007). *Bad girls: Cultural politics and media representations of transgressive women*. New York, NY: Peter Lang.

Ringrose, J., & Walkerdine, V. (2008). Regulating the abject: The TV make-over as site of neo-liberal reinvention toward bourgeois femininity. *Feminist Media Studies*, *8*(3), 227–246.

Rowe, K. (1997). *The unruly woman: Gender and genres of laughter*. Austin, TX: University of Texas Press.

Sieczkowski, C. (2012, October 19). Lee Thompson, Honey Boo Boo's "Uncle Poodle" talks about being gay in the south for spirit day. Retrieved from http://www.huffingtonpost.com/2012/10/19/lee-thompson-honey-boo-boo-uncle-poodle-gay-in-the-south_n_1988820.html

Steeves, H. L. (2008). Commodifying Africa on U.S. network reality television. *Communication, Culture & Critique*, *1*, 416–446. doi: 10.1111/j.1753-9137.2008.00033.x.

Tremlett, A. (2013). Demotic or demonic? Race, class and gender in "gypsy" reality TV. *The Sociological Review*, *62*, 316–334. doi: 10.1111/1467-954X.12134.

Walters, S. D., & Harrison, L. (2014). Not ready to make nice: Aberrant mothers in contemporary culture. *Feminist Media Studies*, *14*(1), 38–55, doi:10.1080/14680777.2012.742919.

Winslow, L. (2010). Comforting the comfortable: *Extreme Makeover Home Edition*'s ideological conquest. *Critical Studies in Media Communication*, *27*(3), 267–290.

# 8. *"Save Your Tears for Your Pillow": Tough Love and the Mothering Double Bind in* Dance Moms

By Stephanie L. Gomez

In July 2014, Debra Harrell, a mother of a nine-year-old girl in South Carolina, was arrested for leaving her child to play by herself in a park while she worked at a nearby McDonald's (Wallace, 2014). Unable to afford child-care, but in need of a job, Harrell felt she had no choice but to leave her daughter alone. People responded to Harrell's arrest with a mixture of outrage at Harrell's negligence and sympathy for her circumstances, yet despite the myriad discourses surrounding Harrell and her arrest, one thing remained clear: Harrell's ability to be a "good" mother was either being questioned or defended; indeed, the entire outcry surrounding the incident centered on what it means to be a "good" or "bad" mother. Mothers are in the media perhaps more now than ever before, from Harrell to Nicole Gainey, a mother in Florida who allowed her seven-year-old son to walk to the park on his own (Schmidt, 2014), to Shanesha Taylor, a mother in Arizona who left her two young children in a locked car while attending an interview for a job she desperately needed (Grinberg, 2014). Motherhood, and what qualifies someone to be a "good" mother, is at the forefront of U.S. consciousness, and is seemingly constantly debated in the media.

The debate over motherhood has been occurring for some time. Akass (2012) discusses the so-called "Mommy Wars," a cultural phenomenon that places women in competition with one another. Working mothers are castigated for not focusing on their children enough, whereas stay-at-home mothers are accused of smothering them with too much attention. As Akass aptly notes, women simply cannot "win" when it comes to motherhood; everything they do is scrutinized to the extreme, particularly within the mass media. Motherhood has become a topic of public consumption, with discourses about what it means to be a "good" mother continually circulating through the media.

One such arena in which discourses about mothering and motherhood are depicted is the reality television (RTV) show *Dance Moms*, which is titled after the mothers of a group of dancers at "The Abby Lee Dance Company" (ALDC), a dance studio located in Pittsburgh, Pennsylvania. *Dance Moms* is a site wherein motherhood and mothering are portrayed, negotiated, and performed. Moreover, *Dance Moms* is particularly salient for an interrogation of the mediated depictions of motherhood because of Abby Lee Miller, the owner of ALDC and the dance instructor/choreographer who is featured most often on the show. Miller is known for her unorthodox teaching methods; she yells at children and their parents, insults her young students, who range in age from 6 to 13 years old, and shows a marked lack of compassion. As a proponent of "tough love," Miller is an interesting counterpoint to the nurturing, often overly concerned mothering style shown by her students' mothers, known as the dance moms, who routinely critique the ways that Miller treats their children. Conversely, however, Miller also constructs herself as a surrogate mother to her students, frequently admonishing the dance moms from her perspective for not caring enough about their children's well-being and dance education.

As a reality television program with a central focus on mothering and motherhood, *Dance Moms* is an important site for an interrogation of the ways in which mothers are portrayed and negotiated in popular media. Thus, I analyzed *Dance Moms* with a particular focus on the following questions: (a) How do Miller and the dance moms perform motherhood and articulate what is appropriate behavior for a mother? (b) How does *Dance Moms* contribute to an understanding of what it means to be a "good" or "bad" mother?

In this chapter, I argue that *Dance Moms* presents mothering as a negotiation that is continually redefined; the mothers (including Miller, as a type of surrogate mother) compete to articulate what it means to be a mother. Moreover, all of the mothers are depicted as lacking in mothering skills and capabilities; they are all "bad" mothers regardless, and in spite of, their behavior. In order to further explicate my claim, this chapter proceeds in four sections. First, I draw upon extant literature regarding mediated representations of motherhood. Second, I detail the performance and critical feminist perspectives that frame this study. Third, I further explain the salient features of *Dance Moms*, before proceeding with my analysis. Fourth, I draw conclusions and implications from my analysis.

## *Mothers in the Spotlight: Mediated Representations of Motherhood*

Research on mothering and motherhood has typically focused on what Hays (1996) refers to as "intensive mothering," or the "ideology of child rearing as labor-intensive, emotionally absorbing women's work" (p. 3), which encourages women to sacrifice their own interests, careers, and other relationships in order to devote themselves to their children. This philosophy of intensive motherhood is part of "the new momism," a system of beliefs shored up by a number of assumptions, including:

> The insistence that no woman is truly complete or fulfilled unless she has children, that women remain the best primary caretakers of children, and that to be a remotely decent mother, a woman has to devote her entire physical, psychological, emotional, and intellectual being, 24/7, to her children. (Douglas & Michaels, 2004, p. 4)

This focus on intensive mothering, as a number of scholars (e.g., Chivers Yochim & Silva, 2013; Douglas & Michaels, 2004; Hayden, 2011; Hays, 1996; McCabe, 2012) have argued, places women in an untenable position; they are only apprehended as "good" mothers if they follow culturally appropriate scripts that proscribe any behavior that is not child-centered.

One way in which these discourses of intensive motherhood are circulated is through the media. In fact, much of the research on mediated representations of mothering and motherhood have focused on three specific elements of intensive mothering: (a) the intensive mother as the "good" mother, (b) the transgressive mother as the "bad" mother, and (c) the "good mother/bad mother" dichotomy. Mothers who devote their time and lives to their children, and who display stereotypically feminine mothering behaviors, are often valorized as the "right" type of mother (Chivers Yochim & Silva, 2013; Douglas & Michaels, 2004; Hays, 1996; Lotz, 2006; Lowe, 2003; McCabe, 2012). For instance, Chivers Yochim and Silva (2013) analyzed the representation of Jenny McCarthy in the wake of her criticism of vaccinations. They argued that McCarthy's opposition to a medical discourse displays her "feminine intuition," and positions her as a "good" mother by virtue of her ability to intuitively know, and provide for—at all costs—her child's needs. Similarly, McCabe (2012), in an examination of Sarah Palin's depictions of motherhood, noted that Palin embodied a stereotypically feminine ideal; Palin was presented as a "real" mother, and was subsequently imbued with what McCabe calls a "feminine power," much like McCarthy. In both of these cases, the women managed to live up to some traditionally feminine ideal of motherhood.

Douglas and Michaels (2004) argue that representations of "good" mothers in the media valorize women who are willing to focus all of their time and energy on raising their children. Motherhood is shown as the most important role a woman will ever inhabit, and women are encouraged to fully immerse themselves in that role. Similarly, Lotz (2006) explains how popular television programming often promotes the notion that women are only fulfilled once they become mothers, at which point they should dedicate their lives to their child/ren. D'Amore (2012) focuses on the trope of the "supermom," and claims that women, as portrayed in the media, are supposed to be able to be a real-life superhero, completing seemingly impossible tasks for the benefit of their child/ren.

Another theme of mothering and motherhood in the media is the positioning of women against each other, labeling "good" mothers in opposition to "bad" mothers. Douglas and Michaels (2004) note that the media have "built an interlocking, cumulative image of the dedicated, doting 'mom' versus the delinquent, bad 'mother'" (p. 7). The media thrive on sensationalistic portrayals of mothers, wherein they are placed at either end of an extreme: Either women are overbearing, intense mothers, or detached, delinquent mothers. Simon (2014), in an analysis of news media coverage of mothers who consume alcohol, argues that so-called "drunken mothers" are portrayed as putting their children in grave and imminent danger. For Simon, these portrayals are symptomatic of a national struggle over the definition of femininity and motherhood, with the end result of separating women from each other and creating a dichotomy between "good" and "bad" mothers. Loke, Harp, and Bachmann (2011) also investigate news media; specifically, they analyze coverage of Governors Jane Swift and Sarah Palin. Similar to Simon's (2014) findings, Loke, et al. (2011) discover that the two women are positioned as dichotomous. Swift distanced herself from traditional ideologies of femininity and motherhood, in that her husband was a stay-at-home father and she planned to continue her career in politics; thus, Loke, et al. claim, Swift was denounced as a "bad" mother. Conversely, Palin upheld traditional notions of motherhood, publicly proclaiming that her first, and most important commitment was to her husband and children, and was thus depicted as a better mother than Swift.

Bedor and Tajima (2012) also note that mothers were often divided into "good" and "bad" categories. The authors studied representations of celebrity mothers in *People* magazine, and found that women who were overweight were considered to be worse mothers than those who were thin. Johnston and Swanson (2003) also claim that magazine coverage unfairly separated women into the categories of "good," intensive motherhood and "bad," detached motherhood. By positioning women as opposing types of mothers, the media ignore the ways in which motherhood is more nuanced than a straightforward "good" or "bad."

As mentioned above, images of mothering and motherhood have evolved over time, and, as Abbey (2003) opines, it is disingenuous to label mothers as simply "good" or "bad." Rather, contemporary mediated representations of motherhood are more complicated, showing mothers as complex and embodying a spectrum of both "good" and "bad" characteristics. Moreover, Karlyn (2011) discusses the rise of the transgressive mother, and argues that unruly women, and mothers, serve to productively disrupt stereotypes of "the new momism" and intensive mothering (also see Mazzarella, this volume). Walters and Harrison (2014) argue that in "the last few years" (p. 40) a more complex type of mother has emerged in popular culture: aberrant mothers who do everything "wrong" (e.g., they do not perform stereotypical femininity, often put their children in danger, and act neglectful towards their children). However, Walters and Harrison claim that rather than being vilified as simply the bad mom, these aberrant mothers are valorized in contemporary popular culture. Regardless of this evolution of the portrayal of "bad" mothers, the fact remains that mothers are still often classified as "good" or "bad" in the first place. In this chapter, I attempt to account for the complexity of motherhood, while also recognizing that amid the complexity, women are still often placed in the dichotomy of "bad" and "good" mother.

## *Motherhood on Stage: Performance and Critical Feminist Perspectives*

In order to investigate the representations of mothering and motherhood on *Dance Moms*, I conducted a critical analysis of the show. Specifically, my approach uses both critical performance studies and critical feminist perspectives. In joining these approaches, I align myself with scholars such as Conquergood (1989, 1992, 2002) who advocates the merging of conventional techniques of rhetorical analysis and performance methodologies. While I have not investigated public performances, I do, as Pezzullo (2003) suggests, "emphasize the usefulness of performance theory" (p. 349) for illuminating facets of discourses not readily apparent through a more conventional rhetorical method. This is not to say that performance is not discourse, but rather that discourse is best captured and understood by looking at it as both rhetoric and performance. An important aspect of a critical performance perspective is the recognition that performances are always in and of the body (Conquergood, 1992, 2002; Foster, 1998; Holling & Calafell, 2007;

Madison, 2010). Embodied performance recognizes the interconnectedness of mind/body and the importance of the body in communicating meaning.

A number of scholars (e.g., D'Amore, 2012; Gilbert, 2008; Karlyn, 2011; Waggoner, 2008) have discussed mothering and motherhood as a performance, and used performance perspectives to analyze mothers. Similarly, I argue that the mothers represented in *Dance Moms* perform motherhood with their words, actions, and bodies. Thus, performance theory is a way of gaining deeper understanding of how motherhood is constantly negotiated, created, and (re)presented through the dance moms' and Miller's behaviors.

In addition to a performance perspective, I used a critical feminist approach to analyze the ways in which motherhood is articulated on *Dance Moms* (Dow, 1995, 1996, 2003; Foss, 2004). Dow (1995) explains that feminism can best be understood as feminism(s), and that critics using a feminist approach may have differing goals; however, feminist rhetorical strategies all attempt to "critique the ways in which these contributions [of women] have been and continue to be marginalized" (p. 106). I used a feminist approach not only because the dance moms and Miller are women, but also, more importantly, because I wish to interrogate the ways that their performances of motherhood situate them, politically, as women and mothers. As Press (2012) states, "The return to the romanticization of motherhood and other 'traditionally female' roles, evident in any cursory examination of popular film and literature, obscures—and deems irrelevant—the fact that the way our society has institutionalized the mother role depends on women's constant emotional and physical labor" (p. 122). According to Press, motherhood is inextricably tied to women and stereotypical notions of what it means to be a woman. More specifically, as West (2007) explains, scholars who use critical feminist approaches to study motherhood attempt to "perform a critical intervention into the ... rhetoric of motherhood by calling attention to the ways in which women have negotiated the possibilities and pitfalls of motherhood as a political identity" (p. 363). Thus, I investigated the discourses of motherhood performed within the RTV show *Dance Moms*, using a critical feminist approach, paired with an attendant focus on the ways in which mothering and motherhood are performed on the show vis-à-vis performance theory.

## *The Mothering Double Bind: The Dance Mom Dichotomy*

Premiering in 2011 on *Lifetime*, the reality television show *Dance Moms* focuses on Pittsburgh's Abby Lee Dance Company (ALDC) and follows the lives of the owner, Abby Lee Miller, the children that belong to one of her competitive dance teams, and the children's mothers, or "dance moms"

(*Dance Moms*, n.d.). While it was not immediately popular, as of fall 2014 the show was ending its fourth season, and in its previous third season, "averaged 2.1 million Total Viewers [*sic*] and was the #1 unscripted program in its Tuesday 9–10p time period among Women [*sic*]" (*About Dance Moms*, n.d.). Each episode features the children preparing for an upcoming dance competition, as well as the subsequent competition and aftermath. While episodes are ostensibly about the intense preparation often needed within the world of competitive dance, the television show mostly focuses on the dance moms and their relationships with each other, their children, Miller, and rival dance studios. As is typical with much reality television, *Dance Moms* often features heightened drama, expressions of intense emotion, and conflict between the stars of the show (Dubrofsky, 2009).

In order to conduct my analysis, I viewed the majority of the episodes from the fourth season. Because the fourth season is the most recent at the time of this writing, it is the most representative of contemporary portrayals of mothering and motherhood on the show. Moreover, even though I have only focused on the fourth season of the show, I am familiar with the entirety of seasons one, two, and three. Due to the timing of the end of the season, I was unable to view the final five episodes of the season. In total, I viewed the first 27 episodes of Season Four via Lifetime.com and Amazon. While conducting repeated viewings of each episode, I made extensive notes of the ways in which mothering and motherhood were negotiated and performed. I then reviewed and coded my notes into predominant themes. Overall, I claim that the mothers on *Dance Moms* are represented dichotomously; nonetheless, *all* of the mothers are often considered "bad," regardless of their behaviors and/or mothering style. In the following analysis, I detail the three major dichotomies regarding mothering and motherhood that I discovered during my examination of *Dance Moms*: (a) Emotional mothers behaving badly versus rational professional behavior, (b) Tough love versus nurturing mothers, and (c) Child-centered versus self-centered.

## *Emotional Mothers versus Rational Professional Behavior*

The infamous "Cult of True Womanhood" (Welter, 1966) ascribes the qualities of "piety, purity, submissiveness, and domesticity" to "true" women (p. 152). However, as Roberts (2002) notes, rather than inherent qualities that all women naturally have, true womanhood is constructed as normal by society. Today, although a "true" woman is different than she was in the nineteenth and early- to mid-twentieth centuries, her characteristics are similarly constructed and limiting. Although these ideas of what it means to be a "true" woman are clearly oppressive and limiting for women in general, they are even more so for mothers more specifically. As some scholars (e.g., Johnston & Swanson, 2003; Ladd-Taylor & Umansky, 1998; Loke et al., 2011) have noted, mothers are not expected to behave badly; they are supposed to be rational, dignified, mature, and in control of themselves. That is, to be a "true" mother, one must also be a "true" woman.

However, the dance moms, collectively, are well known for their emotional behavior, lack of dignity, and loss of control, which includes regularly engaging in physical confrontations. Famously among the show's fans, during Season Three, the dance moms traveled to New Orleans for a dance competition. This trip is included in a flashback in Season Four, where Christi reminisces, specifically, about a dramatic fight in which the dance moms engaged while drinking on Bourbon Street. After being shown imbibing copious amounts of alcohol, the mothers make their way down the street, and eventually begin fighting. Their verbal brawl escalates quickly, and leads to two of the moms, Christi and Leslie, violently punching and kicking each other, and pulling each other's hair. Although the other moms quickly intervene, this episode leads to a number of repercussions, including their children being barred from participating in the dance competition. Christi, remembering this fight, admits that she still feels guilty almost a year later. This fight also proves to be indicative of a larger pattern of the moms fighting with, and competing against, each other. For instance, in one episode, the dance moms begin verbally sparring in the front office of the ALDC dance studio. Eventually, they begin a fistfight in the studio, while Abby Lee Miller looks on disapprovingly ("Double the Moms, Double the Trouble," 2014).

In another dramatic and emotional confrontation, one of the dance moms, Kelly, began hitting and pulling Miller's hair in the dressing room after a dance competition ("Big Trouble in the Big Apple," 2014). Although Miller did defend herself, Kelly instigated the conflict, which led to her eventual arrest and prompted her to leave ALDC. Although the aforementioned examples are, perhaps, the most notable examples of physical confrontations, *Dance Moms* depicts the moms as nearly constantly fighting, and occasionally using physical force. Every single episode of the show highlights at least one controversy, with the women battling amongst themselves and members of rival dance studios.

While the dance moms often behave badly on the show, including emotional and violent outbursts, Miller serves as the calm, rational authority figure who disciplines the moms and often castigates them for their "unprofessional" behavior, reminding them that they should, in fact, behave professionally, in a manner that reflects well on ALDC. After the aforementioned fight in

New Orleans, Miller disciplined the moms by prohibiting their children from participating in the upcoming dance competition. After the fight in her dance studio, Miller admonished all of the moms, making them wait outside while she talked to the two who were mainly involved in the fight. In a separate interview about the fight, Miller stated that the fighting moms "are an embarrassment to women, an embarrassment to the Abby Lee Dance Company, an embarrassment to me" and considered pulling their children out of a dance routine as punishment ("Double the Moms, Double the Trouble," 2014). In another instance, Leslie, one of the dance moms, begins yelling about her daughter's shoes while in the audience of a dance competition. Miller, outraged by Leslie's misbehavior, quickly tells her to stop because Leslie "is making the team look bad" ("Two Can Play This Game," 2014).

Indeed, Miller often chastises the moms as if they are children, and thus becomes an ultimate authority and parental figure to the entire cast of *Dance Moms.* Miller, as the owner of ALDC, is positioned as being responsible for the moms' behavior, particularly when the moms are representing the dance group. As such, she serves as a model of the rational, professional, controlled woman, who is tasked with continually reminding the moms that their children will be punished if they do not comport themselves well. For instance, Miller tells Peyton, one of her students (and Leslie's daughter), that she is only allowed to do a solo if Leslie behaves, noting to Peyton that "your mother is being tested" ("Dance Moms Cares Special," 2014).

While Walters and Harrison (2014) claim that transgressive mothers are now being valorized in popular culture, this is clearly not the case in *Dance Moms.* Although there is certainly space for resistance, along with an opportunity for the dance moms to disrupt dominant narratives about feminine docility and compliance, *Dance Moms* implicitly shames the moms for their bad behavior and invokes the trope of the overly emotional, "hysterical" woman, via the highly emotional and volatile dance moms. By positioning Miller as the rational authority figure who routinely calls attention to the inappropriateness of the moms' behaviors, the show functions to discipline women who dare to transgress societal norms, suggesting that women should maintain the ideal of a rational, calm, and professional (read: well-behaved) woman. This is not to say that society at large should celebrate women drinking excessively and punching each other in the middle of the street; however, *Dance Moms* works to silence any expression outside of the norm. The dichotomy of emotional women behaving badly (the dance moms) vis-à-vis rational women in control of themselves and others (Miller) vilifies any performance of motherhood that does not align with the decorum expected of women more generally, and mothers more specifically.

## *Tough Love versus Nurturing Mothers*

However, despite the aforementioned dichotomy, which positions the dance moms as inferior mothers (overly emotional, unprofessional, immature, child-like), particularly when compared to Miller, portrayals of motherhood on *Dance Moms* are further complicated by the performances of tough love and nurturing motherhood on the show. Intensive mothering is often praised as being the "right" type of mothering (Chivers Yochim & Silva, 2013; Douglas & Michaels, 2004; Hays, 1996; Lotz, 2006; Lowe, 2003; McCabe, 2012). Mothers who nurture and sacrifice for their children may be perceived as far better than mothers who exhibit less outwardly affectionate qualities. Indeed, mothers who appear cold, detached, or harsh, known in the popular imaginary as "Tiger Moms," are usually criticized, particularly within the media (Bronstein & Steiner, this volume; Dillaway & Pare, 2013; Douglas & Michaels, 2004; Park, 2014).

Unquestioningly, Miller exhibits qualities of tough love towards her young students. Miller is often castigated by the dance moms and viewers of the show[1] for her cavalier attitude towards her dancers. Perhaps more insidiously, Miller often pits her students against each other. For instance, a reoccurring feature of the show is "the pyramid," which happens at the beginning of each episode. "The pyramid" consists of Miller calling all of the dance moms and dancers into the main dance floor; awaiting them is each dancer's headshot, facing away from the group and arrayed in a pyramid-shape on the mirror. Once everyone arrives in the room, Miller ritualistically unveils each photograph, beginning from the bottom of the pyramid and moving towards the top. In doing so, Miller ranks each dancer, with the worst dancers featured on the bottom of the pyramid, and the best dancer displayed on the very top of the pyramid. As she reveals the pyramid, Miller explains, in detail, how each dancer failed to meet her high expectations, which often causes one or more of the dancers to cry. For instance, during the pyramid portion of one episode, Miller reveals Chloe at the bottom of the pyramid, and notes, "You came in second at the competition. And you know how I feel about second. That's the first to lose" ("Abby-phobic," 2014). In another episode, Miller reveals Kendall at the bottom of the pyramid, and states, "You and Kalani went onstage and got beat by two girls that *never* shared the stage together, that never danced together, but worked their butts off," then continues, "Next on the pyramid: Nia. We've been doing this for four competition seasons. The very first week I corrected you on your legs and your feet. I'm still telling you the same thing" ("Double the Moms, Double the Trouble," 2014). During all of these examples, the camera often pans to the dancers being discussed, who often appear to be holding back tears.

Moreover, Miller's tough love tactics do not end after the pyramid portion of the show. Indeed, Miller often yells at her students during rehearsal, insults their intelligence, and disregards their feelings and injuries. One of Miller's favorite threatening catchphrases is "everyone's replaceable," and it is used often throughout all of the seasons. In one episode, Miller choreographs a group dance, which she entitles "Just Another Number," explicitly telling her dancers that the title was her way of showing them that they are each replaceable and that she has no loyalty towards any of them ("Double the Moms, Double the Trouble," 2014). Another one of Miller's favorite cold-hearted phrases is "save your tears for your pillow," which she yells harshly at her students whenever they start to cry (which they do at least once per episode). Miller proudly states that she does not coddle her students, and that her tough love strategy is what her students need in order to grow as dancers and people. Moreover, Miller often scoffs at the dance moms for what she sees as behavior that will only hurt their children; for instance, when Christy, Sarah's mom, refuses to let Sarah travel to a dance competition without her, Miller states, "she needs to let Sarah be independent and grow," thereby implying that intensive mothering only stifles children.

Despite Miller's arguably noble intentions, she is still depicted as a harsh taskmaster who disregards the fragile feelings of her young students. Conversely, the dance moms are shown as nurturing, loving mothers who are willing to sacrifice time, money, and energy for the good of their children. For instance, Melissa chooses to homeschool her two daughters, so that they can have more time to dance. Although homeschooling is a difficult, labor-intensive choice, Melissa is willing to make the sacrifice in order for her daughters to progress as dancers. This choice is routinely valorized by the other dance moms, who express their desire to homeschool their own children (even though their children often remind the dance moms they do not actually wish to be homeschooled). The sacrificial ideal for mothers is further upheld when Jill, one of the dance moms, decides to get a long-overdue mammogram ("Dance Moms Cares Special," 2014). Although Jill admits that she does not want to undergo the medical procedure, she repeatedly states that she needs to "do it for her family." Of course, this is not to say that Jill should not have gotten the mammogram; however, her framing of what was ultimately a challenging ordeal, due to Jill's apprehension, as for the good of her family completely obfuscates her own anxieties, needs, and health, positioning Jill as only being useful if she is healthy enough to serve her husband and children, a frequent representation of mothering and motherhood within recent media coverage (Dubriwny, 2013).

In other instances, the dance moms display their nurturing qualities by comforting their daughters after Miller has yelled at them; Holly reassures a crying Nia in the bathroom ("Wingman Down," 2014), Christi gives a crying Chloe a motivational speech ("Nothing's Fair in Abbyville," 2014), Jill comforts a crying Kendall ("No Solo for You," 2014), and the entire group of moms nurtures their children after a crushing loss at a dance competition ("Double the Moms, Double the Trouble," 2014). Overall, the moms are shown as nurturing, protective, and loving, which, particularly as juxtaposed to Miller's brusque demeanor, suggests that nurturing children is the "right" way to mother them.

## *Child-Centered versus Self-Centered*

A final dichotomy within *Dance Moms* is related to intensive mothering. One hallmark of intensive mothering is the complete sacrifice of one's very identity for the good of one's children (Douglas & Michaels, 2004). However, while the dance moms display many characteristics of intensive mothering, including being supportive and nurturing, they fail to completely obviate their own desires and lives. For instance, the moms are often depicted drinking considerable amounts of alcohol at various bars, leaving their children at dance competitions by themselves. As Simon (2014) notes, the media often discipline so-called "drunken mothers" for their negligent behavior (also see Dubriwny, this volume), and *Dance Moms* aligns with this contention. The moms, when drinking, typically do not know where their children are or how they are doing, and are only concerned with enjoying themselves; Miller criticizes this behavior, who points out that dance competitions should be about their children's growth rather than their own enjoyment.

Miller also notes what she perceives as the moms' failure to take their children's dance education seriously. For instance, Miller castigates Jill for failing to take her daughter, Kendall, to a mandatory summer rehearsal ("Guess Who's Coming to the Dance," 2014), and tells Christi that her daughter, Chloe, has to stop missing so many classes ("Nothing's Fair in Abbyville," 2014). In fact, when Christi replies that she has taken Chloe to every required dance class, Miller retorts that maybe Chloe is "going in the back to meet up with some boy" instead of coming to class, implying that Christi has no control over her daughter and is too involved with her own life to make sure that Chloe is attending class.

In contrast to these negligent moms, Miller emerges as a more responsible mother figure. She regularly tells her favorite student, Maddie, how much she loves her and that she would raise her if she could, thus insinuating that Maddie's own mother, Melissa, is unfit. Moreover, in one episode, Miller gives a speech to her students, where she explains that there are a million jobs that dance teachers can do, but they (and Miller herself) choose to teach dance because they love children ("Family Comes First," 2014). In another episode, Miller gives her students an inspiring motivational speech prior to a dance performance, encouraging them to do their best and have a good time on stage ("Nothing's Fair in Abbyville," 2014). Despite Miller's rough manner of behaving towards her students, she does regularly affirm her love for teaching dance and for children, and points out how her love and concern for the children is better than the negligent behavior of their moms. In fact, after a mom forced her daughter to quit ALDC, Miller states that she's glad the mom left because "I certainly don't want a kid whose mother chooses her boyfriend over her own child" ("Guess Who's Coming to the Dance," 2014). Here, Miller explicitly expresses her belief in intensive mothering, and her anger towards a mother who was unwilling to sacrifice a romantic relationship for the "good" of her child.

Moreover, Miller often teaches her students valuable life lessons through her dance choreography, which grapples with issues such as homelessness, poverty, and breast cancer. Because the moms are often shown attempting to avoid these issues, it is particularly salient that Miller fulfills a role that her students' biological moms are not willing to inhabit. Rather than display the valorized qualities of intensive mothering, the dance moms often appear negligent and incompetent, particularly when compared to Miller's desire to help her students succeed as dancers and as people.

## *Curtain Call: Conclusions and Implications*

Motherhood within *Dance Moms* is portrayed as dichotomous, positioning women as either (a) out of control and immature, or in control and composed; (b) tough and uncaring, or nurturing and loving; and (c) attuned to the children's needs, or largely self-absorbed. These three themes, taken together, complicate the "good-bad" mothering dichotomy exemplified in each theme. That is, Miller is portrayed as rational (good), tough and harsh (bad), and child-centered (good), while the dance moms are portrayed as emotional (bad), nurturing (good), and self-centered (bad). Ultimately, Miller, the surrogate mother who functions as the show's alpha mom, "wins," in that she is more often portrayed as a good mother as juxtaposed with the dance moms; however, all of the portrayals of mothering and motherhood are simultaneously complicated.

*Dance Moms* presents mothering as a negotiation that is continually redefined; the moms compete to articulate what it means to be a mother through their performance of motherhood. The mothers embody the often schizophrenic conceptions of women and motherhood circulating in contemporary culture; that is, women are told to be nurturing but not smothering, to help children become independent but not through tough love, and to be "good" women and mothers (e.g., child-centered) while simultaneously having their own identities (read as self-centered). Moreover, regardless of their behavior, all of the mothers are depicted as lacking in mothering skills and capabilities; they are all "bad" mothers regardless of, and in spite of, their behavior. Simultaneously, however, the mothers are positioned as "good"; that is, for instance, the dance moms are portrayed as protective and loving ("good"), but also *too* protective at times ("bad") and absent at other times ("bad"). It appears that there is some standard of maternal "goodness" that all of the moms either exceed or fall short of, often at the same time.

This analysis has two important implications for the ways in which mothering is understood and portrayed in the media. First, being a transgressive mother is criticized, rather than valorized, throughout *Dance Moms.* Moms who perform in an unruly manner are categorized as "bad" mothers, as opposed to some mothering ideal of docility. As both women and mothers, dance moms are continually disciplined into appropriate modes of behavior; when they do not adhere to "appropriate" behavior, they are shamed and punished. This suggests that despite continually changing understandings of what it means to be a mother, there are still societal norms that discipline women to be stereotypically feminine, well-behaved moms.

Second, however, the portrayals of motherhood in *Dance Moms* refuse such a straightforward conclusion. That is, while stereotypical notions of what it means to be a mother (e.g., nurturing, affectionate, and, above all, sacrificial) *are* upheld, these discourses are complicated through a simultaneous repudiation of intensive mothering. That is, all of the mothers are depicted as caring about children, even though none of the mothers completely uphold intensive mothering. However, at the same time, while all of the mothers show caring towards their children, caring is specified in "right" and "wrong" ways, with Miller ultimately serving as the judge of the "correct" way to care about children. This contradictory ethos apparent in the show both upholds and unravels the ideology of intensive mothering, pointing out both its failures and more positive attributes. Perhaps these moms are "bad," but their failures, rather than shoring up intensive mothering as an ideal, point to a more complicated understanding of what it means to be a "good" mother. Although *Dance Moms* does have a disciplinary impulse that encourages women to behave, it also presents intriguing possibilities for understanding motherhood as a complicated, difficult role that is always being negotiated.

Of course, this analysis is limited in that it only focuses on one season of one show, whereas a number of portrayals of motherhood are being circulated through mainstream contemporary media. As Lotz (2006) argues, with the proliferation of representations of women and mothers in contemporary media, each series must be considered relative to other series. However, despite the inherent limits to this single analysis, it does bring to light the competing discourses of mothering and motherhood at play in contemporary media, particularly since *Dance Moms* often positions Miller and the dance moms as opposite in terms of mothering style. This series, then, serves as a microcosm of competing motherhood discourses and the ways they are negotiated within the media.

## Note

1. *Dance Moms* has a broad online following, with audience members responding to the show on blogs, episode reviews, and Twitter. While I have read many of the online content surrounding the show, it is not part of this analysis.

## References

Abbey, S. M. (2003). Deconstructing images of mothering in media and film: Possibilities and trends for the future. *Journal of the Motherhood Initiative for Research and Community Involvement*, *5*(1), 7–23.

Abby-phobic. (2014, August 19). *Dance Moms*. Lifetime. Retrieved February 1, 2015, from http://www.mylifetime.com/shows/dance-moms/video/season-4/episode-24/abby-phobic

About *Dance Moms*—Official Site. (n.d.). Retrieved January 31, 2014, from http://www.mylifetime.com/shows/dance-moms/about

Akass, K. (2012). Motherhood and myth-making: Dispatches from the frontline of the US mommy wars. *Feminist Media Studies*, *12*(1), 137–141.

Bedor, E., & Tajima, A. (2012). No fat moms! Celebrity mothers' weight-loss narratives in *People* magazine. *Journal of Magazine & New Media Research*, *13*(2), 1–26.

Big trouble in the big apple. (2014, February 11). *Dance Moms*. Lifetime. Retrieved August 1, 2014, from http://www.mylifetime.com/shows/dance-moms/video/just-added-full-episodes/season-4/episode-7/big-trouble-in-the-big-apple

Chivers Yochim, E., & Silva, V. T. (2013). Everyday expertise, autism, and "good" mothering in the media discourse of Jenny McCarthy. *Communication and Critical/Cultural Studies*, *10*(4), 406–426.

Conquergood, D. (1989). Poetics, play, process, and power: The performative turn in anthropology. *Text and Performance Quarterly*, *9*, 82–95.

Conquergood, D. (1992). Ethnography, rhetoric, and performance. *Quarterly Journal of Speech, 78*, 80–123.

Conquergood, D. (2002). Performance studies: Interventions and radical research. *The Drama Review, 46*(2), 145–156.

D'Amore, L. M. (2012). The accidental supermom: Superheroines and maternal performativity, 1963–1980. *The Journal of Popular Culture, 45*(6), 1226–1248.

*Dance Moms.* (n.d.). Retrieved January 1, 2014, from http://www.imdb.com/title/tt1991410/?ref_=nv_sr_1

*Dance Moms* cares special. (2014, January 13). Lifetime. Retrieved August 1, 2014, from http://www.mylifetime.com/shows/dance-moms/video/season-4/episode-3/dance-moms-cares-special?cmpid=MRSS_Hulu_MYL

Dillaway, H. E., & Pare, E. R. (2013). A campaign for good motherhood? Exploring media discourse on Sarah Palin, Hillary Clinton, and Michelle Obama during the 2008 presidential election campaign. In M. H. Kohlman, D. B. Krieg, & B. J. Dickerson (Eds.), *Notions of family: Intersectional perspectives (advances in gender reasearch)* (Vol. 17, pp. 209–239). Bingley, UK: Emerald Group Publishing Limited.

Double the moms, double the trouble. (2014, July 29). *Dance Moms.* Lifetime. Retrieved August 1, 2014, from http://www.mylifetime.com/shows/dance-moms/video/season-4/episode-21/double-the-moms-double-the-trouble?cmpid=MRSS_Hulu_MYL

Douglas, S. J., & Michaels, M. W. (2004). *The mommy myth: The idealization of motherhood and how it has undermined women.* New York, NY: Free Press.

Dow, B. J. (1995). Feminism, difference(s), and rhetorical studies. *Communication Studies, 46*(1–2), 106–117.

Dow, B. J. (1996). *Prime-time feminism: Television, media culture, and the women's movement since 1970.* Philadelphia, PA: University of Pennsylvania Press.

Dow, B. J. (2003). Feminism, Miss America, and media mythology. *Rhetoric & Public Affairs, 6*(1), 127–149.

Dubriwny, T. N. (2013). *The vulnerable empowered woman: Feminism, postfeminism, and women's health.* New Brunswick, NJ: Rutgers University Press.

Dubrofsky, R. E. (2009). Fallen women in reality TV: A pornography of emotion. *Feminist Media Studies, 9*(3), 353–368.

Family comes first. (2014, April 1). *Dance Moms.* Lifetime. Retrieved August 1, 2014, from http://www.amazon.com/45-Second-Solos/dp/B00H9N24U0/ref=sr_1_1?ie=UTF8&qid=1412205771&sr=8-1&keywords=dance+moms

Foss, S. K. (2004). Feminist criticism. In *Rhetorical criticism: Exploration and practice* (pp. 151–191). Long Grove, IL: Waveland.

Foster, S. L. (1998). Choreographies of gender. *Signs, 24*(1), 1–33.

Gilbert, J. (2008). Why I feel guilty all the time: Performing academic motherhood. *Women's Studies in Communication, 31*(2), 203–208.

Grinberg, E. (2014, August 7). When justice is "merciful" in child abuse cases. Retrieved September 27, 2014, from http://www.cnn.com/2014/08/07/living/shanesha-taylor-plea-deal/index.html

Guess who's coming to the dance. (2014, January 1). *Dance Moms.* Lifetime. Retrieved August 1, 2014, from http://www.amazon.com/45-Second-Solos/dp/B00H9N24U0/ref=sr_1_1?ie=UTF8&qid=1412205771&sr=8-1&keywords=dance+moms

Hayden, S. (2011). Constituting savvy aunties: From childless women to child-focused consumers. *Women's Studies in Communication, 34*(1), 1–19. http://doi.org/10.1080/07491409.2011.566531

Hays, S. (1996). *The cultural contradictions of motherhood.* New Haven, CT: Yale University Press.

Holling, M. A., & Calafell, B. M. (2007). Identities on stage and staging identities: ChicanoBrujo performances as emancipatory practices. *Text and Performance Quarterly, 27*(1), 58–83. http://doi.org/10.1080/10462930601046053

Johnston, D. D., & Swanson, D. H. (2003). Invisible mothers: A content analysis of motherhood ideologies and myths in magazines. *Sex Roles, 49*(1–2), 21–33.

Karlyn, K. R. (2011). *Unruly girls, unrepentant mothers: Redefining feminism on screen.* Austin, TX: University of Texas Press.

Ladd-Taylor, M., & Umansky, L. (1998). *"Bad" mothers: The politics of blame in twentieth-century America.* New York, NY: New York University Press.

Loke, J., Harp, D., & Bachmann, I. (2011). Mothering and governing: How news articulated gender roles in the cases of governors Jane Swift and Sarah Palin. *Journalism Studies, 12*(2), 205–220.

Lotz, A. D. (2006). *Redesigning women: Television after the network era.* Champaign, IL: University of Illinois Press.

Lowe, M. (2003). Colliding feminisms: Britney Spears, "tweens," and the politics of reception. *Popular Music and Society, 26*(2), 123–140.

Madison, D. S. (2010). *Acts of activism: human rights as radical performance.* New York, NY: Cambridge University Press.

McCabe, J. (2012). States of confusion: Sarah Palin and the politics of US mothering. *Feminist Media Studies, 12*(1), 149–153.

No solo for you. (2014, March 4). *Dance Moms.* Lifetime. Retrieved August 1, 2014, from http://www.amazon.com/45-Second-Solos/dp/B00H9N24U0/ref=sr_1_1?ie=UTF8&qid=1412205771&sr=8-1&keywords=dance+moms

Nothing's fair in Abbyville. (2014, February 26). *Dance Moms.* Lifetime. Retrieved August 1, 2014, from http://www.mylifetime.com/shows/dance-moms/video/season-4/episode-23/three-soloists-one-star?cmpid=MRSS_Hulu_MYL

Park, A. (2014, May 5). The tiger mom effect is real, says large study. Retrieved May 14, 2015, from http://time.com/88125/the-tiger-mom-effect-is-real-says-large-study/

Pezzullo, P. C. (2003). Touring "cancer alley," Louisiana: Performances of community and memory for environmental justice. *Text and Performance Quarterly, 23*(3), 226–252.

Press, A. L. (2012). The price of motherhood: Feminism and cultural bias. *Communication, Culture & Critique, 5*(1), 120–125. http://doi.org/10.1111/j.1753-9137.2011.01121.x

Roberts, M. L. (2002). True womanhood revisited. *Journal of Women's History, 14*(1), 150–155.

Schmidt, C. (2014, August 1). Florida mom arrested after letting 7-year-old walk to the park alone. Retrieved September 27, 2014, from http://www.cnn.com/2014/07/31/living/florida-mom-arrested-son-park/index.html

Simon, J. M. (2014). Disciplining drunken mothers: Media representations of women's use of alcohol. *The Communication Review, 17*(1), 45–64.

Two can play this game. (2014, January 7). *Dance Moms.* Lifetime. Retrieved August 1, 2014, from http://www.amazon.com/45-Second-Solos/dp/B00H9N24U0/ref=sr_1_1?ie=UTF8&qid=1412205771&sr=8-1&keywords=dance+moms

Waggoner, C. E. (2008). Academic adultery: Surreptitious performances of the professor/mother. *Women's Studies in Communication, 31*(2), 209–212.

Wallace, K. (2014, July 21). Mom arrested for leaving 9-year-old alone at park. Retrieved September 27, 2014, from http://www.cnn.com/2014/07/21/living/mom-arrested-left-girl-park-parents/index.html

Walters, S. D., & Harrison, L. (2014). Not ready to make nice: Aberrant mothers in contemporary culture. *Feminist Media Studies, 14*(1), 38–55.

Welter, B. (1966). The cult of true womanhood: 1820–1860. *American Quarterly, 18*(2), 151–174.

West, I. (2007). Performing resistance in/from the kitchen: The practice of maternal pacifist politics and La WISP's cookbooks. *Women's Studies in Communication, 30*(3), 358–383.

Wingman down. (2014, February 18). *Dance Moms.* Lifetime. Retrieved August 1, 2014, from http://www.mylifetime.com/shows/dance-moms/video/season-4/episode-23/three-soloists-one-star?cmpid=MRSS_Hulu_MYL

# 9. *"I Forgot How It Was to Be Normal": Decompensating the Binary of Good/Bad Motherhood*

By Beth L. Boser

Motherhood is a form of mental illness, according to Judith Warner's (2005) bestselling book. Unfolding like a re-imagined *Feminine Mystique*, the book surveys the state of motherhood in the United States and finds that the most apt metaphor for "The Mess" of contemporary anxiety-ridden mothering is "perfect madness." Of course, this popular tome is certainly not the first to offer a critique of the cultural expectations of modern-day motherhood; indeed, the pervasiveness and the problematics of the ideology of intensive mothing are well documented (e.g., Hays, 1996; Douglas & Michaels, 2004). Drawing upon these, and other, prior works, this chapter offers an examination of mediated motherhood wherein mental illness is more than a metaphor (see Hatfield, this volume, for a discussion of mental illness and pregnancy). Specifically, I examine two documentary films centering on a mother diagnosed with a form of schizophrenia. Jonathan Caouette's *Tarnation* (2004) and *Walk Away Renee* (2012) offer accounts of the filmmaker's experiences and relationship with his mother Renee LeBlanc. Both films invite viewers into the complex relationship between Renee and Jonathan. Furthermore, in doing so, both offer depictions of transgressive motherhood.

Scholars argue that media depictions of women who transgress the dominant ideological norms of "good" motherhood—and its ever-present counterpart, "proper" femininity—perpetuate and reinforce established ideals of the same. Such depictions do so by presenting a starkly different and obviously "bad" picture of motherhood and femininity, and punishing the transgressors for their misdeeds (e.g., Douglas & Michaels, 2004; Thomas,

2012). At the same time, media depictions of mental illness may stigmatize (Signorielli, 1989), perpetuate stigma (Klin & Lemish, 2008) and reinforce the ideal of normality (Smith, 1999) by portraying the obviously "abnormal" in spectacular ways. In contrast to these analyses, I posit that the portrayals of Renee offer an alternative to this undoubtedly prominent "support the norm by portraying its opposite" phenomenon on both accounts. In other words, while the films certainly present examples of behaviors and actions that would—upon cursory examination—widely be understood as examples of "bad" mothering and "abnormal" mental states, they do so in a way that serves a more complex purpose than reinforcing the "good" or the "normal" in either case.

*Tarnation* and *Walk Away Renee* document Jonathan Caouette's experiences with and without his mother, Renee, who is diagnosed with schizoaffective disorder and acute bipolar disorder. From the intersection of Renee's two intense and artfully depicted roles—as a loving mother and a woman struggling to engage the world—emerges a novel depiction of transgressive motherhood. The portrayal of Renee, I argue, does not uphold the "good" and the "normal" by depicting their opposite. Instead, the films rhetorically "decompensate" the good/bad mother binary, thereby troubling the foundation upon which such opposing depictions rest. The term "decompensate" is drawn from *Walk Away Renee*, wherein it describes the unravelling of Renee's mental stability. In clinical contexts, it refers to a loss of psychological balance, or a physiological deterioration of a system. Put another way, psychological decompensation is what happens when a person who has been taking steps to "compensate" for some sort of perceived abnormality or insufficiency is no longer able to hold it all together (Kraynak, 2011). In terms of this analysis, decompensation is an apt metaphor for the ways in which the two films work within and against the firmly entrenched ideological "balance" between good and bad motherhood. Through a multifaceted rhetorical strategy of multivocality, depicted in both substantive and stylistic ways, the films break down the established system of ideal intensive motherhood. To do so, they acknowledge the good/bad mother binary, then systemically pull it apart, creating space to build up a relationship of mutual mothering in its place. To unpack this argument, the remainder of the essay will proceed as follows: first, I describe *Tarnation* and *Walk Away Renee*; second, I consider prior work centering on the ideology of motherhood; third, I offer an explanation of multivocality; fourth, I analyze both films to demonstrate how each rhetorically decompensates the good/bad mother binary; finally, I offer some concluding thoughts on decompensated mothering.

## *The Films*

Neither *Tarnation* nor its follow-up *Walk Away Renee* take the form of "traditional" documentary films. An IMDb synopsis claims *Tarnation* is, "part documentary, part narrative fiction, part home movie, and part acid trip" (Varma, n.d.). *Tarnation* is largely comprised of footage Jonathan shot himself, beginning at age eleven, and *Walk Away Renee* has a significant amount of such footage as well. As a boy, Jonathan began documenting interactions with his mother and grandparents, as well as personal reflections on his own identity and sexuality. *Tarnation* begins as Jonathan receives news that his mother, then under the care of her own mentally-fading father, has accidentally overdosed on lithium. The film is a bricolage of Super-8 home movies, photographs, clips of iconic 1980s pop culture, recorded answering machine messages, video diaries, and psychedelic visual effects. *Walk Away Renee* picks up several years later, with Jonathan's realization that his mother is not receiving adequate treatment at her assisted living facility—she is being administered the wrong medication and is miserable. This film—while it employs some of the same intertextual features as the first—is more directly focused on a present day mother-son road trip, as Jonathan brings Renee across-country with him in hopes of securing better treatment for her near his own home. Both films flash between past and present, offering rich, yet fragmented, views of the fraught relationship between mother and son.

Amidst the fragments, Renee's narrative is composed. Her life began in the 1950s in a conventional way. She was the only child of heterosexual, married, White parents, living in a small town outside Houston, Texas. The family business—a small grocery store—provided for all. At the age of twelve, Renee fell off the roof of her house and sustained a serious injury which temporarily paralyzed her. After a few months of paralysis, her parents consented to electroshock treatments, believing the injury to be "all in her head" (Caouette, 2004). She received these treatments twice a week for two years, after which, "she began to suffer from severe psychosis" (Caouette, 2012). In the early 1970s, Renee met Steve Caouette. The two were quickly married, but only remained together for a very short period of time. Renee gave birth to Jonathan in 1973, by which time her husband was already gone. Renee was given more shock treatments, and was in and out of various institutions for the entirety of Jonathan's youth. By the time she was thirty-four years old, Renee had been treated in psychiatric facilities more than one hundred times (Caouette, 2004; Caouette, 2012).

In their depictions of this story, and its consequences, the films are incredibly complex in both message and meaning. A good deal of this complexity is, unfortunately, outside the scope of the present essay. Both films, for example, offer critiques of the United States mental health system and practices of institutionalization; and both films—*Tarnation* in particular—are studies in innovative and unconventional filmmaking. Although these themes certainly are not irrelevant to the present essay, my objective is to highlight what the films have to tell viewers about motherhood outside the social norm. To accomplish this, it is important to first explain previous scholarly work on the ideology of motherhood.

## *The Ideology of Motherhood*

In her landmark critical feminist analysis of motherhood, Rich (1986) presented two different "meanings of motherhood, one superimposed on the other: the *potential relationship* of any woman to her power of reproduction and to children; and the *institution*, which aims at ensuring that that potential—and all women—shall remain under male control" (p. 13). Thus, Rich noted that motherhood is both an oppressive patriarchal ideology and a potentially empowering experience. In another landmark study, Hays (1996) elaborated on the institutional features of motherhood within what she terms the "ideology of intensive mothering" (p. 9). O'Reilly (2004a) further explored this ideology, and renamed it "sacrificial mothering" (p. 14). Douglas and Michaels (2004) built upon Hays and termed media depictions of the ideology of intensive mothering "the new momism" (p. 4). O'Brien Hallstein (2010, 2011) analyzed the rhetorical construction and influence of the ideology. The ideology of intensive mothering—the ideal "good" motherhood—is woven into "our national common sense" (Douglas & Michaels, 2004, p. 9); it is, while "not followed in practice by every mother ... understood as the *proper* approach to the raising of a child" (Hays, 1996, p. 9).

Drawing from this prior work, it appears that "good" mothers must fulfill several requirements. They must be the primary caregivers to their children, and they must give this care constantly. In doing so, they must bestow "copious amounts of time, energy, and material resources" on their children (Hays, 1996, p. 8). A good mother must always put her children's needs ahead of her own, and seek instruction from experts to be the best mother possible. She must be "fully satisfied, fulfilled, completed and composed in motherhood" (O'Reilly, 2004a, p. 14; O'Reilly, 2010, p. 369). Good mothers are happy; they smile and laugh; and they selflessly nurture. A good mother must "devote her entire physical, psychological, emotional, and intellectual being, 24/7, to her children" (Douglas & Michaels, 2004, p. 4). At the same time, a good mother must maintain her body according to prevailing standards of feminine beauty (O'Brien Hallstein, 2011). Furthermore, this ideology is heteronormative, middle-class, and saturated with Whiteness (Addison, Goodwin-Kelly, & Roth, 2009; Douglas & Michaels, 2004; Martínez Guillem & Flores, this volume). To this, I would add that the ideology presumes able-bodiedness and mental health-normativity as well.

The ideology of "good" motherhood is created and reinforced through unattainable images of perfection in media. At the same time, it is also supported through media depictions of its opposite—"bad" motherhood. The bad mothers are, unsurprisingly, portrayed as villains. They are cold, uncaring, neglectful, and even murderous women, images of whom would be abhorred by any good mother (Douglas & Michaels, 2004). According to Douglas and Michaels, the media's "parade of maternal delinquents reinforce[s] an increasingly narrow norm of acceptable behavior that help[s] ... to standardize the rules of the new momism" (p. 170). Through media, the ideology of good motherhood and its necessary good/bad mother dichotomy is crafted and maintained. Indeed, as Addison, Goodwin-Kelly, and Roth (2009) note, media offer a "limited repertoire of maternal portrayals" wherein "mothers are repeatedly demonized or deified" (p. 4).

To counter this, Addison, Goodwin-Kelly, and Roth (2009) note that some independent films complicate this demonized/deified binary. They call for more scholarly writing devoted to "spotlighting and examining alternatives" to such limited portrayals (p. 7). At the same time, O'Reilly (2004b), drawing upon Rich (1986), argues that, while "motherhood" as an institution is a site of patriarchal oppression, "mothering" as a practice can be empowering. Thus, she claims, women need to "mother against motherhood" (p. 161). It is here where this essay enters the conversation—by examining two films that offer an important alternative to the limited representations of motherhood still seen across the majority of popular media, through their depictions of a "mothering" relationship.

## *Rhetorical Multivocality*

Rhetorical multivocality, such as that depicted in *Tarnation* and *Walk Away Renee*, offers an alternative to the either/or representations identified and critiqued in previous work. The concept of "multivoicedness" or "polyphony"—drawn from the work of Bakhtin (1984)—is a useful tool for analyzing complex, multilayered artifacts. Polyphony is characterized by a "plurality of independent and unmerged voices and consciousnesses" (Bakhtin, 1984, p. 6). These unmerged voices may manifest as different characters in opposition to one another or within a single character. In contrast to homophonic texts, wherein stable, unified characters exist "against the clearly defined background of a single-tiered world" (p. 17), in polyphonic texts characters and worlds are not collapsible into a single piece. Thus, viewed from a homophonic perspective, polyphony "may seem a chaos" (p. 8) wherein "everything that seem[s] simple" becomes "complex and multi-structured" (p. 30).

Polyphonic characters and ideas resist categorization within other analytical constructs. For example, polyphony is not the same as dialectic—it does not present opposing thesis and antithesis for purposes of merging into synthesis (pp. 9, 30). Polyphony resists synthesis; instead, multiple juxtaposed voices exist at the same time and are not collapsible. In Bakhtin's words, characters must "converse with [their] own double" (p. 28). Furthermore, this resistance to synthesis coincides with a resistance to develop and evolve along a linear plotline. According to Bakhtin, polyphonic characters and ideas do not evolve; in other words, they do not grow and develop across the perpetual motion of linear time. Rather, polyphony is characterized by "*co-existence* and *interaction*" (p. 28, emphasis in original). All things are "side by side and simultaneous, as if they existed in space and not time" (p. 28). Importantly, Bakhtin contends that true polyphony contains "an assumption of *equal rights* for simultaneously existing, experiencing persons" (p. 37). The multiple voices and consciousnesses do not exist in hierarchical relation to one another. Instead, they all inhabit "one plane, as standing alongside or opposite one another" (p. 30).

Polyphony is a felicitous concept for an analysis of schizophrenic motherhood. The complex layering of voices and affects depicted in the films to be examined here, and undoubtedly across many depictions and discourses of schizophrenia, resist unified, stable, homophonic characterizations. Indeed, according to a psychiatrist who authored the book sometimes termed the "schizophrenia bible" (e.g., Jaffe, 2014; "Recommended Readings," 2009), people diagnosed with schizophrenia are said to experience several interwoven phenomena. These include: alterations in sense perception, including over-acuteness of visual and/or auditory senses; difficulty interpreting, synthesizing, and responding to stimuli; experiences of delusional ideas; visual and/or auditory hallucinations; and alterations in sense of self, including an inability to distinguish between the self and interlocutors and/or the self and the rest of the world (Torrey, 2013). Polyphony, like schizophrenia, resists monolithic and stable meanings and understandings. Here, I hope to demonstrate that mothering may do so as well.

In the following sections, I explore the rhetorical multivocality of mediated schizophrenic motherhood by analyzing the portrayal of Renee and her relationship with her child in *Tarnation* and *Walk Away Renee*. The two films, taken together, rhetorically decompensate the good/bad mother binary in several steps. First, they acknowledge the ideology of good motherhood and proper femininity; indeed, decompensation necessitates recognition of an ideal, a "normal," that one may attempt to achieve through various means of "compensation." Then, they posit and express, in a variety of ways, the instability and falsity of these ideals. Finally, they demonstrate how this instability offers opportunities for a more desirable relationship of mutual mothering to be built up in place of the traditional binary. In the sections that follow, I provide analysis and elaboration of each of these steps.

## Tarnation: *Establishing Multivocal Motherhood*

Multivocal motherhood is depicted, in *Tarnation*, through the words and actions of the characters, and is supported and reinforced through stylistic elements. In the film, Renee "speaks" with multiple voices, and is "spoken" about with multiple voices, which depict a collection of subjectivities that, in the context of motherhood, run the gamut from good to bad. Renee, at various points in the space of the film, is the embodiment of, on the one hand, perfected femininity, the happy middle-class homemaker, and the devoted caregiver, and on the other, the neglectful villain. In a process that may initially seem paradoxical, in order to decompensate the good/bad binary the film overtly represents both of its polarized ends.

To initiate the process of decompensating the binary between the good and bad representations, the film acknowledges interconnected and familiar understandings of proper femininity and good mothering. One such acknowledgment comes in the form of narrative, presented through on-screen text. Early on in the film, viewers are presented with Renee's "story" through text in this manner. The story begins:

> Once upon a time in a small Texas town, in the early 1950s, a very good woman met a very good man. The man, Adolph, and the woman, Rosemary, fell in love and got married. They had a beautiful daughter, Renee. Everything in their lives was bright, happy, and promising. Adolph had a prosperous business; a small grocery story. When Renee was 11 years old, she was scouted by a famous photographer from New York City, who happened to be visiting the small Texas town. The photographer made Renee a very famous regional child model. She appeared on local kiddie shows, fashion magazines, and a well-known TV commercial.[1] (Caouette, 2004)[2]

With this happy tale, the film commences with a familiar construction of ideal American life. To reinforce the idyllic vision presented in the text, photographs are interspersed to provide visual evidence of their happy family life.

The small-town Texas origins of the family call up simple interpretations of traditional values. The woman was "good"—a photograph of a bride smiling brightly on her wedding day demonstrates that she conformed to conventional standards of feminine beauty. The man was "good"—while the story does not provide details regarding how he came to have his own business, the implication is that he embodied the proper entrepreneurial spirit and sought to achieve The American Dream. As owner of a "small" business, he must have worked hard and sacrificed to carve out a measure of monetary success. By providing the small town with food, the friendly neighborhood grocer achieved prosperity. Resulting from the loving, married, union of the good man and the good woman was a good child—"a beautiful daughter." Happy images of mother holding daughter, daughter laughing in a pink bonnet, and daughter sitting on Santa's lap demonstrate her beauty. She was so good, so perfect, in fact, that her perfection was judged worthy of being put on display as a model for other children, and other children's parents, to emulate. From this promising beginning, Renee should have been on her way to a life of feminine excellence and well positioned to reproduce the role of wife and mother. As Addison, Goodwin-Kelly, and Roth (2009) humorously note, mothers, quite literally, reproduce dominant ideology (p. 4).

Indeed, the film indicates that, for a brief period, she was on her way: in 1972, Renee met a door-to-door salesman named Steve. A portrait of Steve, which appears in the midst of the on-screen text, indicates that he served in the military. The two fell in love and were married. A wedding photograph shows Renee and Steve happily cutting cake. The image of the happy couple is reiterated by Renee herself, at one point in the film, as she explains to Jonathan that his father, "was a very good provider," and that they had a "beautiful apartment home," "the finest furniture, the best food," and that "he was a good and loyal husband." Renee indicates her own recognition of the ideals of traditional family life, speaking as a proud homemaker. In this way, she speaks from a complicit position of gender essentialism identical to that articulated by O'Reilly (2010) when she writes of the public/private divide central to the most traditional notions of patriarchal motherhood, which is characterized by a clear split between a masculine producer and a feminine nurturer. The reproduction of ideal traditional family life stopped short, however; Steve left town, unaware that Renee was pregnant with Jonathan. Perhaps this type of behavior should have been expected from a door-to-door salesman; but, the desertion is not attributed to wanderlust. Rather, Renee's husband was "unable to deal with her family." Thus, the ideal was but a momentary, fragile, simulation. While *Tarnation* acknowledges images of perfect family life, it concurrently calls those images—and all related associations—into question.

Part of this questioning comes in the form of starkly exhibiting the ideal's opposite, by giving voice to Renee's "bad" mothering. In contrast to Renee's beauty, femininity, and childlike innocence, viewers are presented with incidences of ghastly and oftentimes heartbreaking behavior. In a scene filmed during Jonathan's teenage years, a despondent Renee sits on the ground, disinterested, and says matter-of-factly, "You won't have a family if I die, Jon. You'll have no one [...] It is true. I'm all you've ever had. You never really appreciated me." Her uncaring, manipulative voice stands in stark opposition to the tenets of good motherhood; she certainly does not put the needs of her son before her own as she lays guilt and shame upon him. She does not yet embody the maternal monster trope that Douglas and Michaels (2004) identify, but other events and actions in the film move in that direction. Viewers learn that, over the course of thirty-four years, Renee was treated in psychiatric hospitals over one hundred times, meaning that she was absent for much of Jonathan's childhood, youth, and young adulthood. In other moments, viewers are clued into incidences where Renee's actions placed her son in genuine physical danger. For example, when Jonathan was very young, Renee, "in a psychotic state" according to the film, took her son and went to Chicago. This action set off a series of events—including Renee being sexually assaulted, in front of her son, by a man who picked them up off the street, and arrested for causing trouble on a bus—which led to Jonathan's placement in foster care. While in Renee's care, Jonathan was exposed to horrific sexual violence and criminal behavior. Of course Renee cannot be blamed for these events; yet, they illustrate her capacity to be grossly negligent, a danger to her son. This capacity, seen alongside embodiments of good motherhood, troubles the foundation of the good/bad binary. The host of incongruous voices and actions, all given equal expression through Renee, cannot be synthesized into a coherent representation of either a good or bad mother.

Renee assumes yet another voice in relation to the good/bad mother binary. This voice indicates her personal understanding of ideal mothering and its opposite, from the perspective of a child. She tells the camera:

> I was an extremely abused child. It was a ... an ongoing thing, there was no end to it. I never knew from one minute to the next when I was gonna be slapped, or drug by my hair. By ... my ... the people who raised me. Sick parents raise sick children. [...] Rosemary was the woman who raised me, she was schizophrenic, she was very neurotic, and she was very psychotic. She would hit me on my back, she would hit me with her fist, for no apparent reason. I was extremely abused, and, uh, hopefully I didn't bring any of the abuse to my children. I wanted to be the one to break the cycle.

Here, Renee speaks with a complicated voice that projects her own subjectivity onto her mother. The film does not present any other evidence that Renee's parents were physically abusive, and makes no mention of her mother having schizophrenia. Therefore, viewers are invited to conclude that this story has been concocted by Renee, whether she is being intentionally untruthful or not. Yet, the story does more than this: as she speaks with the voice of an abused child, she is also a concerned caretaker who wants to do better for her own child. In this way, she negotiates the intergenerational space between her mother and her child. In one sense, she speaks with a voice of "matrophobia"—fear of becoming one's mother—which O'Brien Hallstein (2007), drawing upon Rich (1986), describes as "the splitting of daughters from mothers" (p. 270). Her desire to "break the cycle" reinforces this split. However, the fact that her story projects elements of herself onto her mother counteracts the splitting; Renee is, to use Burke's (1969) terminology, consubstantial with her mother. At the same time, her statements further acknowledge what bad motherhood looks like—what it means to both *have* and to *be* a bad mother—and, simultaneously, they articulate a desire to live up to the standards of ideal motherhood. She embodies all these positions at once; thus, she cannot be collapsed into any single one of them.

Renee's construction as a multivocal character is supported through visual juxtapositional strategies. Frequently, the film conveys parts of the story through on-screen text interwoven with visual split-screen effects and fast-cutting techniques. One such effect presents a split-screen mirroring of video footage. At times, in this way, Renee is depicted as reflecting herself across the screen; to use Bakhtin's (1984) words she is "convers[ing] with [her] own double" (p. 28). Other times, a single image of Renee appears; then, the image either changes or the angle rapidly widens to reveal multiple copies of the image displayed in a tiled effect. This visual strategy oftentimes accompanies text that conveys tragedy: one image of a young and conventionally pretty Renee becomes four as text layered over the image reveals that she was raped in front of her son; one image of Renee looking melancholy becomes twenty-five as text speaks of her parents choosing to authorize consent for additional electric shock treatment. She symbolically splits, one into many, in concert with tragic events. Such visual multiplication offers a figurative representation of Renee's multivocality, wherein voices are "side by side and simultaneous," unable to be united (Bakhtin, 1984, p. 28).

Other times, juxtaposition takes on a powerfully ironic tone, as it does when photos of Renee as a young joyful mother, holding happy baby Jonathan, are interwoven with text revealing heart-wrenching details of Renee's young adult life. Such photos, for example, accompany the information that

Jonathan was removed from his family by child welfare. Frequently, in instances such as these, fast-cutting edits are employed to display a barrage of images in rapid succession. Following the revelation that Renee has endured years of shock treatments, a divorce, and treatment more than one hundred times in psychiatric hospitals, and that there was "nothing initially wrong with her," a series of happy, conventional-looking photos of Renee quickly flash past. This sort of juxtaposition—wherein happy, "normal," "good," images are layered over stories of trauma and despair—begins to unravel the stability of such "normal" images in a more general sense. The images, on their own, convey aspects of the conventional "good" mother: she is loving, she is affectionate, she is happy, and she is devoted to her child. Thus, the juxtaposition of incongruous information invites viewers to directly question the images and defamiliarize with notions of what comprises a "good" mother in the first place. It is important to note here that the "normal" is not mere façade, covering over a deep layer of genuine trauma. Instead, the normal, the traumatic, the picturesque, and the painful are all given equal representation, all appear as equally "real," and all exist at the same time and in the same space.

Although *Tarnation* creatively disintegrates stable notions of "good" motherhood, the film's work does not end here. At the same time that representations challenge viewers to reexamine familiar notions of motherhood, the film offers up a complex mother-child connection, creating the conditions necessary for a relationship of mutual mothering. This dynamic is hinted at from the very beginning of the film, when an adult Jonathan receives news that Renee has overdosed on Lithium and makes plans to travel back to Texas to help care for her. Right off the bat, audiences are presented with a reordering of the traditional mother-child relationship, as child takes on the responsibility of caring for mother. Jonathan does not hesitate in this regard—his mother is in crisis, and he immediately responds as the obvious and natural caretaker. The implication is that this is not the first (nor likely the last) time that Jonathan has embodied the role of "mother." The urgent need to care for his mother causes Jonathan significant, visible, emotional stress—he has "like a hundred and two fever," which he thinks has been caused by "all the stress," and he feels like he is "gonna have an anxiety attack." He enacts a mothering voice that is encumbered, worried, and dutiful. Yet, at the same time, the responsibility to care for his mother is not presented as abnormal, unnatural, or even as an overly-excessive burden. Caring for his mother is, simply, something that he does.

In this way, viewers see that Jonathan's identity is constituted in part by this caretaker role and that this inextricably ties him to his mother. Themes of mother-child interconnection surface at other points in the film, as well.

This interconnection is sometimes presented in not-obvious ways, particularly since much of *Tarnation* documents Jonathan's experiences *without* his mother. In one such instance, thirteen year-old Jonathan describes his experience smoking PCP-laced marijuana. This, he says, "depersonalized" his mind. He says, "I am depersonalized, I think it is permanent brain damage. I feel like I'm in a dream all the time. I forgot how it was to be normal, you know." He continues on in a fragmented stream-of-consciousness, speaking of being gay, of being lusty for everything, of loving his mother, of being molested, of not wanting to die, of wanting to die, of stubbing his toe, of feeling that he is in another dimension. His early words point to a time in an imagined past where he "knew" how to be normal; the disjointed statements that follow enact the crumbling of that construct in his own mind and for viewers. Jonathan's multiple voices reproduce Renee's, and demonstrate that Renee is always present. Her voices are always apparent, even when she is physically absent. Of course, physical absence precludes all tenets of good motherhood (Douglas & Michaels, 2004; Hays, 1996; O'Reilly, 2004a; O'Reilly, 2010); but this scene demonstrates a mother's shaping of her child in the face of prolonged periods of absence. Undoubtedly, children mimic their parents. Here, instead of more conventional, expected representations of childlike mimesis—daughter dons apron and joins mom in the kitchen to bake, son straps on tool belt and joins dad in the garage to pound nails into wood—viewers are faced with contradiction, profound uncertainty and exploration.

A quintessential representation of mother-child consubstantiality comes at the very end of the film. Jonathan is alone, talking to the camera; he even makes mention of the fact that he wants the present scene to be like the ones he shot of himself when he was younger. He says:

> I don't ever want to turn out like my mother. And I'm scared because, um, when I was little, and she was my age, that I am now, which is thirty-one, um, she seemed a lot better than she does now. I love my mother so much. As fucked up as it is. I can't escape her. She lives inside me. She's in my hair, she's behind my eyes. She's under my skin. She's … downstairs.

Here, viewers witness Jonathan enacting multivocality. In Bakhtin's (1984) language, the past has "not ceased to be present" (p. 29) as Jonathan "stand[s] alongside" (p. 30) his child-self, his mother at thirty-one, and his mother who is literally downstairs at his house, "side by side and simultaneous[ly]" (p. 28). He "converse[s] with [his] own double" (p. 28) as he speaks with contradictory voices. He does not want to turn out like his mother; yet, his mother lives inside him—he *is* his mother. This illustrates the confounding position one might experience when living a relationship of mutual mothering within the confines of a dominant ideology that leads one to not want to turn out like one's mother. Rich (1986) writes, "Our personalities seem dangerously to blur and overlap with our mothers'" (p. 236). In this scene, Jonathan acknowledges this danger, and seems for a moment to want to "perform radical surgery" (p. 236), to matrophobically split himself from his mother to avoid becoming her. Yet, this move is immediately rendered impossible. Jonathan cannot cleanly split from an intersubjective being.

The multivocal connection, shared by Renee and Jonathan, will be further explored in the analysis of *Walk Away Renee*. *Tarnation*, for its part, establishes the conditions and multivocal dynamics of mutual mothering. To reiterate, it does so by acknowledging the ideological construction of a good/bad mother binary, and demonstrating that both poles of the binary exist in the same place, in the same time, in the same person. Thus, Renee enacts a multiplicity of voices that throw into relief the illusory nature of both the binary and the unified distinction between mother and child. Multivocality and the embodiment of fluid roles constitute consubstantial interconnectedness between Renee and Jonathan. The following section will examine ways in which the follow-up film, *Walk Away Renee*, picks up these themes and elaborates upon them.

## Walk Away Renee: *Elaborating Mutual Mothering*

Although *Walk Away Renee* is comprised of the same cast of characters as *Tarnation*, and even recounts some of the same footage and events, it is a very different sort of film. Whereas *Tarnation* enacts multivocal dimensions of motherhood and establishes interconnection between Renee and Jonathan as they are parallel yet apart, *Walk Away Renee* almost entirely deals with the relationship between mother and son as they interact with one another in co-presence. The narrative centers on a mother-son road trip. At the beginning of the film, Jonathan learns that Renee is not getting adequate treatment from the Houston facility in which she lives. As he did in *Tarnation*, Jonathan goes to Texas to care for his mother, once again enacting an inversion of familiar mother/child roles. This time, the plan is to move Renee back to New York—which they do, via an adventure-filled road trip across the country in a U-Haul truck. This premise allows viewers to witness more directly the relationship of mutual mothering that exists between Renee and Jonathan. Moreover, while this film, like *Tarnation*, uses a significant amount of flashback footage filmed by Jonathan, the present day scenes are filmed by others. Thus, viewers are able to see Renee and Jonathan acting together. As with the prior film, mutual mothering is given space to grow out of the decompensatory acknowledgment and pulling apart of the good/bad mother binary.

Acknowledgment and pulling apart happens in ways that parallel depictions in *Tarnation*. However, the specific situations differ in ways that offer elaboration of—or additional evidence in support of—the workings of decompensation. In one flashback scene, viewers see Renee speak with a protective mother voice. Jonathan's grandfather (Renee's father) Adolph, who suffers from dementia, begins to verbally abuse Jonathan. Adolph is clearly confused about Jonathan's identity; he angrily tells him to get out of the house and that he's "gonna die."[3] Renee immediately and viciously responds, "*You're* gonna die! Don't you ever tell my son that as long as you live!" Prior work demonstrates that, alongside nurturing behaviors, mothers may appropriately enact "protective fury" and "aggressive confrontation" in the service of guarding their children from harm (Tonn, 1996, p. 16). However, Renee's enactment of fiercely protective motherhood goes beyond that which most would consider appropriate. She acknowledges that she is supposed to protect her son from harm and abuse; yet, her son is not in grave danger. The inappropriate contextualization of this protective voice renders such motherly action confounding. She is good (protecting her son) and bad (abusing her father) all in the same breath.

A present-day scene of a different sort, which nonetheless has a similar effect, comes as Renee and Jonathan drive down the freeway in their moving truck. Renee sits in the passenger seat with her glasses perched crookedly on her nose and her broad smile revealing several missing teeth. She confidently sings, in a manner that is silly and almost bawdy, the song "He's got the whole world in his hands." The song—a familiar, simple, religious children's tune—is one that kids who grow up Christian are likely to sing at Sunday school and with their parents. Singing this song with one's child might traditionally signal a mother's intention to pass along a religious worldview and proper morals. As Jonathan sits quietly smirking alongside, Renee's performance gives new meaning to the song. Her disheveled appearance and irreverent style divorces the song from its familiar meaning and remakes it as ironic camp; hence, another symbol of good motherhood is cast down as Renee speaks with the voices of good and bad motherhood simultaneously.

A scene that takes place once Renee and Jonathan arrive in New York, in Central Park, further troubles the binary of good/bad motherhood. The two walk together through a tunnel, and Renee says to Jonathan, "This is like, see the showers, you take a shower in here on both … carwash. Carwash. That's how you think of it. Look. Pretend. You're driving your car through here and the water's shooting out and cleaning your car." Certainly, imaginative mothers engage in games of make-believe with their children. Jonathan, now thirty-eight years of age, has probably largely outgrown his ability to appreciate the notion of an ordinary walk through a tunnel transforming into an opportunity to drive an imaginary car through an imaginary carwash. Once again the dislocation of act from appropriate context is revealing, and demonstrates the instability of the symbols of good/bad motherhood. Acknowledgments of the ideal materialize, and almost as soon as they appear they are shattered by Renee's persistent multivocality.

In place of appropriate, traditional, patriarchally consistent demonstrations of the mother-child relationship, viewers once again—and this time more directly—see the contours of a different sort of relationship emerge. The fluid nature of the mother-child dynamic is illustrated when Renee and Jonathan make a stop in New Orleans on the way from Houston to New York. They walk together through the French Quarter, hands clasped. Suddenly, Renee lets go of Jonathan's hand, turns to step out into the street, and is almost hit by a car. Jonathan pulls her back. As both then prepare to cross, Renee says to Jonathan, "Be careful crossing, it's a busy street. Be very careful crossing," to which Jonathan earnestly replies, "I will." Renee says, "Hold my hand," and the two clasp hands again and cross the street together. Here, viewers witness mutual mothering and reciprocal caretaking as both Jonathan and Renee interchangeably care for one another. This sort of mutual mothering emerges as a product of their shared history and fluidly voiced roles. It is a necessity, and it is also desirable.

Such desirability manifests in scenes that demonstrate the undeniably loving nature of the connection between Renee and Jonathan. As the two make stops along the way from Houston to New York, they have all sorts of fun together. Side by side, they gleefully swing together on a swing set. Squeezed tightly together in a small train car, and smiling at one another, Renee excitedly points out different animals to Jonathan as they ride through a zoo. At an amusement park, they huddle together as they spin on the Tilt-o-Whirl. In addition to representing mutual affection, scenes such as these demonstrate the capacity of both mother and adult child to assume a child-like voice as they engage in lighthearted fun and simply enjoy the company of the other. Both Renee and Jonathan are, once again, fluid in these enactments—they both speak with the voice of both mother and child, and the sharing of these voices bonds them indelibly together.

This point is reproduced in two dramatized scenes, which are woven into the film after Renee and Jonathan arrive in New York. Following an intense argument between the two, Jonathan sits alone watching television. In the dramatized program, a scientist introduces the notion that the cosmological theory of the "universe" has been replaced by that of the "multiverse." The scientist says, "Now think about it. The baby universe emerging from the womb ... when we get these baby pictures of the instant of creation, maybe there'll be an umbilical cord, connecting our universe to a parent universe." The program's image of the "multiverse" is a rhetorical device which connotes elements of the mothering relationship that manifests between Renee and Jonathan over the course of the two films. Through figurative representation of the literal bodily connection made by an umbilical cord, it overtly indicates the intense and enduring connection between mother and child. The connection is one that is undeniable and primal. It stands in contrast to the superficial connections implied by images of picture-perfect, ever-happy, ideal mothers dutifully and intensively raising picture-perfect children. This connection is representative of a wholehearted embracing, honoring, and acceptance between mother and child; indeed, it acknowledges that mother and child are one and the same. This embodied, anti-matrophobic, metaphor encapsulates Jonathan and Renee's mutual mothering relationship.

The second dramatized scene comes after Renee has moved into an assisted living institution north of New York City. Jonathan, once again, realizes that Renee is not being well cared for. Unsure of how to proceed, Jonathan ostensibly attempts to relax by taking a bath. He falls asleep in the bathtub and dreams of the umbilically connected universes. In the dream, he sees the two universes floating in space as two swirling masses of constituent parts connected by a long cord. He enters the cord, and is rapidly propelled toward one of the universes. Once inside, he floats above the earth briefly, and then zooms all the way down to New York, where blurry characters stand outside a luxurious-looking suburban home. The characters appear to be representations of Jonathan and Renee, except their roles have been reversed. Jonathan looks haggard. He is missing teeth, and he is unshaven and unkempt. Renee, who is almost entirely blurry, is smartly dressed in a wool coat. Her hair is neatly styled. She says, "Jonathan, we have to go," to which he replies with nonsensical babbling. Later in the dream, Jonathan and Renee seem back to their "normal" selves as they drive toward what looks to be a psychiatric hospital. Renee turns to Jonathan and says, "You're gonna lose me. I'm gonna lose you." The sound of Renee's voice on an answering machine pleading "Jonathan, *please* call me back, would you *please* call me, please" fades in, and a barrage of fast-cut images representing Jonathan's many voices and Renee's many voices flash across the screen. The sound of an electrical current is heard, and Jonathan awakens. This scene, like the first, reinforces the mothering relationship established in other portions of the film. The connection between Renee and Jonathan's two "universes" makes the ways in which they relate to one another mutually reinforcing and fluid. In the scene, Jonathan "becomes" Renee; but as he made clear in *Tarnation*, he already *is* her. She "lives inside" of him. They are not separate beings; they are one and the same. Thus, they cannot help but care for one another. Caring for the other is the same as caring for the self; it is a desirable necessity. Of course, Renee and Jonathan do not perfectly enact this caring. Their relationship is messy, and each constantly fails to meet the other's expectations. Yet, the failure and the messiness is part of what makes their relationship, and the films, so powerful. By committing Renee to yet another institution, Jonathan realizes that he has committed part of himself. His sense of self, and Renee's, become disordered when the two are disconnected. When connected, both mentally and physically, their mutual care provides a reimagined sense of stability. Hence, immediately following this "dream," Jonathan goes to get Renee from the institution and brings her back to his home to live.

In this film, viewers see how the unravelling of a stable understanding of the meaning of good/bad motherhood—and a stable voice shaped within such meaning—creates the possibility for a relationship of mutual mothering. As in *Tarnation*, this relationship grows out of the acknowledgment and pulling apart—the decompensation—of the good/bad motherhood binary. In the following section, I offer some concluding thoughts and implications of this analysis.

## Conclusion

The preceding analysis demonstrates how a rhetorical text may transform what might otherwise be interpreted as disordered representations of bad patriarchal "motherhood" into progressive, feminist, representations of "mothering." In doing so, both films answer O'Reilly's (2004b) call to mother against motherhood. Or, to put it in terms that she has elsewhere used, both films do the work of "outlaw[ing] motherhood to make possible outlaw motherhood" or mothering (O'Reilly, 2010, p. 379). By decompensating the good/bad mother binary, the films transgress patriarchal motherhood and put forth a representation of mutual mothering. Importantly, this mutual mothering also engages in the feminist work of degendering motherly care by featuring a relationship between mother and son. O'Reilly (2010) reminds us that the destabilization of patriarchal motherhood depends upon our ability to "dislodge the gender essentialism that grounds and structures it" (p. 378). Both films do this, and *Walk Away Renee* carries its overt anti-essentialism beyond the relationship of Renee and Jonathan; viewers see Jonathan enact mothering with his own son, Joshua. To this need for anti-gender essentialism, I would add that the destabilization of patriarchal motherhood—which is inextricably bound to ideologies of White, middle-class, heteronormative, able-bodied, and mental health–normative supremacy—also depends upon our ability to theorize models of mothering that pull apart such a system from multiple directions. This analysis, by piecing together a model of mothering in a context of mental "difference," undertakes a small portion of this work.

The beginnings of a model of decompensated mothering are suggested by this essay, and are grounded in the positions embodied by the people who enact it. As a woman diagnosed with schizophrenia, psychiatrists would tell us that Renee likely experiences trouble interpreting, synthesizing, and responding to messages, and an "altered" sense of self wherein she has trouble distinguishing between herself and others (Torrey, 2013). The Mayo Clinic would tell us that she "interpret[s] reality abnormally" and has "extremely disordered thinking and behavior" ("Mayo Clinic," 2014 January 14). As a man who experienced "depersonalization" following a bad experience with drugs, Jonathan is fragmented; he "feel[s] like [he is] in a dream," and he "forgot how it was to be normal." The Mayo Clinic tells us that Jonathan might feel that he is an "outside observer" of his "thoughts, feelings, [and] body" ("Mayo Clinic," 2014 May 24). Both of these imply a splitting, a multiplicity of consciousness. This multiplicity of consciousness leads to the embodiment of multiple subjectivities, expressed through multivocality. Such split subjectivity is problematic in a homophonic world, wherein stable categories determine unified characterizations within fixed possibilities. For example, a mother whose subjectivity is split between a desire to be a good mother and a desire to pursue a successful career will perpetually be faced with confounding double binds. In a homophonic world, one must be either/or within a clearly established hierarchy. However, split subjectivity, as it is presented in the polyphonic world of these films, becomes an opportunity: an opportunity to transgress boundaries, to forge strong and meaningful connections, to enact feminist mothering, to happily forget "how it was to be normal." Decompensated mothering privileges the "abnormal interpretation," revels in "disordered thinking," and learns from the opportunity to see the self from the perspective of another and *as* another. In these ways, a model of decompensated mothering pushes beyond some other critiques of the dominant ideology of motherhood in its refusal to recreate binary patterns of interpretation. In her analysis of two feminist books on motherhood, one of which is Douglas and Michaels (2004), O'Brien Hallstein (2006, 2007) demonstrates how feminist critiques may reproduce "patriarchal either/or binaries" (2007, p. 291) and perpetuate problematic split subjectivity by focusing either on the institution of motherhood or on the relationship of mothering. By engaging in the transformative work of decompensation, perhaps this trap may be avoided.

It may seem as though this analysis paints an overly rosy picture of the mothering in *Tarnation* and *Walk Away Renee.* It is certainly true that, along with the alternative model of mothering that I have sought to elaborate here, both films depict significant pain, neglect, suffering, anger, contempt, and trauma. These themes have not been given equal treatment here. I would posit, however, that it is precisely these themes alongside and within decompensated mothering that so powerfully invite viewers to participate in the model. In monolithic depictions of good/bad motherhood, viewers have the option to either fail in living up to the "good" standard, or take some comfort in knowing that they are not quite as bad as the "bad." As opposed to these options—both of which depend on identifying one's difference or division from the representation—mutual motherhood, in all its messiness, invites everyone to participate. For Renee and Jonathan, mothering happens amidst a constant barrage of unrelenting challenges. Hence, it invites connection by allowing viewers the opportunity to see themselves mirrored in and amongst the complexities of life. It is Renee and Jonathan's particular positions and enactments of multivocality that create this possibility, but anyone can join in. In this way, perhaps we all would do well to forget "how it was to be normal."

## Notes

1. This narrative is presented, in the film, one short phrase at a time. Punctuation and capitalization have been added and modified here for clarity.
2. All subsequent uncited quotations in this section are from Caouette, 2004.
3. All subsequent uncited quotations in this section are from Caouette, 2012.

## References

Addison, H., Goodwin-Kelly, M. K., & Roth, E. (2009). Introduction. In H. Addison, M. K. Goodwin-Kelly, & E. Roth (Eds.), *Motherhood misconceived: Representing the maternal in U.S. films* (pp. 1–11). Albany, NY: State University of New York Press.

Bakhtin, M. (1984). *Problems of Dostoevsky's poetics* (C. Emerson, Trans.). Minneapolis, MN: University of Minnesota Press.

Burke, K. (1969). *A rhetoric of motives.* Berkeley, CA: University of California Press.

Caouette, J. (Director). (2012). *Walk away Renee* [Documentary]. United States: Sundance Selects.

Caouette, J. (Director). (2004). *Tarnation* [Documentary]. United States: Wellspring Media.

Douglas, S. J., & Michaels, M. W. (2004). *The mommy myth: The idealization of motherhood and how it has undermined all women.* New York, NY: Free Press.

Hays, S. (1996). *The cultural contradictions of motherhood.* New Haven, CT: Yale University Press.

Jaffe, D. J. (2014, April 5). Best book on schizophrenia: *Surviving schizophrenia*, 6th edition. *The Huffington Post.* Retrieved from http://www.huffingtonpost.com/dj-jaffe/best-book-on-schizophreni_b_4719176.html

Klin, A., & Lemish, D. (2008). Mental disorders stigma in the media: Review of studies on production, content, and influences. *Journal of Health Communication, 13*, 434–449.

Kraynak, J. (2011). Have you decompensated lately? *Psych Central.* Retrieved from http://blogs.psychcentral.com/bipolar/2011/02/bipolar-disorder-decompensate/

Mayo Clinic Staff. (2014, May 24). Diseases and conditions: Depersonalization-derealization disorder. Retrieved from http://www.mayoclinic.org/diseases-conditions/depersonalization-derealization-disorder/basics/symptoms/con-20033401

Mayo Clinic Staff. (2014, January 14). Diseases and conditions: Schizophrenia. Retrieved from http://www.mayoclinic.org/diseases-conditions/schizophrenia/basics/definition/con-20021077

O'Brien Hallstein, D. L. (2011). She gives birth, she's wearing a bikini: Mobilizing the postpregnant celebrity mom body to manage the post–second wave crisis in femininity. *Women's Studies in Communication, 34*(2), 111–138.

O'Brien Hallstein, D. L. (2010). Public choices, private control: How mediated mom labels work rhetorically to dismantle the politics of choice and white second wave feminist successes. In S. Hayden & D. L. O'Brien Hallstein (Eds.), *Contemplating maternity in an era of choice: Explorations into discourses of reproduction* (pp. 5–24). Lanham, MD: Lexington Books.

O'Brien Hallstein, D. L. (2007). Matrophobic sisters and daughters: The rhetorical consequences of matrophobia in contemporary white feminist analyses of maternity. *Women's Studies, 36*(4), 269–296.

O'Brien Hallstein, D. L. (2006). Conceiving intensive mothering. *Journal of the Association for Research on Mothering, 8*(1 & 2), 96–108.

O'Reilly, A. (2010). Outlaw(ing) motherhood: A theory and politic of maternal empowerment for the twenty-first century. In A. O'Reilly (Ed.), *21st century motherhood: Experience, identity, policy, agency* (pp. 366–380). New York, NY: Columbia University Press.

O'Reilly, A. (2004a). Introduction. In A. O'Reilly (Ed.), *Mother matters: Motherhood as discourse and practice* (pp. 11–26). Toronto, ON: Association for Research on Mothering.

O'Reilly, A. (2004b). Mothering against motherhood and the possibility of empowered maternity for mothers and their children. In *From motherhood to mothering: The legacy of Adrienne Rich's* Of Woman Born (pp. 159–174). Albany, NY: State University of New York Press.

Recommended readings from the Cadigans. (2009). *People Say I'm Crazy.* Retrieved from http://www.peoplesayimcrazy.org/living-with/cadigan-reading-list

Rich, A. (1986). *Of woman born: Motherhood as experience and institution* (2nd ed.). New York: W. W. Norton.

Signorielli, N. (1989). The stigma of mental illness on television. *Journal of Broadcasting & Electronic Media, 33*(3), 325–331.

Smith, C. J. (1999). Finding a warm place for someone we know: The cultural appeal of recent mental patient and asylum films. *Journal of Popular Film and Television, 27*(1), 40–47.

Thomas, E. M. (2012). Punishing unfaithful wives and working mothers: Messages of postfeminism in contemporary film. In A. A. Ruggiero (Ed.), *Media depictions of brides, wives, and mothers* (pp. 77–89). Lanham, MD: Lexington.

Tonn, M. B. (1996). Militant motherhood: Labor's Mary Harris "Mother" Jones. *The Quarterly Journal of Speech, 82*(1), 1–21.

Torrey, E. F. (2013). *Surviving schizophrenia: A family manual* (6th ed.). New York, NY: Harper Perennial.

Varma, S. J. (n. d.). *Tarnation* plot summary. *IMDb.* Retrieved from http://www.imdb.com/title/tt0390538/?ref_=fn_al_tt_1

Warner, J. (2005). *Perfect madness: Motherhood in the age of anxiety.* New York, NY: Riverhead Books.

# 10. *A Tale of Morality, Class, and Transnational Mothering: Broadening and Constraining Motherhood in* Mammoth

By Rachel D. Davidson & Lara C. Stache

In the past few decades, transnational mothering has been a topic that has garnered growing interest from scholars due to the large numbers of mothers who are leaving their home countries and families to seek employment in the United States (e.g., Hondagneu-Sotelo & Avila, 1997; Horton, 2010; Parrenas, 2001; Parrenas, 2010). Bahira Sherif Trask (2013) suggests that "although migration is not a new occurrence, it has expanded with respect to numbers and significance since 1945" (p. 20). Further, Trask (2013) reports, "As of 2005 approximately 191 million individuals, or 3.0% of the world population, were living outside of their native countries" (p. 20) and "approximately 38 million foreign-born individuals, constituting about 13% of the population" are currently residing in the U.S. (p. 21). Transnational mothering often enters conversations regarding migration because transnational mothers leave their home countries and families in order to gain better opportunities and money earning potential in the U.S. Many transnational mothers take on domestic work, such as caring for children in Western homes, and Parrenas (2010) suggests this "migration takes women outside of the confines of the home, thus disrupting the ideology of female domesticity" (p. 1826). Transnational mothering, according to Quintero Escobar (2010), challenges "mainstream western ideas about family configuration and in particular, about women's mothering role" (p. 2) because migrating mothers are physically separated from their children in order to financially provide for the family. Thus, for transnational mothers, caring for their own children removes them from the context of their homes, as opposed to a Western framework that suggests mothering occurs in the domestic home.

The notion of transnational mothering stands in stark contrast to intensive-mothering standards that are commonplace in Western culture. For example, Hays (1996) and O'Brien Hallstein (2010) argue that ideals of intensive mothering, including assumptions that a mother is the only suitable primary caregiver and that mothering happens in the private, not the public sphere, are still ideas that are well entrenched in society and are manifest in the ways motherhood is talked about and evaluated. As such, the transnational mothering paradigm is a framework that disrupts the norms of intensive mothering, because transnational mothering does not only occur within the confines of the domestic space.

As representations of Western mothering in popular culture continue to be interrogated by academic scholars (see, e.g., Dancey, 2009; Dobris & White-Mills, 2006; Johnston & Swanson, 2003; Kinnick, 2009; Silbergleid, 2009), it is also important that representations of transnational mothering are included in this academic conversation because such analyses can potentially lend valuable insight into the complexities of understanding definitions of motherhood in the United States. Texts that invoke rhetorics of transnationalism draw upon, open up, and encourage a public discussion about the complications that arise when motherhood intersects with issues of class. In this chapter, we contend that when the transnational mother is placed in direct contrast to a wealthy, professional Western mother, definitions of mothering are at once broadened and constrained. One such textual example is the 2009 independent film *Mammoth*.

*Mammoth* (2009) is a popular culture text that rhetorically disrupts definitions of motherhood on two levels: (1) it presents a non-Western vision of motherhood alongside Western mothering practices, and (2) it complicates the ways in which the "bad mother" is evaluated. The film *Mammoth* (2009) is a viable text to observe the clash between the two mothering paradigms because they are juxtaposed throughout the film and spectators are invited to directly compare and contrast the paradigms. *Mammoth* (2009) depicts a mother, Ellen Vidales, played by Michelle Williams, who is a busy physician living with her daughter, Jackie, and her husband, Leo, played by Gael Garcia Bernal. A hired nanny, Gloria, played by Marife Necesito, lives with the Vidales family and cares for Jackie when Ellen and Leo are busy working. Jackie is portrayed spending more time with Gloria than with either of her biological parents. Gloria is a transnational mother as she has left her two biological sons, Salvador and Manuel, in the Philippines with her mother. The film reveals that Gloria is in the United States working for the Vidales family in an attempt to earn money for her sons to have a better life in the Philippines.

In this analysis, we primarily focus on Gloria's and Ellen's experiences as we suggest the film constructs an argument about the consequences of the maternal choices they make. The film highlights the mothers' similarities throughout: (1) both make maternal sacrifices by letting another individual take over her role as primary caregiver; (2) both sacrifice time with their children to make occupational gains; (3) both suffer anguish about the lack of time they spend with their biological children; and (4) both experience negative consequences for their lack of time spent with their biological children. Despite the mothers' significant similarities, Gloria's mothering practices result in her oldest son, Salvador, being brutally beaten and raped; however, Ellen's same steps result in less direct consequences that do not threaten the life of her own child.

Through an evaluation of the functions of allegiance and dissociation in the film, we argue that spectators are encouraged to align within a structure of sympathy regarding motherhood, where "bad mothers" are punished more harshly based on their socioeconomic status as opposed to public/private-sphere expectations. We argue the film presents this dissociative argument through the mothers' opposing points of view that function as a morality tale of class. The film highlights a theme in representations of motherhood, where distance from children deserves punishment. However, there is a discrepancy for the severity of punishment based on class. Physical distance between mother and children is the crime of the poorer mother, who suffers direr consequences for her children, whereas emotional distance is the crime committed by the wealthy mother, and she and her child are punished less severely. Ultimately, *Mammoth* can be read as an example of popular discourse that highlights disadvantages of class by contrasting two different mothering paradigms via two disparate mothering point of views.

## Good/Bad, Public/Private: Constructions of Motherhood in Popular Culture

Historically, Western culture dichotomizes between the public and private spheres, where men are encouraged to participate in the public sphere and women are encouraged to be in the private sphere. Such a public/private-dichotomy maintains biases in maternal roles and expectations grounded in differences of gender. Because of the traditionally gendered nature of the public and private spheres, Western working mothers operate within two competing and contradictory logics: The ideology of intensive mothering, where childrearing is valued, and getting ahead in the public sphere, where childrearing is undervalued (Hays, 1996). Intensive mothering has evolved out of a separate-spheres ideology regarding gender that dates back to the nineteenth century where women's work was domestic and relegated to a private sphere, and men's work and political activity was valued in a public sphere.

Although Kerber (1988) emphasizes that there has been much slippage in the use of "public" and "private" to imply material or literal spheres, a separate-spheres ideology is more ideological than material. Kerber (1988) argues that the public/private-sphere language persists, however, in spite of increased "overlap" between "men's 'spheres' and women's 'spheres'" because "vast areas of our experience and our consciousness do not overlap" (p. 39). Furthermore, "The boundaries may be fuzzier, but our private spaces and our public spaces are still in many important senses gendered" (p. 39). In other words, social constructions of gender are still informed by a separate-spheres ideology, and "good" and "bad" mothering continues to be measured based on adherence to or deviation from public/private expectations.

Hays's (1996) intensive-mothering principles give scholars a language to understand how mothers are evaluated based on private-sphere expectations informed by a separate-spheres ideology. For example, Hays (1996) argues that intensive mothering is characterized with mothers as the primary caregiver and mothers taking a child-centered, as opposed to parent-centered approach to rearing. This can be translated as a mother constructing her "good mother" persona by giving up her own needs in order to fulfill the needs of her children and by being the primary caregiver of her children; however, this is threatened when mothers enter the public workforce because of the physical and emotional distance that occurs as a result.

Many feminist studies that trace the intersection of motherhood and work indicate that mothers are punished or face undesirable consequences when they attempt to encroach on the male-dominated public sphere and abandon their duties in the private-sphere (e.g., Bizzell, 2010; Dancey, 2009; Dubrofsky, 2009; Fishbein, 1987). These authors explore how rhetoric functions to instruct women about the misfortunes and dire consequences that occur upon deviation from their private-sphere role. Such consequences result in a disciplining of the mothers to abide by mothering norms that suggest a mother's place is in the private sphere.

This traditional notion of public/private is frequently maintained in popular discourse whereby consequences exist for mothers not abiding by the separate-spheres ideology. Johnston and Swanson (2003) suggest that, "culture defines and rewards 'good mothers,' and it sanctions 'bad mothers'"

(p. 22). The rewards and sanctions against mothers is nowhere more prevalent than in popular culture, but especially in film. For example, Glenn Close's psychopathic career-woman character, Alex Forrest in *Fatal Attraction* (1987), has been read in direct contrast with that of Anne Archer's character, Beth Gallagher, a stay-at-home devoted-to-family mother, indicating a reinforcement of traditional norms and the good mother (Bromley & Hewitt, 1992). This good/bad mother struggle has continued to play out in various films and television shows and can be read as a representation of cultural conversations about women and the role of motherhood in public discourse. Much scholarly research has focused on the ways Western mothering plays out in popular culture. Given the rise in transnational mothers migrating to the U.S., we suggest that a closer look at rhetorically constructed mothers who do not square with this Western vision is not only timely, but also necessary in order to better understand the fluctuations that exist when fictional mothers deviate from intensive-mothering principles. In other words, many feminist studies focus on how fictional mothers are portrayed as "bad" mothers when they are absent from the primary caregiver role, but we argue that fictional depictions of transnational mothering calls for a more nuanced evaluation of the how the "bad" mother is evaluated. This is especially important to interrogate in terms of the class differences between the transnational mother, who must seek work out of necessity, and the Western mother who can afford not to work, but has still chosen to pursue professional goals and has hired the transnational mother to take care of her child.

In *Mammoth*, within the Vidales home, the Western working mother is frequently positioned as the less involved, less capable caregiver, whereas the transnational working mother is depicted as abiding by the traditional role of intensive motherhood, where mothering occurs in the home taking care of domestic concerns. However, *Mammoth* offers a unique reading of the dual role of the transnational mother as both the good and bad mother simultaneously, as she leaves her own family to care for another.

When Gloria gives up her primary caregiving responsibilities of her own children to care for another family's child, this move rhetorically constructs two different value hierarchies based on the home country. In Western mothering, according to intensive-mothering norms, physically caring for a woman's own children in the private sphere is more valuable than work in the public sphere; in contrast, in Third World countries, financially providing for children in the public sphere is prioritized higher than primary care in the private sphere. These hierarchies are constructed in the film by contrasting how Jackie and Gloria's children are separately supervised. For example, Jackie is always escorted to school by Gloria. She is never alone except for the concluding moments of the film when Gloria abruptly leaves to go back to her home country. Not only is Jackie always escorted to school, Ellen is never the one to take her but is shown longingly watching Gloria and Jackie walking to school from the window of their high-rise. In other words, although Ellen does not physically walk Jackie to school, she wants to and she expresses guilt over not being the one to do so. In contrast to this experience, Gloria's sons are never shown being supervised by adults in similar situations. In one scene, the boys are walking to school together, but have no adult supervision. In another scene, they are together at a beach, but again, are not supervised. These juxtapositions discursively construct two alternate prioritizations for mothers where in Western motherhood, the priority lies with physical proximity to and supervision of the child, and, for Third World countries, the priority is not on primary supervision of the child. This contrast demonstrates class differences in mothering expectations. Ellen may be absent from her role as primary caregiver but she still longs to care for her child and provides a surrogate supervisor, whereas Gloria makes a much bigger sacrifice and is physically absent from her role as primary caregiver. Although Gloria is absent from her role as primary caregiver to her boys, she displays great anguish over being absent. For instance, every time she talks to Salvador on the phone she ends the phone call in tears and she also expresses to her mother that "This is not what God wants ... God wants me to be with my children." The film thus complicates how "bad" mothers are evaluated because for both mothers in the film, the working mothers suffer consequences within their private sphere for absenteeism in their own domestic family. However, the reasons why they are absent and the type of absence (i.e., physical vs. emotional) suggest a close reading of why each mother has abandoned her primary caregiver role and the consequences for doing so.

In the next section, we articulate how the film can be read both as broadening notions of motherhood, by presenting a dissociative argument about the changing standards for evaluating mothers, but also, constraining notions of motherhood by adding to the list of reasons why mothers should be evaluated, as well as reinforcing that mothers should be the primary caregiver in parenting situations. Through an analysis of the rhetorical functions of allegiance and dissociation, the intersection of the Western and transnational mother in *Mammoth* complicates this notion of the good/bad mother. First, we explain how a structure of sympathy creates identification with the characters and establishes a complex framing of the good and bad mother, and then we articulate how this construction creates a dissociative argument within the film.

## *Complicating the Good/Bad Mother: Allegiance and Dissociation as Functions of Argument in* Mammoth

### *A Structure of Sympathy*

The concept of identification between the audience and fictionalized characters in a narrative is an important scholarly pursuit. As Smith (1994) explains when detailing the components of his structure of sympathy, media scholars have theorized identification from a variety of philosophical lenses, including psychoanalysis, "a mixture of central and acentral imagining" (p. 49), where audience members imagine themselves at the center and emotionally distanced from the characters, and secondary and primary identification. Although there are many approaches to understanding the concept of spectator identification to fictional characters, the importance of identification for understanding what the audience takes away from a text is rarely challenged. We contend that Smith's version of identification, which occurs through a structure of sympathy, is one that is particularly useful to better understand the constructions of motherhood within *Mammoth*.

Smith's (1994) seminal work offers a viable framework to understand the identification, or to use his preferred term, "engagement," that exists between spectators and fictional characters in film. He suggests that recognition, alignment, and allegiance are all levels of engagement within a cinematic text that create a structure of sympathy. According to Smith, recognition is a function of engagement with the text that allows the spectator to correlate what they are seeing in the narrative with what they know to be true in real life. It allows the audience to engage with the characters as whole beings, while still acknowledging that they are fictional. Recognition is necessary for spectators to align themselves in sympathy with or against the characters' predicaments and choices.

The next component, alignment, relates to the amount of information the audience is given about and by the characters in a film. This can occur through both spatial attachment and subjective access (Smith, 1994). Spatial attachment refers to which character the spectator is expected to follow as the primary storyteller and/or whose story the narrative allows spectators to see. In *Mammoth*, the film oscillates equally between Ellen's and Gloria's stories. Audiences are encouraged to understand the narrative through each of their stories, at times intertwined, when they interact directly, but also separately when meeting Gloria's children, or seeing Ellen at work. Spatial attachment creates a sense of alignment because audiences are getting the story through specific characters' perspectives, but spectators can also align with the characters via the information that comes from how well audiences get to know the characters in the film via their subjectivity.

Subjective access, another component of alignment, is the "degree of access we have to the subjectivity of characters" (Smith, 1994, p. 41). The audience is given subjective access to both mothers in *Mammoth*, but in two different ways. For Ellen, audiences understand her as a subject via the conversations she has with her husband, specifically about her misgivings as a working mother. The camera focuses on her facial expressions, a mix of disappointment and longing, as she watches Jackie go off to school. The audience is also given access to understand her as a caring partner, when she leaves a kind note for her husband, and when she shows compassion to her patients in the emergency room where she works. We understand that she is, or at least could be, a good caregiver, but we rarely see her interact with her own daughter. For Gloria, her kindness with Jackie and her loving touches of her face and hands show both care and intimacy. However, the subjective access that most clearly encourages audience sympathy towards her character is when she tries to explain to her oldest son that she cannot come home yet. Her tears are heartbreaking, and although it is likely that most people in the audience have not had to personally have such a conversation, this construction of Gloria as a subject is designed to create sympathy.

The third component in Smith's (1994) structure of sympathy is allegiance, and this is the function that is the primary focus for the remainder of our analysis. Allegiance is "the moral and ideological evaluation of characters by the spectator" (p. 41). Through recognition and alliance, spectators are encouraged to make judgments about the characters within a text. None of the three components are static; recognition, alliance, and allegiance may fluctuate as the narrative progresses. In *Mammoth*, allegiance occurs when the role of the mother and the evaluation of what it means to be a good/bad mother are most apparent in the narrative, and this fluctuates throughout the film. For example, spectators are encouraged to feel allegiance with Gloria as evidenced by the access given to audiences to both her pain at being away from her children and her children's pain at being away from their mother. The narrative only gives the spectator access to Gloria's desire to leave her situation and the pressure from her own mother to stay in America and make money for the family after her son begs her to come home and she denies him. Within just a few short scenes, allegiance with her son, and the obvious questions about what kind of a person could leave her young children and allow them to plead for her, gives way to an allegiance with Gloria when the complexity of her situation is revealed. Her own mother frames Gloria's choice to work in America as the decision that makes her a good mother. Gloria's mother tells her that she must be strong for her children and stay away, thus reinforcing the role of the good mother, which implies a positive moral judgment. The fact that she is so despondent over her decision to leave her children reinforces a sympathetic vision of Gloria as a good mother, one who believes she is doing the right thing by leaving her children to make a better life for them.

Similarly, the spectator's allegiance with Ellen fluctuates within the frame of the good and bad mother. The audience aligns with Ellen's disappointment when Jackie continually chooses to spend time with Gloria over her own mother, Ellen. The narrative sets up Ellen as a compassionate but frustrated woman, and one who wants to spend more time with her daughter. This recognition of her desire to be a good mother creates allegiance with the audience; her intentions are morally good. However, when Ellen later passively aggressively confronts Gloria, arguing that time with Gloria may be distracting Jackie, but clearly masking her own jealousy of the time they spend together, the spectator's allegiance with her is placed in flux. Her choice to reprimand Gloria is selfish and places judgment of her morality in question.

It is through the creation of a structure of sympathy, and specifically the fluctuations of allegiance, that spectators are asked to identify with the mothers in compatible, but different ways. The frequent tension between subjectivities of the mother characters and the moral judgments expected by the spectators via allegiance underscores the capriciousness of definitions of motherhood. The structure of sympathy underscores the complexity of understanding both Western and transnational motherhood within and outside of the context of the good/bad mother, and for the critic, reveals an opportunity to read the film through the argumentative scheme of dissociation, to explore the nuances of allegiance as it is associated and dissociated with issues of class.

## *Dissociating Mothering Experiences*

Within an intensive-mothering paradigm, because mothering is gendered, and consequently evaluated according to adherence to or deviation from public and private assumptions, it is expected that women will experience maternal consequences when they give up their primary caregiver role. In *Mammoth*, both mothers can be understood as violating their domestic role by choosing to be absent as the primary caregiver to their biological child[ren]. The notion of choice, however, as presented in the film, complicates the allegiance to Gloria and Ellen. Using insights from Smith's (1994) structure of sympathy, we now explore how *Mammoth* breaks apart aspects of maternal consequences through dissociation in order to illuminate the levels of oppression experienced based on class, which reveals how the intensive-mothering paradigm ignores issues of class and financial necessity. More specifically, we argue the film *Mammoth* (2009) employs an argument of dissociation with regard to the socioeconomic distinction between the Western and transnational mother, in conjunction with the structure of sympathy. In doing so, the film shifts the frame for understanding hierarchical levels of inequality in contemporary mothering in a way that reflects a more progressive narrative informed by the current historical and cultural context of increased globalization.

Definitional arguments are a useful method of analyzing the presentation of messages within public discourse, such as film. Critics can observe definitional arguments, like what constitutes a "good" vs. "bad" mother, in public discourse and identify a "definitional struggle" (Jasinski, 2001, p. 152). This rhetorical dichotomy of a struggle between two seemingly different definitions relies on dissociation. Perelman and Olbrechts-Tyteca (1969) provide the starting point for observing how dissociation works persuasively as an argument, positing, "Dissociation … assumes the original unity of elements comprised within a single conception and designated by a single notion" (pp. 411–412). If we attempt to understand *Mammoth* through the framework of a Western notion of intensive mothering, the idea that a mother is socially sanctioned and evaluated negatively if she fails to be the primary caregiver of her child is the original single notion. However, *Mammoth* can be read as attempting to disrupt this framework, when it places the Western mother and transnational mother in direct contrast. This disruption creates an argument of dissociation, by emphasizing what Perelman and Olbrechts-Tyteca (1969) call "appearance-reality." In other words, a rhetor might use argument by dissociation to break apart links between concepts, emphasizing what appears to be true, with what is actually true (Zarefsky, 1997). In *Mammoth*, an argument of dissociation is deployed to emphasize two disparate aspects of how "bad" mothers are evaluated when revealed through the lenses of "appearance" and "reality," thus constructing the film's dissociative argument through the following framework:

| | | |
|---|---|---|
| Term I | Appearance | Public/Private-Sphere Expectations |
| Term II | Reality | Wealthy/Poor Socioeconomic Class |

Term I suggests that the consequences of maternal choices are aligned with the traditionally Western idea of intensive mothering, creating definitions of the "good" and "bad" mother according to adherence to private-sphere expectations. This constructs the issue as that which occurs within a private/public-sphere tension. Term II reveals the reality of the situation by understanding motherhood through socioeconomic class standing. Warnick (1996) argues that Perelman and Olbrechts-Tyteca's "appearance-reality" is particularly helpful in rhetorical criticism because it "provides rhetorical critics with a powerful tool for exposing a text's hidden agenda, the ways it is designed to respond to other texts, and the reasons for its success in reframing audience perceptions" (p. 184). The dissociation framework of appearance-reality is useful here to explain how *Mammoth* breaks the links in maternal consequences to illuminate the levels of oppression experienced depending on class, rather than a public/private-sphere boundary, thus broadening the notion of motherhood beyond Western standards.

The film can be read as employing an argument of dissociation to explain why Ellen and Gloria suffer different consequences, even though their mothering experiences are emphasized as similar. Perelman and Olbrechts-Tyteca (1969) indicate that "Term I [appearance] corresponds to the apparent, to what occurs in the first instance, to what is actual, immediate, and known directly" (p. 416). In the film, the public- and private-sphere constraints experienced by both Gloria and Ellen are presented as "actual"- and-"immediate" to viewers, thus rhetorically constructing the appearance of maternal consequences based on their absence from their primary caregiver role. These similarities are presented throughout the film. For instance, Ellen's work as an emergency room doctor takes her away from spending quality time with Jackie. This causes growing anxiety in Ellen as Jackie begins to prefer time and activities with Gloria. One evening, Ellen is excited to spend some quality time making homemade pizzas with Jackie, however, Jackie is visibly disappointed when her mother tells her about their pizza party because she was hoping to go to church with Gloria to practice her new Filipino words that Gloria had been teaching her. Ellen expresses disappointment and worry because she wanted to spend her rare night off with Jackie, and this is an example where Jackie demonstrates her preference for Gloria. In short, through allegiance with Ellen, spectators are encouraged to sympathize with the private-sphere anguish that is a result of her demanding occupation in the public sphere and the consequences she experiences as a result of her emotional absence in her primary caregiver role. Although Ellen is not as physically removed from Jackie, her time spent at work has clearly created emotional absence between herself and Jackie as emphasized through Jackie's choice to prefer time with Gloria over her own biological mother.

Similar to Ellen, Gloria works in the public sphere, although it is domestic work, and this work prevents her from seeing her two children, Manuel and Salvador. Her occupation physically removes her as primary caregiver for her children because she is not caring for them on a daily basis but rather, across the globe caring for another family's daughter. Gloria experiences significant guilt throughout the film, similar to Ellen, for not being home with her young boys. Her anguish is also depicted visually in the form of tears, worry, and lonesomeness that she experiences in the Vidales's home. A structure of sympathy is similarly created for Gloria through her experience of being away from her private-sphere duties to her own biological children.

At first glance, Ellen and Gloria stand in as an analogy for the public/private-sphere expectations faced by all mothers. They both are generally absent from their role as primary caregivers and both experience grief over their absence. Gloria becomes the primary caregiver to Jackie rather than to her own sons, and Ellen relinquishes her role as primary caregiver to Gloria as her job demands most of her time to be spent away from home. They both experience significant guilt throughout the movie for not fulfilling their primary caregiver duties. Thus, the film suggests that deviation from their private-sphere duties might *appear* to be the reason behind the consequences experienced by the mothers. However, if we analyze this reading through the lens of dissociation, the public/private-sphere expectations (appearance) are only an illusion for why they are punished for their "bad" mothering (reality). Stated another way, the mothers are violating their role in the private sphere, within the intensive-mothering framework, but the reality is that they are punished very differently based on their socioeconomic status. Gloria, and Ellen's absence from their primary caregiver role is presented as a choice to make money in the public sphere, although the film emphasizes why this choice is very different for Gloria than for Ellen. Gloria's absenteeism and work in the U.S. is presented as necessary for her family's survival whereas Ellen's husband also works and both parents can be considered breadwinners.

This illusion of choice undergirds term II, or the reality of why Ellen and Gloria are alternatively punished due to their mothering decisions. Perelman and Olbrechts-Tyteca (1969) claim that

> after the dissociation has been made, term II makes it possible to retain or to disqualify the various aspects under which term I is presented. It makes it possible to distinguish, out of a number of appearances of doubtful status, those which are merely appearance and those which represent reality. (pp. 416–417)

In contrast to reinforcing appearance (public/private-sphere expectations), the film can be read as illuminating reality when the mothers are punished differently not because of the violation of their private-sphere duties, but rather, due to the differences in their socioeconomic status. Both women have given up their private-sphere role as primary caregiver, and both have entered the public sphere, so the appearance of the situation would suggest that women should suffer similar consequences in the private sphere. Since dissociation allows the critic to analyze the hidden meaning or agenda within the text, the film instead can be read as emphasizing the socioeconomic differences between the two mothers by juxtaposing the class differences between the mothers as well as presenting varying degrees of punishment that each mother faces at the end of the film. These textual choices reveal a dissociation from the public/private-sphere issue, and emphasize socioeconomic issues at stake for transnational mothers in particular, but more broadly, mothers who are economically disadvantaged.

The reality portion of the "appearance-reality" pair is emphasized, in part, by contrasting Ellen's and Gloria's living and mothering experiences. Ellen, Leo, and Jackie live a high-class life in New York City. They live in a high-rise apartment with an elevator that opens directly to their home. Both Ellen and Leo have professions that afford disposable income for the family. Leo's well-paying job is made apparent at the beginning of the movie when he is saying goodbye to Jackie before he heads out of town and she goes to the Planetarium with Gloria. As he is telling Jackie goodbye he says, "Don't go to the planetarium, come with me on my private plane." The film reveals that Leo is not just traveling out of town, but doing so on a private plane. In addition to Leo's profession, the Vidales family's status is also depicted through the details of the apartment shown in the film. For instance, the Vidales family appears to have a private rooftop that is used only for exercise, when Ellen is shown jogging on a treadmill twice. The Vidales's kitchen is spacious, a high commodity in an expensive city, with top-of-the-line appliances and a fully stocked refrigerator. The Vidales's kitchen is contrasted with Gloria's boys' kitchen, which is very small in comparison. The Vidales's home is luxurious and spacious and Jackie has her own room with an incredible view overlooking the city. The spaciousness of the home is foregrounded in the beginning scenes of the movie where Ellen, Leo, and Jackie are playing hide-and-go-seek in their home with plenty of room. Gloria's children live with their grandmother and their uncle. Gloria's brother is shown building a new home for the family, but it is a small cinderblock structure that is situated nearby other homes on a dusty road.

The lives of Jackie and Gloria's children are also contrasted throughout the film emphasizing the reality of the class discrepancies between the families. Gloria eats a dinner that she has prepared with Jackie. This vision of Gloria and Jackie dining together is immediately contrasted with Salvador and Manuel, who are unsupervised, on the beach together. The boys share a small room where their beds are touching and shrouded with a netting, likely a mosquito netting, which implies that the home does not have central air conditioning. One image of the boys' room is juxtaposed with Jackie's room. Jackie is sitting on her bed with a map of the world behind it as she is discussing her thoughts about astronomy. Jackie's experience here, in the comfort of her home and her life, stands in stark contrast to Salvador and Manuel's experiences as children in the Philippines. Ellen buys seven-year-old Jackie a very nice telescope after Jackie indicates she wants to be an astronomer. This "just because" gift is paralleled with Gloria buying a simple basketball for Manuel's upcoming birthday. Overall, the director's choice to juxtapose these experiences of class invites viewers to think about the reality of class over the appearance of an absent primary caregiver.

After juxtaposing each mother's experiences throughout the film, the narrative climaxes with maternal punishment. With Gloria, the punishment is severe. In an attempt to get his mother to come back home, Salvador tries to find ways to earn money so that his mom will not have to, and thus she would be able to come home. Throughout the film, Salvador is distraught about his mother's absence. He is shown going through town asking townspeople for a job. He cries to his mother on the phone and begs her to come home. After Gloria's mother hears that Salvador has been calling his mother, she scolds him for making Gloria feel guilty. He wakes up one morning to his punishment from his grandmother that begins with no breakfast. The grandmother then takes Salvador to the local garbage dump and shows Salvador that kids his age are scavenging through garbage. Later, she explains to Salvador that "something worse happens here at night ... kids sell themselves to tourists." She begins to explain this but when Salvador begins to ask too many questions such as "Why are they taking kids to their hotel? Do they get paid? What else do they do?" she says, "Let's not talk about it. They don't do anything. They just sleep there." It is at this point that Salvador begins to think that he can make money by coming to the same place at night and only sleeping in a hotel room. The next morning, the grandma comes to wake up Salvador and Manuel but Salvador is missing from his bed. The family begins to look everywhere inside and outside the home, then through town for Salvador. In a very disturbing conclusion to the film, a townsperson finds Salvador's body under a bridge the next morning. He has been brutally beaten and raped. Gloria's family calls her to come home and when she sees her son in the hospital, acknowledging her role in his tragedy, she tells Salvador, "I will never leave you again, son." This is the completion of the narrative for Gloria. Because this is the final time that spectators witness Gloria, her concluding lines imply that this experience is of central importance for viewers to remember about Gloria. It is inferred in this scene that Gloria is taking responsibility for what has happened to Salvador. Saying "I will never leave you again, son" reminds spectators that Gloria was physically absent from her role as primary caregiver to Salvador and that her presence could have prevented this experience.

It is this no-win situation that highlights a major discrepancy between the options available to Gloria and Ellen. For Gloria, if she is physically absent in order to provide financially for her family, her son is hurt. Logically, she is fulfilling her role to provide for her sons, and in this sense is a "good mother." However, if the "good mother" is supposed to be the primary caregiver for her own children, her "choice" to work away from her own home constructs her as a "bad mother." By making this promise to Salvador, Gloria reinstates herself as a "good mother," by becoming physically present, but now, the options available to her, to provide a good home and food for her family, have been diminished. Gloria's conclusion in the film highlights the double bind that the transnational mother faces, when she must make choices about the importance of physical versus financial caregiving.

Ellen's punishment is also revealed at the end of the film, but it is less direct than the punishment that Gloria experiences. The film reveals to spectators that Ellen takes special interest in a young child who comes to the emergency room after being stabbed in the stomach by his own mother. Ellen's special care of and empathy for the boy suggests her potential to be a caring and devoted mother. In these scenes, the boy's mother is cast as a "bad" mother, because she inflicted brutal violence against her own son. Ellen vocally condemns the woman to her coworkers, and promises the young unconscious boy that as soon as he gets better, she will buy him ice cream. At the end of the film, the boy dies and Ellen visibly struggles to handle the grief that comes with the loss of her patient. Ellen's punishment functions as a rhetorical "wake-up call" for her because her patient died as a result of the actions of his own "bad" mother. Ellen recognizes the material repercussions of a bad mother and thus has a new opportunity to be a good mother to Jackie.

Ellen's opportunity is enacted at the end of the film. Similarly, at the conclusion of the film, Gloria is at the Vidales household tucking Jackie into bed. When she gets the phone call about Salvador, she immediately packs a bag and tells Jackie to call her mom because she must leave. Ellen rushes home to Jackie and the film concludes with an idealistic vision of a reunion of the Vidales family, when Jackie, Ellen, and Leo are laughing together in their home. In this revelation, Ellen receives a second chance to be a better, more present mother to Jackie. In contrast to what Gloria experiences with her son, Ellen's punishment is not so much a punishment in the same way that Gloria is punished because Jackie is not harmed due to Ellen's emotional absence as a primary caregiver. Additionally, there is no indication that Ellen has to quit her job in the public sphere; she simply has to be more present in the private sphere. This dissociation asks viewers to understand the consequences as rooted in differences of socioeconomic class as opposed to the similar steps taken to provide for their respective families.

The film's employment of a dissociative argument functions in conjunction with the structure of sympathy as a morality tale of class. The film asks viewers to engage with Ellen and Gloria throughout the film through recognition, alliance, and especially, allegiance. The narrative is structured so that audiences understand both women to be good and bad mothers within the definitions of an intensive-mothering framework, fluctuating between the moral judgments that cast women with one or the other label. This serves the purpose of highlighting the constriction of a good/bad binary, thus broadening our definition of motherhood. Viewers are asked throughout the film to understand the mothers as facing similar plights under the unity of the theme of gender and the subsequent assumptions of the mother in relation to the public and private spheres because both mothers relinquish their role as primary caregiver.

By juxtaposing Western mothering and transnational mothering, the film offers the appearance of punishment to both of the mothers based on their similar choices to relinquish their private-sphere duties in an attempt to provide for their corresponding family. However, the film's juxtaposition between the lives and mothering experiences as well as the final moments of the narrative reveal the film's attempt to present the spectator with the "reality" of a cross-cultural mothering experience in association with the mother's socioeconomic status. As such, the film invites viewers to interrogate a new vision of mothering, one that is simultaneously complex, and also defined by a mother's class status as opposed to her choices in relation to the public and private spheres.

## *Broadening and Constraining Motherhood: Shifting the Frame through Character Allegiance*

Ultimately, we suggest that it is a frame-shifting approach within the film that broadens and redefines mothering experiences in a contemporary cultural climate where different mothering paradigms are becoming more prevalent and more widely discussed. When a new frame of reference is created for "a subject that usually is defined from a certain perspective … the effect is that people see the thing 'in a different light' and their attitudes about it therefore change" (Zarefsky, 1997, p. 8). The film redirects the audience's attention to observe a transnational perspective of mothering. Given this, the film widens "the scope of a conflict by making it relevant to those not initially involved or irrelevant to some of those who were" (Zarefsky, 1997, p. 8). Widening the scope, in this case, reveals problems in evaluating mothers as either good or bad and suggests that in between these extremes lie complex factors by which society actually evaluates mothers. *Mammoth* suggests that reality is particularly oppressive to women with less social privilege.

However, although this film broadens conceptualizations of contemporary motherhood by introducing complexities that arise when motherhood intersects with issues of class, not just gender, the film also constrains notions of motherhood because it suggests that mothers can and will be judged based on their mothering "choices"—regardless of whether or not the choices are within or outside of their control. We can assume that differences in class are strong predictors of "choosing" or "not choosing" to seek income. For many individuals of lower socioeconomic status, this "choice" will likely seem forced upon him or her by the necessity to survive, and in some cases, to support other dependent parties, such as the typical case in transnational families. These markers of class differences invite viewers to see the class discrepancies between the mothers as the primary maternal disadvantage in spite of their similarities in being physically and/or emotionally absent as the primary caregiver. To be emotionally absent, but financially secure enough to hire a caregiver is acceptable, but to be physically absent from children, even if it is to secure a better financial future for the benefit of the children, is subject to harsher punishment. By engaging the audience with a structure of sympathy, allegiance with the characters forces an evaluation of the similar actions of the two mothers, but reveals issues of privilege with the differing severity of punishments.

We conclude this chapter with two important lessons. First, through the use of identification/engagement, we were able to highlight dissociation within the text that works as a frame-shifting device. We contend that popular culture texts lend themselves well to this type of critical project. We found that identifying the function of Smith's concept of allegiance within a structure of sympathy reveals Perelman and Olbrechts-Tyteca's concept of dissociation. Allegiance and dissociation are two compatible theoretical frameworks that can assist critics' understandings of the persuasive tactics of media. As such, our analysis suggests that a critic has possibilities to open up interdisciplinary dialogue and engagement through both rhetorical and media studies perspectives.

Second, we suggest this film represents a desirable focus on mothering representations that deviate from what is prescribed within the intensive-mothering model. As demonstrated in our analysis, *Mammoth* complicates the good/bad mother binary and disrupts tenets of intensive mothering by underscoring the complexity of these categorizations. This film reinforces the necessity to understand the variety of factors that influence mothers in the private and public sphere. The "choice" involved for a mother to work and to be absent, in some form, in her role as mother, is not the same across class. The public/private-sphere aspect of mothering is gendered, but just one issue under a much larger umbrella. The more frequently that texts about motherhood aim to represent this complexity, the more spectators have an opportunity to question the over-simplification of ideas that are much more nuanced than they traditionally appear.

In sum, *Mammoth* invites viewers to interrogate the hierarchical levels of inequality in contemporary mothering by suggesting that the appearance of traditional public/private gender issues hides behind the larger social inequality of class. Throughout the film, Ellen's material-filled life is contrasted with Gloria's children's materially austere conditions. The Western upper-class refrigerator is filled with food, whereas members of Gloria's community wade through garbage to find dinner. We suggest the film functions as an argument that encourages a shift in the public conversation about motherhood to move away from the direction of public/private gender inequalities and move toward the socioeconomic inequities that function to disadvantage a growing number of transnational mothers in our culture.

The messages about mothering within the film shift the cultural frame of motherhood in new and more nuanced ways. An intensive-mothering framework generally constrains the ways in which we evaluate mothers. We contend that *Mammoth* broadens definitions of motherhood in this respect because it complicates the ways in which we evaluate mothers by reinforcing a fluctuation of moral assessment of the characters by the audience. However, there is a constraining aspect here as well, because although the film can be read as implying that standards of motherhood are in flux, especially in the way that we evaluate Ellen and Gloria as subjective characters, the mothers are still ultimately disciplined in level of severity based on socioeconomic class. Furthermore, the central tenet of intensive mothering that suggests mothers are the primary caregivers of children is left unchallenged and actually reinforced, which reveals that despite the broadening, it is difficult to get around the constraining notion that mothers are (and should be) the primary source of care for their children. This analysis, then, also reveals the naturalization of rhetorics of motherhood where even texts that challenge definitions of motherhood still reify certain assumptions that are difficult to alter. It is this broadening and constraining of motherhood that makes this text an important and progressive narrative and demonstrates the importance of interrogating the intersection of class and motherhood in popular culture.

## *References*

Bizzell, P. (2010). Chastity warrants for women public speakers in nineteenth-century American fiction. *Rhetoric Society Quarterly, 40*(4), 385–401.

Bromley, S., & Hewitt, P. (1992). *Fatal Attraction*: The sinister side of women's conflict about career and family. *The Journal of Popular Culture, 26*(3), 17–23.

Dancey, A. (2009). Killer instincts: Motherhood and violence in *The Long Kiss Goodnight* and *Kill Bill*. In A. C. Hall & M. Bishop (Eds.), *Mommy angst: Motherhood in American popular culture* (pp. 81–92). Santa Barbara, CA: Praeger.

Dobris, C., & White-Mills, K. (2006). Rhetorical visions of motherhood: A feminist analysis of the *What to Expect* series. *Women and Language, 29*(1), 26–36.

Dubrofsky, R. E. (2009). Fallen women on reality TV: A pornography of emotion. *Feminist Media Studies, 9*(3), 353–368.

Fishbein, L. (1987). The fallen woman as victim in early American film: Soma versus psyche. *Film and History, 17*(3), 50–61.

Hays, S. (1996). *The cultural contradictions of motherhood*. New Haven, CT: Yale University Press.

Hondagneu-Sotelo, P. & Avila, E. (1997). "I'm here, but I'm there:" The meanings of Latina transnational motherhood. *Gender & Society, 11*(5), 548–571.

Horton, S. (2010). A mother's heart is weighed down with stones: A phenomenological approach to the experience of transnational motherhood. *Culture, Medicine, and Psychiatry, 33*(1), 21–40.

Jasinski, J. (2001). *Sourcebook on rhetoric: Key concepts in contemporary rhetorical studies*. Thousand Oaks, CA: Sage.

Johnston, D. D., & Swanson, D. H. (2003). Invisible mothers: A content analysis of motherhood ideologies and myths in magazines. *Sex Roles, 49*(1/2), 21–33.

Kerber, L. (1988). Separate spheres, female worlds, woman's place: The rhetoric of women's history. *Journal of American History, 75*(1), 9–39.

Kinnick, K. N. (2009). Media morality tales and the politics of motherhood. In A. C. Hall & M. Bishop (Eds.), *Mommy angst: Motherhood in American popular culture* (pp. 1–28). Santa Barbara, CA: Praeger.

O'Brien Hallstein, L. (2010). *White feminists and contemporary maternity: Purging matrophobia*. New York, NY: Palgrave Macmillan.

Parrenas, R. S. (2001). Mothering from a distance: Emotions, gender, and inter-generational relations in Filipino transnational families. *Feminist Studies, 27*(2), 361–390.

Parrenas, R. S. (2010). Transnational mothering: A source of gender conflicts in the family. *North Carolina Law Review, 88*, 1825–1856.

Perelman, C., & Olbrechts-Tyteca, L. (1969). *The new rhetoric: A treatise on argumentation*. Notre Dame, IN: University of Notre Dame Press.

Quintero Escobar, J. (2010). *Transnational mothers and the construction of alternative meanings of motherhood* (unpublished master's thesis). Indiana University Purdue University—Indianapolis, Indianapolis, IN.

Silbergleid, R. (2009). Hip mamas: *Gilmore Girls* and Ariel Gore. In A. C. Hall & M. Bishop (Eds.), *Mommy angst: Motherhood in American popular culture* (pp. 93–111). Santa Barbara, CA: Praeger.

Smith, M. (1994). Altered states: Character and emotional response in the cinema. *Cinema Journal, 33*(4), 34–56.

Trask, B. S. (2013). Locating multiethnic families in a globalizing world. *Family Relations, 62*(1), 17–29.

Warnick, B. (1996). Argument schemes and the construction of social reality: John F. Kennedy's address to the Houston Ministerial Association. *Communication Quarterly, 44*(2), 183–196.

Zarefsky, D. (1997). Definitions. In J. F. Klumpp (Ed.), *Argument in a time of change: Definitions, frameworks, and critiques* (pp. 1–11). Annandale, VA: National Communication Association.

# 11. *Mommy Blogs and the Disruptive Possibilities of Transgressive Drinking*

By Tasha N. Dubriwny

A 2012 episode of *Anderson Live*, reporter and news personality Anderson Cooper's daytime talk-show on CNN, began with this announcement from Cooper: "Today's show is all about moms and stress. But first I've been noticing a lot of news stories about moms acting out in surprising and frankly shocking ways" (Cooper, 2012). Cooper's introduction promises a titillating exploration of mothers engaging in outrageous acts. In fact, the episode concentrates on just two arenas of acting out by mothers: shoplifting and drinking alcohol. Regarding the second, Cooper declares, "Drinking. Not the behavior you might expect from a mom" (Cooper, 2012). *Anderson Live* makes quick work of demonizing and disciplining mothers who drink, framing drinking as always a threat to children's well-being and punishing mothers for acting outside of the boundaries of good motherhood. Mothers who enjoy a glass of wine at play dates are, according to Cooper, "just the latest example of some moms acting like out-of-control teenagers" (Cooper, 2012). *Anderson Live*'s episode is entirely typical of media coverage of mothers who drink. As Jenni M. Simon (2014) explains, "The way in which drinking mothers are portrayed in the news suggests that there is a crisis in the United States wherein children are consistently put in danger by their drunken mothers" (p. 46).

That mothers who drink receive negative media coverage is not surprising. Even when the drinking mother is only enjoying one glass of wine after putting her children to bed, she still engages two different gendered discourses that position her use of alcohol as a violation of social norms. The first is the discourse of good motherhood, perhaps still best described by Adrienne Rich:

The natural mother "is a person without further identity, one who can find her chief gratification in being all day with small children, living at a pace tuned to theirs" (1986, p. 22; see also Douglas & Michaels, 2004; Wolf, 2007). If mothers who drink do so in a cultural moment saturated by a discourse of good motherhood that insists upon mothers leading entirely child-centered lives, they also drink in a cultural moment in which alcohol use continues to be primarily constructed as both morally and physically dangerous for women. Helen Keane (2013) explains, "Female drinkers are routinely addressed in terms of their vulnerability to the harmful effects of alcohol, a vulnerability which is understood as both biological and social" (p. 151). Positioned both in relation to the discourse of good motherhood and a cultural standard in which women's alcohol consumption is often gender deviant, mothers who drink are easy lightning rods for a media-created moral panic. Drinking mothers are thus exemplars of what Owen, Stein, and Vande Berg (2007) describe as "transgressive women," women whose existence constitutes a transgression against nature (p. 2). The case of the drinking mother as a transgressive woman, however, is more complicated than the easy disciplining enacted on *Anderson Live* and other related coverage might suggest, and that complexity is embodied by one of Cooper's guests: Kristen, described as a "mom who drinks in front of her kids" (Cooper, 2012).

Kristen is actually a mommy blogger who has been actively blogging since the birth of her first son in 2005, and her notoriety as a drinking mother is such that she has appeared both on *Anderson Live* and *Good Morning America*. Mommy bloggers who blog about drinking are numerous, and while blogging is a form of new media, the voices of mommy bloggers—particularly those that use multiple media platforms (Kristen also maintains a presence on Twitter)—are "needling their way into the mainstream" and becoming part of the larger cultural conversation about motherhood (McKenna, 2012). As a "forum for broadcasting women's voices" (Ratliff, 2009, p. 142), mommy blogs are the original mediated home of the drinking mother, and I suggest in this chapter that the transgressive subject of the drinking mother is articulated differently in mommy blogs compared to mainstream media. This difference is apparent to mommy bloggers themselves, including Kristen who reports with some anger (and a bit of bemusement) that she was asked to guest on *Anderson Live* because of her "Mommy needs a cocktail" T-shirt business, but she was surprised to find her segment called "Are Moms Behaving Badly?" She reports, "I sacrificed my dignity for your entertainment" (Kristen, 2012).

This chapter is an exploration of mommy blogs and mommy bloggers' books as they relate to motherhood and alcohol use. My approach to alcohol in this chapter is deliberately non-pathological; while I recognize that alcohol use can lead to alcohol abuse, and that alcohol use does have substantial health implications, here I am interested in alcohol's symbolic use by mommy bloggers. In other words, I approach drinking alcohol (and blogging about drinking alcohol) as practices "through which personal and group identity are actively constructed, embodied, performed, and transformed" (Dietler, 2006, p. 235). In the new media landscape of mommy blogs, mothers like Kristen create a contrasting discourse about mothers and alcohol, one that celebrates, rather than demonizes, mothers who drink through amusing stories of filling sippy cups with wine and attending playdates with bottles of champagne.[1] Mommy bloggers, I argue, are resisting the traditional caregiving practices of motherhood and recreating their identities as mothers in their accounts of alcohol use, and while the transgressive potential of this resistance is limited by the post-feminist context of mommy blogging, their new vision of motherhood is one worthy of our attention.

## Mommy Blogging, Risky Motherhood and Uses of Alcohol

In the relatively masculine world of the blogosphere, mommy bloggers have charted out a distinct space of their own, drawing "thousands of readers daily to websites that document countless tales of parenting joys and woes" (Lopez, 2009, p. 729; see also Friedman, 2013). I use "mommy blogger" in this chapter to capture those bloggers who tend to focus on the daily practices and experiences of mothering, although I recognize that even with this description the blogs and related material I approach represent vastly different blogging styles. Some mommy bloggers have successfully integrated themselves into the new parent market, selling advertising on their blogs and expanding their blogging voice to different platforms, while other mommy bloggers engage in the reciprocal process of blog writing and responding on a much smaller and more intimate scale. These large market-driven ventures and smaller blogs perform in an "overlapping collection of conversations" that revolve around shared themes: "self-deprecating stories about parenthood, cute stories about children, musing on what it means to mother in contemporary society, [and] calls for advice or support in solving parenting or other dilemmas" (Morrison, 2010, para. 6). Apart from the potential of earning money from blogging (a feat only a few bloggers do well), the function of mommy blogging is one tied directly to community and identity. Mommy bloggers take part in developing what Aimee Morrison (2011) describes as a "politically and personally empowering women's culture" (p. 38).

The functions of constructing both community and identity through blogging suggest that mommy blogs can be sites of resistance to contemporary constructions of good motherhood (Douglas & Michaels, 2004). This is certainly acknowledged and embraced by some mommy bloggers; the 2006 BlogHer conference included an entire panel session devoted to "Mommy Blogging as a Radical Act" (Lopez, 2009, p. 730). Mommy blogger Alice Bradley explains that mommy blogs are radical because "we're redefining the roles with our blogs," in part by writing about the "unexciting, every day" parts of motherhood (as quoted in Lopez, 2009, p. 732). However, mommy blogging's potential for resisting constructions of good motherhood is constrained by several dimensions of blogging. First, as Morrison (2011) notes, mommy bloggers (with a few exceptions) are reluctant to move from blogging to political participation; the alternate vision of motherhood offered on mommy blogs all too often stays on mommy blogs. Second, blogging is itself a highly specialized activity in which select people take part; mommy bloggers (particularly those who become blogging "stars") are overwhelmingly White and middle class, and their reconstruction of motherhood is thus circumscribed by their privilege (Lopez, 2009). Indeed, mommy bloggers largely operate within—not outside of—the discourse of good motherhood in all of its raced and classed dimensions. Mommy bloggers perform what I call "risky motherhood," a postfeminist iteration of good motherhood in which mothers routinely engage in "imperfect" (risky) behavior but continue to assert love and substantial self-definition through their children (Dubriwny, 2013). Risky mothers in the blogging world are not afraid to critique the mythical good mother; instead, they are mothers who relish their "bad mommy" moments such as sneaking to the bathroom to enjoy a moment of quiet. As postfeminist subjects, the risky mothers who detail the trials and tribulations of motherhood are White and middle class, and their self-reflexivity about their status as good mothers even while having "bad mommy" moments points to an ongoing investment in self-discipline and self-surveillance.

What is significant for understanding the risky mother as a postfeminist mother in relation to alcohol is the expanded role given to the postfeminist subject in public, more traditionally male-dominated spheres. Angela McRobbie (2009) explains that postfeminism offers women a new sexual contract in which women can recognize themselves as "privileged agents of change" (p. 58) with an increasing role in the global economy, although traditional gender roles are still maintained through an emphasis on hyperfemininity and a focus on heterosexual desire. Young women's alcohol use can be seen as one way that women are increasingly inhabiting public culture. Helen Keane (2013) explains, "Drinking as a leisure activity has been one of the freedoms taken up by women," and in many post-industrial nations "public drinking and intoxication have become markers of youthful modern femininity" (p. 155). Alcohol use by young women remains the target of negative mainstream media reports and social scientific research, but alcohol has also become a means for young women to construct a new "positive femininity avoiding traditional, more conservative gender constructs" (Killingsworth, 2006, p. 363). Drinking is "meaningful" to young women, offering a way for women to build relationships with each other and identities for themselves that include—even embrace—transgressions of standard feminine codes (Sheehan & Ridge, 2001).

Although the postfeminist subject remains constrained by gender norms and a larger rhetoric of choice and consumption, the feminization of nightlife and the increasing visibility of women drinking for pleasure has positioned alcohol as a "symbolic marker of freedom and equality" (Keane, 2013, p. 155). This is the contemporary context in which postfeminist women become mothers, and this is the context in which young risky mothers live and blog. However, if for postfeminist women alcohol is a "form of transgression which is licensed at the same time it is condemned," postfeminist mothers face a different situation (Keane, 2013, p. 159). Killingsworth (2006) explains that for "pregnant women, the mothers of young children, and even women thinking of having children, the taboo against drinking remains as strong as ever, if not stronger" (p. 363). This taboo presents a contradiction in expectations for the postfeminist subject; she is promised freedom through alcohol as a single woman followed by strict moral prohibitions against alcohol as a mother. As the blogs and other texts by mommy bloggers I analyze in the next two sections demonstrate, alcohol does not disappear from postfeminist mothers' lives. Instead, as Killingsworth (2006) notes in his ethnographic work with mommy groups, alcohol again becomes important in the creation of positive identities for women as mothers. Drinking alcohol while a mother is a symbolically important transgressive act, one that holds power to disrupt typical discourses of good motherhood precisely because of the continuing strength of the public prohibitions against mothers—even postfeminist risky mothers—drinking.

My analysis centers on six blogs and three books written by mommy bloggers that engage frequently with the topic of mothers drinking alcohol.[2] The sample of blogs and other related work is admittedly limited and skewed toward what is most publicly visible, but I do not seek to lay claim to broad truths about mommy bloggers in this chapter. Instead, I offer an argument about the potential of alcohol as a transgressive symbol to move conversations about motherhood in new directions, a potential amply demonstrated in this set of texts. I approach the texts from the standpoint of a feminist rhetorical critic. David Zarefsky (2006) explains that rhetorical criticism is less a fixed method than an attitude; rhetorical critics seek to illuminate a text through interpretation and argument. As a feminist rhetorical critic, I am particularly attentive to the dimensions of power and identity in the texts that I analyze. I understand the blogs as productive "meaning making" texts that shape our collective understanding of both the identities of mothers and the everyday practices associated with the institution of motherhood (Dubriwny, 2013). Mommy bloggers recraft meanings for mothers and motherhood through stories of their daily lives, and thus it is appropriate that I approach the texts from within a narrative paradigm. Narratives, Kenneth Burke (1967) explains, are "equipment for living" in that they help humans make meaning and act on that meaning. In the next two sections, I analyze the two dominant narratives constructed by mommy bloggers about alcohol, a nostalgic narrative and a coping narrative. Together, these two narratives position the postfeminist risky mother who drinks as a transgressive subject who crafts her identity around her interests (not just her children's interests) and who engages in critique of one particular practice associated with motherhood, women's presumed affinity for caregiving.

## *Recrafting Identity in the Nostalgic Narrative*

Motherhood "represents a significant, and often stressful, change in a woman's life, with increased responsibilities and expectations, as well as changes in women's relationships with their friends, family and partner" (Laborde & Mair, 2012, p. 1810). Becoming a mother, however, signals a shift not merely in daily activities, expectations, and relationships, but also in identity. "Mother" as an identity is perhaps unique in the way in which it overshadows, or even replaces, women's previous identities. As Jessica Collett (2011) explains, "women lose their personal identities and motherhood monopolizes their time" (p. 329). Mothering represents for women a significant contradiction in expectations: while both mothers and children exist within contemporary discourses of individualism, mothers are faced with "the realization that their individual selfhood is necessarily constrained by their parenting labour" (Friedman, 2013, p. 121). Indeed, a key quality of the identity of "mother" is the expectation that mothers are almost entirely other-centered, focused primarily on their children's needs. Where there may be some flexibility—especially for the postfeminist subject—to pursue individual achievements (to care for the self, not for others), this flexibility is simply not present for mothers. Douglas and Michaels (2004) explain, "At the heart of the new momism is the insistence that mothers inhabit what we in the academy would call the 'subject positions' of our children as often as possible. (In the parlance of childcare experts, this means always climbing inside your child and seeing the world only and entirely through his or her eyes)" (p. 19). The identity of "mother" is thus one that is often void of agency for mothers to act for themselves.

All identities are "discursively constructed and performed and thus in flux" (Friedman, 2013, p. 26), and mommy blogs are engaged in the reconstruction of "mother" as an identity. Friedman (2013) explains that mommy blogs work to "shift understandings of maternal subjectivity by presenting a public and multitudinous account of many mothers' practices" (p. 27). In their writings about alcohol, mommy bloggers use alcohol to articulate a self-interested identity, or an identity centered on their interests. They do so within a nostalgic narrative that positions the risky mother as a woman with a happy past life without children who experiences motherhood as a dramatic upheaval. Nostalgia is a particular form of memory, a remembering that bridges nostos, or "return home," with algia, or "longing" (Barney, 2009, p. 135). Although nostalgic memories often serve a socially conservative function, the "acknowledgement of pain and longing for something that cannot be obtained in the present" (Barney, 2009, p. 136) so characteristic of nostalgia can also work for more progressive ends. Svetlana Boym (2001) distinguishes between two types of nostalgia, a conservative, restorative nostalgia that promises a return to the golden age, and a reflective nostalgia that engages in a more critical appraisal of the past. Reflective nostalgia is characterized by a "self-conscious humor and irony" (as cited in Barney, 2009, p. 137), and although looking to the past, it moves individuals to consider a new future. The nostalgic narrative in mommy blogs engages in precisely the sort of reflection that Boym identifies; rather than reifying a pre-child identity as the only possible means to happiness, the yearning for that pre-child identity in the narrative works to reposition women's sense of what the identity of mother can encompass in the present and future.

Like nostalgic memories more generally, one way to understand this narrative is as a "search for continuity" (Tannock, 1995) in this case where mothers "mend" their sense of self by reflecting on the past as they try to find peace with the present. The past life of the mommy bloggers is described through reference to all of the many things—body, house, career, interests, friends—that have changed since the arrival of children. For example, Lyranda Martin-Evans and Fiona Stevenson (2013) in *Reasons Mommy Drinks* offer an extended discussion of hand bags as they reflect on the past: "Before you were born, Mommy used to splurge on the season's latest handbag … Her adorable Chanel clutch has been replaced by an oversized Skip Hop messenger tote which, like you, she carries everywhere" (p. 70). Although the topic of hand bag versus diaper bag is relatively lighthearted, the larger picture depicted is serious in terms of its representation of women's autonomy. The well-off woman without children can choose her bag based on her personal preferences, while the mother's choice is constrained. The transformation of woman to mommy is one marked by lack of freedom and choice, and this is nowhere more clear than in memories that specifically involve alcohol. As Martin-Evans and Stevenson (2013) remember, "Mommy used to party irresponsibly. She used to wear pleather and dance on the bar to 'Pony' by Ginuwine, and once while overserved $2 Amaretto sours she ate a whole apple pie off some random dude's table" (p. 42). That type of activity, perhaps irresponsible but also fun, is expected to end as women age and mature, especially as signaled by motherhood.

Framed in wistful, humorous language, memories of the past—including past drinking—collide in mommy blogs with frank discussions of the present. As Tannock (1995) explains, nostalgia functions temporally, dividing past and present into three stages: a "prelapsarian world" of the golden days, the "lapse," or catastrophic event that disrupts the rosy world, and the "postlapsarian world," the insufficient world of the present (p. 458). Nostalgia only occurs when the present is less than satisfying, and the present of the risky mother who remembers with fondness her handbags, date nights, and drinking exploits is one that is unrelentingly tedious, a point that Stefanie Wilder-Taylor (2008) makes by labeling motherhood as "Your New and Improved but Strangely Less Exciting Life" (p. 1). Unlike the prelapsarian golden days of autonomy, motherhood presents women with an identity that is circumscribed on all sides by the needs of others. Wilder-Taylor (2008) points to the need to adjust as she discusses the experience of staying at home with her children: "I'm just going to say it: It's a bitch to stay home with a pre-school-age child all day. We have very different agendas. It seems that they want to do stuff all the time, and I, well, don't want to do stuff ever. But we need to meet them in the middle, right?" (p. 11). Wilder-Taylor's take on the problem—that her agenda might be different than that of her toddler—is a good summation of the problem of "mother" as an identity: while it makes sense that a woman and a child might have different agendas, a mother is expected to share the same agenda as her child, or at the very least put her child's agenda before her own. The life mothers lead is new and different, and that difference is given specific meaning in comparisons to their old life; the mundane aspects of spending all day, every day with a pre-schooler are amplified by the knowledge that, as blogger Christie Mellor (2004) explains, "You were here first" (p. 12).

What is significant about the function of nostalgia at work in this narrative is that although mommy bloggers look to their past with a good deal of yearning, they do not necessarily want to return to living lives without their children. Consider, for example, the poem written by one blogger about her failed attempt to write a "beer of the week" blog post. Three stanzas capture the unique dynamic of the looking backward in mommy blogs—the yearning for the past, the dissatisfaction with the present, and, importantly, a desire to live in the present.

> Baby wakes up three times / The toddler only twice / Remember a full night's sleep? / Good God wouldn't that be nice
>
> Hit the park then time for dinner / Peaches in the baby's hair / Bath time, story time, tuck in time / Hugs and prayers sent with care
>
> No beer in the fridge? Fine by me / I'm just happy to take a seat. / Maybe next week I'll try again / But for tonight it's Penguin Feet. (Christie, 2010, April 28)

In the first stanza above, Christie remembers fondly the good night's sleep of her previous child-free life, and her frustration with the present is also evident. However, she also expresses some contentment (hugs and prayers) and ends by sitting and enjoying a glass of Penguin Feet wine. As good mothers, mommy bloggers performing risky motherhood may indicate frustration with their children but they do not cross the line by indicating that they regret motherhood. This lack of regret works in a productive fashion in the nostalgic narrative of adulthood by prompting mommy bloggers to refashion their identities in the present.

In staking a claim to her Penguin Feet at the end of the day, Christie demonstrates what a more self-interested identity for mothers might look like. Alcohol is positioned as a way for Christie to care for herself, to take the time and space to enjoy something that is clearly an adult activity. Alcohol provides the mothers of mommy blogs a means to be more than a mother; alcohol is in this case the link between a past identity and their new identity. Thus, the identity symbolized by the diaper bag in the example I offered above is linked to the identity of the Chanel clutch by the recipe offered on the next page for a "Coco Chanel" martini. Martin-Evans and Stevenson (2013) explain, "Combine all ingredients in a shaker with cracked ice. Shake well and strain into a crystal martini glass. Take off those mom jeans and remember what Coco said: 'A girl should be two things: classy and fabulous' (read: not wearing front pleats)" (p. 71). A symbol of independence, alcohol falls in line with other elements of adulthood that are held distinctly apart from children: "Whether or not for you 'naptime' falls in the middle of the day or after the kids are finally in bed, this is the time you'll finally be able to have that bottle of wine, pay your bills, and update your Netflix queue" (Wilder-Taylor, 2008,

p. xii). The transgressive potential of alcohol as a symbol of independence is enhanced by the mommy bloggers' nostalgia for their past, for the new self-interested identity for mothers constructed in this narrative is an explicit refusal of the other-centered mother identity, but not a refusal to mother. It is expected for this new self-interested mother to open her fridge and find "one baby cucumber, some half-rotten mushrooms, and gobs of wine and beer" (Elizabeth, 2013), a state that may force her to the grocery store, but only because she cannot feed her children the half-rotten mushrooms.

## *Critiquing Caregiving in the Coping Narrative*

In the second narrative about alcohol constructed in the mommy blogs, the coping narrative, alcohol is positioned not as symbol of independence, but as a coping mechanism. The two narratives about alcohol overlap in the temporal space of the present; the sense of dissatisfaction or unhappiness in mothers' lives that prompts a looking backward in the nostalgic narrative is the focus of the coping narrative. Risky mothers in the coping narrative describe alcohol as an essential aspect of motherhood because it provides relief and takes the edge off of the daily caregiving experiences of mothering. Notably, the coping narrative constructs a critique of mothers' caregiving experiences by engaging, and then upending, the popularized medical construction of stressed mothers as in need of a "mother's little helper."

The Rolling Stones described "mother's little helper" in 1966 as a "little yellow pill" that provided a woman "shelter" as it helped her get "through her busy day." This depiction of women's use of tranquilizers during the 1960s reflected the reality of medical practice at the time: the over-prescribing of addictive tranquilizers (benzodiazepines) to women between 1965 and 1979 (Metzl, 2003). Mothers in particular were targeted by medical authorities as a key patient population because of the assumption that a mother's "moodiness" would "affect her ability to provide the conditions that were vital to ensuring her child's healthy psychological development" (Held & Rutherford, 2012, p. 111), but unhappy and stressed mothers were only part of a long line of transgressive women—frigid women, wanton women, unmarried women—who were encouraged to partake in pharmaceutical intervention (Metzl, 2003). The trend of offering women help in the form of a pill continues today in the form of SSRIs; antidepressants are prescribed to women at a 3:1 ratio (Metzl & Angel, 2004). Mother's little helpers are part of a larger medicalization of motherhood that decontextualizes women's distress and stress—taking such emotions out of the social context of motherhood—and re-contextualizes them in terms of brain chemistry (Dubriwny, 2013).

Such a re-contextualization allows for the treatment of postpartum disorders (for example) in individual women but gives very little space for reflection about the structural dynamics of motherhood. The individualizing tendency of medicalization that is a characteristic of "mother's little helper" discourse is part of what the coping narrative resists by directing attention away from individual mothers and toward the shared practices of mothering.

Like all risky mothers, mommy bloggers are frank in their appraisal of the daily stressors of mothering, and they are frank in their desire to find a way to ease their stress. Notably, the daily stressors that these mommy bloggers describe are almost all in relation to the tedium of caregiving. At times, this tedium can be linked (at least implicitly) to structural issues, such as the continued expectation that mothers do the vast majority of childcare. For example, bloggers Martin-Evans and Stevenson (2013) describe one problem faced by mothers as MF, or "Mommy Fear." This type of anxiety, they explain, is the reason why mommies might believe things like "the day care is a covert meth lab" and "the babysitter is sexting her math teacher" (p. 196). Held solely responsible for their children's well-being, mothers can only relax if they have a bit of help. Thus, Martin-Evans and Stevenson (2013) suggest that mothers "take a deep breath and enjoy a crisp Chardonnay" (p. 197). Mothers may need help to relieve their "MF" anxiety, but they also need help getting through smaller moments that may be frustrating, if not anxiety producing: "The swim meet was awful. 100 degrees out and it went until 10 pm. But I was hittin' the sippy by the baby pool so I managed" (Kate & Lydia, 2010). This latter example is a more typical expression of frustration: at issue is not the burden of responsibility, but rather the unpleasantness of living through a swim meet.

In response to the unpleasantness of a swim meet, or a toddler going into a rage for any number of reasons ("I made him put on socks," "I made him put on pants"), the coping narrative positions alcohol as the easy way for a mother to relax and to put things back into perspective (Julie, 2014, April 15). Julie, writer of "I Like Beer and Babies," explicitly describes her "box-o-wine" as her "Mommy's Little Helper," promising her readers that wine is "happiness at an amazing price" (Julie, 2013, February 28). In the coping narrative that emerges around alcohol, women are not coping with physiological depression or anxiety (as they do in blogging about postpartum depression), but rather they are coping with motherhood, specifically the routine caregiving associated with motherhood. The turn to alcohol as a "mommy's little helper" in this case is significant because drinking is not medicalized by the bloggers; instead, having a drink is an adult means by which mothers make it through what are often described as necessary but unpleasant tasks. For example, Julie (2013, May 21) encourages moms to make sure they have "at least one case of beer, a box of wine and a handle of vodka on hand" before beginning potty training because potty training is "torturous." She explains, "There is about to be pee and poop everywhere. The bathroom, the bedroom, the living room, the kitchen. And guess who has to clean it up? You" (Julie, 2013, May 21). Mothers in this narrative drink not because they are ill, but because they are doing a job that is full of "mess and mayhem" (Christie, 2010, April 1). In their explicitness about the frustrations with the caregiving associated with motherhood—and in their active seeking out a means to cope with those frustrations—mommy bloggers refuse to succumb to a mythical version of motherhood in which the mother/child unit exists in peaceful and perfect happiness. More specifically, by singling in on the frustrations associated with caregiving, risky mothers debunk at least one essential leg on which the institution of motherhood operates: namely, that women are innately suited to and enjoy the mundane tasks associated with child-rearing.

The venting of frustrations regarding caregiving is a characteristic of mommy blogging more generally, and it is certainly one way in which the coping narrative critiques the institution of motherhood. However, mommy bloggers who drink are not critiquing the institution of motherhood as individuals; they voice their critique as a collective of women who share similar frustrations with the daily practices of caregiving. Evidence of this collectivity can be seen in blog entries and books that move from reflection about day-to-day experiences to giving advice. Christie of "Mommy Drinks" is a prime example of this textual movement. In one entry, "Whine and Cheese" (2010, May 27) she describes the hour she spends trying to get her daughter to go to bed, ending with an exasperated "I need a glass of wine minus the whine." In a different entry, she advises readers to "take a breath" and recognize that Goldfish and Muscato make a great "mommy wine pairing" (2010, April 7). Constructing the act of drinking as a collective act of transgression is also apparent in explicit references to the drinking mommy community. Mommy friends—and the larger drinking mommy blogging community—recognize the need to "go through it [motherhood] together ... With the occasional after-the-kids-have-gone-to-bed cocktail" (Martin-Evans & Stevenson, 2013, p. 15). When mommy bloggers who drink are understood as a collective group actively coping with the caregiving associated with motherhood, the pathological story of the individual woman with her psychiatric problem turning to a "mother's little helper" is displaced by a community of women coping with a problematic institution. In short, the script of the more typical "mother's little helper" narrative is flipped;

where women were positioned as pathological previously, mommy bloggers who drink have carved out the space through discussions of the necessity of drinking to suggest that it is motherhood itself that is problematic, especially in the assumption that women would only find joy and self-fulfillment through caregiving. As one blogger suggests, mothers and their mommy friends "understand that having children often requires the consumption of copious amounts of alcohol" (Julie, 2012, May 3).

## *Good Mothers, Drinking*

The use of alcohol as a collective means of coping by mommy bloggers positions the coping narrative in direct conversation with the nostalgic narrative. The same substance that grounds the self-interested identity of mothers is also represented as the necessary source of collective relaxation after a long day of caring for children. Indeed, it is perhaps because the risky mother is articulated as self-interested that some form of coping is needed. Faced with the constraints and tedium of the expected daily caregiving for small children, the self-interested mother needs an outlet for herself. That outlet—a glass of wine to relax, a beer to take the edge off—is not perfect; drinking alcohol can have negative health consequences and will do little to change the structural inequalities that situate women as the primary caregivers of small children. Indeed, the dangers of drinking are well documented in media coverage of alcoholic mothers (see, for example, the coverage of television news personality Elizabeth Vargas's "coming out" as an alcoholic) and the pain they can cause their children and families. Perhaps the most striking media story of this sort in recent years is the tragedy of Diane Schuler, a mother who killed herself and seven others (including her two-year-old daughter) by driving intoxicated. Within mommy blogs at least, alcohol becomes a means to push back against the expectation that caregiving is always enjoyable, thus undermining at least one ideological facet of the institution of motherhood. The re-crafting of identity and the critique of caregiving in mommy blogs is particularly valuable when considered in light of more mainstream media condemnation of mothers and drinking. Such condemnation—including the coverage of the Schuler case—rarely takes into consideration the social context of why women may abuse alcohol, instead condemning individual alcoholic mothers as failing in their most essential duty: taking care of their children.

Together, the coping narrative and the nostalgic narrative re-imagine both what mothers can be (women can be self-interested) as well as what mothers can do (they can relax by enjoying an alcoholic drink). That this re-imagining happens within the larger context of postfeminist expectations for women is both problematic and promising. On the one hand, because they are enacting a version of risky motherhood, mommy bloggers are necessarily reifying problematic aspects of good motherhood, including but certainly not limited to issues of race and class privilege. On the other hand, the taking up of alcohol as a positive tool for the construction of identities and the critique of practices of mothering demonstrates how mothers can use culturally available (if still problematic) means of empowerment to disrupt expectations for mothering. Young women use alcohol to frame themselves as "empowered pleasure-seeking social beings" (Lyons & Willott, 2008, p. 709), and while that pleasure seeking occurs within the hyper-sexualized context of postfeminist culture, it is significant that pleasure-seeking and self-interested behavior does not disappear for the postfeminist drinking mother. Indeed, alcohol's illicit nature—drinking remains gender-deviant for women, even while it is propelled as a sign of postfeminist young women's independence—may give the use of alcohol by mothers for relaxation and self-definition more symbolic power than other more culturally accepted forms of relaxation (yoga, exercise). The contrasting discourse constructed by mommy bloggers leverages postfeminist expectations for young women's independence and empowerment as symbolized through the transgressive act of drinking alcohol as the groundwork for a more self-interested enactment of motherhood.

## *Notes*

1. Mansson (2014) describes the positive depictions of women drinking as a "contrasting discourse" to the messages about women and alcohol in mainstream media. Contrasting discourses offer women a "wider range of subject positions in which to invest" (p. 57).
2. I analyzed approximately 30 entries (based largely on tagged words, such as "alcohol," "drink," "martini," "wine," and "cocktail") from the following blogs: "Mommy Drinks Because You Cry" (http://www.mommydrinksbecauseyoucry.com/), "I Like Beer and Babies" (http://www.ilikebeerandbabies.com/), "Reasons Mommy Drinks" (http://reasonsmommydrinks.com/), "Rants from Mommyland" (http://www.rantsfrommommyland.com/), "Mommy Needs a Cocktail" (http://mommyneedsacocktail.com/), "The Three Martini Complaint Department" (http://www.mommytracked.com/features/christiemellor), and "Motherhood: A Descent into Madness" (http://motherhoodadescentintomadness.blogspot.com/). In addition, I included two books written by bloggers whose blogs I included in the analysis, Christie Mellor's (2004) *The Three-Martini Playdate* and Lyranda Martin-Evans and Fiona Stevenson's (2013) *Reasons Mommy Drinks*. Finally, I included Stefanie Wilder-Taylor's (2008) book, *Naptime Is the New Happy Hour*. As one of the first drinking mommy bloggers, Wilder-Taylor made a name for herself by promoting drinking while parenting. For many years she blogged at "Make Mine a Double: Tales of Twins and Tequila." In 2009, she surprised readers by announcing she was an alcoholic and

was no longer drinking. While I focus in this chapter on the symbolic use of alcohol by mothers, Wilder-Taylor stands as a cautionary tale of the very real problems that can emerge when alcohol is abused.

## References

Barney, T. (2009). When we was red: *Good Bye Lenin!* and nostalgia for the "Everyday GDR." *Communication and Critical/Cultural Studies*, *6*(2), 132–151.

Boym, S. (2001). *The future of nostalgia*. New York, NY: Basic Books.

Burke, K. (1967). *The philosophy of literary form: Studies in symbolic action*. Baton Rouge, LA: Louisiana State University Press.

Christie. (2010, April 1). Baby on back, camera on front. [Web log comment]. Retrieved from http://www.mommydrinksbecauseyoucry.com/?p=272

Christie. (2010, April 7). Wine pairing—mommy style. [Web log comment]. Retrieved from http://www.mommydrinksbecauseyoucry.com/?p=287

Christie. (2010, April 28). Beer of the week—almost. [Web log comment]. Retrieved from http://www.mommydrinksbecauseyoucry.com/?p=328

Christie. (2010, May 27). Whine and cheese. [Web log comment]. Retrieved from http://www.mommydrinksbecauseyoucry.com/?p=362

Collett, J. (2011). What kind of mother am I? Impression management and the social construction of motherhood. *Symbolic Interaction*, *28*(3), 327–347.

Cooper, A. (Producer). (2012, May 25). *Anderson live* [Television broadcast]. Atlanta, GA: Cable News Network.

Dietler, M. (2006). Alcohol: Anthropological/archaeological perspectives. *Annual Review of Anthropology*, *35*, 229–249.

Douglas, S., & Michaels, M. (2004). *The mommy myth: The idealization of motherhood and how it has undermined women*. New York, NY: Free Press.

Dubriwny, T. N. (2013). *The vulnerable empowered woman: Feminism, postfeminism, and women's health*. New Brunswick, NJ: Rutgers University Press.

Elizabeth. (2013, July 8). What parents want when we take our kids to the store. [Web log comment]. Retrieved from http://motherhoodadescentintomadness.blogspot.com/2013/07/what-parents-want-when-we-take-our-kids.html

Friedman, M. (2013). *Mommyblogs and the changing face of motherhood*. Toronto, ON: University of Toronto Press.

Held, L., & Rutherford, A. (2012). Can't a mother sing the blues? Postpartum depression and the construction of motherhood in the late 20th century. *History of Psychology*, *15*(2), 107–123.

Julie. (2012, May 3). Why you need your mommy friends. [Web log comment]. Retrieved from http://www.ilikebeerandbabies.com/2012/05/why-you-need-mommy-friends.html

Julie. (2013, February 28). Box-o-Wine to the rescue! [Web log comment]. Retrieved from http://www.ilikebeerandbabies.com/2013/02/box-o-wine-to-rescue.html

Julie. (2013, May 21). Are you ready for potty training? [Web log comment]. Retrieved from http://www.ilikebeerandbabies.com/2013/05/are-you-ready-for-potty-training.html

Julie. (2014, April 15). Harvey and the terrible, horrible, no good, very bad twos. [Web log comment]. Retrieved from http://www.ilikebeerandbabies.com/2014/04/harvey-and-terrible-horrible-no-good.html

Kate & Lydia. (2010, January 18). Mommyland desk reference. [Web log comment]. Retrieved from http://www.rantsfrommommyland.com/2010/01/mommyland-desk-reference.html

Keane, H. (2013). Health adults and maternal bodies: Reformulations of gender in Australian alcohol guidelines. *Health Sociology Review*, *22*(2), 151–161.

Killingsworth, B. (2006). "Drinking stories" from a playgroup. Alcohol in the lives of middle-class mothers in Australia. *Ethnography*, *7*(3), 357–384.

Kristen. (2012, May 23). Anderson Cooper loves mommy needs a cocktail tees. [Web log comment]. Retrieved from http://mommyneedsacocktail.com/2012/05/anderson-cooper-loves-mommy-needs-a-cocktail-tees/

Laborde, N., & Mair, C. (2012). Alcohol use patterns among postpartum women. *Maternal and Child Health Journal*, *16*, 1810–1819.

Lopez, L. (2009). The radical act of "mommy blogging": Redefining motherhood through the blogosphere. *New Media & Society*, *11*(5), 729–747.

Lyons, A., & Willott, S. (2008). Alcohol consumption, gender identities and women's changing social positions. *Sex Roles*, *59*, 694–712.

Mansson, E. (2014). Drinking as a feminine practice: Post-feminist images of women's drinking in Swedish women's magazines. *Feminist Media Studies*, *14*(1), 56–72.

Martin-Evans, L., & Stevenson, F. (2013). *Reasons mommy drinks*. New York, NY: Three Rivers.

McKenna, L. (2012, August 1). Mommyblogging, Inc.: Why women rule the social web. *The Atlantic*. Retrieved from http://www.theatlantic.com/business/archive/2012/08/mommyblogging-inc-why-women-rule-the-social-web/260566/

McRobbie, A. (2009). *The aftermath of feminism: Gender, culture and social change*. Los Angeles, CA: Sage.

Mellor, C. (2004). *The three-martini playdate: A practical guide to happy parenting*. San Francisco, CA: Chronicle.

Metzl, J. (2003). "Mother's little helper": The crisis of psychoanalysis and the Miltown resolution. *Gender & History*, *15*(2), 228–255.

Metzl, J., & Angel, J. (2004). Assessing the impact of SSRI antidepressants on popular notions of women's depressive illness. *Social Science & Medicine*, *58*, 577–584.

Morrison, A. (2010). Autobiography in real time: A genre analysis of personal mommy blogging. *Cyberpsychology: Journal of Psychosocial Research on Cyberspace*, *4*(2). Retrieved from http://www.cyberpsychology.eu/view.php?cisloclanku=2010120801&article=1

Morrison, A. (2011). "Suffused by feeling and affect": The intimate public of personal mommy blogging. *Biography*, *34*(1), 37–55.

Owen, A. S., Stein, S., & Vande Berg, L. (2007). *Bad girls: Cultural politics and media representations of transgressive women*. New York, NY: Peter Lang.

Ratliff, C. (2009). Policing miscarriage: Infertility blogging, rhetorical enclaves, and the case of House Bill 1677. *Women's Studies Quarterly*, *37*(1&2), 125–145.

Rich, A. (1986/1995). *Of woman born: Motherhood as experience and institution*. New York, NY: Norton.

Sheehan, M., & Ridge, D. (2001). "You become really close … you talk about the silly things you did, and we laugh": The role of binge drinking in female secondary students' lives. *Substance Use & Misuse*, *36*(3), 347–372.

Simon, J. (2014). Disciplining drunken mothers: Media representations of women's use of alcohol. *The Communication Review*, *17*, 45–64.

Tannock, S. (1995). Nostalgia critique. *Cultural Studies*, *9*(3), 453–464.

Wilder-Taylor, S. (2008). *Naptime is the new happy hour and other ways toddlers turn your life upside down*. New York, NY: Simon Spotlight.

Wolf, J. (2007). Is breast really best? Risk and total motherhood in the National Breastfeeding Awareness Campaign. *Journal of Health Politics*, *32*(4), 595–636.

Zarefsky, D. (2006). Reflections on rhetorical criticism. *Rhetoric Review*, *25*(4), 383–387.

# 12. *"Devil Mamas" of Social Media: Resistant Maternal Discourses in Sanctimommy*

By Valerie Palmer-Mehta & Sherianne Shuler[1]

Feminist rhetorical scholars have characterized the diverse discourses of motherhood that pervade U.S. culture as "polyvalent" (Kinser, 2013, p. xv), "slippery" (Buchanan, 2013, p. xvii), "conflicting", and "complex" (O'Brien Hallstein, 2010, p. 6). Inherent in such characterizations is the ultimate paradox of maternal rhetoric: It is imbued with, and commands, both symbolic force and peril. As Kinser (2013) avers, motherhood invokes "widely shared cultural codes that operate in tension with each other, expanding women's political voice and igniting social change, but also reifying gendered norms that contract and attenuate women's agency and possibility" (p. xiii). Across time and space, motherhood discourses have functioned variously to ensure that women stay in their place. In response, women have strategically deployed maternal metaphors to envision alternative social orders and have creatively resisted confining notions of motherhood while imagining new ones in their place (Buchanan, 2002; Hayden, 2003; Knudson, 2009).

Despite such efforts to reinvent motherhood discourses, contemporary expectations for mothers continue to expand (Douglas & Michaels, 2004; Warner, 2005). Although the new momism of the 1980s was wrapped in a neoliberal rhetoric of choice, Douglas and Michaels (2004) argue that it supported a domesticated, intensive mothering, a descendent of the feminine mystique Freidan identified in the 1960s, which encouraged mothers to revolve their lives around their children at the expense of themselves. More specifically, intensive mothering discourses advance the ideas that mothers are naturally the most capable parent, that mothers must lavish enormous amounts of time and energy on their children, and that mothering is outside the scope of public, professional, paid work, existing as a special provision within the private sphere (O'Brien Hallstein, 2006). In contrast to the ostensible choices offered by the neoliberal era, O'Brien Hallstein (2010) traces how real choice continues to erode for women as each new label or mommy conceptualization emerges—soccer mom, mommy wars, and alpha mom. As expectations, labels, and metaphors of motherhood expand and morph, Knudson's (2009) warning of U.S. culture's obsession with making mothers "hypervisible" (so as to critique them better) becomes more potent (p. 168).

The list of mothers' paradoxical responsibilities *continues* to grow, and the greater hypervisibility afforded by social media provides opportunities for transmitting higher expectations and holding women to those expectations. The intensive-mothering ideal suggests, for example, that mothers are expected to breastfeed for at least a year while not allowing their children to become overly attached; not yell at or spank their children while employing firm discipline; avoid being helicopter moms and yet monitor their children in school, with peers, and in media choices; throw elaborately themed birthday parties while making sure the birthday child doesn't become too spoiled or entitled; pack lunches that are both healthy and artistic; involve their children in chores while keeping their homes immaculate; allow kids to roam free and develop "grit" while shielding them from carcinogens and strangers and also not making them fearful. The list goes on and on. Social media forums such as Facebook, Instagram, and Pinterest have provided creative outlets, social connection, and resources for mothers. Unfortunately, they also have the potential for increasing competition, judgment, and guilt among them.

Thus, the policing mothers endure is not confined to an external, judging patriarchal gaze. Women are adept at self-subjugation, internalizing norms for femininity and motherhood to such an extent that it forms their very subjectivity. But what about women who reject the interpellation into an agreeably feminine mother persona or who have doubts about its construction? In years past, the mother withering under the expectations of what Douglas and Michaels (2004) refer to as the "Motherhood Religion" might have privately shared her doubts and concerns with other mothers, in the hope of not being judged. Today, social media sites push this private discourse into the public sphere, providing a transgressive—and hypervisible—space for mothers to question traditional motherhood and to revel in being "bad mamas." In so doing, they demonstrate how the very hypervisibility that has functioned to police mothers also provides a space for women to critique motherhood discourses.

The "mommy blog" genre, often ridiculed by the mainstream media (Rahoi-Gilcrest, 2012), has inspired an array of social media sites for mothers, some of which challenge the cultural practice of intensive mothering. One particularly potent site is Sanctimommy, a public Facebook page with over 27,000 followers.[2] Perhaps the note entitled "Should you submit to Sanctimommy" from June 19, 2013, best defines both "sanctimommy" and the purpose behind the Sanctimommy page:

> The idea here is to poke fun at moms who think their way is the best way. For instance, your sister posting "I'm so happy we made it to 6 months breastfeeding. It was harder than I thought and I'm glad I stuck it out" is not sanctimonious; don't bother sending it in. Your sister saying "I'm so glad we made it to 6 months breastfeeding, it was so hard and I know lots of lazy moms would have come up with excuses to stop because they aren't as committed to being a good parent" IS sanctimonious; send that in for sure. With screenshots. (Sanctimo, 2013b, para. 2)

By mocking the self-righteousness that is often attributed to intensive mothering, Sanctimommy[3] provides a cultural critique of the dominant ideology while making space for alternative mothering practices. Buchanan (2013) argues that the rhetoric of motherhood "not only encourages identification and a predetermined emotional response but also discourages critical distance, in effect shutting down analysis, discussion, deliberation, reflection, and nuance" (p. 7). Social media sites open up that critical distance, which is so often foreclosed, and enable a deeper analysis of motherhood as a symbolic space where convention can be subverted.

Using feminist rhetorical analysis, this chapter identifies the rhetorical inventiveness employed by participants in the Sanctimommy Facebook community who subvert symbolic codes of motherhood and develop alternative ones. We examine what it means when the private doubts of mothering practices become public, and how such hypervisibility both enables and delimits the critique of maternal discourses. Specifically, we draw on Buchanan's (2013) unique redeployment of Richard Weaver's god and devil terms in the form of the god-term Mother and devil-term Woman, as well as her articulation of maternal ethos and woman-centered collaboration. As we identify how this site transgresses traditional notions of motherhood, we note how it fuses the Mother/Woman binary to create an alternative version of motherhood, which we call the "Devil Mama." This burgeoning form of motherhood is hip and cool, but intolerant in her own way, as Strauss (2014) discusses in her assessment of the parenting books *All Joy and No Fun* and *Bad Mother*. As the Sanctimommy Facebook page both resists the intensive-mothering ideal and articulates its own new modality of judgment in the Devil Mama, it serves a both/and function, challenging and extending in new ways the discourses that so often serve to contain women. In so doing, the site becomes the latest location, the ground zero, of the mommy wars. O'Brien Hallstein (2010) argues that the varying mom labels we see in existence today have been "developed for and by advertisers to sell products" and "applied to women rather than created by women" (p. 9). The Sanctimommy Facebook page offers a unique opportunity to examine the so-called mommy wars because, this time, it is real mothers, rather than advertisers, who are attempting to define the terms of the debate. To begin, we examine the rhetorics of motherhood before investigating how Thea Sanctimo and the Sanctimommy community work with and against them.

## *The Rhetorics of Motherhood*

We take as our point of departure Buchanan's (2013) conceptualization of the rhetorical framing of motherhood and womanhood as circulating around two conceptual and rhetorical poles, and the potential influence this framing has on maternal ethos and women's forms of collaboration. In her book, *Rhetorics of Motherhood*, Buchanan (2013) contends that the constitutive discourses of motherhood operate in a Janus-like fashion, opening up possibilities for women, giving them credibility and authority to achieve their sociopolitical agendas, while also impeding them by "reinforcing limiting stereotypes and inequitable gender relations" (p. 14). This occurs, Buchanan argues, through the framing within public discourse of "Mother" as a god-term and "Woman" as a devil-term. The god-term Mother is positioned to suggest sacrifice, altruism, morality, strength, and the home. It functions as "a rhetorical expression of the code of motherhood" that places "audience members into familiar subject positions and encourage[s] established emotional responses, ranging from respect and allegiance to anger and fear" (p. 117). While the god-term Mother can reinforce stereotypical thinking about women and their limited role in society, it also enables rhetors to "create common ground, provoke feeling, and inspire trust ... Its social centrality explains why the Mother is easy to introduce but difficult to resist or refute within public discourse" (p. 117).

Its opposite, Buchanan (2013) avers, is the concept of Woman, which operates as a devil-term. Woman connotes selfishness, materialism, immorality, weakness, sensuousness, childlessness, and the public sphere. The conceptual terrain of Woman is situated as the antithesis to the Mother figure, operating as "the dark to its light, the failure to its success—and a necessary internal scapegoat" (p. 8). The two terms, operating in a binary fashion, enable audiences to tap into a sort of rhetorical shorthand that paints a picture of the "sainted mother or selfish career woman" (p. 9). Buchanan taps into the cultural significance and weight of these conceptualizations for speakers, noting their implications for audiences as well: "They provide speakers with immediately recognizable (and culturally resonant) stereotypes, each comprised of well-known qualities and associations. When either figure is invoked, much is suggested even if little is said" (p. 8). The god-term Mother and the devil-term Woman, and the rhetorical terrain that exists and operates between them, provide the broader public with the rhetorical means through which to praise/exalt or blame/denigrate women. By extension, they become the measuring stick with which women judge themselves and each other in a demonstration of internalized oppression.

These terms do not function exclusively to oppress women and limit their spheres of influence. In addition to providing a rhetorical shorthand for judging or praising women in general and mothers in particular, these terms—and all that they invoke—might be exploited by women to advance their own perspectives and goals. However, women must deploy these rich rhetorical resources carefully, Buchanan (2013) argues, since "maternal rhetorics sometimes have disastrous consequences for women" (p. 14). One way that women can harness the cultural and rhetorical significance of the Mother term for their own ends is to strategically deploy a "maternal ethos" in favor of their particular socio-political agenda. Invoking a maternal ethos can be productive because U.S. audiences are so familiar with it, as it dovetails into dominant discourses: "Maternal ethos is typically simple and straightforward, transforming a complex multifaceted woman into a familiar, reassuring character. This flattening effect derives from motherhood's affiliation with dominant social, historical, and ideological constructs of gender, which the code presents as natural, eternal, and inevitable" (Buchanan, 2013, p. 118). Of course, the association of maternal ethos with hegemonic social structures suggests its complexity and peril. That is, as it enables women to possess an authoritative voice to advance their objectives, it also potentially confines their power and expertise to the domestic sphere, reduces the nuances of being a woman and a mother, and reifies stereotypical notions of woman's place. Consequently, women who deploy it must be careful not to simply reinforce uncritical modes of thinking about gender.

Strategically employing a maternal ethos is not the only, albeit slippery, route to rhetorical inventiveness for mothers. Collaboration also offers women a method to overcome the complexities of motherhood in a culture that is male-centered and male-identified. Because U.S. culture largely separates the public and private spheres, and struggles to properly value and integrate birth and childrearing into the daily functions of the public world, motherhood inherently complicates women's professional lives. Buchanan (2013) notes that motherhood frequently has "an adverse impact on women's careers, halting, interrupting, or postponing them" (p. 119). While it is often assumed that men will take little time off to attend to the birth and rearing of children, for women, the decision whether to work outside the home is one that is fraught with guilt and difficulty. For those women who have no choice but to work, there are additional complexities to consider. Despite public and private obstacles, women have long created imaginative ways of balancing work and home to remain active in the public sphere. Perhaps the most effective strategy women have developed is collaboration, a "cooperative endeavor" that involves the "direct and/or indirect assistance of others" and ultimately "results in a rhetorical product, performance, or event" (Buchanan, 2013, p. 119). Through collaboration, mothers can continue to participate in and value both their public and domestic lives.

We employ Buchanan's insights to illuminate the rhetorical inventiveness of Thea Sanctimo and her cadre of community members on the Sanctimommy Facebook page. In what follows, we examine how the administrator of Sanctimommy deploys a maternal ethos in order to justify her community's collaborative critique of the intensive-mothering trend that continues to ratchet up in the U.S. context. Next, we turn our attention to how the Sanctimommy Facebook membership negotiates the praise/blame terrain that exists between the god-term Mother and the devil-term Woman. We argue that the collaborative rhetoric of Sanctimommy mocks the god-term Mother as it relates to intensive-mothering practices and elevates the devil-term Woman by deploying a new version of "bad" motherhood that engages in its own form of judgment. We look first to Thea Sanctimo, the assumed identity behind Sanctimommy.

## *Thea Sanctimo: Deploying the Maternal Ethos and Facilitating Collaboration*

The administrator[4] of the Sanctimommy Facebook page illuminates how one might deploy a traditional maternal ethos in order to justify a community's collaborative critique and reframing of motherhood. Although on the Sanctimommy Facebook page she utilizes the name "Sanctimommy," in other media platforms like Pinsta.me and Instagram, she uses Thea Sanctimo.[5] In her role as the page's founder and administrator, Sanctimo invokes the maternal ethos to justify and defend Sanctimommy's attack on the intensive-mothering ideal. O'Brien Hallstein (2008) argues that "intensive mothering gives women 'powerless responsibility'; it assigns mothers all the responsibility for mothering but denies them the power to define and determine their own experiences of mothering" (p. 107). It does so in part by defining how "women are to mother and how they should feel about mothering" while also "isolat[ing] women from each other and ultimately deny[ing] women 'personhood'" (p. 107).

One can see immediately on the Facebook page that Sanctimo is striking against this narrow approach to mothering by cultivating a community where mothers can define and share their own experience of mothering. First, Sanctimo could have written a blog or book about her perspective on mothering that would not have enabled dialogue; however, she chose a community format in Facebook that enables mothers to come together to share their experiences. In so doing, she works against the isolation that mothers might feel by bringing them together to contribute their voices, humor, and perspective. Second, the Sanctimommy Facebook group is categorized, tongue in cheek, as an educational group. This framing suggests that Sanctimo is trying to educate women about the perils and pitfalls of being a sanctimonious mother, while also satirizing the intensive mother's drive to "educate" others about correct parenting choices. To render her critique palpable within the comic frame, on the "About" page, Sanctimo satirically lists the awards she—and by extension Sanctimommy members—have won: "Mom of the year" and "Martyr of the millennium" (Sanctimo, 2013a, para. 5). Under "personal information" and "personal interests" Sanctimo (2013a) lists, respectively, "I'm not saying you're a bad mom but …" and "I have no time for my own interests. My baby is my greatest accomplishment" (para. 9–10). Most importantly, Sanctimo posts photos and status updates that poke fun at the intensive-mothering ideal, inviting members to comment on them. It is this activity that forms the centerpiece of the site.

With a common enemy of intensive mothering and a shared goal of promoting realistic and judgment-free mothering, the members of the Sanctimommy Facebook group make it their mission to critique these anonymous, offending sanctimommies with force. A representative example[6] is from September 22, 2014; Sanctimo (2014c) posted the following comment: "It's never too late (or too early) to do a little shaming! If only this mom had the same information as I do, I'm sure she'd make better choices." This comment works to frame a screenshot of a disposable diaper on which an anonymous offending sanctimommy had written with a Sharpie, "it's not too late to cloth. He he." The offending sanctimommy's accompanying status says, "At a baby shower … we needed to write a 'message' on a diaper. I didn't even want to touch it! So this is what I wrote … I thought I would share. ☺"

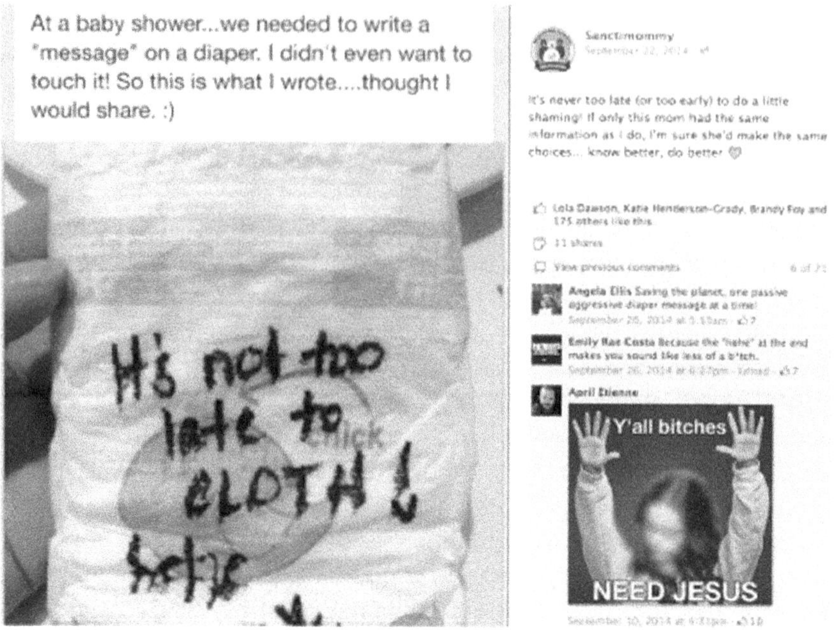


*Thea Sanctos, September 22, 2014 blog post. Reprinted by permission of the publisher.* 

This Sanctimommy post received 178 likes and 71 comments.[7] The comment authored by Rachel Ferris (2014), was well received, with 94 likes. It reads "I know that you've made your decision [to use disposable diapers instead of cloth ones], but since its not the same one I made i thought i'd call you out right in the middle of your baby shower anyways. How can you tell if someone cloth diapers? Don't worry they'll tell you." Jasmine Marrero-Pratt's (2014) comment accumulated the most likes (97) from community members. Marrero-Pratt writes: "I'm so glad she [the offending sanctimommy] put "hehe" at the end, wouldn't want people to think you're a completely humorless twat." A comment contributed by Christy Dannheim Castro (2014) reads, "Too bad it was too late to un-invite you" and Jessica Miller (2014) adds, "Yes, I like to start mommy wars at all my friends baby showers. It's debate time bitc)&$!!" In such moves, the Sanctimommy Facebook community works to resist the judgment and presumptuousness inherent in the offending sanctimommy's post. By taking the original poster to task for being judgmental of moms who use disposable diapers, the Sanctimommy community tackles the cultural supremacy of the intensive-mothering ideal and critiques the mommy wars with humor and force.

In these rhetorical moves, Sanctimo leads her membership in lodging critiques of the intensive-mothering ideal that demands mothers center all their attention on their children at the expense of themselves and their personhood. Through mocking "sanctimommies," the community works together to create and maintain a more realistic ideal of mothering. This critique of the intensive-mothering ideal has not gone unnoticed by audiences who are actively hostile to the Sanctimommy Facebook page. It is worth noting why the woman behind the page does not list her real name, but rather goes by the title, "Sanctimommy," or variations of the name "Thea Sanctimo" or "Sanctos." Sanctimo (2014b) explains the reasons behind the decision to use a *nom de plume*:

> I don't operate under an alternate profile because I'm afraid of being "outed" or ashamed of what we do here. I use an alt for two reasons: my real personal account has gotten a Facebook time out and been in danger of deactivation because hundreds of moms report me for "bullying" when they didn't understand the page, and because from the very beginning I have gotten real threats from people. I remember the first time someone threatened to find me and circumcise me, I remember the first time someone said they wanted to "light my face on fire and stab it out with a fork." And maybe they're kidding! But ... maybe they're not. (para. 13–14)

That the Sanctimommy Facebook community has come under enough hostile scrutiny to compel Sanctimo to use an alternate profile indicates that their critique of traditional motherhood has been pushed to its conceivable limits. The resistance she receives demonstrates how invested the broader U.S. culture is in traditional notions of motherhood as articulated by Buchanan's conceptualization of Mother as a god-term.

Sanctimo justifies her mocking of sanctimonious moms by invoking a traditional maternal ethos and fashioning herself as a struggling mother who has suffered from the expectations of intensive mothering. In so doing, she illuminates Kinser's (2013) observation that, "mother rhetors will often appease audiences somehow, evoking familiar images for women's identities and social place" (p. xv). In "A Long Overdue Introduction," which was posted as a "Note" on September 4, 2014, Sanctimo (2014b) explains the motivations behind starting the Sanctimommy Facebook page. She states in the first paragraph that she decided to post this explanation after her profile was shut down for the sixth time and she had been unable to answer messages. Recognizing her critics, she states, "For some of you, this will be great news, met with cheers, you've done it! You've taken down Sanctimommy!" (para. 1). It is interesting that although the Sanctimommy Facebook page was launched on January 24, 2013, this introduction was not provided until September of the following year, demonstrating that she felt pushed, perhaps even forced, to provide a sentimental explanation for why she started this page that lodges harsh criticisms of intensive motherhood. Delivering on the sentimental expectations she thinks her unfavorable audience requires, while also tapping into the emotions of favorable audience members, the post provides a rare glimpse into the pain that Sanctimo has experienced, which has formed her perspective. Sanctimo states that "being a new mom is disorienting" before detailing her own struggles with infertility and expectations for motherhood:

> No matter how you planned to parent or what your life was like pre-baby, everything will turn out differently than you imagined. My partner and I struggled with infertility for several years, we lost 3 pregnancies in that time and I became obsessed with the idea of myself as a mother. What would I be like? Well, for starters I wouldn't be like those lazy moms with dirty kids and messy hair. Of course I'd have one of those orgasmic natural births, right? And breastfeed exclusively. Oh, and we'd have lots of time for crafts and cloth diapering. Maybe I'd start one of those work at home mom businesses and even sell cloth diapers! And wooden rattles! (para. 2)

Sanctimo cultivates a traditional maternal ethos by detailing how she imagined motherhood would be before she gave birth. She invokes pathos and attempts to cultivate identification as she reveals that she struggled with infertility and suffered from three miscarriages. After relaying this private information, she goes on to suggest the folly of her dedication to the intensive-mothering ideal by situating her commitment in her anguish: "This was the motherhood I spent years building in my grief. I was very hard on moms I saw struggling in grocery stores, at parks. I judged them and their formula bottles. *I would do better*" (para. 4–5).[8] Sanctimo suggests that the intensive-mothering ideal she bought into was erroneously built on the irrationality and emotionality of her own despair; further it was based on a lack of experience of actual motherhood. By laying out her journey in such a manner, she invokes traditional themes of motherhood and a maternal ethos. She *sought to be* a traditional mom, one who tried to meet the intensive-mothering ideal. However, it was an ideal, she argues, that cannot be met. As such, she cultivates a maternal ethos based in her experiences vis-à-vis traditional expectations, but then questions the ideal that is supposed to proceed from them.

In the "Long Overdue Introduction," Sanctimo (2014b) also strives to cultivate identification between herself and the various audiences the site has accumulated as she works to build a community of struggling mothers and promote her particular brand of motherhood. She suggests that her audiences must identify with her struggle on some level and that is why they seek out her site: "When I had my first baby everything changed in an almost comically formulaic way. I know most of you will be familiar with this because it's why you found my page, why you liked [it]. Your story is probably somewhat similar" (para. 6). By linking her story with their stories, she creates a common bond of struggle that works to justify her new approach to motherhood, moves it beyond her personal struggle to overcome, and connects it to women's broader experiences. In effect, this is not her personal problem; it is a problem other mothers are facing because of this unrealistic approach to mothering. To edify readers on the need for a new mode of motherhood, she lists the specific struggles women face as mothers, underscoring the disorientation and judgment that new mothers endure when the ideal that they had imagined does not mirror the reality that they experience:

> Forget that adorable little nursing nightie you packed, just buy the fucking Depends and give up a little more of your pride. In a few weeks when you have to talk to a lactation specialist about your bloody nipples the word "pride" won't even register anymore. Baby's not gaining weight and cries ALL.THE.TIME and you have to supplement with formula. ... Maybe you go back to work (and abandon your children?!) or maybe you settle into a routine and find a few friends (lazy stay at home moms like you). Maybe you start to feel like you can do this. Or maybe you struggle. When your doctor gently mentions postpartum depression you have finally hit the bottom. Where are the mom friends who can bring over dinner and talk you through this? They're judging you for medicating yourself when there are so many omega 3s and essential oils that can help! (para. 6, 8)

As she lays out the difficult choices mothers are compelled to make, she demonstrates that from whatever angle you look at this multifaceted prism of motherhood, there are unexpected challenges that are often met by judgment. She affirms and validates her community's experiences of motherhood by saying, "Every mom has a story like yours, no matter what they say. I feel so guilty for every mom I judged when she talked about cry-it-out or snapped at her toddler in Target" (para. 9). That moms often face such hostility and judgment from others (particularly other moms) is taken as a given. If this is so, perhaps the rhetoric of intensive mothering can only be challenged by the creation of alternative communal mothering rhetorics. As she lays out her story and connects it with her audiences' experiences, she creates a space, based on a maternal ethos, in which she and her newly built community can critique intensive-mothering practices and traditional expectations for motherhood.

Finally, Sanctimo (2014b) deploys pathos once more, invoking the Catholic sacrament of Penance in which the faithful receive mercy for the sins they have committed and are rejoined to the community of the church:

> In a lot of ways I started writing Sanctimommy as penance. I was lonely and I couldn't figure out how to forgive myself for not being the mom I thought I would be, for not having the life I thought I would have. In the beginning a lot

> of the statuses hit close to home for me too, but it was like therapy mocking all the things I blamed myself for! It was liberating! (para. 10)

As she situates her struggle in pain, and in religious imagery, she connects her grief to the experiences of other women. She indicates that her judgment of other women and of herself was so severe that she needed to purge the guilt she felt through penance in order to reconnect with herself and her female community. The Sanctimommy Facebook page is her penance, a way to eliminate the guilt for the judgment she enacted before she was a mother herself. By invoking her pain, she also provides a defense for the site's mocking of intensive mothering. It's not "bullying," it's therapy! Yet while the Sanctimommy Facebook page could be an aspirational, liberating space where a more humane motherhood is articulated, one that divests itself from judgment and the scrutiny of the public eye, a different design seems to be taking shape. Indeed, Sanctimo's heartfelt explanation and judgment-free ideal is undercut by caustic communal mocking of sometimes even minor "sanctimonious" statuses of other mothers, making the Sanctimommy Facebook page a fairly ruthless and judgmental space in its own right. Thus, the site deploys a both/and dynamic: It undermines intensive-mothering practices through critique and ridicule, but also implements its own brand of judgment of certain mothering practices, thus contributing in its own way to the mommy wars. We explore both rhetorical practices in the next section.

## *The Sanctimommy Collective: Mocking the Sanctimonious Mother, Elevating the New Devil Mama*

One reason the Sanctimommy site draws such a large following is likely because so many women are tired of being subjected to the judgment that comes from the dominance of intensive mothering, as Sanctimo points out in her introduction. She argues that mothers are looking for an alternative that is practical, based in the reality that mothers live every day, and that does not take itself too seriously. If intensive mothering requires that mothers put in the time and do the research necessary to become experts in all areas related to the health and safety of children and refuse to simply accept mainstream customs or advice, the Sanctimommy Facebook community offers a more relaxed and humane perspective. In other words, television will not kill your kids, junk food is all right sometimes, disposable diapers' convenience can occasionally trump environmental concerns, and vaccines provide lifelong protection against debilitating diseases. The type of intensive mother that Sanctimommy deconstructs often operates with an anxious mindset that the world is a scary place and that mothers can trust no one but themselves to take care of their kids. You can neither trust the government nor trust corporations; not even the schools are beyond reproach. As a counter to this stance, Sanctimommy participants urge mothers to relax, to resist an overanxious approach to parenting, and to maintain their own sanity by doing what is easy and reasonable for their families. As Sanctimo and other community members lodge their satirical comments, they create a space where the tenets associated with the devil-term Woman—such as selfishness, weakness, and immorality—are exalted. Practicality is valued over conscientiousness and humor over earnestness. Participants make the seemingly altruistic and moralizing (and, of course, judgmental) "sanctimommy" the object of scorn and ridicule, while reclaiming the motherhood moniker for themselves.

As indicated earlier, the way the page functions is that Sanctimo, the administrator of the Sanctimommy page, offers up an anonymous "offending sanctimommy" status update and screenshot that was originally posted elsewhere by someone who was being judgmental of other moms and not intending it to be satire. The Sanctimommy administrator adds satirical commentary, and then opens the post for community comment. This is where the community's challenge to the intensive-mothering ideal is most apparent as the group mocks earnest and judgmental mothers and offers up a more profane, irreverent, and realistic (or "Devil Mama") vision of motherhood, and wraps it all up in humor, which is deployed as both a means of coping and resistance.

The Sanctimommy Facebook page focuses on a range of topics, including food, baby-wearing clothing,[9] safety, transportation, children's behavior, and mothers' attitudes, thoughts, and behavior. For example, the post from October 30th, 2014, includes a screenshot of an enraptured mother kissing her smiling baby's hands with the phrase, "Motherhood is a forever love story … Enjoy every minute and treasure it," in a flowery cursive font.

The introduction to this photo by Sanctimo (2014e) is, "Motherhood is the gift that keeps on giving. What are you doing today to #cherisheverymoment?" This original post was "liked" 73 times and commented on 84 times. The first comment, from Eric Mendelsohn (2014), states "Yes, that's what the film Psycho is all about." The most "liked" comment at 32 likes is "scheduling my husband's vasectomy," submitted by Julie Elizabeth (2014b), the same woman who also jokes:

> Uncle Panasonic is watching the boys so I can catch up on eating donuts and attempting to survive on 2 hours of sleep, 1.5 of which involved a baby kicking me in the head and neck repeatedly. #cosleepingneverinvolvessleep #whereisthegiftreceipt

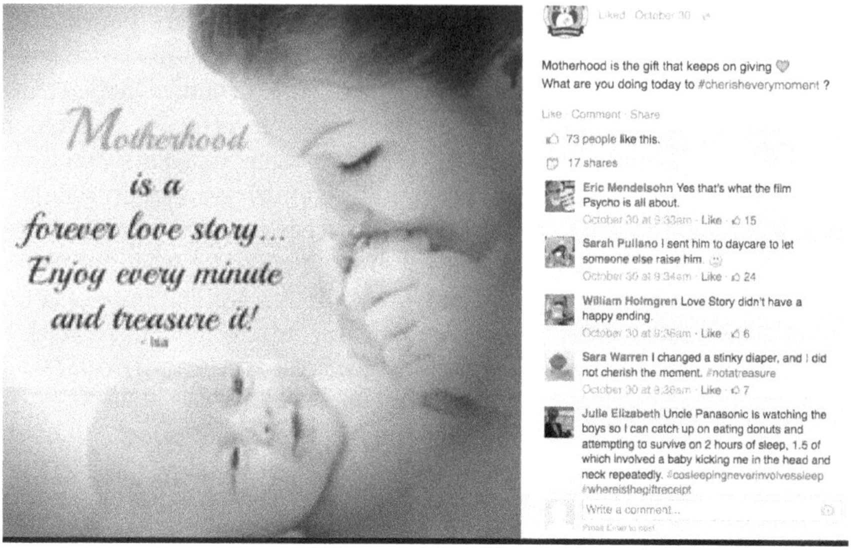


*Thea Sanctos, October 30, 2014 blog post. Reprinted by permission of the publisher. All rights reserved.*

The comment by Lynn Dyer (2014), which was "liked" 31 times, asserts, "I'll cherish all the moments later when the daycare tells me all about them." In a similar vein, Jennifer Richert (2014) writes, "I generously slowed the car down this morning before making them jump out at school. #blessings." As these comments attest, the intensive-mothering ideal that is promoted by the original photo is subject to mockery that undermines its cultural force with a more realistic picture of motherhood that also situates these women commenters as Devil Mamas who joke about their own non-idealized behaviors like drinking, swearing, and plopping their kids in front of the television without apology. In such moves, the Sanctimommy site works not only to indicate that mothers' needs matter too, but also to contest—even pathologize—the idea that motherhood is the most important element in women's lives.

Despite the claim by Sanctimo (2013b) in the post, "Should You Submit to Sanctimommy?" on June 19, 2013, that, "my aim is not to belittle a specific type of parenting" (para. 4), members of the community sometimes do cross this line in their use of satire and go beyond the goal of taking judgmental people to task. For example, in response to the post discussed above that asks members "what are you doing today to #cherisheverymoment?" several commenters poke fun at particular motherhood activities that they see as overly earnest or as requiring inordinate amounts of time and energy. For example, Nathalie Chenault (2014) states, "We are currently kneading our grain free Paleo bread together while singing earth hymns. Later we will weave marigold crowns and do rain dances in our birthday suits." Such comments mock the highlighted activities themselves rather than mocking a parent who is judgmentally pushing their own parenting agenda. The next comment, contributed by Alexandra Critvis (2014), states:

> Well, I woke up an hour before her so she could wake up to a freshly made, all organic breakfast and a sippy of freshly pumped breastmilk. Later, we'll be following our strict 1 year old education program, but if she gets upset it's ok, because it's just her expressing herself. Then I think we'll go to the local park ... not to play on the filthy equipment, but so she can see what a good mom she has compared to some of the snot-nosed ragamuffins there. I might bring some reading material about the dangers of vaccines, to put on car windshields. While properly baby-wearing, of course! When you know better, you cherish better.

Here, it seems that the commenter is not restricting her mocking to particular offending sanctimommies or poking fun at her own non-idealized maternal performances; rather, she is taking her critique a step further to mock a particular set of parenting practices associated with the intensive-mothering regime.

In addition to resisting the oppressive intensive-mothering ideal and particular parenting practices, the group also critiques ideas that seem uninformed or potentially elitist or racist. On October 16, 2014, for example, Sanctimo (2014d) posted a screen shot that read, "Punch me in the throat if I'm not on to something, but maybe, just maybe, Breastmilk can assist in healing Ebola patients? Doesn't hurt to try right?" This post was "liked" by Sanctimommy followers 285 times and garnered 105 comments. Tiffany Cochran's (2014) comment reads, "Kale is the cure all, you ignorant twit," picking up on a frequent target of mockery, as does Meg Braskett's (2014) comment, which avers, "No no no! Essential oils is the best known treatment. #shityourdoctorwonttellyou." Robyn Greenwell's (2014) comment moves deeper than the earlier responses when she lodges a critique of the ostensible paternalism and racism inherent in the original post: "But of course! People in Africa never ever breastfeed. Only smug white mommies know the intricate mysteries of this curative miracle." Again, rather than restricting their comments to mocking judgmental parents, this post and its comments instead mock what they deem as an ignorant idea. Certainly, those who are dogmatic about breastfeeding or hypercritical of the use of formula are fair game for participants within the Sanctimommy Facebook community, according to the group's own stated parameters. In this case, however, it is less clear that the original poster falls into either of those categories. Given what seems to serve as the punch line to many jokes, it is hard to imagine that a mom who enjoys kale, doesn't vaccinate her kids, uses cloth diapers, or breastfeeds beyond a year would feel very comfortable in the group. In an effort to present a more humane, relaxed, and nonjudgmental form of motherhood, the group (at least at times) seems to create its own exclusive clique that not everyone is funny or cool enough to join.

Occasionally, a participant who is not aware that the page is satirical stops by and is confused by the comments. On the September 22, 2014, disposable diaper post mentioned above, a comment written by April Etienne (2014) reads:

> None of you know better than the rest of us. Your just a bunch of a**holes who judge everyone else and think your a better parent. I feed my baby breast milk and fresh food only but I do not judge those who use formula and I use disposable diapers. Get the flying F*ck over yourselves.. Your all so close minded and rude! All our babies are beautiful and all our babies are happy no matter what they're wearing or being fed. God tells us do not judge thy neighbor well clearly NONE of you are Christians or Catholics because your the judgiest bunch of twats I've ever seen. Rant over.

Immediately following this comment, Rebecca Zulu (2014) writes, "Aww did some real sanctimommys come in and get all offended??" Sometimes these mistaken commenters are dealt with through humor and, other times, community members point out the satirical nature of the site. Other times, however, moms who do not seem to play nicely by the norms of the group are excluded from the community. On August 22, 2014, Sanctimo (2014a) posted a typical Facebook meme that states, "I hate the phrase 'kids will be kids.' I think it should be replaced with 'Bad Parenting results in assholes.'" Marci Lynn Thompson (2014) pens this in response:

> I'd love to find something funny to say, but this is the least sanctimonious, least ironic, truest thing Sanctimommy has ever posted and I couldn't agree more. I can't even satirize it, is how right-on this is. I firmly believe that children are naturally kind, not mean. Sure, they lack impulse control and have meltdowns, but they are not deliberately cruel. Any parent who co-signs that kind of behavior past a certain age is asking for it. Deliberate meanness is unacceptable in the extreme. If you're raising little assholes, better take a good look at yourself. Signed, Debby Downer.

In subsequent comments, a few other moms post similar sentiments and defend them. The pushback from regular community members comes in the form of comments like, "Wow. You really are a Debbie Downer. Sanctimommies will be sanctimommies" (Czarnuszewicz, 2014) and, "I may be generalizing, but I think there could be someone here who is zero fun at parties" (Elizabeth, 2014a). Finally, the most direct call out of the more "serious" moms who do not seem to get the joke comes from LuCretia Kennedy (2014), who says, "Anastasia and Marci ... Go, just go. You can't sit with us." So while the collaborative spirit appears to be rather free flowing, community members are willing to directly call out and exclude those who disagree with the direction of the comments and the goals of the group.

In another twist to the nature of collaboration among women, after an offending Sanctimommy post doubting that colic exists was posted on October 12, 2014, many of the 92 commenters began uncharacteristically sharing their own stories of babies with colic instead of just mocking the offending sanctimommy. Toward the end of the comment thread is this string of comments from three different women, "I thought this was sanctimommy, not story time …" (Chops, 2014), "sooo many many words …" (Binadel, 2014), and "I had to double check where I was. Thought I was on baby center" (MacArthur, 2014). The insistence that "this is not Baby Center" is a frequent reference on the Sanctimommy Facebook page that attempts to maintain the site as one that is not built on a more traditionally supportive, woman-centered community model, but instead is less relational and much more caustic than what might be expected from a "mom group." This is a place to be casually connected—not a support group, but somewhere to go to laugh and be funny. These norms are an additional way the members of the group are undermining typical gendered associations that come with the god-term Mother and elevating the devil-term Woman instead.

Despite its resistance to typical woman-centered community norms, some participants do find the site to be supportive or helpful to their own experience as mothers. On just about every post, there will be at least one and usually several comments simply appreciating the humor of the other participants and replying with "LMAO" (laughing my ass off) or the like. More substantively, hundreds of participants took the opportunity to respond to Sanctimo's "Long Overdue Introduction" with supportive comments like, "This page has taught me that I'm not a bad mother … It's also taught me that my way of raising my children is just that … My way. Everyone doesn't have to agree with me or do things as I do" (Bolt, 2014); "It's really refreshing to just say 'fuck it' and stop being a soldier in the mommy wars. And just laugh at the ridiculousness of it all" (O'Loughlin, 2014); and "Sanctimommy, as my kids are eating McDonald's for dinner for the second time this week instead of the organic grown up food I dreamed of, I just want to say thank you, I love you, and for God's sake don't ever quit" (Juliano, 2014). Clearly, though the style of interaction is often quite caustic, the community that is formed is not only doing some rhetorical work to remake our notions of what counts as "good mothering" on a cultural level, but also it is making members feel less alone in their own personal struggles with motherhood. The rhetorical practices of this community are complex, invoking a both/and modality on a number of levels: Liberating and yet also judgmental, reassuring and yet exclusionary, caustic and yet supportive, and irreverently humorous, yet with a serious purpose.

## *Motherhood's "Evolution"?*

The rhetorical activity on the Sanctimommy Facebook page represents an interesting cultural dynamic and a shift in representations of motherhood. As O'Brien Hallstein (2010) has indicated, the mommy labels bandied about in U.S. culture typically stem from advertisers seeking to sell their products; they are not created by women, but applied to them. On the Sanctimommy Facebook page, the women (and the occasional man) who inhabit the site determine the terms of the debate. We argue that the site serves as a means of resistance to traditional mothering practices, as theoretically represented by the god-term Mother and which is manifest in the intensive-mothering ideal. Sanctimo strategically leverages a maternal ethos in order to justify her, and her community's, deep critique of intensive mothering and the idea that motherhood is the most important component of women's lives. The members of the page satirically deploy people's oppressive messages in a manner that undermines them for their own amusement and fantasy gratification, and to displace an ideal in which they no longer believe. They replace that ideal with a more realistic, bawdy, and seemingly selfish and immoral version of motherhood that situates them in what Buchanan (2013) would label the devil-term Woman domain. As the community makes this shift, they render ridiculous the requirements of traditional motherhood as defined by the intensive-mothering ideal and fuse the Mother/Woman binary to create an alternative version of motherhood: The Devil Mama. Ironically, the creators of Sanctimommy seem to support our analysis through the site's logo. Pictured in the center is a figure of a mother holding a baby, with a devil on one side and an angel on the other side. While there is likely another intended meaning driving the creation of their logo, it seems apropos that their logo mother figure serves as an intermediary between the angel (god-term Mother) and devil (devil-term Woman), similar to the rhetorical position created by the community.

By making private doubts about intensive-mothering practices public, the group serves as a form of social support for those mothers who are struggling and also serves as a site where resistance to the norm can be articulated. Yet it is the very visibility of the site, and the perception of the participants as Devil Mamas that causes the group to occasionally receive hostile critique, potentially limiting the force of their efforts. As Sanctimo has indicated, she has received threats and her profile has been forcibly shut down. This suggests

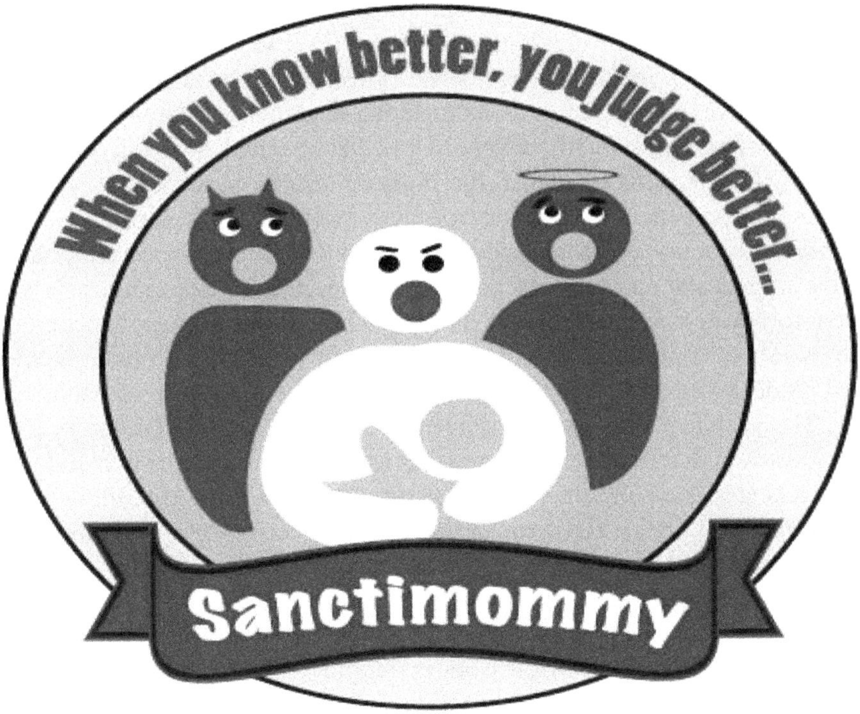


*Thea Sanctos, Sanctimommy logo. Reprinted by permission of the publisher.* 

that U.S. audiences remain invested in the god-term Mother ideal and have difficulty understanding, or are actively resisting, Sanctimommy's critique of it. It also suggests that the Sanctimommy Facebook page's method of critique creates a context in which only those who are willing to participate, unfailingly, in the satirical commentary of intensive-mothering practices are welcome. Whereas the page could offer a space that articulates a new philosophy of womanhood, mothering, and parenting, in addition to forcefully critiquing the intensive-mothering ideal and asserting that mothers' needs matter, this is not the objective of the group. Consequently, the group is limited in its social contribution; it offers some productive reactionary critique, but builds little concrete in its place.

Further, in its attempt to create a space for a more humane and realistic version of motherhood, the members of Sanctimommy create a hip and cool Devil Mama image that is judgmental of moms who are earnest about certain parenting practices. Eating kale or a paleo diet, extended breastfeeding, not vaccinating, cloth diapering, and donning baby-wearing clothing are examples of activities that are routinely mocked, even when advocates of these practices are not necessarily being judgmental sanctimommies themselves. It would seem that if one is not willing to feed kids fast food and allow them unlimited screen time while mama Facebooks and drinks, then one is simply not quite hip or fun enough at parties to be included in the Sanctimommy Facebook community's reframed and preferred Devil Mama image of motherhood. Although the site seeks to reduce the pressure created by society's seemingly endless and polyvalent judgment of mothers, ironically, at the same time, many members seem to reproduce tired battle lines by themselves being judgmental about a particular set of parenting practices, as well as excluding mothers who seem too earnest or unable to get the joke. Thus, in this manner, Sanctimommy is participating in the mommy wars that do so much to contain women and render more difficult their experiences of motherhood and womanhood.

The very fact that there is a need for a Sanctimommy Facebook page demonstrates that mothers are struggling under unrealistic pressures and they are seeking a space in which to deconstruct these norms. We still live in a world that, as O'Brien Hallstein (2010) states, directs women homeward and sees the work/life struggle as a woman's problem, not a parents' problem. Sanctimommy gestures towards a radical reconceptualization of motherhood in its critique, but stops short of creating a new version of humane motherhood. However, this rhetorical work is ongoing, and their long-term influence remains to be seen. Sanctimommy points to the need to expand our critique of motherhood's centrality to womanhood, to create more spaces where actual mothers (not advertisers) can articulate their concerns, and to build a new version of parenthood that speaks to the complexities of the 21st century and women's increasing role in the public sphere.

## *Notes*

1. The authors wish to indicate that they contributed equally to this work.
2. As of June 9, 2015.
3. While Sanctimommy is a public page that is heavily moderated, it is important to note that an affiliated private Facebook group exists. That group, entitled, Sanctimommy Said What?, has over 15,000 members who may directly post to the timeline. The content on the original Sanctimommy page, on the other hand, is controlled by administrators. Perhaps because its content is created in a more decentralized fashion, the private group includes several notes and videos outlining the rules. This group is more profane and vulgar than the original Sanctimommy site and has a more caustic style of interaction. A March 11, 2014 post on the original Sanctimommy public group reads, "If you think my page is offensive, you should see the Sanctimommy Said What? private group." This remark is followed by several comments characterizing the private group as offensive and mean. Though our analysis focuses on the public group, we mention the private group here because the two are often thought of interchangeably.

For example, an introductory video to Sanctimommy Said What? (which appears on YouTube and thus allows for public viewing), begins with, "Welcome to Sanctimommy!" Many of the same people are active in both groups, including the Sanctimommy founder, Thea Sanctimo, though she claims in her "Long Overdue Introduction" to have "very little involvement in" the private group (Sanctimo, 2014b, para. 12). We have made the ethical decision to focus here on the publicly available site, though we acknowledge that some of the public site's flavor is inextricable from the private site.

4. We understand that it is within the realm of possibility that someone might help the Sanctimommy administrator, also known as Thea Sanctimo, with the posts that emerge on the page. However, because the posts are framed or positioned as coming from one centralized person, we will refer to the posts as hers, while recognizing it could be a group of people.
5. Although the page's administrator goes by the name "Sanctimommy" on the Sanctimommy Facebook page, we will use the moniker that she uses on other media platforms, Thea Sanctimo, for the sake of readability in this paper.
6. Posts and comments to Sanctimommy are reproduced here as posted to the site, without corrections to spelling, punctuation, or inclusion of "[*sic*]" and the like in an effort to preserve as much of the flavor of the community discussion as possible.
7. The "likes" and "comments" provided were last updated on February 14, 2015.
8. Emphasis in original.
9. Baby-wearing clothing refers to garments that enable parents to carry their children, often in sling or wrap.

## References


Binadel, B. (2014, October 12). Yes deeply connected mamas ... Talk to her about colic [Online forum comment]. Retrieved from https://www.facebook.com/523533471000365/photos/pb.523533471000365.-2207520000.1433864124./819711754715867/?type=3&theater

Bolt, J. (2014, September 4). A long overdue introduction [Online forum comment]. Retrieved from https://www.facebook.com/notes/sanctimommy/a-long-overdue-introduction/800578093295900

Braskett, M. (2014, October 16). Punch me in the throat if I'm not on to something [Online forum comment]. Retrieved from https://www.facebook.com/523533471000365/photos/pb.523533471000365.-2207520000.1433864124./821673911186318/?type=3&theater

Buchanan, L. (2002). Regendering delivery: The fifth canon and the maternal rhetor. *Rhetoric Society Quarterly, 32*(4), 51–73.

Buchanan, L. (2013). *Rhetorics of motherhood.* Carbondale, IL: Southern Illinois University Press.

Castro, C. D. (2014, September 22). It's never too late (or too early) to do a little shaming [Online forum comment]. Retrieved from: https://www.facebook.com/523533471000365/photos/pb.523533471000365.-2207520000.1433864124./809493715737671/?ype=3&theater

Chenault, N. (2014, October 30). Motherhood is the gift that keeps on giving [Online forum comment]. Retrieved from https://www.facebook.com/523533471000365/photos/pb.523533471000365.-2207520000.1433864124./828176203869422/?type=3&theater

Chops, C. (2014, October 12). Yes deeply connected mamas… Talk to her about colic [Online forum comment]. Retrieved from https://www.facebook.com/523533471000365/photos/pb.523533471000365.-2207520000.1433864124./819711754715867/?type=3&theater

Cochran, T. (2014, October 16). Punch me in the throat if I'm not on to something [Online forum comment]. Retrieved from https://www.facebook.com/523533471000365/photos/pb.523533471000365.-2207520000.1433864124./ 821673911186318/?type=3&theater

Critvis, A. (2014, October 30). Motherhood is the gift that keeps on giving [Online forum comment]. Retrieved from https://www.facebook.com/523533471000365/photos/pb.523533471000365.-2207520000.1433864124./828176203869422/?type=3&theater

Czarnuszewicz, A. (2014, August 22). I hate the phrase "kids will be kids" [Online forum comment]. Retrieved from https://www.facebook.com/523533471000365/photos/pb.523533471000365.-2207520000.1433864136./794100903943619/?type=3&theater

Douglas, S. J., & Michaels, M. W. (2004). *The mommy myth: The idealization of motherhood and how it has undermined all women*. New York, NY: Free Press.

Dyer, L. (2014, October 30). Motherhood is the gift that keeps on giving [Online forum comment]. Retrieved from https://www.facebook.com/523533471000365/photos/pb.523533471000365.-2207520000.1433864124./828176203869422/?type=3&theater

Elizabeth, J. (2014a, August 22). I hate the phrase "kids will be kids" [Online forum comment]. Retrieved from https://www.facebook.com/523533471000365/photos/pb.523533471000365.-2207520000.1433864136./794100903943619/?type=3&theater

Elizabeth, J. (2014b, October 30). Motherhood is the gift that keeps on giving [Online forum comment]. Retrieved from https://www.facebook.com/523533471000365/photos/pb.523533471000365.-2207520000.1433864124./828176203869422/?type=3&theater

Etienne, A. (2014, September 22). It's never too late (or too early) to do a little shaming [Online forum comment]. Retrieved from https://www.facebook.com/523533471000365/photos/pb.523533471000365.-2207520000.1433864124./809493715737671/?type=3&theater

Ferris, R. (2014, September 22). It's never too late (or too early) to do a little shaming [Online forum comment]. Retrieved from https://www.facebook.com/523533471000365/photos/pb.523533471000365.-2207520000.1433864124./809493715737671/?type=3&theater

Greenwell, R. (2014, October 16). Punch me in the throat if I'm not on to something [Online forum comment]. Retrieved from https://www.facebook.com/523533471000365/photos/pb.523533471000365.-2207520000.1433864124./821673911186318/?type=3&theater

Hayden, S. (2003). Family metaphors and the nation: Promoting a politics of care through the Million Mom March. *Quarterly Journal of Speech, 89*(3), 196–215.

Juliano, C. (2014, September 4). A long overdue introduction [Online forum comment]. Retrieved from https://www.facebook.com/notes/sanctimommy/a-long-overdue-introduction/800578093295900

Kennedy, L. (2014, August 22). I hate the phrase "kids will be kids" [Online forum comment]. Retrieved from https://www.facebook.com/523533471000365/photos/pb.523533471000365.-2207520000.1433864136./794100903943619/?-type=3&theater

Kinser, A. (2013). Clever deployments: A foreword. In L. Buchanan, *Rhetorics of motherhood* (pp. xiii–xvi). Carbondale, IL: Southern Illinois University Press.

Knudson, L. (2009). Cindy Sheehan and the rhetoric of motherhood: A textual analysis. *Peace & Change, 34*(2), 164–183.

Marrero-Pratt, J. (2014, September 22). It's never too late (or too early) to do a little shaming [Online forum comment]. Retrieved from: https://www.facebook.com/523533471000365/photos/pb.523533471000365.-2207520000.1433864124./809493715737671/?type=3&theater

MacArthur, R. N. (2014, October 12). Yes deeply connected mamas … Talk to her about colic [Online forum comment]. Retrieved from https://www.facebook.com/523533471000365/photos/pb.523533471000365.-2207520000.1433864124./819711754715867/?type=3&theater

Mendelsohn, E. (2014, October 30). Motherhood is the gift that keeps on giving [Online forum comment]. Retrieved from https://www.facebook.com/523533471000365/photos/pb.523533471000365.-2207520000.1433864124./828176203869422/?type=3&theater

Miller, J. (2014, September 22). It's never too late (or too early) to do a little shaming [Online forum comment]. Retrieved from: https://www.facebook.com/523533471000365/photos/pb.523533471000365.-2207520000.1433864124./809493715737671/?type=3&theater

O'Brien Hallstein, D. L. (2006). Conceiving intensive mothering. *Journal of the Association for Research on Mothering, 8*(1&2), 96–108.

O'Brien Hallstein, D. L. (2010). Public choices, private control: How mediated mom labels work rhetorically to dismantle the politics of choice and white second wave feminist successes. In S. Hayden & D. L. O'Brien Hallstein (Eds.), *Contemplating maternity in an era of choice: Explorations into discourses of reproduction* (pp. 5–26). Lanham, MD: Lexington.

O'Brien Hallstein, D. L. (2008). Second wave silences and third wave intensive mothering. In A. E. Kinser (Ed.), *Mothering in the third wave* (pp. 107–118). Toronto, ON: Demeter Press.

O'Loughlin, J. L. (2014, September 4). A long overdue introduction [Online forum comment]. Retrieved from https://www.facebook.com/notes/sanctimommy/a-long-overdue-introduction/800578093295900

Rahoi-Gilcrest, R. L. (2012). Momtinis, not martyrs: Examining "Anti-Mom" blogs, muted groups, standpoints, and the struggle over motherhood. In A. A. Ruggerio (Ed.), *Media depictions of brides, wives, and mothers* (pp. 197–208). Lanham, MD: Lexington.

Richert, J. (2014, October 30). Motherhood is the gift that keeps on giving [Online forum comment]. Retrieved from https://www.facebook.com/523533471000365/photos/pb.523533471000365.-2207520000.1433864124./828176203869422/?type=3&theater

Sanctimo, T. (2013a, January 24). About [Online forum comment]. Retrieved from https://www.facebook.com/pages/Sanctimommy/523533471000365?sk=info&tab=page_info

Sanctimo, T. (2013b, June 19). Should you submit to Sanctimommy [Online forum comment]. Retrieved from https://www.facebook.com/notes/sanctimommy/should-you-submit-to-sanctimommy/588055751214803

Sanctimo, T. (2014a, August 22). I hate the phrase "kids will be kids" [Online forum comment]. Retrieved from https://www.facebook.com/523533471000365/photos/pb.523533471000365.-2207520000.1433864136./794100903943619/?type=3&theater

Sanctimo, T. (2014b, September 4). A long overdue introduction [Online forum comment]. Retrieved from https://www.facebook.com/notes/sanctimommy/a-long-overdue-introduction/800578093295900

Sanctimo, T. (2014c, September 22). It's never too late (or too early) to do a little shaming [Online forum comment]. Retrieved from https://www.facebook.com/523533471000365/photos/pb.523533471000365.-2207520000.1433864124./809493715737671/?type=3&theater

Sanctimo, T. (2014d, October 16). Punch me in the throat if I'm not on to something [Online forum comment]. Retrieved from https://www.facebook.com/523533471000365/photos/pb.523533471000365.-2207520000.1433864124./821673911186318/?type=3&theater

Sanctimo, T. (2014e, October 30). Motherhood is the gift that keeps on giving [Online forum comment]. Retrieved from https://www.facebook.com/523533471000365/photos/pb.523533471000365.-2207520000.1433864124./828176203869422/?type=3&theater

Strauss, E. (2014). The tyranny of the "bad mother": Slacker moms are just as intimidating as perfect ones. *Salon.* Retrieved from http://www.salon.com/2014/02/17/the_tyranny_of_the_bad_mother_slacker_moms_are_just_as_intimidating_as_perfect_ones/

Thompson, M. L. (2014, August 22). I hate the phrase "kids will be kids" [Online forum comment]. Retrieved from https://www.facebook.com/523533471000365/photos/pb.523533471000365.-2207520000.1433864136./794100903943619/?type=3&theater

Warner, J. (2005). *Perfect madness: Motherhood in the age of anxiety.* New York, NY: Penguin Books.

Zulu, R. (2014, September 22). It's never too late (or too early) to do a little shaming [Online forum comment]. Retrieved from https://www.facebook.com/523533471000365/photos/pb.523533471000365.-2207520000.1433864124./809493715737671/?type=3&theater

# 13. *When Tiger Mothers Transgress: Amy Chua, Dara-Lynn Weiss and the Cultural Imperative of Intensive Mothering*

By Linda Steiner & Carolyn Bronstein

Recent attention to intensive mothering—often referred to as "helicopter parenting" or the "soccer mom on steroids"—has emphasized demands on mothers to devote what are essentially professional-level skills and never-ending attention to their children. This ideology encourages mothers—but not fathers—to take full responsibility for their children's physical and psychological health as well as their emotional and intellectual development, always putting their children's needs above their own. Within this paradigm, a mother's success is measured by her children's academic, athletic, and social achievements, which range from scoring the winning goal at a soccer game to gaining admission to an elite college. Intensive parenting insists that mothers are essential as parents in ways that fathers are not; mothers should feel completely fulfilled by their children and let their lives revolve around them; mothers should always provide their children with intellectual stimulation; and both mothers and fathers should recognize that good parenting is always difficult and exhausting (Rizzo, Schiffrin, & Liss, 2012). Susan Douglas and Meredith Michaels (2004) underscore how "standards of perfection" of this "new momism" (p. 1) are impossible and contradictory, requiring the "cross cloning of Mother Teresa with Donna Shalala" (p. 5). Jennifer Senior summed up the forced-march parenting climate in the title of her 2014 book: *All Joy and No Fun*.

The well-known shift in the 1970s and 1980s to (or, more correctly, back to) laissez-faire economic neoliberalism brought an emphasis on free trade, deregulation, and reductions in government spending. As neoliberalism's focus on the private sector intensified, resulting in cuts in state support for child and family-oriented programs such as food stamps and publicly funded preschool, parents were encouraged and even required to fill in the gap, taking up the responsibilities abandoned by the state. Intensive parenting can thus be read as a socially mandated response to a new economic order. Sharon Hays (1996) characterizes the selfless practice of intensive mothering as "a gendered model that advises mothers to expend a tremendous amount of time, energy and money in raising their children" (p. x). Hays adds that intensive parents must "acquire detailed knowledge of what the experts consider proper child development and then spend a good deal of time and money attempting to foster it" (1996, p. 8), privately paying for speech, behavioral, and occupational therapy in the absence of high-quality, state-supported child care and health and welfare services.

Neoliberalism puts responsibility for children solely on their parents, tending to blame children's failures not on intrinsic limits to their abilities, but on their mothers' lack of effort and attention. To wit, a national epidemic of child obesity is connected to the selfishness of working mothers who fail to prepare healthy meals. This logic ignores structural causes, such as the rising cost of fresh fruits and vegetables in a recession-prone economy and a crumbling urban infrastructure that leaves children without safe outdoor play spaces. Extending the neoliberal rationale, if healthy children represent the outcome of good mothering, mothers may even be to blame when their children are sick (Blum, 2007). An inflated sense of the dangers posed to children's health by a "toxic" social environment, visible in such threats as unregulated "sexting" and online access to pornography, require increased parental surveillance as well as consultation with specialized parenting experts (Furedi, 2008). Every parenting decision is vulnerable to attack; mothers are continuously "bombarded with judgment" (Peskowitz, 2005, p. 13).

Precisely how far "good mothers" should go to undertake their responsibilities is not intuitively obvious, whether that responsibility concerns academic achievement or bodily perfection. Not surprisingly, some scholars criticize intensive motherhood as not only unnecessary, but also bad for mothers, their children, and society (e.g. Nelson, 2010). The "good mother" ideology produces guilt and shame, and several researchers have linked intensive forms of parenting and that resulting sense of guilt to unhealthy increases in stress, depression and lower life satisfaction (Rizzo, Schiffrin, & Liss, 2012; Sutherland, 2010). In aggressively advocating on behalf of their children's health, mothers may come to see themselves as uniquely qualified, perhaps more so than medical professionals, thus bringing societal risks. Reich (2014) found that mothers who disobey state mandates for childhood vaccinations saw themselves as equipped to weigh medical risks in the name of protecting their children. By focusing solely on their own children, per intensive-mothering practices, they ignored both how their children benefit from others' immunity and how their choices undermine community health; each mother's insistence that her individual choice proved her maternal commitment replicated structural inequality. While the risks of this for others are usually invisible, the 2015 Disneyland measles outbreak brought this into stark view.

Resisting such critiques, advocates of intensive mothering maintain that no investment of time, money, energy or attention is excessive, given mothers' duty to help children reach their highest potential. Amy Chua's *Battle Hymn of the Tiger Mother* (2011) and Dara-Lynn Weiss's *The Heavy: A Mother, A Daughter, A Diet* (2013), are leading exemplars of the intensive-parenting literature written for the popular market. Chua details a strict regimen to turn her daughters into academic and musical superstars; Weiss describes a draconian effort to control her seven-year-old daughter's food intake and weight. Both mothers received considerable public support for their intensive parenting. Nonetheless, others questioned whether these well-meaning parents went too far. Indeed, the extremism of these two memoirs raises the possibility of a limit, an outer border beyond which "good mothers" will be criticized as transgressive, as violating socially sanctioned neoliberal parenting norms. Interested in the extent to which parents themselves, or at least non-academic commentators, reference those norms and accuse a mother as either too controlling, or, conversely, as too casual, this chapter analyzes online reader responses, posted to Amazon.com and the *New York Times*' Motherlode parenting blog, regarding Chua and Weiss.

Both mother-authors had already incited considerable controversy prior to publication of their books. Yale law professor Chua's excerpt, "Why Chinese Mothers are Superior," appeared in *The Wall Street Journal* (January 8, 2011) where it drew 10,285 comments, many hostile to her strict parenting philosophy. *Tiger Mother* subsequently became a *Time* cover story, a *New York Times* bestseller, and a bestseller in Europe and Asia. It was translated into 30 languages. In April 2012 Weiss, a freelance journalist, published "Weight Watcher," in *Vogue*, which also carried photographs of Weiss and newly slim daughter, Bea, both in designer dresses. Her article and subsequent book claimed she devised the diet after the family pediatrician (and bullying peers) sounded an alarm. Many of Weiss's critics did not object to the diet per se. Instead, they were alarmed by the public shaming of Bea. They pointed to the potential psychological damage of such widespread and permanent exposure, and accused Weiss of unfairly exploiting Bea for profit. Chua was likewise criticized for capitalizing on a family issue and specifically trying to stir up controversy with horrifying anecdotes, such as threatening to incinerate her daughter's stuffed animals, to stimulate book sales. Two Motherlode posters linked Weiss and Chua as leading authors of a new genre, the "mom-fessional" (boo, 2012, March 28). Poster Golf Widow (2012, March 28) decried the "mom-fessional" as "Sensationalism at the mercy of young innocents: Dance Moms, Tods and Tiaras, etc. It's not for the children. Not at all. It's for the desperate parents."

We did not expect even the most critical readers/posters to deploy the term "transgressive," which we understand here to mean a mother who violates socially accepted boundaries for behavior. Nonetheless, we sought to discover how much leeway mothers are allowed, and the extent to which mothers operate under a condition of surveillance, their actions open for public comment, both supportive and condemnatory. Furthermore, we wondered whether falling off the tightrope on either side of the boundary between good and bad carries equally high stakes. According to convention, children of lax parents suffer; they are unsupervised, excessively independent, easily lured into trouble, fat, or otherwise undisciplined. Would children of overly intense parents analogously be seen as victims of a form of parental negligence, or as damaged by parental fervor?

Our analysis of reader comments turned up a range of responses, showing very different sets of ideas about what constitutes good (or bad) mothering and the best interests of children. We find tremendous constraints on the behaviors considered acceptable for mothers, who are subject to the ideologies of intensive parenting even if they see the flaws in this demanding approach. Overall, we find that mothers have little freedom to transgress; they are subject to severe condemnation for operating outside the highly patrolled bounds of conduct prescribed for the "good mother." The many who vociferously attacked and condemned Weiss and Chua confirmed that mothers can be highly judgmental of one another's approaches. Many parents demonstrated that they were able to navigate the rather onerous demands of intensive parenting, although apparently they cannot reject it wholesale. The fact that a healthy percentage of the posters sought out and read Chua and Weiss's accounts, but then critiqued at least some of the demands of intensive parenting suggests a level of resistance among parents. In other words, many parents, especially mothers, are anxious enough about their roles and responsibilities to read a range of advice books, but they do not necessarily absorb said advice passively; they are not cultural dupes. Posters strongly disagreed over where the line between good and bad mothering fell. They vigorously debated the philosophy of intensive parenting, with most noting that a mother must go very far in adopting these practices before she has gone too far, transgressing social norms. Both critics and supporters agreed, however, that fathers are typically subject to few such rules, nor do their actions warrant surveillance.

## *Tiger Mothers*

On her website (http://amychua.com/) Chua claimed that she wrote *Battle Hymn of the Tiger Mother* as a form of family therapy during "a moment of crisis." Chua's parents were Chinese immigrants who came to the U.S. as graduate students and maintained strict rules and high standards for their children; she and her three sisters were forced to practice math and piano every day, were criticized for earning A minus grades, and were not allowed to attend birthday parties or sleepovers or have boyfriends. The Harvard-educated Chua experienced greater resistance raising her own daughters, especially the younger one, in the same way. Chua emphasizes that *Tiger Mother* is not a parenting book per se, but rather a memoir about her "transformation as a mother" negotiating the normative parenting styles of two cultures. Yet, Chua has shifted her position in the face of public criticism. At first, she embraced the subculture of intensive parenting, quickly becoming the poster mother for Harvard-hopeful, helicopter moms everywhere. She later retreated in the face of a backlash against a parenting trend connected to child anxiety, depression, and even suicide. *Tiger Mother*, Chua insisted, was supposed to be funny, "filled with zany showdowns between me and my daughters, who have all the best lines and are always calling my bluff" (Chua, 2014). In publicizing her subsequent book, *The Triple Package*, co-authored with her husband, she suggested that *Tiger Mother* was self-parody.

*The Heavy* offered intimate details of the diet program Weiss created and Bea's shifting emotional and physical states as she endured her mother's round-the-clock enforcement. Under pressure, Weiss (2013) also retreated a bit from what she did in *Vogue*. Although she defended the book as not harmful to Bea and helpful to other mothers dealing with their children's weight struggles, she expressed regret about allowing the *Vogue* photo shoot. Some readers applauded Weiss as a courageous, responsible and loving mother who would not allow her daughter to be fat in a culture that denies social opportunities to girls and constantly denigrates overweight women. Others criticized Weiss as a narcissistic, appearance-obsessed socialite who cared more about her own image as a "perfect mother" than her daughter's emotional well-being and feelings of self-worth. Both camps compared her to Chua, describing her as "tigeresque" and "the tiger mother of diets." Many of the Amazon posters who praised *The Heavy* emphasized that thinness is such a mandate for American females that a "good mother" has no choice but to devote herself selflessly to this cause. Largely left unsaid is that only middle- and upper-class mothers like Chua and Weiss have the material and cultural resources to invest intensively in their children's development (Reich, 2014). The intensive ideology affects mothers at all socioeconomic levels, but only certain mothers can afford to adopt these practices wholesale (for additional insights into the intersection of class and intensive mothering, see Davidson & Stache, this volume; Mazzarella, this volume).

## *Intensive-Mothering Ideology*

After World War II, with the growth in developmental psychology, child-rearing advice literature required mothers to set aside their own desires in favor of their children's needs. By the early 1990s, parenting advice shifted toward even greater emphasis on stimulating infant and young children's cognitive skills (Wall, 2010). Wall documented the uptick in increasingly child-centered public discourse about the importance of secure attachment and stimulation for pre-school children, not only for children's emotional and psychological health, but also intellectual potential; mothers were thus even expected to use new "brain research" to further children's optimal development.

The demands of intensive mothering left the working women Hays (1996) studied "feeling pressed for time, a little guilty, a bit inadequate" (p. 151); they justified their paid work by emphasizing its benefits for their children. Johnston and Swanson (2007) similarly found that, despite their "cognitive acrobatics," mothers were not able to reconcile the tension between their identities as mothers and workers. Recent studies suggest that employed mothers renegotiate the expectations of intensive mothering by deploying additional financial resources. Working women navigate the "intensive mother" and "ideal worker" ideologies by constructing scripts of "supervisory" or "extensive mothering," which involve delegating day-to-day child care, like school drop-offs, to others (Christopher, 2012). Some women executives emphasized the primacy of family life, although others developed a "work devotion schema" emphasizing commitment to paid work and a definition of motherhood "more delegatory than intensive" (Blair-Loy, 2003, p. 184). That said, very few mothers have the freedom to define their mothering practices in the "outlaw" way that Adrienne Rich proposed in *Of Woman Born* (1976). Rich said good mothers needed to be outlaws, to resist the patriarchal institution of motherhood. Contemporary mothers, however, lack much freedom and space to be outlaws. Instead they must walk lockstep with other mothers in prescribed ways. The outlaw today might be the middle class mother who eschews standardized test prep in favor of unscheduled free time, or who allows her daughter McDonald's French fries for a snack. Yet the threat of a misstep—the potential for child failure—is a powerful deterrent. Mothers are expected not only to be ever vigilant, but also ever anxious. The irony, of course, is that in always agonizing over how aggressively they should monitor and patrol—that is, control—their children, the mothers themselves are disciplined and held in check. The intensive philosophy enforces mothers' role as enforcer.

Intensive parenting is gendered in two specific ways. First, daughters' behaviors, interactions, and especially their bodies seem to require more surveillance. Girls must look feminine but not too sexy; they must be active, but not be tomboys; they should perform well in school, but not to the exclusion of being well-rounded and likeable. Second, and central to our thesis, the responsibilities for making sure home and children are properly outfitted—attaining precisely the right appearance—fall primarily, nearly exclusively, on mothers. A longitudinal study of fathers (Shirani, Henwood, & Coltart, 2012) found that men are relatively insulated against the demands of intensive parenting; despite increased involvement in childcare, men's major contribution is financial.

## *Methods*

Mothers, who have been avid consumers of expert and professional advice about parenting, are now able to provide it; indeed, using the online tools that make user-generated content more easy and accessible, mothers have avidly used digital sites for, of, and by parents. Therefore, this chapter provides a qualitative thematic analysis of readers' online comments on Amazon and Motherlode in response to Chua's *Tiger Mother* and Weiss's *The Heavy*. Amazon no longer hires professionals to review books and now relies solely on readers. Edited by KJ Dell'Antonia, Motherlode is an influential parenting blog maintained by the *New York Times* covering child care, food, sports, technology, sex, and work-family balance. On both sites, the majority of posters seemed to be women based on their names (of course, the online format allows for creative self-identification). Many claimed to be mothers.

We analyzed all comments, reviews, and responses to *The Heavy* posted on the two sites as of July 1, 2014: *The Heavy* drew 123 comments on Motherlode and 52 reviews on Amazon, where 25 gave it five stars, the highest number of stars possible; 9 gave one star, 5 gave two stars, 6 gave three; and 7 awarded four. As of July 1, 2014 Chua's book got 931 reviews on Amazon; we analyzed the first 200 of these reviews, plus all the comments on the reviews. Many listed as "Most helpful customer reviews" were recommended by more than 300 readers. Nearly all Amazon reviews drew comments, some of them quite extensive, and provoking debate among the readers; for example, one drew 54 comments. Williams (2011, February 18) claimed that some negative reviews of Chua's book had been removed; several other posters also alleged that negative reviews were removed or withdrawn. We cannot now determine whether negative reviews were removed, although this seems unlikely; we can say, however, that during the first month following the book's publication, 305 customer reviews had been posted, of which 136 gave five stars; 44 gave four stars; 26 gave three stars, and 99 gave one or two stars. Lisa Belkin's first Motherlode article on Chua's book (January 11, 2011) generated 293 posts; her piece three days later (January 14, 2011) generated 384 posts. We analyzed the first 125 posts responding to Belkin's first article, and the first 125 responding to her second.

We took several "long soaks" (Hall 1975, p. 15) in the materials to look (independently, and in joint meetings to check for consistency and agreement in coding and interpretation) at what respondents said about Chua and Weiss, and about mothering, particularly what they emphasized in their posts. Stuart Hall's (1980) analysis of different decoding positions was even more crucial to our reading. Hall famously noted that readers do not always accept and use the dominant code, the code that media producers or "encoders" expect to be deployed. Indeed, even while fully understanding the hegemonic encoding, which supports dominant ideologies about such variables as gender, race and class, readers may apply an oppositional code, deconstructing the message in a globally contrary way. Highly relevant for our findings, Hall also theorized a negotiated encoding position, where readers acknowledge the general legitimacy of the hegemonic definitions, but bring their own positions, experiences and interests to the interpretation of the text. Many parents, following Hall's theory, resisted and modified the philosophy of intensive parenting using their own experiences to offer exceptions to the general rule. Hall argued that this negotiated position involved contradictions, and indeed, many posters were unable to declare Chua or Weiss "good" or "bad" mothers, but described them to varying degrees as mothers who were trying their best amid complex expectations for mothers today.

### *Reader Assessments of Chua*

Many reviewers praised Chua as a good mother, endorsing her strict parenting as a form of tough love that would ultimately benefit the children. Typical of the five-star endorsements, Sylvia Smoller (2011, January 12) called

*Tiger Mother* "funny, wise and wonderful"; her review incorporated many of the terms of intensive mothering: "This is about a mother who believes her daughters are capable of excellence—if they work hard enough and if she works hard enough to make them do it." On Motherlode, poster RPR (2011, January 15) praised Chua's selfless devotion to her daughters: "She is willing to sacrifice every drop of her happiness for their success." A five-star review by AdoreLire (2011, January 11) applauded Chua for giving her children the best tools possible for navigating their lives: "It is time that we stop celebrating mediocrity. ... This should be a true universal value for all culture, be it Chinese or western!" Someone's Mom (2011, January 15) commented that "moms" seemed to be the most likely to question Chua's wisdom; conversely, those who like her book the most are "dads who are at work most of the time" but still think they know how mothers should raise their children. Indeed, a greater percentage of men endorsed Chua's tough love approach. A Chinese father (Hei Liu, 2011, January 11) endorsed Chua's parenting, and claimed that "strict discipline is the foundation for anyone who wants to be successful." Lofthouse (2011, January 23) mocked "the soft, positive language, self-esteem method of parenting that caused my thirty years in the classroom to be torture." Chua, the retired teacher added, was willing to do what most American parents are not: "Say no and tell it like it is when a child needs to hear they are not doing their best."

It should be noted that Amazon reviewers (i.e., as opposed to blog posters) often evaluate books using conventional literary standards and, with Chua, therefore emphasized literary merit over content. DAK (2011, January 11) worried that controversy over intensive mothering would drown out appreciation for Chua's writing: "The author's voice is like none you have ever encountered: at once wince-inducing yet winning, horrifying yet hilarious, alienating yet affecting, unbelievable yet undeniable. ... You may still hate the book—or the author!—at the end of your read, but you won't be able to deny the sheer magnetism of her voice." Some 81 of 126 Amazon readers found this review helpful. But, several people accused DAK of being a plant. Critics regularly expressed suspicion that five-star raves were fakes, perhaps written by Chua's students.

This distinction between style and substance partly, but not wholly, explains some of the ambivalence over Chua. Several posters praised some aspects of Chua's approach but also cited concerns. After describing Chua's book as compelling, "told with wit and self-deprecation," New Yorker (2011, January 11) said: "Even if you wouldn't do childrearing exactly as she did, Chua makes a compelling case that the pendulum in America has swung too far toward lazy indulgence and low expectations." Conceding that Chua was "nuts" and "too pushy to the extreme," Bing Jiang (2011, January 13) acknowledged Chua did one thing right that many mothers fail to do," to "fight the grueling battles, side by side with their children." On Motherlode, DM (2011, January 11) wrote: "I'll grant you that the overly indulgent, helicopter-style parenting which seems so prevalent among the upper classes in the US these days does kids no favors. But I work with abused kids, and the piano incident Chua describes is clearly emotionally abusive." Perhaps one of the most interesting was by "Top 500 Reviewer" K. Corn (2011, January 26), who appreciated Chua's honesty and her recognition that no single parenting method works for all children. Corn felt sorry for Chua's daughters—but also for Chua. Not only did Chua face other parents' disapproval, she said, but Chua evolved and had second thoughts, feeling caught between "how she'd been raised and what she felt was best for her children." On one hand, Corn noted that Chua's style may seem "cruel, degrading and even horrifying" by American standards. On the other hand, Corn, giving voice to Hall's (1980) theory of the impact of personal experiences, conceded that her own beliefs "are influenced by my culture, how I was raised, and the attitudes of other parents with whom I relate."

On the other hand, most posters refused to cut Chua any slack on the basis of her Asian background and cultural traditions. Williams (2011, February 18) called Chua a "tyrannical mother" who controls every aspect of her daughters' lives and wrote the "manifesto" to justify her "abusive" behavior. This 2,000-word review, which 411 of 499 people found helpful, agreed with Chua's position that "self-esteem boosting" and overly permissive parenting are social problems. Nonetheless, this poster savaged Chua, pointing out that the answer to laxness is not the opposite extreme, just as the solution to obesity is not anorexia. Indeed, the word "abuse" came up 532 times in the 200 Amazon reviews and related posts. Gray (2011, January 11) labeled his review "Chua should be committed to an institution for child abuse." A Reader (2011, January 11) said Chua "is basically abusing her kids and getting paid to delude others that it's parenting." Chua was called pathological, insane, or crazy 20 times on Amazon (although others mentioned the "crazy" reactions to Chua). Chua and/or her method was dubbed cruel 24 times by Amazon readers; she was derided as rigid, terrible, harsh, and narcissistic. On Motherlode, adjectives such as "maniacal," "heartless" and "twisted" abounded. Pinewood (2011, January 11) compared Chua to the infamous Joan Crawford depicted in *Mommie Dearest*, who terrorized her children. MFAP (2011, February 2) worried that Chua's daughters might similarly become "a monster of a mother." Deeming *Tiger Mother* a "mean-spirited, crass" handbook to conformity, D.G.R. (2011, January 11) opined that "many dysfunctional, terrible people have mastered the violin and graduated from Yale Law."

Posters were equally vitriolic on Motherlode. Among the 68 posters (appearing within 250 sampled posts) who dubbed her parenting a form of abuse, many questioned the legality of Chua's actions. "I want child protective services to investigate the health and safety of Chua's children," demanded FrugalMom (2011, January 14). Poster Mickeyrad (2011, January 14) claimed to have identified "at least three instances that constitute felonious child abuse" in each of the three chapters she read. S. Murphy (2011, January 15) called out the class privilege that allowed Chua to boast of her cruelty without fear of legal consequence: "If a poor woman admitted doing some of these things to her children, we'd call in Child Protective Services; when a tenured Yale professor admits it, she gets a six figure advance from a major publisher."

Several critics attributed entirely selfish motives to Chua, even saying she exploited her daughters purely for profit. NP1 (2011, January 12) rejected the idea that Chua's philosophy was a response to an over-permissive culture: "All this is, is one deranged mother trying to justify her choices, and a bunch of deranged enablers (WSJ, the book publisher) trying to make a buck out of a tale of abuse." Lucy (2011, January 11) compared Chua to "reality TV stars try[ing] to be exceedingly mean, rude, or painfully stupid to ensure attention and air time. … [S]he is pimping out her daughters, and shaming Asians everywhere to make some money." ZZtop (2011, January 15) concurred: "I don't want anyone to buy her book. Nobody should make money off child abuse. Every dollar she gets is a slap in the face to me and every other Asian kid who has suffered under this ideology." Parkermann 347 (2011, January 11) wondered "How low has our culture gotten when we will pay half a million to someone to tell their child abuse stories." Defending Chua, however, JL (2011, January 11) denied that a $500,000 advance for a tough parenting book indicates cultural abasement, when "millions [are] paid to reality TV stars" to glorify "sex, greed and violence."

Many of the debates about Chua turned on whether or how her approach was Chinese, whether Chua herself was Chinese, and precisely what Chua had said about all of this. No consensus emerged on these questions. Some denied the approach was Chinese, either because attributing an authoritarian, possibly abusive, parenting style to an entire culture was irresponsible, or because many cultures endorse strict parenting. S. L. Kim (2011, January 12) pointed out that Chua was born and raised in the United States; her book, moreover, was "a classic American product" designed to "provoke and attract the anxious middle-class American parents" concerned about their children's prospects in an increasingly competitive global economy. Chua's "Chinese" parenting, Kim explained, was really nothing more than "an extreme version of what many children of immigrants will recognize as a … style of parenting that is focused on class and social mobility for the children." James (2011, January 11) asserted that Chua represented "one way" of parenting, and was not representative of all Chinese mothers. "Does she speak for every Chinese parent in the world? Is she Chinese or Taiwanese or of other heritage? This is as 'Chinese' as chicken and broccoli."

On the other hand, T. Carroll (2011, January 11) speculated that Chua's parenting style was authentically Chinese, and correlated with a culture that undervalued creativity, problem-solving ability, and social skills. Others cited parental strictness and discipline to explain why the Chinese were succeeding both at universities and in the Olympics. Rose (2011, January 11) emphasized that Asians comprise 12% of the population of California, but Asians are 40 to 50 percent of the undergraduates at UC-Berkeley, UCLA, and UC-San Diego. However, a series of Chinese commenters on both sites reported that their parents never deployed such cruel techniques, although a greater number said they had suffered because their parents—some Chinese, some not—were similarly harsh. And while fans insisted that no one should criticize without first reading the book, mrka (2011, January 27) said she refused to buy the book "because it would support this woman's delusional belief that her ethnicity is the reason behind her cruel parenting."

The idea that Chua had done a disservice to all Chinese people by labeling her extreme parenting as "Chinese" appeared frequently. In a review that 366 of 445 people found helpful, "a mom" (2011, January 12) who self-described as Chinese, called the book "disturbing in its negative stereotyping of Chinese and Chinese American parents": Chua's admission that she used the term "Chinese mother" loosely "does not save her from a perception among many that she has exploited her ethnicity—and Chinese people—to sell this book." Kim (2011, January 12) worried that "way too many people both here and on the WSJ site … are conflating Chua's 'Chinese' parenting with all of China and Chinese people, and are making ridiculously racist comments based on crude stereotypes." Chua's perpetuation of "simplistic race- and ethnicity-based stereotypes that don't do anyone any good—particularly the children of Chinese (and other Asian) mothers" was called "outrageous and sad" (student, 2011, January 11)

This line of commentary often turned into a debate over "Eastern" vs. "Western" values and long-term prospects for achievement. Condemning "typical" American parenting, Chris (2011, January 14) asked: "Well, what do you prefer? The 'extreme parenting' discussed in this book, or the pop psychology/anything goes/TV parenting that seems to be the rage today in this country. Our kids may be in touch with their emotions but, by and large, they are going to fail in the test of life against the Chinese, Indians, Eastern Europeans and anyone else who emphasizes discipline and results." D'agostino (2011, January 12) supported Chua's perspective on a culture grown "lazy": "[A]s a parent and a raised American I am petrified about raising children in what we have now grown to call 'normal' Western life. … Perhaps some of her approaches are extreme in nature but I also agree with her reasons for not allowing sleepovers and playdates." Jackson (2011, January 11) was one of several fathers to agree that while Westerners over-coddle their children, Chua's approach was "disturbing."

In sum, the formal reviews of Chua's book offered what they explicitly called a fair-minded approach to the book, avoiding extreme criticisms in summarizing her content and emphasizing writing style. Evidencing the same harsh discourse that often emerges on such sites, Chua's most severe critics were as appalled by her defenders as they were by her parenting. On both sites, however, commentary on those reviews and responses to the comments sparked a robust debate over "tigeresque" mothering and intensive parenting. About half the posters, both Asian and non-Asian, saw Chua's approach as essentially a valid (albeit exaggerated) solution to laziness in American culture, given the increasing competition among middle- and upper-middle-class families for such privileges as admission to selective schools. But the other half either denounced parenting that blindly urges children forward, and societal efforts to accommodate or valorize it; or accepted that contemporary U.S culture is competitive but nonetheless attacked Chua's particular extremism. On Motherlode, eight posters highlighted high rates of depression and suicide among Asian American students, and the despair in store for those who failed to meet overly strict parental standards. Hall's "negotiated" reading was clearly evident here: Nearly all readers of the books and of the comments agreed that parents, and especially mothers, are responsible for their children's success, or lack thereof. The bad mother was the lazy, inattentive woman who refused to sacrifice herself and her needs for her children. Yet, without challenging the dominant notion that mothers should always be wholly devoted to their children's welfare, readers specified that mothers must carefully navigate such standards in the context of their own parenting philosophies and family situations.

## *Reader Assessments of Weiss*

Some critics called Weiss "delusional" for her rigid stance toward her daughter's weight. In her one-star review self-titled "Worst MOM of the century!" (2013, March 1) Montegani called Weiss "disgusting, controlling and overwhelmingly vain." Jacqueline R. Avid Reader (2013, February 9) called her "over-the-top insane." One post criticized Weiss both for expecting too much service and not doing enough herself; according to whammus (2013, May 14), although Weiss recognized her privilege as an upper-middle-class woman, she too often expected other people, like camp counselors, to monitor Bea's behavior and provide healthy snacks. Some Motherlode posters gave Weiss no quarter, pointing out that Bea's Internet-savvy classmates would someday dredge up the account of her weight struggles and tease her mercilessly. Characterizing Weiss as the worst sort of mother, Karah asked: "I wonder if Ms. Weiss [will] be able to forgive herself when her daughter's decimated self-esteem lands her on the suicide watch list" (2012, March 29).

At the other extreme, however, and countering accusations that Weiss was too strict, some commenters condemned her for inadequate, "lazy" parenting. M. Peterson (2013, April 5) blasted Weiss for "continual excuses and lackadaisical approach," especially around unrestricted fruit consumption. "Several bananas or apples in one day, let alone in one sitting? Ludicrous." Reba Mae (2103, April 10) criticized Weiss in both directions: She was a "tightly-wound, over-zealous mother [who] may have inadvertently damaged [Bea] for life"; at the same time, Weiss should have set more limits and been more willing to say "no."

Meanwhile, in essence negotiating some middle ground, the majority of commenters on Amazon and Motherlode applauded Weiss even as they simultaneously articulated a range of criticisms—for example, making public in a book the daughter's private struggles. Admirers often invoked the language of intensive motherhood. One of the five star Amazon reviews came from GAMom (2013, January 17), who commended Weiss for her "dedication, vigilance, and persistence," her "labor of love" and attention to the "day-to-day grind" of meal planning. Tara Libby (2013, February 25) wrote: "This is a great example of tough love and the person responsible for carrying out the tough love is of course 'the Heavy,' the mother, however misguided she appears to be at times." As did others, Tara Libby denied that Weiss had depicted herself or her husband as perfect parents. Liz's review (2013, January 22), which 35 of 37 people deemed helpful, acknowledged that Weiss might be "projecting some of her food issues on to her daughter." On the other hand, Liz defended Weiss against criticisms that she was abusive and shaming. Rather, "she's deciding what's healthy for her daughter in a sea of contradictory information in an affluent, food-obsessed culture, and also trying to equip her daughter for the future."

Many explicitly thanked Weiss for her courage and honesty. John C. Lawrenz (2013, January 24) said: "I cried through almost the entire book because I can relate to it all. ... We feel like failures as parents, like we are doing something wrong." Jill Currey Shermer's 864 word essay (2013, January 27) also credited Weiss "for her raw honesty with such a touchy parental subject." Writing as the "very lonely" mother of daughters with even worse eating habits, Elizabeth Klein (2013, January 30) expressed eternal gratitude to Weiss for her candor, courage, and devotion to Bea.

Motherlode commenters tended to be more critical of Weiss than were Amazon posters, but she also found strong supporters on the *New York Times* site. Many posters focused on what mothers should feed their children, and how unfair controversy can ensnare parents who try to ensure a healthy diet. Sierra (2013, January 22) observed, "I don't understand why people complain about childhood obesity then complain when this woman decides to do something about it for her daughter. You can't have it both ways." JGMurphy (2012, April 14) also noted that mothers face a double bind. They are condemned as negligent if they let a child's eating habits spiral out of control, but now, "a mom [is] condemned for taking action to control her kid's weight. It seems a mom can't win no matter what she does!" Kevin Apte (2012, April 10) was unequivocal in his praise. "I am VERY IMPRESSED with her. Parenting is not a popularity contest, and controlling what you eat is part of a good value system that a mother needs to inculcate in her child. ... Compared with parents in East Asia and Eastern Europe, American parents are disgusting."

At the same time, Weiss came under attack. Descriptors from Motherlode critics included: "crazy Vogue mom," "uncaring" and "clueless." A number of critics scathingly mocked the assertion that Weiss's parenting techniques were exemplary. MBT (2012, March 28) sneered: "Congratulations on your superior parenting and your obvious financial sacrifices so that you and only you may raise your children with organic fruits and vegetables and the occasional healthy grain. Me and my average (formula fed, in daycare and at a normal weight to height ratio) children are going to go cry in our juice and have donuts to feel better." Weiss also came under fire for what readers presumed was a selfish choice to work outside the home and resulting inattention to her child. Invoking the ideal of intensive motherhood, GP (2012, March 28) posted: "I bet the mom, before this, was uninvolved, probably formula fed and the child was in daycare or with a nanny all day. Crisis hits and suddenly mom gets engaged. Puke!"

At both sites, readers accused Chua and Weiss of causing significant physical and emotional damage. On Motherlode, jh (2011, January 15) expressed concern for Chua's daughters: "I hope those poor girls don't resort to coping mechanisms like eating disorders, or self-mutilation." In highly similar language, Weiss's detractors predicted long-term therapy for Bea; they described crying at the thought of Bea's future, suffering low self-esteem. Reba Mae (2013, April 10) characterized *The Heavy* as sealing Bea's fate: "Poor Bea's tightly-wound, overzealous mother may have inadvertently damaged her for life. [S]he has projected? dumped? her own unhealthy food issues and obsessions on her daughter." Across both cases, a mother's misguided and extreme acts were condemned as perhaps inescapably damaging to a child's potential for a happy, well adjusted future.

The most common response to Weiss, however, evidenced an acceptance that mothers bear the responsibility for enforcing and reproducing the ideal of the slender body, given both physical health risks and the punishing social costs of obesity for girls. Some supporters specified improved health as the primary reason to support Weiss's actions. One Amazon reader wrote that she "could feel a mother's love for her children so strongly, that she was willing to do everything within her power to help her daughter get healthy" (mom of four, 2013, January 19). Yet a far greater proportion of posters endorsed the "dominant" reading of beauty, and admired Weiss for "trying desperately to spare her daughter from a life of shame, self-hatred, mocking, ridicule, body issues, loneliness, exclusion, and missed opportunities" (Goldstein, 2013, February 6). Most posters were sympathetic, given that fat girls are typically ostracized and Weiss's actions arose from maternal love. Moreover, they recognized how this is highly gendered: It is girls who pay the greatest price for failing to achieve the beauty ideal, and it is mothers' responsibility to enforce the ideal for their daughters.

Bea's plight struck a universal chord among women who had dieted or who had been forced to diet or who worried about their children's weight. Class was an issue: critics of *The Heavy* were prone to speculating that Weiss was concerned about Bea because she was a "socialite," whose social standing was damaged by a fat daughter. None of the Amazon or Motherlode posters mentioned race or ethnicity or commented that the weight issue affected White women in particular (or, for that matter, not). Indeed, a prior analysis (Bronstein & Steiner, 2015) of comments about *The Heavy* at several other sites found surprisingly few references to race or ethnicity. At *A Black Girl's Guide to Weight Loss*, a blog about dieting, beauty, food, and sex from the perspective of women of color, several bloggers, especially the blog owner, wrote that reading about Bea was very painful, because it recalled how their own mothers made them feel ashamed or worthless because of their weight problems. On Babble.com, a Latina (Condes, 2013) described overhearing her mother disparaging her as a "gordita" (little fat one) with big "nalgas" (buttocks). So, the few comments addressing ethnicity turned out to be the critical of cruelty of their own mothers. Even so, this was a rare and minor theme, suggesting that both weight issues and ideas about mothers' responsibilities for them transcend culture. Meanwhile, the negotiated reading is evident in the most common response: Readers accepted intensive parenting and a mother's responsibility for monitoring her daughter's weight and appearance per se even if they rejected a particular mother's harsh—even damaging—ways of implementing the philosophy.

## Conclusion

In Hall's (1980) terms, reviewers and posters engaged with Chua and Weiss from both dominant and negotiated approaches. The dominant position was adopted by those who celebrated intensive mothering, which meant devoting oneself single-mindedly to perfecting children. Some posters claimed to live by the intensive mother's credo, taking it on personally as an aspirational goal. More to the point, they applied the imperative to other women, knowing that no mother could literally achieve the ideal, but condemning the mother who did not try her best to enforce very high standards for children, in terms of both intellectual and embodied achievement. To them, a mother was transgressive if she failed to take her responsibilities seriously and flouted the code of conduct for the "good mother." Much in U.S. culture would seem too complex and flexible for the term "hegemonic" to be valid, and the trend to irony might seem to mitigate against hegemony. Nonetheless, in this case, the posters who praised Chua and Weiss for their commitment to intensive-mothering practices exemplify a hegemonic position.

Chua and Weiss offered a new twist on an old cautionary tale, presenting what could go *right* if only mothers would invest more fully. Chua and Weiss engaged in extended self-criticism regarding their flawed mothering practices before their respective epiphanies. Whether this was promotional gimmick or genuine modesty, they set up a previous stage of misguided casualness in order to heighten the argument for the imperative of the intensive model. Both authors wrote their husbands off as essentially useless. Both fathers were incapable and or unwilling to step up to the demands of intensive parenting, thus heightening the responsibility for each author-mother, although only Chua lambasted her husband for lacking clear goals for their daughters. Chua and Weiss insisted that, no matter how unpopular and even controversial their techniques were, they were the only ones who would act (selflessly) to ensure their children's success. This demanded persistent hypervigilance, being the "heavy" who literally monitored each spoonful in Weiss's case and each piano practice in Chua's. Chua and Weiss condemned anything less. That is, they and their supporters both invoked the dominant neoliberal position, and judged mothers who transgressed such standards as bad mothers.

The negotiated position emerged in the comments of posters who accepted, endorsed, and called for intensive mothering but took the position that Chua and Weiss had gone too far and caused harm. Our sample of Amazon and Motherlode posts turned up only a few criticisms of either woman for not going far enough. On the other hand, these sites and others we read regarding Weiss's *The Heavy*, did show debates over the standard, even challenging Weiss's claims about intensive mothering and suggesting that, by acting too late and/or ineffectively to address weight gain, she had been insufficiently intensive and was thus a bad mother now making good. Far more often, of course, these mothers were seen as transgressive, exceeding the outer boundary, whether this emerged from misguided love, or entirely selfish motives. In criticizing them, women did not abandon the principle of intensive mothering. Instead, they condemned Weiss and Chua as either far too extreme, whether this was because of personal neuroses or selfishness, or, in the case of Weiss, coming to an understanding of intensive mothering far too late.

Critics of Chua and Weiss on both the Amazon and *New York Times* sites routinely predicted that the Tiger Mother approach would cause children to suffer psychological distress. Many predicted Bea, and to a lesser extent, Chua's daughters, would suffer some combination of eating disorders, depression, and relational or romantic failures. Sometimes, although even less frequently, they suggested that intensive mothers had their own psychological problems. Siloing Weiss and Chua as sick was another way to defend the paradigm. This emerged in posters' accusation that Weiss (who, after all, admitted having long obsessed about her own weight and appearance) cared primarily about her own reputation, which, according to this diagnosis, would be undermined by a fat daughter. These posters claimed that for Weiss, the issue was not the physical health dangers of obesity, but only the social risks to Bea and especially to herself. That said, just as some adults—this certainly includes fathers—suffer "achievement by proxy distortion" (ABPD) in sports, and thus derive their primary satisfaction and pride through the sports successes of their children, so Weiss exemplifies what Martina Cartwright (2012) calls "Princess by Proxy" syndrome, whereby parents achieve their primary satisfaction from the beauty-related accomplishments of their children. Notably, no Amazon or Motherlode posts referred to ABPD. But a Huffington Post poster suspected that Munchausen Syndrome by Proxy caused Weiss's "pathology" (nightingale11, 2013, January 15). If so, Chua may illustrate the intensive mother who requires hyper-performance, which we might call "Superstar by Proxy."

Both the dominant and the negotiated positions insisted that ongoing monitoring was necessary even if it required sacrificing the mother's careers, friendships, and personal time. The intensive mothers' lives were wholly subsumed by the demands of child rearing, and one's children's achievements and successes filled in any resulting gaps. We saw no indications here that mothers might be conflicted over the need for unending self-sacrifice or that mothers might have legitimate interests separate from their children. Rather, the mother who did not devote herself to intensive mothering was attacked as lazy, selfish, likely a socialite or a working mother or both. No one challenged the notion that fathers, the state, or society in general cannot be expected to shoulder significant responsibility for children's welfare. Husbands' laxness provoked little ire, much less vitriol; it hardly mattered and was unsurprising. Finally, no posters questioned the idea that parenthood is highly fulfilling and that parents should be fully devoted to their children, although some research finds parenting, and especially intensive mothering, to be detrimental to a mother's personal satisfaction and well-being. That is, while mothers enjoyed opportunities to negotiate the dominant philosophy of intensive mothering, at least the posts about Chua and Weiss suggest that they do not express what Hall would have called an oppositional viewpoint. For all their other differences, the readers agreed that mothers bear the ultimate responsibility.

Amazon and Motherlode posters regularly acknowledged the difficulties and complexities of mothering, and the sheer volume of responses speaks to how parents worry over this. Several posters voiced their fears about how, or how well, they would handle the job. Many asserted that they knew what a "good mother" looked like; they were confident in their respective appraisals of Chua or Weiss. But many others, mothers in particular, expressed considerable anxiety, revealing a sense of inadequacy and confusion. Even male posters astutely observed that self-righteous people like to criticize mothers for how they are raising their children, no matter what they do. Weiss earned sympathy from those who recognized that she was condemned both for having a fat daughter, and for doing something about it.

More importantly, in focusing on and judging individual mothers—as Chua and Weiss did themselves—posters largely ignored the crucial class dimensions of intensive parenting, although a few people mocked the two authors for their status pretentions. The issue is not that Weiss was incorrectly labelled a socialite. Rather, as Senior (2014) explains, "middle-class parents not only regard their children as assets, but also enhance their value by pouring increasing amounts of capital—both emotional and economic—into them" (p. 10). Characterizing such efforts as "good mothering" disguises the connections of this time-consuming and expensive "parenting out of control" model (Nelson, 2010, p. 4)—which relies on parents' private labor and economic resources and demands that each mother find her way alone—to the rise of privatization and of market values throughout everyday life, and to class (and relatedly, race) privilege. Lower-income families cannot afford to perform "out of control" parenting, unlike wealthy parents, who can trade on their workplace flexibility to spend time with their children; and can afford high-quality education, tutors, extracurricular activities, and new technologies (Nelson, 2010).

Meanwhile, neither site offered a sustained critique of neoliberal ideas about mothers' responsibilities to their children. Chua provoked debates over the wisdom of setting forth unreasonable standards for children. Evaluations of Weiss often centered on the ubiquity of unhealthy fast food, large portions, and, far less often, narrow and potentially unhealthy standards of beauty for women. "The media" was a favorite villain to demonize; the media had no defenders on either (media) site. If Weiss and Chua were exploiting their children's problems, "the media" were also cashing in, and perhaps even further sensationalizing the stories. Such criticisms, however, did not lead to calls for structural reform—ending subsidies for corn syrup or revamped nutrition and physical education programs in schools. Nor did criticisms call for structural reforms in the ways that high school students are taught, tested, or selected for college, the focus of Tiger Mothers. More to the point, the neoliberal expectation that individual parents—primarily mothers—will bear the onus and be judged on this basis went unchallenged. These online sites provide valuable opportunities for parents to seek, offer, and share advice and support about the increasingly complex requirements of parenting. They enable parents to negotiate the definitions of good and bad mothering, and may ultimately enlarge the space available for transgressive mothering, which would allow children and parents greater freedoms. Nonetheless, at present, these sites neither encourage collective mobilizing around structural reform nor present realistic alternatives to the myth of the "good mother."

## *References*

AdoreLire. (2011, January 11). Make the right choice that we can afford [Review of the book, *Battle hymn of the tiger mother*, by A. Chua]. Retrieved from http://www.amazon.com/review/R1B18OBLDFVHL89/ref=cm_cr_rdp_perm

a mom. (2011, January 12). Stereotyping at its worst—is this responsible publishing? [Review of the book, *Battle hymn of the tiger mother*, by A. Chua]. Retrieved from http://www.amazon.com/gp/customer-reviews/R180XSBCBH3O89/ref=cm_cr_pr_rvw_ttl?ie=UTF8&ASIN=1594202842

Apte, K. (2012, April 10). Re: Putting a 7-year-old on a diet [Web log comment]. Retrieved from http://parenting.blogs.nytimes.com/2012/03/27/how-to-or-how-not-to-put-your-child-on-a-diet/#postComment

A Reader. (2011, January 11). An alternately hilarious and heart-wrenching story, a literary piece with complexity and depth [Review of the book, *Battle hymn of the tiger mother*, by A. Chua]. Retrieved from http://www.amazon.com/review/R3HYP-GVMSBS8PP/ref=cm_cr_rdp_perm

Belkin, L. (2011, January 11). On Chinese mothers and American kids [Web log post]. Retrieved from http://parenting.blogs.nytimes.com/2011/01/11/on-chinese-mothers-and-american-kids/

Belkin, L. (2011, January 14). The "Tiger Mother" speaks [Web log post]. http://parenting.blogs.nytimes.com/2011/01/14/the-tiger-mother-speaks/?_r=0

Bing Jiang. (2011, January 13). Re: A truly remarkable piece of writing [Web log comment]. Retrieved from http://www.amazon.com/review/R48FRQWZDS19A/ref=cm_cr_rev_detmd_pl?ie=UTF8&asin=1594202842&cdForum=FxY709B-KFOJW8D&cdMsgID=Mx3QBDMS46LKG02&cdMsgNo=11&cdPage=2&cdSort=oldest&cdThread=Tx3PZKL0YZ3A2HU&store=books#Mx-3QBDMS46LKG02

Blair-Loy, M. (2003). *Competing devotions: Career and family among women executives.* Cambridge, MA: Harvard University Press.

Blum, L. (2007). Mother-blame in the Prozac nation: Raising kids with invisible disabilities. *Gender & Society*, *21*(2), 202–226.

Boo. (2012, March 28). Re: Putting a 7-year-old on a diet [Web log comment]. Retrieved from http://parenting.blogs.nytimes.com/2012/03/27/how-to-or-how-not-to-put-your-child-on-a-diet/

Bronstein, C., & Steiner, L. (2015). Weighing mothers down: Diets, daughters, and maternal obligation. *Feminist Media Studies*, http://dx.doi.org/10.1080/14680777.2015.1006134

Carroll, T. (2011, January 11). Source of this parenting [Review of the book, *Battle hymn of the tiger mother*, by A. Chua]. Retrieved from http://www.amazon.com/review/RJ5ZQYBNUCAB/ref=cm_cr_rdp_perm

Cartwright, M. M. (2012). Princess by proxy: What child beauty pageants teach girls about self-worth and what we can do about it. *Journal of the American Academy of Child and Adolescent Psychiatry*, *51*(11), 1105–1107.

Chris. (2011, January 14). Re: The "Tiger Mother" speaks [Web log comment]. Retrieved from http://parenting.blogs.nytimes.com/2011/01/14/the-tiger-mother-speaks/

Christopher, K. (2012). Extensive mothering: Employed mothers' constructions of the good mother. *Gender & Society, 26*(1), 73–96.

Chua, A. (2014). [Home page]. Retrieved from http://amychua.com/

Chua, A. (2011, January 8). Why Chinese mothers are superior. *The Wall Street Journal.* Retrieved from http://www.wsj.com/articles/SB10001424052748704111504576059713528698754

Chua, A. (2011). *Battle hymn of the tiger mother.* New York, NY: Penguin Press.

Condes, Y. (2013). When I was put on a diet at 8 years old [Web log post]. Retrieved from http://www.babble.com/babble-voices/when-i-was-put-on-a-diet-at-8-years-old/

Corn, K. (2011, January 26). It is a bestseller and most likely you won't be able to put it down BUT [Review of the book, *Battle hymn of the tiger mother*, by A. Chua]. Retrieved from http://www.amazon.com/review/R25JFGV468XCSB/ref=cm_cr_rdp_perm

Currey Shermer, J. (2013, January 27). This book was exactly what this mother needed! [Review of the book, *Battle hymn of the tiger mother*, by A. Chua]. Retrieved from http://www.amazon.com/review/R2FEJNUS5XWTRC/ref=cm_cr_rdp_perm?ie=UTF8&ASIN=B0092EE92A

D'agostino, T. (2011, January 12). Re: Chua makes her case [Web log comment]. Retrieved from http://www.amazon.com/review/R329QE9MW1FVZF/ref=cm_cr_rev_detmd_pl?ie=UTF8&asin=1594202842&cdForum=Fx2M59QNZB4JA8I&cdMsgID=Mx5TVUMDN70VDY&cdMsgNo=10&cdPage=1&cdSort=oldest&cdThread=Tx28U244PCOSFNX&store=books#Mx5TVUMDN70VDY

d.a.k. (2011, January 11). A truly remarkable piece of writing [Review of the book, *Battle hymn of the tiger mother*, by A. Chua]. Retrieved from http://www.amazon.com/review/R48FRQWZDS19A/ref=cm_cr_rev_detmd_pl?ie=UTF8&asin=1594202842&cdForum=FxY709BKFOJW8D&cdMsgID=Mx3QBDMS46LKG02&cdMsgNo=11&cdPage=2&cdSort=oldest&cdThread=Tx3PZKL0YZ3A2HU&store=books#Mx3QBDMS46LKG02

D.G.R. (2011, January 11). Re: A truly remarkable piece of writing [Web log comment]. Retrieved from http://www.amazon.com/review/R48FRQWZDS19A/ref=cm_cr_rev_detmd_pl?ie=UTF8&asin=1594202842&cdForum=FxY709BKFOJW8D&cdMsgID=Mx1XMIGZ3G4M1CZ&cdMsgNo=9&cdPage=1&cdSort=oldest&cdThread=Tx3PZKL0YZ3A2HU&store=books#Mx1XMIGZ3G4M1CZ

DM (2011, January 11). Re: On Chinese mothers and American kids [Web log comment]. Retrieved from http://parenting.blogs.nytimes.com/2011/01/11/on-chinese-mothers-and-american-kids/

Douglas, S., & Michaels, M. (2004). *The mommy myth: The idealization of motherhood and how it has undermined all women.* New York, NY: Free Press.

Frugal Mom. (2011, January 14). Re: The "Tiger Mother" speaks [Web log comment]. Retrieved from http://parenting.blogs.nytimes.com/2011/01/14/the-tiger-mother-speaks/

Furedi, F. (2008). *Paranoid parenting: Why ignoring the experts may be best for your child.* London, UK: Continuum.

GAMom. (2013, January 17). Honest and loving struggle with a child's obesity [Review of the book, *The heavy: A mother, a daughter, a diet—a memoir*, by D.-L. Weiss]. Retrieved from http://www.amazon.com/gp/customer-reviews/RNE4DYFMYTQCN/ref=cm_cr_pr_rvw_ttl?ie=UTF8&ASIN=0345541340

Goldstein, M. (2013, February 6). I don't agree but I get it [Review of the book, *The heavy: A mother, a daughter, a diet—a Memoir*, by D.-L. Weiss]. Retrieved from http://www.amazon.com/gp/customer-reviews/R1GJIGTCVSPP2V/ref=cm_cr_pr_rvw_ttl?ie=UTF8&ASIN=0345541340

Golf Widow. (2012, March 28). Re: Putting a 7-year-old on a diet [Web log comment]. Retrieved from http://parenting.blogs.nytimes.com/2012/03/27/how-to-or-how-not-to-put-your-child-on-a-diet/#postComment

GP. (2012, March 28). Re: Putting a 7-year-old on a diet [Web log comment]. Retrieved from http://parenting.blogs.nytimes.com/2012/03/27/how-to-or-how-not-to-put-your-child-on-a-diet/#postComment

Gray, A. D. (2011, January 11). Chua should be committed to an institution for child abuse [Review of the book, *Battle hymn of the tiger mother*, by A. Chua]. Retrieved from http://www.amazon.com/gp/cdp/member-reviews/A2XVCOQHKAJT4J/ref=pdp_new_read_full_review_link?ie=UTF8&page=1&sort_by=MostRecentReview#R1PI0LWP5YLWRP

Hall, S. (1975). Introduction. In A. C. H. Smith (Ed.), *Paper voices: The popular press and social change, 1935–1965* (pp. 11–24). London, UK: A. C. H. Smith, Chatto and Windus.

Hall, S. (1980). Encoding/decoding. In S. Hall, D. Hobson, A. Lowe, & P. Willis (Eds.), *Culture, media, language: Working papers in cultural studies, 1972–1979* (pp. 128–138). London, UK: Hutchinson.

Hays, S. (1996). *The cultural contradictions of motherhood.* New Haven, CT: Yale University Press.

Hei Liu. (2011, January 11). *Battle Hymn of the Tiger Mother* [Review of the book, *Battle hymn of the tiger mother*, by A. Chua]. Retrieved from http://www.amazon.com/review/R84A9F19XLC5T/ref=cm_cr_rev_detmd_pl?ie=UTF8&asin=1594202842&cdForum=Fx1HRK1DTGWC7KU&cdMsgID=Mx2QWNP7R2XP0EA&cdMsgNo=1&cdPage=1&cdSort=oldest&cdThread=Tx3EILFWJ3HC0KY&store=-books#Mx2QWNP7R2XP0EA

Jackson, R. (2011, January 11). All for mom's ego? The dogs made out ok … but the kids suffered [Review of the book, *Battle hymn of the tiger mother*, by A. Chua]. Retrieved from http://www.amazon.com/review/R17B4U7FDURV04/ref=cm_cr_rdp_perm?ie=UTF8&ASIN=1594202842

Jacqueline R. Avid Reader. (2013, February 9). I am flabbertgasted … [Review of the book, *The heavy: A mother, a daughter, a diet—a Memoir*, by D.-L. Weiss]. Retrieved from http://www.amazon.com/gp/customer-reviews/R2E6YAR6ZUSYVM/ref=cm_cr_pr_rvw_ttl?ie=UTF8&ASIN=0345541340

James. (2011, January 11). Re: On Chinese mothers and American kids [Web log comment]. Retrieved from http://parenting.blogs.nytimes.com/2011/01/11/on-chinese-mothers-and-american-kids/

JGMurphy. (2012, April 14). Re: Putting a 7-year-old on a diet [Web log comment]. Retrieved from http://parenting.blogs.nytimes.com/2012/03/27/how-to-or-how-not-to-put-your-child-on-a-diet/?_r=0#postComment jh. (2011, January 15). Re: The "Tiger Mother" speaks [Web log comment]. Retrieved from http://parenting.blogs.nytimes.com/2011/01/14/the-tiger-mother-speaks/?_r=0

JL. (2011, January 11). Re: A truly remarkable piece of writing [Web log comment]. Retrieved from http://www.amazon.com/review/R48FRQWZDS19A/ref=cm_cr_rev_detmd_pl?ie=UTF8&asin=1594202842&cdForum=FxY709BKFO-JW8D&cdMsgID=Mx2X5A1BKUX6NIU&cdMsgNo=2&cdPage=1&cdSort=oldest&cdThread=Tx3PZKL0YZ3A2HU&store=books#Mx2X5A1BKUX6NIU

Johnston, D. D., & Swanson, D. H. (2007). Cognitive acrobatics in the construction of worker–mother identity. *Sex Roles*, *57*(5–6), 447–459.

Karah. (2012, March 29). Re: Putting a 7-year-old on a diet [Web log comment]. Retrieved from http://parenting.blogs.nytimes.com/2012/03/27/how-to-or-how-not-to-put-your-child-on-a-diet/

Kim, S. L. (2011, January 12). Re: On Chinese mothers and American kids [Web log comment]. Retrieved from http://parenting.blogs.nytimes.com/2011/01/11/on-chinese-mothers-and-american-kids/

Klein, E. (2013, January 30). Thank you so much Dara-Lynne Weiss [Review of the book, *The heavy: A mother, a daughter, a diet—a memoir*, by D.-L. Weiss]. Retrieved from http://www.amazon.com/review/R1YRYCGZATDXKO/ref=cm_cr_rdp_perm?ie=UTF8&ASIN=0345541340

Lawrenz, J. C. (2013, January 24). Absolutely wonderful [Review of the book, *The heavy: A mother, a daughter, a diet—a memoir*, by D.-L. Weiss]. Retrieved from http://www.amazon.com/review/R12BGCZFWX7A3Y/ref=cm_cr_rdp_perm

Liz. (2013, January 22). Hold your criticisms [Review of the book, *The heavy: A mother, a daughter, a diet—a memoir*, by D.-L. Weiss]. Retrieved from http://www.amazon.com/gp/customer-reviews/R3P6Y9LNHJ9BUS/ref=cm_cr_pr_rvw_ttl?ie=UTF8&ASIN=0345541340

Lofthouse, L. (2011, January 23). [Web log comment]. Retrieved from http://www.amazon.com/review/R1FGVQUBVAX8AX/ref=cm_cr_rev_detmd_pl?ie=UTF8&asin=1594202842&cdForum=FxDGW5K43GY25E&cdMsgID=Mx1AIULK3W3BU0L&cdMsgNo=47&cdPage=5&cdSort=oldest&cdThread=TxXJUP0ILHZZIU&store=books#Mx1AIULK3W3B

Lucy. (2011, January 1). No different than reality TV [Review of the book, *Battle hymn of the tiger mother*, by A. Chua]. Retrieved from http://www.amazon.com/review/R2JEXEL5T4TMKN/ref=cm_cr_rev_detmd_pl?ie=UTF8&asin=1594202842&cdForum=Fx15YTM8GOG9EKV&cdMsgID=MxZLEDY90LD9XW&cdMsgNo=1&cdPage=1&cdSort=oldest&cdThread=Tx1KAPUEIF6D74&store=books#MxZLEDY90LD9XW

MBT. (2012, March 28). Re: Putting a 7-year-old on a diet [Web log comment]. Retrieved from http://parenting.blogs.nytimes.com/2012/03/27/how-to-or-how-not-to-put-your-child-on-a-diet/#postComment

MFAP. (2011, February 2). Re: Child abuse makes money for Chua! [Web log comment]. Retrieved from http://www.amazon.com/Child-abuse-makes-money-Chua/forum/

Fx2TW1617UZNULU/TxAHDS028U9V6M/7?_encoding=UTF8&asin=0142429104

Mickeyrad. (2011, January 14). Re: The "Tiger Mother" speaks [Web log comment]. Retrieved from http://parenting.blogs.nytimes.com/2011/01/14/the-tiger-mother-speaks/

mom of four. (2013, January 19). Thank you Dara-Lynn Weiss for being willing to go where others will not [Review of the book, *The heavy: A mother, a daughter, a diet—a Memoir*, by D.-L. Weiss]. Retrieved from http://www.amazon.com/gp/customerreviews/R7P15ZYABC61C/ref=cm_cr_pr_rvw_ttl?ie=UTF8&ASIN=0345541340

Montegani, J. (2013, March 1). Worst mom of the century! [Review of the book, *The heavy: A mother, a daughter, a diet—a memoir*, by D.-L. Weiss]. Retrieved from http://www.amazon.com/gp/customer-reviews/RYGCI8B7TGX4P/ref=cm_cr_pr_rvw_ttl?ie=UTF8&ASIN=0345541340

mrka. (2011, January 27). Disturbing [Review of the book, *Battle hymn of the tiger mother*, by A. Chua]. Retrieved from http://www.amazon.com/review/R3F87GMIYTBP7E/ref=cm_cr_rev_detmd_pl?ie=UTF8&asin=1594202842&cdForum=Fx3OI5Z3B-3FMO1X&cdMsgID=Mx2O2FN7LXK95B9&cdMsgNo=1&cdPage=1&cd-Sort=oldest&cdThread=TxCNU36HQREXN7&store=books#Mx2O2FN-7LXK95B9

Murphy, S. (2011, January 15). Re: The "Tiger Mother" speaks [Web log comment]. Retrieved from http://parenting.blogs.nytimes.com/2011/01/14/the-tiger-mother-speaks/

Nelson, M. K. (2010). *Parenting out of control: Anxious parents in uncertain times.* New York, NY: New York University Press.

New Yorker. (2011, January 11). Chua makes her case [Review of the book, *Battle hymn of the tiger mother*, by A. Chua]. Retrieved from http://www.amazon.com/review/R329QE9MW1FVZF/ref=cm_cr_rev_detmd_pl?ie=UTF8&asin=1594202842&cdForum=Fx2M59QNZB4JA8I&cdMsgID=Mx3HL0BD9JR5N9P&cdMsgNo=1&cdPage=1&cdSort=oldest&cdThread=Tx28U244PCOSFNX&store=books#Mx3HL0BD9JR5N9P

nightingale11. (2013, January 15). [Web log comment]. Retrieved from http://www.huffingtonpost.com/social/nightingale11?action=comments

NP1. (2011, January 12). Re: The "Tiger Mother" speaks [Web log comment]. Retrieved from http://parenting.blogs.nytimes.com/2011/01/14/the-tiger-mother-speaks/

Parkermann 347. (2011, January 11). Re: A truly remarkable piece of writing [Web log comment]. Retrieved from http://www.amazon.com/review/R48FRQWZDS19A/ref=cm_cr_rev_detmd_pl?ie=UTF8&asin=1594202842&cdForum=FxY709BKFO-JW8D&cdMsgID=Mx2X5A1BKUX6NIU&cdMsgNo=2&cdPage=1&cdSort=oldest&cdThread=Tx3PZKL0YZ3A2HU&store=books#Mx2X5A1BKUX6NIU

Peskowitz, M. (2005). *The truth behind the mommy wars: Who decides what makes a good mother?* Emeryville, CA: Seal Press.

Peterson, M. (2013, April 5). Sad [Review of the book, *The heavy: A mother, a daughter, a diet—a memoir*, by D.-L. Weiss]. Retrieved from http://www.amazon.com/review/R26TWANW58YF9F/ref=cm_cr_rdp_perm

Pinewood. (2011, January 11). Re: The "Tiger Mother" speaks [Web log comment]. Retrieved from http://parenting.blogs.nytimes.com/2011/01/14/the-tiger-mother-speaks/?_r=0

Reba Mae. (2013, April 10). Poor Bea ... [Review of the book, *The heavy: A mother, a daughter, a diet—a memoir*, by D.-L. Weiss]. Retrieved from http://www.amazon.com/gp/customer-reviews/R1GK1XGIU4UXAZ/ref=cm_cr_pr_rvw_ttl?ie=UTF8&ASIN=0345541340

Reich, J. A. (2014). Neoliberal mothering and vaccine refusal imagined gated communities and the privilege of choice. *Gender & Society, 28*(5), 679–704.

Rich, A. (1976). *Of woman born: Motherhood as experience and institution.* New York, NY: Norton.

Rizzo, K. M., Schiffrin, H. H., & Liss, M. (2012). Insight into the parenthood paradox: Mental health outcomes of intensive mothering. *Journal of Child and Family Studies, 22*, 614–620.

Rose. (2011, January 11). Re: The "Tiger Mother" speaks [Web log comment]. Retrieved from http://parenting.blogs.nytimes.com/2011/01/14/the-tiger-mother-speaks/?_r=0

RPR. (2011, January 15). Re: The "Tiger Mother" speaks [Web log comment]. Retrieved from http://parenting.blogs.nytimes.com/2011/01/14/the-tiger-mother-speaks/?_r=0

Senior, J. (2014). *All joy and no fun: The paradox of modern parenthood.* New York, NY: Ecco.

Shirani, F., Henwood, K., & Coltart, C. (2012). Meeting the challenges of intensive parenting culture: Gender, risk management and the moral parent. *Sociology, 46*(1), 25–40.

Sierra. (2013, January 22). Re: Putting a 7-year-old on a diet [Web log comment]. Retrieved from http://parenting.blogs.nytimes.com/2012/03/27/how-to-or-how-not-to-put-your-child-on-a-diet/?_r=0#postComment

Smoller, S. (2011, January 12). In pursuit of excellence [Review of the book, *Battle hymn of the tiger mother*, by A. Chua]. Retrieved from http://www.amazon.com/review/RWHI67U407SS9/ref=cm_cr_rev_detmd_pl?ie=UTF8&asin=1594202842&cdForum=Fx1NUYD3QD0FEA2&cdMsgID=Mx18CL6LXFI2VF4&cdMsgNo=2&cdPage=1&cdSort=oldest&cdThread=TxAXH7M8KVIQR7&store=books#Mx18CL6LXFI2VF4

Someone's Mom. (2011, January 5). Re: Battle Hymn of the Tiger Mother [Web log comment]. Retrieved from http://www.amazon.com/review/R84A9F19XLC5T/ref=cm_cr_rev_detmd_pl?ie=UTF8&asin=1594202842&cdForum=Fx1HRK1DTGWC7KU&cdMsgID=Mx2QWNP7R2XP0EA&cdMsgNo=1&cdPage=1

&cdSort=oldest&cdThread=Tx3EILFWJ3HC0KY&store=books#Mx2QWN-P7R2XP0EA

student. (2011, January 11). Re: On Chinese mothers and American kids [Web log comment]. Retrieved from http://parenting.blogs.nytimes.com/2011/01/11/on-chinese-mothers-and-american-kids/

Sutherland, J. A. (2010). Mothering, guilt and shame. *Sociology Compass*, *4*(5), 310–321.

Tara Libby. (2013, February 25). Helpful read [Review of the book, *The heavy: A mother, a daughter, a diet—a memoir*, by D.-L. Weiss]. Retrieved from http://www.amazon.com/review/RU27QZDPB8B1Z/ref=cm_cr_rdp_perm

Wall, G. (2010). Mothers' experiences with intensive parenting and brain development discourse. *Women's Studies International Forum*, *33*, 253–263.

Weiss, D. L. (2012, April). Weight watcher. *Vogue*, pp. 122–130.

Weiss, D. L. (2013). *The heavy: A mother, a daughter, a diet.* New York, NY: Ballantine.

whammus. (2012, May 14). The privilege was hard to bear [Review of the book, *The heavy: A mother, a daughter, a diet—a memoir*, by D.-L. Weiss]. Retrieved from http://www.amazon.com/gp/customer-reviews/R3V6WAZLMS4WE/ref=cm_cr_pr_rvw_ttl?ie=UTF8&ASIN=0345541340

Williams, S. (2011, February 18). A mother's manifesto [Review of the book, *Battle hymn of the tiger mother*, by A. Chua]. Retrieved from http://www.amazon.com/review/R126R4ZJ6W1DSO/ref=cm_cr_rdp_perm?ie=UTF8&ASIN=1594202842

ZZtop. (2011, January 15). Re: The "Tiger Mother" speaks [Web log comment]. Retrieved from http://parenting.blogs.nytimes.com/2011/01/14/the-tiger-mother-speaks/?_r=0

# *Contributor Biographies*

**Beth L. Boser** is a Visiting Assistant Professor at The College of Wooster in Ohio. Her scholarship focuses primarily on political rhetoric and rhetorics of reproduction, birth, and motherhood. Currently, she is focused on discourses of mental health and medicine within these contexts. She earned a Ph.D. from the Annenberg School for Communication and Journalism at the University of Southern California in 2013. Her dissertation, titled *Miracles of Birth and Action: Natality and the Rhetoric of Birth Advocacy*, explores the complexities of women's agency in contexts of childbirth through analyses of historical case studies. Her work also appears in *Rhetoric & Public Affairs.*

**Carolyn Bronstein,** Ph.D. is a Professor of Communication in the College of Communication at DePaul University. She is the author of *Battling Pornography: The American Feminist Anti-Pornography Movement, 1976–1986* (Cambridge University Press, 2011), for which she received the 2012 Emily Toth Award for the Best Single Work in Women's Studies, given by the Popular Culture Association/American Culture Association. Her scholarship on gender and media representation, social responsibility, and contemporary feminism has been published in a wide range of media, history and communication journals, including *Journalism and Mass Communication Quarterly*, the *Journal of Women's History*, *Feminist Media Studies*, the *Journal of Mass Media Ethics*, and *Camera Obscura*. Her popular writing on feminism has appeared in *The Atlantic.* She is currently coediting a collection of essays that analyzes the impact of pornography on American culture and politics in the 1970s.

**Patrice M. Buzzanell** (Ph.D., Purdue University) is a Distinguished Professor in the Brian Lamb School of Communication and the School of Engineering Education by courtesy at Purdue University. She also is the Chair and Director of the Susan Bulkeley Butler Center for Leadership Excellence at Purdue and the Endowed Visiting Professor in the School of Media and Design at Shanghai Jiaotong University in China. Co/editor of three books and author of 165 articles and chapters, her research centers on the everyday negotiations and structures that produce and are produced by the intersections of career, gender, and communication, particularly in STEM (science, technology, engineering, and math). Her research has appeared in such journals as *Communication Monographs*, *Management Communication Quarterly*, *Human Relations*, *Communication Theory*, *Human Communication Research*, and *Journal of Applied Communication Research*, as well as handbooks on professional, organizational, gender, applied, family, ethics, and conflict communication. Her work also has appeared in ASEE and IEEE proceedings for engineering education. Fellow and past president of the International Communication Association, she has received awards for her research, teaching/mentoring, and engagement. She also has served as president of the Council of Communication Associations and the Organization for the Study of Communication, Language and Gender.

**Rachel D. Davidson** (Ph.D., University of Wisconsin-Milwaukee) is a Visiting Assistant Professor in the Department of Communication at Hanover College. Her research is broadly focused in the area of rhetoric and public culture with particular interest in rhetorics of motherhood, caregiving, and social advocacy. In particular, her research explores the ways in which values about issues assumed to be private are manifested in public culture in a broad range of diverse texts from film and television to online and print public advocacy efforts. Rachel's research has appeared in *GEMS* (*Gender, Education, Music, and Society*).

**Suzy D'Enbeau** (Ph.D., Purdue University) is an Assistant Professor in the School of Communication Studies at Kent State University. Her research explores the contradictory and complex goals of feminist organizing and problematizes dominant ways of thinking about, constructing, and performing gender in different organizational contexts and popular culture. Suzy's work has appeared in leading journals such as *Communication Monographs*, *Human Relations*, *Journal of Applied Communication Research*, *Qualitative Inquiry*, and *Women's Studies in Communication*.

**Tasha N. Dubriwny** is an Associate Professor of Communication and Women's and Gender Studies at Texas A&M University. Her research focuses on the intersection of feminism, politics, and women's health and her essays have appeared in journals such as *Quarterly Journal of Speech*, *Feminist*

*Media Studies*, and *Women's Studies in Communication*. Her 2013 book *The Vulnerable Empowered Woman: Feminism, Postfeminism, and Women's Health* received the Bonnie Ritter book award from the Feminist and Women's Studies Division of the National Communication Association. Dubriwny's recent work on motherhood has problematized the medicalization of motherhood in essays that have focused on postpartum disorders, cesarean sections, and breastfeeding.

**Lisa A. Flores** is an Associate Professor in the Department of Communication at the University of Colorado. Her research and teaching interests lie in rhetoric, critical Whiteness and critical race studies, and gender. She has published in *Text and Performance Quarterly*, *Communication and Critical/Cultural Studies*, and the *Quarterly Journal of Speech*. Her most recent work examines the rhetorical dynamics of domination, particularly as manifest in Whiteness and masculinity and in historic narratives of immigrants and immigration. This project accounts for the intersections of race/ethnicity and nation, and it offers a site through which to theorize belonging and citizenship. The project theorizes race and racialization with specific attention to race and Mexican-ness.

**Stephanie Gomez** (Ph.D., University of Utah) is an Associate Instructor in the Department of Communication at the University of Utah. Her research and teaching focus on media studies, U.S. popular culture, critical/cultural studies, and representations of identities. Her current research includes work on the ways in which racial and ethnic hybridity are rhetorically articulated through food in cooking shows featuring women on the *Food Network*, the shifting means of disciplining women's behaviors depicted in comedic films, and the ways in which audiences interact with reality television to negotiate and create meanings about identities using Internet message boards. Her essay about identities as portrayed in the reality television show *So You Think You Can Dance*, entitled "Choreographing the Real, Essentializing Difference: The Transformation of Dance within Neo-Liberal Capitalism," was competitively selected as a Top Paper in the Performance Studies Division of NCA in 2013.

**Elizabeth Hatfield** (Ph.D., Texas A&M) is an Adjunct Professor at the University of Houston–Downtown. Her work focuses on family, gender and culture in the mass media. In particular, she considers how parenting messages in the mass media impact the lived experience of mothers and fathers, including issues such as work/life balance and gender roles. Her research has been published in journals such as *Communication, Culture & Critique* and

*Communication Law Review*. Her dissertation focused on the media's coverage of celebrity pregnancy and parenthood, and identified ways in which the media use celebrities to perpetuate intensive mothering as an unrealistic ideal. Elizabeth served as the Graduate Student Representative for the National Communication Association in 2009–2010. Prior to earning her Ph.D., Elizabeth worked in marketing and public relations serving the financial industries.

**Sara Hayden** (Ph.D., University of Minnesota) is a Professor of Communication Studies at the University of Montana. Her scholarship and teaching focus on the rhetoric of U.S. feminisms, maternity, and reproduction. Her research has been published in journals including the *Quarterly Journal of Speech*, *Communication and Critical/Cultural Studies*, *Women's Studies in Communication*, and the *Western Journal of Communication*. Her coedited book *Contemplating Maternity in an Era of Choice: Explorations into Discourses of Reproduction* (with D. Lynn O'Brien Hallstein) received the Organization for the Study of Communication, Language, and Gender's 2011 Outstanding Edited Book Award.

**Natasha R. Howard**, Ph.D., is an Assistant Professor of Communication at Bronx Community College. She is a coauthor of the anthology, *Black Women and Popular Culture: The Conversation Continues* (2014). Her research interests include: hip hop culture; media effects; and how race, gender, and sexuality are portrayed in the media. Dr. Howard earned her doctorate in Mass Communications & Media Studies, with a Graduate Certificate in Women's Studies, from Howard University in 2012. She is also a freelance writer for various publications and websites outside of the academy.

**Heather L. Hundley** (Ph.D., University of Utah) is a Professor of Communication Studies at California State University, San Bernardino. Her scholarship and teaching focus on media studies, critical/cultural studies and representations of identities. Her research has been published in journals including *New Media & Society*, *American Communication Journal*, *Communication Quarterly*, *Visual Communication Quarterly*, and *Journal of Men's Studies*. She has coauthored *Views from the Fairway: Media Explorations of Identity in Golf* and coedited *Examining Identity in Sports Media* (both with Andrew Billings). In 2013 she contributed chapters to *Fallen Sports Heroes, Media, and Celebrity Culture* (edited by Lawrence Wenner and published by Peter Lang) and *The International Encyclopedia of Media Studies: Content and Representation* (edited by Angharad Valdivia and Sharon Mazzarella and published by Blackwell).

**Katherine J. Lehman** (Ph.D., University of New Mexico) is an Associate Professor of Communications at Albright College in Reading, Pennsylvania, where she also codirects the Women's and Gender Studies program. She is author of the book *Those Girls: Single Women in Sixties and Seventies Popular Culture* (University Press of Kansas, 2011). Her essay "Woman, Divided: Gender, Family and Multiple Personalities in Media" appears in the *Journal of American Culture* (March 2014). She recently contributed chapters on media portrayals of single women to the anthologies *Lucky Strikes and a Three-Martini Lunch: Thinking about Television's* Mad Men (Cambridge Scholars, 2015) and *HBO's* Girls*: Questions of Gender, Politics and Millennial Angst* (Cambridge Scholars, 2014).

**Susana Martínez Guillem** is an Assistant Professor in the Department of Communication & Journalism at the University of New Mexico. Her research interests are in cultural studies and critical discourse studies, focusing mainly on rhetorics of immigration, race, and racism. Her work has appeared in several internationally recognized journals, including *Discourse & Society*, *Journal of International and Intercultural Communication*, *Critical Studies in Media Communication*, and *European Journal of Cultural Studies.* Her most recent work examines beliefs and practices related to contemporary cultural keywords such as "multiculturalism," "(anti)racism," or "tolerance" are embedded in practices such as law making, public television programming, and social movements, with especial attention to the European Union and in the United States.

**Sharon R. Mazzarella** (Ph.D., University of Illinois at Urbana-Champaign) is a Professor of Communication Studies at James Madison University. Her research focuses on youth culture and mass media, specifically in the field of Girls' Studies. She is editor of five academic anthologies as well as the book series "Mediated Youth" (Peter Lang). She previously served as founding and lead co-editor of the journal *Popular Communication* (Taylor and Francis), and her published articles appear in a range of journals including *Popular Music and Society*, *Women's Studies in Communication*, the *Journal of Broadcasting & Electronic Media*, *Communication Research*, the *Journal of Children and Media*, the *Journal of Communication Inquiry*, *Communication Quarterly*, the *Journal of Radio and Audio Media*, and *Girlhood Studies.* At present, she is at work on a large-scale research project examining journalistic constructions of girls, in particular as they relate to a moral panic about girls growing up too fast.

**Valerie Palmer-Mehta** is an Associate Professor in the Department of Communication & Journalism at Oakland University. Her research and teaching interests sit at the intersection of rhetorical studies and gender studies. Her current research examines the diverse rhetorical strategies women employ to influence public culture, question entrenched orthodoxies, and transform intellectual traditions and everyday practices. Her work may be found in a variety of journals and edited collections, such as *Communication, Culture & Critique*, *Text and Performance Quarterly*, *Women's Studies in Communication*, *Journal of American Culture*, and *Women and Ethos: Identifying a Feminist Ecological Imaginary.*

**Sherianne Shuler** (Ph.D., University of Kansas) is an Associate Professor in the Communication Studies Department at Creighton University. Her teaching and research interests focus on the intersections of organizational communication and gender studies as well as representations of work and home in the media. Recent research projects have involved the exploration of the emotional rules and coping strategies constructed by such diverse organizational groups as 911 dispatchers, domestic violence employees, and reference librarians. She has also published critiques of the portrayal of executive women in *Fortune* magazine and of the depiction of women's friendships on *Desperate Housewives.* Finally, her growing interest in autoethnographic methods has led to publications exploring emotional labor in academic life and social support in the health care context. Past research has appeared in such publications as *Management Communication Quarterly*, *American Communication Journal*, *Women's Studies in Communication*, *Health Communication*, *The Electronic Journal of Communication*, *Communication Studies*, and in several edited volumes.

**Lara C. Stache** (Ph.D., University of Wisconsin–Milwaukee) is an Assistant Professor in the Department of Communication at Governors State University. Her research emphasizes media, rhetoric, and representations of gender in popular discourse. Lara's research has appeared in journals, including *Feminist Media Studies* and *New Technology, Work, and Employment*, and a book chapter in *Fan Girls and the Media: Creating Characters, Consuming Culture.* Lara's popular press writing has appeared on *The Feminist Wire.*

**Linda Steiner,** Ph.D. is a Professor of Journalism at the Philip Merrill College of Journalism at the University of Maryland. Steiner was Editor of *Critical Studies in Media Communication*, and remains on eight editorial boards. She has coauthored or coedited six books, including *Women and Journalism*, *Key Concepts in Critical Cultural Studies*, and *The Routledge Companion to Media and Gender.* Steiner was president of the Association for Education in

Journalism and Mass Communication. Within AEJMC, she twice won the James Murphy Award for Top Faculty Paper and the MaryAnn Yodelis Smith Award for Research; and was named Outstanding Woman of the Year in Journalism and Mass Communication Education. Her current major project is about women war reporters.

# Index

## *D*



## *E*



## *F*



## *G*



## *H*

## *I*



## *J*



## *K*



## *L*



## *M*

## *N*



## *O*



## *P*

## *R*



## *S*



## *T*

www.ingramcontent.com/pod-product-compliance
Ingram Content Group UK Ltd.
Pitfield, Milton Keynes, MK11 3LW, UK
UKHW021852100926
8556IPUK00020B/1184

9 781433 131660